Essays and Journalism
Volume 2
Carradale

Carradale House

Naomi Mitchison

Essays and Journalism

VOLUME 2

CARRADALE

Edited with an introduction by
Moira Burgess

Kennedy & Boyd

Kennedy & Boyd
an imprint of
Zeticula
57 St Vincent Crescent
Glasgow
G3 8NQ
Scotland.

http://www.kennedyandboyd.co.uk
admin@kennedyandboyd.co.uk

First published in this form 2009

Text Copyright © The Estate of Naomi Mitchison 2009
Photographs Copyright © The Estate of Naomi Mitchison 2009
Introduction Copyright © Moira Burgess, 2009

ISBN-13 978-1-84921-011-9 Paperback

Contents

List of illustrations	*ix*
Introduction	*xi*
Acknowledgments	*xv*
Glossary	*xvii*

Part I: Kintyre (1) — **1**

On the Edge of the Highlands (1944)	3
Kintyre News (1944-5)	12
Lovely, long Kintyre (1960)	20
In Sight of the Sea (1964)	25
Wartime at Carradale (1991)	27

Part II: The village and the Big House — **31**

Village Play-Making (1941)	33
What to Do with the Big House (1943)	42
Garden Fete (1950)	50
Christmas at the Big House (1951)	53
Highland Funeral (1953)	57
Platform Party (1953)	59
Living in Scotland Today (1955)	62
Pigeon Shoot (1955)	68
The Garden Opening (1955)	71
Weather (1955)	76
Hogmanay in a Fishing Village (1955)	80
The Farmers' Dance (1955)	85
Mistress Jean and I (1956)	89
Life Begins at Balloch (1957)	95
On the Council (1957)	98
Does this make sense? (1963)	101
Planning a Kitchen Complex (1972)	107
Caravans to Carradale (1979)	114
Carradale catch (1987)	118

Part III: The farm —

A Small Farmer Looks at her Farm (1942)	123
The End is the Beginning (1942)	131
Down on the Farm (1943)	134

Marginal Land (1) (1944) 140
My Farming and My Neighbours (1944) 143
Marginal land harvest (1944) 147
Marginal land crop (1945) 150
Philip Ram (1945) 153
Marginal land: second year (1945) 155
Marginal land: sowing out (1946) 158
My weeds (1946) 161
Marginal Land (2) (1946) 163
Marginal field: hay crop (1947) 166
Marginal Field (1947) 169
Threshing (1949) 172
The Year of the Late Harvest (1950) 175
A Binder of One's Own (1951) 178
I'll Never Forget (1952) 181
Sheneval (1952) 185
Harvesting in Kintyre (1952) 188
Trials and Rewards of Becoming Attested (1953) 193
Mild Winter (1954) 197
Wet July (1954) 200
Visitor (1954) 202
Leaning on a Gate (1955) 204
Maggots and Potatoes (1955) 207
Thoughts on Growing Grass (1955) 210
The Year of the Good Hay (1955) 213
Cautionary Story (1955) 216
A Year's Work Done (1955) 220
The Big Mill (1955) 223
Think of a Number (1956) 226
The Cow and the Calf (1956) 229
Rough Weather (1956) 232
The Buck Rake (1956) 235
The Price of a Binder (1956) 238
Threshing in Carradale (1956) 242
Summer Work (1957) 245
Beating the Rain (1957) 248
Lambs for the Fair (1957) 251
Cattle Sales at Oban (1957) 254
Building a Haystack (1958) 257

The Weather and the Crops (1958)   260
The Calves (1958)   263
The Threshing Team (1959)   267
Science and the small farmer (1959)   271
The Sales (1960)   276
Namely Lambs at Tarbert Sale (1961)   280
The New Shed (1961)   284
Happiness on the Farm (1961)   287
The Fortunate Isles (1963)   290
The Deadly Bracken (1965)   293
The Day I Took a Fellow Tribesman to Tarbert Fair (1966)   297
Skills and Changes (1977)   301
No more porridge (1982)   306

Part IV: The fishing   **309**
Herring Country (1961)   311
Bringing Home the New Boat (1949)   313
Spindrift at the Citizens' (1951)   321
Winter Fishing (1952)   326
A Lean Harvest (1955)   330
The Crafty Darlings (1956)   333
Twelve-mile Limit (1958)   336
Carradale Harbour Opened (1959)   339
The Old Canal (1961)   341

Part V: The garden   **345**
The Gale (1953)   347
Highland Water Garden (1955)   350
The Golden Year (1960)   355
Winds and Seedlings (1960)   358
A Garden in Argyll (1980)   363

Part VI: Kintyre (2)
The Tinkers and their Language (1952)   369
The Haldanes in Kintyre (1979)   374
Rural Reconstruction (1942)   378

Title index   *395*
Sources   *403*

Mitchison typing in the drawing room at Carradale House

List of illustrations

Carradale House ii

Mitchison typing in the drawing room at Carradale House viii

Carradale House bookplate x

The cast of the Carradale play 'A Matter Between Macdonalds' 32

Denis Macintosh and Mitchison in costume for the play 36

Mitchison's daughter Val performing the sword dance. 38

Christmas card, drawn by Gertrude Hermes, depicting Carradale
House 54

Christmas card with a poem by Mitchison 56

Dry rot, Carradale House 77

Neighbour and farmer Alec Mackinven playing the accordion
for dancing in the library 86

Drawing-room mantelshelf with Hermes' bronze head of a
young Denny, Carradale House 111

The new extension to Carradale House 111

Drawing-room facing West. Murdoch in chair facing out to terrace.
Prof. Mo Bedawi talking to Val on the sofa 113

Drawing-room mentelshelf with Hermes' soapstone heart and
seagull sculpture in centre above fireplace 120

Harvest at Carradale 189

A Galloway cow and her calf 264

Mitchison milking an Ayrshire cow 272

Mitchison and a lamb 281

Anthony Edwards (Percy's son) in the tractor, pulling up a
section of fence 303

Percy Edwards, gardener and friend, in the walled garden 303

Denis Macintosh, part-owner and skipper of the fishing boat
Maid of Morvern 315

Mitchison in front of the glasshouses in the garden of
Carradale House 346

Mitchison in her 60s with Prof Victor Gugenheim by the back
door, with the oil-tank painted by Sir Charles (Charlie) Brett. 354

Mitchison with *Sunflower*, a sculpture by Gertrude Hermes. 362

A fishing-themed bookplate 398

Carradale House bookplate

Introduction

The writing career of Naomi Mitchison (1897-1999) stretched over some seventy years, encompassing at least seventy works of fiction (no definite total has yet been agreed) as well as non-fiction, poetry and plays. Individual works in this extensive oeuvre have all too often been allowed to fall out of print, but at least they are known about, and the publishers of the present volume, Kennedy & Boyd, have begun a programme of republication in *The Naomi Mitchison Library.*

Almost unknown, however, is the mass of shorter prose pieces – journalism, essays, polemics, reminiscences – which Mitchison produced, alongside the books, during her long career. There are many hundreds of these pieces, covering a tremendously wide range of topics, for Mitchison was something of a polymath and interested in everything that came under her eye. If it happened she wrote about it, and generally got it published, in newspapers and periodicals both in Britain and abroad. This edition of Naomi Mitchison's essays and journalism aims to present as much as possible of this fascinating, valuable and hitherto neglected work.

The edition will extend to several volumes, their coverage and size to be established as material comes to hand. One volume will certainly be devoted to Mitchison's writing about Scotland. Born in Edinburgh, from at least the 1930s onwards she was not only passionately interested in Scottish landscape and history but involved in Scottish politics and current affairs. Another will comprise her writing on Africa, particularly Botswana, where in later life she found another homeland. It seemed right, however, to devote this first volume to Carradale (with some extension to the rest of Kintyre), where she lived for over sixty years.

She writes about many aspects of Carradale. The largest section here concerns the mixed arable and dairy farm (with some diversions into sheep and pigs) which she ran, not just as a manager but with hands-on involvement in every aspect of the work. There is a smaller section of pieces about the fishing – she was part-owner of a boat for some years – and another about the big garden which was particularly dear to her heart. A few descriptions of beautiful Kintyre open the book, with Mitchison's own retrospective of early days in Carradale to help orient any reader who comes fresh to the story, and at the end is the long essay 'Rural Reconstruction', both a snapshot of Carradale in the 1940s and a spirited presentation of Mitchison's dreams for its future. Most attractive of all, perhaps, is the section I have called 'The village and the Big House'; community drama, garden fetes, dances, hitch-hiking, stocking the freezer – there is something for everybody here.

The tone is generally fairly upbeat. Mitchison appears to make light of most practical problems, and perhaps there is little room for introspection in two thousand words for a daily newspaper or a weekly magazine. But at times – see 'Winter Fishing' – the practical and the thoughtful sides of her writing are both there, to touching effect. Similarly, she may appear at times to be slightly, if affectionately, making fun of the villagers (whom, it seems, she didn't expect ever to read her columns). But she cared deeply for them and for Carradale. Her war diary *Among You Taking Notes* (1985) and the novels *The Big House* (1950) and *Lobsters on the Agenda* (1952) supply other insights and angles for the enquiring reader.

Some duplication will be found in the topics covered, particularly perhaps in the farming section. Haystack building, cattle sales, the visit of the threshing team, these recur. But so they do in the cycle of the farming year, an observation Mitchison makes several times. Besides, no two articles are identical, or anywhere near it, and each, thanks to a somewhat digressive style of writing, has its own hidden gems. An article on a garden opening veers right off the subject to talk about poaching salmon, but nobody could possibly wish these lively, lyrical pages away. Omit a piece which appears to be just a second or third amble down the Tarbert road, and you lose the irresistible picture of Mrs Mitchison, County Councillor, perched by an eagle's eyrie and musing that the housing committee would probably object to it on health and safety grounds. Omit yet another discussion of milk yield and butter fat, and you lose the casual remark about Barbara Castle, MP, helping to bring a calf home in the back of the car. I have kept everything in.

Some technicalities: this is not a scholarly edition, its main purpose being to retrieve and present the work, and it uses the printed versions of the pieces in newspapers and periodicals, which may therefore contain the occasional misprint and be subject to the sub-editor's whim. Mitchison's own usage as to capital letters and hyphenisation, understandably, varies over the years, and a few discrepancies have been silently amended where they seemed likely to distract the reader, though undoubtedly some remain. The scholars who will surely follow will go back to the manuscripts (in the National Library of Scotland, the Harry Ransom Center in Texas, and other libraries, in some cases not yet fully catalogued) which I have not pursued.

I have footnoted fairly lightly to explain some references to people and events, then topical but now perhaps less clear, as well as local Kintyre references. I have not identified local people, since a few are still alive and most have surviving family still in Kintyre. There is a glossary of Scots and Gaelic words and agricultural terms.

The Gaelic and Norse place names of the Carradale area have usually reached us in a form which seemed plausible to some early mapmaker who spoke neither of these languages. That form can vary quite widely in Ordnance Survey maps over the years; effectively, there is no correct spelling. Auchenbreck and Auchnabreck, for instance, are used impartially for the same farm in Carradale Glen. Auchenfraoch (or Auchanfraoch), 'the heather field', sometimes appears (in Mitchison's writing and on maps) as Auchenreoch (or Auchanrioch); local information indicates that this was the usual pronunciation, representing another variant, Auchnafhraoch, in which by the rules of Gaelic spelling the 'fh' is silent. I have allowed all these versions to remain in the text as they occur.

In some cases – see for instance 'The Tinkers and their Language' – there has been further work and research on the topics Mitchison wrote about half a century ago. I have not attempted to update her remarks. They stand, I think, as a testament to her insatiable curiosity and to the undaunted way she would plunge into whatever subject had caught her interest at the time.

These articles and essays comprise a valuable resource both in Mitchison biography and in the wider field of social history. Mitchison's own multi-faceted intelligence and her world-wide, universe-wide view have long been recognised in her fiction. In the rediscovered pieces contained in this and future volumes of her non-fiction writing, such qualities are evident again.

For rather similar reasons, readers should probably treat local history references with caution. The armed abbots, for instance, who appear in at least two of these pieces, most likely spring from Mitchison's romantic imagination: the warriors and the ecclesiastics on the Saddell stones can be seen to be separate. Again, I have generally let such statements and judgements stand, leaving comment and possible correction to future researchers.

Moira Burgess

Acknowledgements

Lois Godfrey-Mitchison, Naomi Mitchison's elder daughter and literary executor, has most generously given permission to reprint material for this edition of her mother's essays and journalism, and has taken a keen interest in the project throughout; sincere thanks are due to her first of all.

Invaluable help has been supplied by staff at Argyll and Bute Library Service; Edinburgh Central Library; Glasgow University Library; The Mitchell Library, Glasgow; the National Library of Scotland; and by Brigadier (Ret'd) C.S. Grant, Highland Division Website Historian, and Tommy Smyth, Archivist, Black Watch Museum. I am also indebted to the Society of Authors for advice, and to the editors of *The Campbeltown Courier* and *The Kintyre Magazine* who printed appeals for material and information.

Individuals who have supplied information, advice and material include Mary Arnold-Forster; Val Arnold-Forster; Ian Davies; Frances Hood; Angus Martin; Ronald Renton; Bob Smith and Ronald Togneri. Without their interest and involvement this book would lack several pieces of text and photographs, the name of a sculpture, the correct spelling of a Gaelic phrase, and the definition of 'scoocher', among other things. I hope they, as well as anyone I have omitted to name here, will approve of the finished result.

And I am most grateful to Alison Brown for supplying the comprehensive index.

Glossary

aftermath	a second growth of grass in a season
AI	artificial insemination
airt	direction, compass point
allemande	a move to change position in Scottish country dancing
back-end	late autumn, the end of the farming year
battel	a bundle of hay or straw (sometimes battle, bottle)
blintering	glimmering
brailer	a net used to transfer herring from fishing-boat to shore
braird	the first green shoots of a crop
bullock	a castrated bull
ceilidh	in the Highlands, an informal evening of music, song and storytelling, to which traditionally everyone contributes (Gaelic *cèilidh*)
cleg	horse-fly
condy	a covered drain or sewer (sometimes cundy)
cowp	to overturn (sometimes coup)
cromag	a shepherd's crook, generally with a carved head (Gaelic)
dagg	the dirty wool on a sheep's rump
daylight saving	a measure introduced during World War II to increase working hours in summer by putting the clock forward; see also double summer time
double summer time	a daylight saving measure in which the clock was put forward two hours; unpopular with cows
Dutch barn	a barn open at the sides
early bite	the first growth of grass in spring
fank	an enclosure for sheep (Gaelic *faing*)

first-footing   visiting neighbours in the early hours of the New
                Year, bearing gifts of food, drink and fuel; ideally the
                first foot should be tall, dark and male
foggage   the grass that grows after the hay is cut

garron   a small Highland horse
gey   very, quite
girnal   a chest for storing grain (sometimes girnel)
glean   to gather corn left by the harvesters, traditionally on
                behalf of the old or destitute (cf the Bible story of
                Ruth and Naomi, Book of Ruth chapter 2)
grilse   a young salmon on its first return from the sea
grip   the gutter or drain in a byre

haar   a term for sea mist, most used on the east coast of
                Scotland
haims   curved pieces of wood or metal forming part of a
                horse collar (sometimes hems)
hansel   (v) to use or wear something for the first time; (n) an
                inaugural gift
harling   roughcast finish on a wall
haulm   a stalk of straw
haysel   haymaking season
head rigg   the part of the field where the plough turns
hirsel   a herd of sheep, or the ground it occupies
hogg   a yearling sheep not yet shorn
Hydro Board   The North of Scotland Hydro-Electric Board,
                formed in 1943 to construct and manage hydro-
                electric projects in the Highlands; dissolved in 1990
                and re-formed as Scottish Hydro-Electric

jabble   a slight rough movement of the sea

keel   to mark a sheep with red ochre (to indicate
                ownership)

laggan   an area of flat, fertile ground; specifically here the
                Laggan of Kintyre, between Campbeltown and
                Machrihanish, famous for barley growing

ley, lea   (n and adj) (land) under grass or pasture
loching   (of herring) swimming up a sea loch, notably Loch Fyne

MacBrayne a steamer company serving the west of Scotland from the mid 19th century; now Caledonian MacBrayne
mantua-maker dressmaker
machair   sandy grassland by the sea (Gaelic)
messages   errands, shopping etc
midden   a dungheap or rubbish heap
Mod   in the Highlands, a festival of music, song and poetry; the National Mod is held annually in different Scottish towns (Gaelic *Mòd*)

NFU   National Farmers' Union
Nissen hut a corrugated iron hut used during World War II

peewit   the lapwing (probably from its cry)
PEN   an international writers' organization
piece   sandwich, packed lunch
pike   a small hay-rick with a conical top
puckle   a small amount

quey   a young cow which has not yet calved

redd-land   the bare soil of land cleared after a crop
rigg   a male sheep (or other animal) with only one testicle
ring-netting a fishing method in which a pair of boats works together to net a shoal of herring and haul it aboard one of the boats
road   in harvesting, a path cut by hand round the perimeter of a field to allow the mechanical reaper to move in
runrig   a Scottish form of land tenure, the land divided into individual strips

sarking   a layer of felt or other material under the slates of a roof

scale   to scatter (e.g. fertilizer, dung) over a field
schottische   a type of Scottish country dance, similar to a polka
scunner   a feeling of disgust or nausea (also used as verb)
seine-netting   a fishing method in which individual boats cast
                nets and bring the ends together to catch a shoal of
                fish
seuch   a sighing noise, as of wind or the sea
shearling   a sheep that has been shorn for the first time
skew   the coping-stone of a gable
slype   a narrow passage between two walls
smirr   gentle rain
sock   (of a plough) ploughshare
solan (goose)   the gannet
sourocks   sorrel (the plant)
spate   (of a river) a rushing torrent, a flood
stirk   a bullock or heifer between one and two years old
stob   a stake of wood
stook   a group of sheaves of cut grain propped up to dry
stour   dust
swither   to be undecided

tangle, sea tangle   seaweed
TT   (of milk or a dairy herd) tuberculin tested
tup   a male sheep, a ram

wale   to choose, select
wedder, wether a castrated male sheep
wrack, sea wrack   seaweed
WRI   Women's Rural Institute

yarr, yare   corn spurrey (the plant)
yeld   (of a female animal) barren

PART I

KINTYRE (1)

On the Edge of the Highlands

(1944)

Battered and splashed on the west by great waves and great wet winds, and on the east by smaller waves – yet fierce and sudden enough to wreck a fishing-boat – and a colder, drier wind, the stubborn backbone of Kintyre runs north and south, humping itself into small grass and heather bens, the Atlantic rain constantly filling its small lochs. Farther down, Knapdale has more protection from the west; you look out on to island after island and always the great Paps of Jura.

There is some limestone in Kintyre, and a vein of coal near Campbeltown, not yet worked out, though the pit was shut down and the miners thrown out of work, and at the foot of the hills everywhere and in the small straths, there is some decent arable land. Down by Campbeltown it is better than that; this was great barley-growing land in the old days of local, unmonopolised distilleries, when Campbeltown swam into a brief prosperity on seas of whisky. To this prosperity we owe both the remarkable ugliness of Campbeltown – on one of the most exquisite sites imaginable – and the patches of semi-industrial slum which lurk behind the half-ruined warehouses and old distilleries. It is a badly hurt town, a small distressed area, and it is only in the last few years that a few local people have begun to hope and work for rebuilding a new and better life for their town. But whether it will be based on whisky, and whether the Scots barley will ever wave and whisper again on the laggan of Kintyre, that remains to be seen. Some people would rather see cream and butter, seed potatoes, early vegetables, and fruit.

Tarbert, Ardrishaig, and Lochgilphead were never so prosperous, nor do they now bear such scars. They were mainly market towns and ports. For there has been fishing all round these shores since the farthest times, since the gold-collared heroes came from Ireland, since the pirates built their fort on Carradale Point, firing the walls till the sand ran into a glassy paste, gluing the stones together, since MacDonalds and Campbells fought and killed. Nowadays there is little inshore fishing. That went with the crofts. But the herring fishing is still very much alive. There are not so many boats as there used to be; they are more expensive and far more efficient. A modern ring-net herring-boat with a reliable diesel engine costs between a thousand and two thousand pounds (more inflated war prices!), with five or six of a crew. Campbeltown and Carradale are the main ports, with Tarbert falling behind.

Queer how things change! A century ago there were over a thousand herring-boats between Inveraray and Lochgilphead, for the Loch Fyne fishing mostly – now there are hardly any, and none modern. At the same period there were more than five hundred between Campbeltown and Islay. There are still some forty pairs in Campbeltown counting those that have been commandeered, and only a few pairs less in Carradale – well-known boats whose owners are part of a solid and intelligent community.

You will hardly find a man or woman in Kintyre and Knapdale who is not interested in news of the fishing; mostly all have relations who are or were part of a crew. The small farms up the glens will have a barrel of salt herring for winter eating: 'Tatties and Herring' is the song we all know! Equally, the fishermen will have an eye for the crops, and most will have given a hand at harvest one year or another. And the shore folk and sea folk alike will have a good notion of the whereabouts of the deer and the glossy blackcock, and the bonny, autumn-leaf-coloured pheasants.

The road down from Lochgilphead to Campbeltown twists south mostly between hills and sea, sometimes up on the bare moorland level of heather, bog myrtle and asphodel, sometimes plunging down through rough rocky copses of birch, scrub oak, rhododendron, or golden whin to black rocks, orange and tawny weed, and the slight rocking of wild swans on the sea lochs: a tourist asset if ever there was one! But for all it was remade a few years back, the surface has been torn up since by war transport, and the poor county of Argyll with an enormous mileage of roads and quite inadequate rates, cannot possibly make or keep up the corniche way we might have. But a bonny road it is, at least where Nature, rather than the small Highland house-builder, has had her way! – and always with the strange richness and softness of western colour, even in mid-winter or bitter February when the half-starved woodcock crouch on the top of the road and the sheep flounder into snow-choked ditches.

Lochgilphead town lies round the shallow semicircle of old harbour, and the first thing you will see at low tide is a broken causeway from one side to the other, by which at one time an ill-liked laird could get from his gate to the main road without encountering the Lochgilphead fishermen. The same as the rest of the Highlands, we in the south-west are only now lifting our heads from a long oppression by landlords, and indeed the thing is not over yet, though a few are trying to make up for the sins of their predecessors. But all along this road you will see the dark squared stones of ruined crofts and steadings, lost homes with the enemy sheep grazing over them, landlords' doing for a few ruinous generations.

At Ardrishaig the Crinan canal comes down into a placid basin and locks, with maybe a small yacht or an odd fishing-boat lying there. It is little used now, though it is a nice wee canal, pretty on a summer's day. There are few ways across the hills, and the small road to Achahoish goes up and up into remoteness before it drops to the shore of Loch Kellisport [Caolisport]. It is easily snowed up and it is not so long ago that the dark-haired MacDonald who farms there needed to ride one of her farm horses and lead another through drifts into Lochgilphead to get bread for the village.

There is a cave on the edge of Loch Kellisport [Caolisport] with a rough altar and a cross on the wall just to be seen, one of the earliest churches in Scotland. They say St Columba came here, but on a clear day he saw Ireland yet, and needed to go on once more. Each of these lochs and inlets has its own character, its own colour: each has its own singers and most will have their own songs. The Gulf Stream warms them all, and down to the water's edge the gardens show flaming rhododendrons and inappropriate palms.

A little way out before Tarbert the road is rather surprisingly edged with purple-spiked buddleias; clumps of montbretia, too, have gone wild. There are far more of the common rhododendron than we know what to do with, though the forestry folk say they can be planted out and crushed once the young spruce gets going. But they seed across on to the hillsides everywhere, and nobody likes them in spite of their purple summer magnificence, for the leaves are poisonous to cattle and sheep.

Above Stonefield the road takes a loop through some fine timber, great beeches and Douglas firs mostly, and just where it begins to drop towards Tarbert, you can look down on the walled garden of Stonefield, like a charming toy with its rows of vegetables and bright glass houses. Then Tarbert loch, islanded and sheltered, with maybe half the Clyde fleet of ring-netters lying in for the day, each marked with the letter of its port of registration and its official number, but each, too, with her private and special name, *Maid of Honour, Rolling Wave, Alban,* and *Cluaran, Queen of the Fleet, Watercress, Stella Maris,* or homelier *Polly Cook, Betty,* and *Ina Bell* —[1] but ah! these are all Carradale boats and half are away now, called up as their crews too were called up, and some to foreign service, maybe never to come back to Kintyre, never to slip out of port in the tail of daylight nor come back in the dawn, heavy with herring.

Nowadays the herring are bundled out of the fishing ports by lorry, and with control prices there is little of the old auctioning and still less of the heartbreak and bitterness when decent men had to race and cheat to get a price for their catch that would make them a living; or, worse still, needed to dump the lot, good food and all the labour and danger that had gone to the getting of it, because there was no price at all. All this is remembered; it must not be again.

By now there will be thousands of service men and women who will remember Tarbert for its free canteen – kept up largely by the local folk. It is more than possible to be seasick in the boat between the Kyles and Tarbert on a rough day, and a good cup of tea in the canteen has made many an English sailor think less ill of his first day in the Highlands! They will be mostly going on to Campbeltown, or to Islay by the ancient steamer from the west loch. The two lochs have almost opposite tides, but it seems as though the west loch were too shallow for any hydro-electric scheme. There is only the narrowest ridge between the two lochs, though, and the road goes on with the sea on the right hand now, sometimes ridiculously transparent and sometimes, in summer, an opaque paint blue. The farther side is wooded and romantically far by road, although a few minutes' rowing would carry one across. There are one or two beautiful houses there, among them Ardpatrick, with yet another walled garden full of rare west-coast flowers and shrubs, and Beauty of Bath red-streaked summer apples. But beyond the remoteness of Knapdale lie the islands, blue and purple and endless mist shades.

The main road follows the western side of Kintyre, sometimes through good farm land, sometimes through fields that have been roughest pasture for generations now, but last year or this were ploughed again by the government tractors and heavy single-furrow ploughs. This is marginal land, with half the cultivation costs subsidised; something may be made of it yet. There is a limestone deposit here and the mills are hard at work grinding it down; all sensible farmers are liming heavily, for the lands need it, and again half the cost comes from the subsidy.

Most of the farms in Kintyre carry accredited herds; there is an expanding market for clean milk, and stock from such farms fetch top prices. It means taking trouble, both over buildings and methods, but it is well worth while. In the old days there was much butter-making, and Kintyre cheeses were well thought of; but today whatever milk is not drunk locally goes into the creamery at Campbeltown. Farms have to be self-supporting and all must grow their quota of oats and turnips and potatoes; some try kale or beans. On the west side cartloads of the sea tangle are brought up from the beaches for manure; the horses stand knee-deep in the stuff, snuffing it over and chewing an odd bit.

Sea birds nest along the rocks everywhere. The beautiful bright colours of sheldrake and eider show up on the black. In spring the air is full of the tumbling of the peewits, the farm birds, over the newly brairding land. The hedges are full of finches, and there is an occasional kingfisher up the burns.

The small villages along the west road are each a centre of life and gossip and emotions, but lying back, not to be grasped by the casual visitor. The big houses are loosely attached. Largie Castle, standing a little behind Tayinloan, is the MacDonald centre. Here Flora came, as a girl, to stay and be educated with her young cousins. The MacDonald spirit, the brounie, is immanent here and in Cara Island opposite. The brounie is the greatest enemy of the Campbell fairy on the other side, who also has two dwellings. MacDonalds and Campbells can live in peace with one another now, but when a Campbell from the east side married the niece of the housekeeper at Cara House and went to stay with his wife's auntie, the unforgetting brounie would have none of it and turned the poor lad out of his bed.

One asks oneself now whether were the Campbells any worse than the rest of the clans. It is hard for a Campbell that he should be always needing to answer for old sins, for Glencoe and Dunaverty. Yet the thing is not quite over and folk speak as though the spirit of the Campbells were always one of oppression and crookedness. Yet it was the Campbell fairy that comforted the poor widow whose two bonny sons had been pressed into the army and were away in Spain fighting Napoleon and sending no letters to their mother for the good and sufficient reason that neither of them could write.

There used to be a road over the hills from Tayinloan to Auchnabreck, and so down to Carradale. You can still follow it up from either end till it fades out into bog and waste. There used to be a village half-way across – Narrachan. Now only the shells of houses remain and the sheep wandering among them.[2]

On a stormy day I have seen the Atlantic spray blowing in sudden rainbows across the west road. Once, going by the bus, I smelt seals, and there, sure enough, were a dozen of the fellows lying out on the rocks close to us, sunning themselves. The plane goes punctually to Islay, nothing to make a ploughman lift his head nor to fright the plough horses, although the same man may never have seen a railway train. Looking south, one sees the great shadowy bulk of the Mull, and out to the west Rathlin Island and maybe a glimpse of Ireland herself. The ups and downs of the road flatten out and it turns inland across the laggan and the wide fields dotted with poles against enemy landing craft. At last one comes into Campbeltown by Longrow, which is just what its name implies.

Campbeltown loch is a beautiful inlet between grass hills, with here and there a plantation and flowers growing easily; it is guarded by a great rock, Davaar Island, and a low causeway. Some day, maybe, a town worthy of its site will be built there, and indeed the first little fishing port may have been pretty enough. There are glimpses of man-made beauty yet, the great brown curves and drapes of the drying ring-nets on the high poles or along the harbour railings, and the boats themselves lying against the quay. The fishing community is on its own, with its special stories and nicknames and its deep kindliness and courage and a loyalty at bottom that goes beyond small rivalries and cheatings, and the devilment of the wild lads with time in hand and nothing good to do with it.

Campbeltown can be cheery enough, too, on a market day when we farmers come in and have our great cracks, speaking of stock and crops and the doings of one or another, and buyers and sellers get together and there is as much honesty, nearly, as you will find anywhere else! It is a great place, too, for skilled tradesmen, families and firms whose account books go back for a hundred years or more, men with a real liking for and pleasure in their craft, and, at the back of that, considerable culture, above all in matters to do with their own country. You will hear fine singing in Campbeltown, both of Gaelic songs and of the lovely psalm tunes of the Covenanters.

At the farther side of the fertile Atlantic plain, facing the Atlantic, are the windy, sunny Machrihanish links and a great pale beach of sand, good for bathing. Another road goes south down a central glen to Southend. There are several burns coming down out of the hills here and few Southend folk that have never had a piece of salmon to their tea. But farthest south of all is the great height of the Mull itself. It is said that when the moles get to the end of the Mull the Campbells will be driven out of Kintyre, but it would be a clever mole that could burrow through these solid rocks. There are plenty of caves, too, and stories about them of a sufficiently improbable kind. The sack of Dunaverty Castle was real, but has left little to see. If we go back to Campbeltown and north by the east road, we are again between sea and hills, but always, a few miles across from us, beyond Kilbrannan Sound, the beautiful, ever-changing colours and shadows of Arran. The road is smaller and twistier, banked high with primroses and fern, ditched with yellow flags, slipping under rowan branches, and bridging small violent torrents.

Here below us are the remains of an old fort, and there is Saddell Abbey, scene of the contest between the tailor and the devil. We come past Torrisdale bay and over Dippen brae to the bright loops of the Carradale river, up through a strath of small ploughed fields and grazing cattle. A branch of the road goes down to Carradale pier, where we hope to see the finest fishing-boat harbour of the Clyde.

Visitors go on coming to Carradale year after year; it is a fine place for wandering round, but we do wish people would remember to shut the gates – my own black Galloways are for ever getting where they shouldn't be! There is a herd of wild goats on Carradale Point – white fellows, with long coats and great curved horns; they must have gone wild many generations ago, though they are Saanens,[3] not the indigenous wild goat of Scotland. One of my sheep is wandering round with them, being, like his mistress, unable to separate himself from the goats. The deer are partly fallow and partly Japanese, so there is a great variety of colouring; they range over the hills in summer, but in the winter come down to the turnips and stacks and make a great nuisance of themselves.

The woods round Carradale have been heavily cut during the war, though the best of them – a lovely mixture of planting – still stands. Meanwhile the Forestry Commission have been planting up along the hillsides, and in another twenty years the open heathery sides of Carradale Glen will be as dark with pines as the Black Forest. The road, which follows the glen up, drops down to the sea by a steep, wriggly hill at Grogport, and then follows the coast up and down and in and out, and if you keep the tail of an eye open on Kilbrannan Sound you will likely see a basking shark rise and splash. At Clonnaig [Claonaig] one branch goes over the hill and back to the main road and the west loch, and the other goes out to Skipness, once a prosperous fishing village, now with no industries and no prosperity. Here in the early nineteenth century Robert and James Haldane, the evangelists, landed from a small boat as a first step towards their evangelising of 'heathen Kintyre', where the established church was completely under the control of the lairds and cared nothing for human souls.[4]

These wee maps are the queerest things! Here they lie on the page and they will give you a shape and maybe the exact height of the hills. They will give you the big names. But they will not give you the small secret names, the Gaelic names of rock and hillock, needed on a farm where you will maybe want to say that a ewe has lambed here or that you will find a coil of rope or a scythe there. These names will not have been told to the folk that made the maps, nor heeded by them. But they are there all the same.

SMT Magazine, v. 33, June 1944, pp. 35-9

[1] Mitchison names most of these boats in her poem 'The Alban Goes Out: 1939'; see *The Cleansing of the Knife* (1978), pp. 2-11.

[2] See Mitchison's account of walking this track in *Among You Taking Notes* (1985), pp. 148-150.

[3] A breed of white goat originating in Switzerland.

[4] See 'The Haldanes in Kintyre', later in this volume.

Kintyre News

(1944-5)

These ten short pieces on Carradale, Campbeltown and Kintyre matters were contributed by Mitchison, generally under the heading 'Kintyre News', to *Piobaireachd*, the newsletter of the 51st Highland Division, at monthly intervals between July 1944 and April 1945.

We've been in a state of excitement about our water spout in Kilbrannan Sound and cloudburst just over Peninver, which ended a spell of splendid farmer's weather, during which time some of a fine hay crop had been cut but only the luckiest got it up. It started off with a wild hail storm that blocked the drains and whitened the fields, then down came the burst, tearing a swathe of young turnips out, sweeping tons of hay out to sea, making near as much mess of early potatoes as a tank would, and cutting off Robert McNair at Low Peninver. But by and large the crops look good and the summer fishing has begun with most of the Campbeltown and Carradale boats getting good quality herring.

There's been a great to-do about the Piper's Cave,[1] where various folks have been exploring and bringing out bones – and when the vet says they're one thing and the butcher says they're another, and the Head Yins at Edinburgh won't commit themselves yet, I can't tell you what they are – except that they're neither the piper nor his dog!

Man for man, Kintyre contributed most of any district in Argyll to Save the Soldier Week. But there are some who think you deserve just a wee bit more than our money in the safest kind of securities, and the National Debt correspondingly increased! Quite a few of the Home Guard and others gave the money they raised as a free gift. Though that's little enough, and you know it, and so do we, listening to the wireless, hurrying back from milking or out in the boats ourselves.

Piobaireachd 28, 12 July 1944

Some more news from Kintyre. In a week of fine weather all farmers worked till late on the hay, and now most is up, with corn and turnips both promising well – also a fine growth of weeds everywhere!

The Campbeltown and Carradale fleets are out and getting good quality herring near in, though mostly in small shots. No dumping so far, and everyone discussing the Herring Industry Bill with its important clause 4(c) – lending money to any society of fishermen, kipperers and so on – as well as the possibility of a straight charter of govt.-owned fishing boats to ex-service men. But surely the fishermen will have the sense to co-operate this time. We all say the lads coming back will have more sense than their fathers.

The usual crowds at Glasgow Fair-time, and hundreds left behind at Wemyss Bay, buses crammed, lads camping and some helping the farmers. We hope to get three Youth Hostels in Kintyre after the war; they're needed and we hope you'll come to them. The one at Carradale is a firm promise.

A stray copy of your *Piobaireachd* turned up here and was eagerly seized on by a couple of last war veterans, one saying how he'd got home news from an old paper thrown away in a dug-out up by Ypres. He said this time the lads would know far more of what was going on, even in Scotland, and hoped you'd all filled up your forms to get votes in the next election – which mayn't be so far off now.

Piobaireachd 50, 4 August 1944

Everyone is upset about the Argyll Council's post-war housing scheme, and of course it's primarily you that it will affect. The Kintyre Divisional Committee has suggested a certain number of houses for each place, and goodness knows it would have been a tight fit getting in the boys coming back, and half of them married or promised – Carradale for instance was to have fifty houses, though we hope to get eighty boys back, and some of our existing houses are condemned. But the Council has cut everything – Carradale from fifty to forty, Southend from twenty-four to sixteen, Skipness from twelve to six, and so on. What happens in Campbeltown will depend on whether the Drumlemble pit is re-opened. There are various rumours about that, and of course the men it's really going to affect aren't going to have any say about it!

Scarcely any herring these weeks, though plenty of mackerel – for which there's often no market. A good deal of investigation going on about freezing and processing of herring; Provost Macnair has done a lot of work on that and anyone with good ideas will have Tom Johnston's[2] backing.

Harvest prospects good, and the Government reaper-binders going round everywhere doing a good job; the drivers hereabouts are a very decent lot and deservedly popular. I'm sure farmers will want that kind of thing to go on in peace-time, and there'll be jobs for good mechanics in country districts. I think, too, that the Hydro Board has its eye on the West for post-war electricity schemes, though probably nothing quite immediate.

Housewives are all hoping not to have to renew their blackouts for another winter: thanks to you. We're all thinking of you. Hurry home.

Piobaireachd 78, 2 September 1944

The great thing this month for us has been the coming of Tom Johnston. You have no idea the sense that man talked – away different from most politicians. He says that we in the Highlands have got too much into the habit of asking for grants and special treatment and then sitting back: we must help ourselves – but he will see that our efforts get what they deserve. He spoke to the fishermen, the farmers, and the Town Councillors of Campbeltown, and to a crowded village meeting at Carradale, where everyone is shouting for a harbour. He spoke of Scotland 'never free so long as we have poverty, unemployment and sickness' and his plans for ending that, with 'goodwill and coherence among our folks'. He wants to end the insecurity of fishing by making the fishermen into 'civil servants catching fish' and their best market 'in the stomachs of our people'. Talking to the Scottish Office men who were round with him, I felt he must be a grand chap to work for.

Otherwise, the place has been quiet, with the harvest mostly in and the stock sales going on; with 'The Duke' [of Argyll] bidding up most of the prize rams. What would happen if another Duke turned up at the Lochgilphead ram sales?

The farmer Home Guards are very happy to be finished with parades, though they did manage to catch two escaped Italian prisoners of war, who had cleverly been snaring rabbits with their boot laces.

And the mothers are daring to ask – Will we get any of our boys home for the New Year? We hope so.

Piobaireachd 113, 7 October 1944

Sad news. Poor old Campbeltown has been flooded by a lot of particularly smelly rain. The sewers didn't work, dogs swam about in Longrow, and lorries making a dash for it only made matters worse. There were bad floods elsewhere, especially in the Laggan, where thirty Parkfergus cross-bred lambs, all ready for grading, were drowned. But potato lifting wouldn't be itself in Kintyre without rain every other day! The 'potato holidays' were mostly too early, and anyway, there's little to be said for them – stopping all the children's school work for the sake of ten per cent who aren't so very good on the tatties when all's said and done.

There has been dumping of herring again at Tarbert – with any amount of folk in Glasgow and elsewhere who never see a herring or a kipper. They were not the best for keeping as they were full of feed and went soft, but that shouldn't hurt in chilly weather if the transport is properly organised. They were the first in Loch Fyne for months and the fishermen are angry and asking why it is that there are still no canning factories here in the west. The Clyde Fishermen's Association are trying to meet the situation by limiting catches in various ways, but of course it's not only with them: the buying end of the trade is very elaborately organised but not entirely on the lines of getting the herring quickly and cheaply to the breakfast table. There's another big thing that needs sorting in Scotland. Oh yes, and the Rex[3] is open again.

Piobaireachd 147, 10 November 1944

The frosts came early this year, and we had to hurry to get our potatoes earthed up. It has been a cold wet month and ploughing has scarcely started, though most of the dung has been carted out, and on the West side and at Peninver they have been spreading sea tangle on the potato land. There may be a big future for early and seed potato-growing in Kintyre. High prices held for stock and implements at all the farm sales, especially for TT Ayrshire; more and more farmers are going in for accredited herds. It is rather more trouble but much more profitable, as well as being better for everyone's babies. We've still got to keep up our acreage of food crops for another season.

Good fishing, mostly Loch Fyne way, where there was an accident, one of the Campbeltown boats turning sharply and sinking an old Tarbert boat: but all the crew were saved. There is even a market for saithe and lythe just now.

It is being authoritatively said now that the pits at Drumlemble are going to be re-opened; there are rumours of a rich new seam. That should mean wages and profits! A lot of talk about making the Admiralty re-build the Grammar School which they took over early in the war, turning the scholars out into all sorts of church halls. But of course it's not only good buildings that are needed to make a good school. Some people are wondering where the new 'People's Colleges' for Argyll are going to be built. We surely ought to have one for Kintyre.

All the political parties are getting busy, with a view to an election next summer. Do make sure you're going to be able to vote! It's just a matter of filling in a wee form, and it will be no use at all as an election if we don't have you all as voters.

Piobaireachd 185, 18 December 1944

You'll guess how much we're all thinking of you out there in the mud, now that New Year is coming round again, and most of all maybe the fathers who were out in the same kind of fighting last time. We wish our thoughts could keep you warm and safe, and this time I want to send you news of education because the fathers among you will be thinking plenty about their bairns. Well, Argyll seems to be beginning to realise that its education is in a pretty good mess. One sign of the times is a parents' association in Campbeltown which is shouting about all that is wrong with the various school buildings, equipment and so on – partly due to the Navy having taken over the Grammar School at the beginning of the war (and when there were lots of big houses empty!) but even more to original 'economies' – no playgrounds, bad lighting, wretched lavatories and so on.

Teachers' salaries have been voted up – though perhaps not as much as they will go up anyhow when the new scales come into force – but so far most of the benefit goes to the young ones just entering, and faithful service of many years is so far not rewarded. Teachers get smaller pay than most skilled workers and have to keep up appearances on it, as well as getting new books and so on if they are to do their job well.

A bit of Cowal news! There's a young headmaster, John Fleming, a scientist ex Army and heavy industry (in fact he's still on the Army Reserve) who has got going at Tighnabruaich. His school, like most Argyll country schools, is a disgrace, but he has got his school Management Committee to think so too and they are prodding the County Council. There's a ratepayers' advisory committee on education there, which has shaped itself out of the folks interested, and there's talk about adult education and Young People's Colleges. Keep an eye on Tighnabruaich!

Piobaireachd 206, 8 January 1945

Snow and hard frosts, everything held up, including mail and papers. Southend was quite cut off and there were exceptionally heavy drifts at Smerby and Grogport. But it was great the way the buses rammed their way through. Of course it's been pure hell for the grown-ups with the snowballing that's been going on! Meantime the Argyll County Council Housing Committee has come out with its post-war housing proposals, which have horrified everyone – Tarbert is the only place to get any houses in the first year, and none in the rest of Kintyre until the third year. But Carradale, for instance, doesn't get the whole of the miserable forty that have been allotted to it till the seventh year! Tarbert needs the houses – but then so do other places, and the Welcome Home Fund is a bit of a farce if you aren't to have houses to be welcomed in. We're all asking ourselves what you would like done with the Fund, whether it should be divided up at once or made into a fund for folk to draw on, if for instance, they are setting up in business or getting married. When you're writing home, remember to tell us what you think. Your opinion is the most important, you know.

It looks as if the Carradale Harbour scheme will go through fairly soon after the end of the war; it should bring prosperity to Kintyre, especially if we can get a decent steamer service. It will be big enough to take the whole of the Clyde fishing fleet. Perhaps you will know how big that is, you who hail from our quarter, or you who have spent a holiday somewhere on Clydeside. We hope for a refrigerating plant for herring, and that might lead to kippers and a cannery. We hope for a general spread of light industries, so that there will be a choice of jobs all in decent conditions. If there was a sufficient industrial lode, we'd get electricity throughout Kintyre. That wouldn't be so bad, would it? But it's the houses we want for you first.

We know now that you're back in the battle. Our thoughts and our prayers are with you.

Piobaireachd 247, 19 February 1945

It seems definite that the Drumlemble pit will re-open, and that may mean subsidiary industries. But I wonder if it isn't almost as important that the Cambridge research people have been quietly working on the growing of virus-free potatoes, over in Islay. This month they have been meeting the farmers and suggesting that Islay should specialise in seed-potato growing; that means quite a lot of employment for fairly skilled people.

How many of you want to go back to the land? I was at a Young Farmers' Club meeting over at Largieside and they were all asking what could be done for soldiers coming back – many of them will have been thinking of their own big brothers and cousins. There's little good land to spare and I don't advise anyone to take over a hill flock unless they know a lot about it. If we knew what the real demand was, we might do something about it. These clubs are doing grand educative work among some of the lads and lasses, who are debating, studying and taking responsibility. But there are a lot of wild young toughs in Campbeltown who have been up in Court recently – who need their elders back to skelp them – and to give them a lead! Meanwhile, the Education Committee have been having a teacher up on the mat for complaining – quite rightly – about the condition of his school, and 'writing letters'! We need you back to bring democracy into Argyll!

Piobaireachd 271, 15 March 1945

A few of the boys have been coming home on leave and making us really see what you're up against. You know, it takes a lot of imagining from here; very few country folks have seen anything terrible and shocking, anything to make them wild with anger and hate; words don't mean the same thing to us as they do to you. But we're trying to understand and at the same time trying to hang onto a few ideas of general decency and kindliness that are apt to get lost in wars, but will be wanted afterwards. And we all listen in day after day, night after night, and we hear of what you're doing – and wonder what's happening to our own special one.

The fishing season is about over and most of the boats in for yearly overhaul. A spell of fine weather has let us get ahead with the ploughing, and some sowing has been done; the early potatoes are in everywhere. You can tell by the growth and brightness of the green which fields had artificials. Every year now, more farmers are using the Government outfits on their arable land, especially where they have had to plough up difficult fields that have long been out of cultivation. Of course any Kintyre man will expect the clan Semple to do something special, so it will be no surprise to hear that Harry had a calf with two heads at Lephincorrach! There's still thunder in the air about the Campbeltown schools, and we keep wondering what will happen when the school [leaving] age is raised – as it should be – to sixteen, but there aren't either the school buildings or the teachers.

The Press has been quiet about you since your stirring first-over-the-Rhine battles – but we know you are there and will be in until the end.

Piobaireachd 299, 10 April 1945

[1] A cave on Bengullion, above Campbeltown, associated with a version of the widespread folk tale about the disappearance of a piper and his dog.

[2] Thomas Johnston (1881-1965), politician and writer; at one time Secretary of State for Scotland, and involved in Scottish public and economic affairs, such as the establishment of the Hydro-Electric Board.

[3] The Rex Cinema in Campbeltown had been damaged by fire in February 1944.

Lovely, long Kintyre

(1960)

Kintyre – the head of the land: that is what it meant in the Gaelic, and so we who live there know it to be, ringed round with breaking seas, only tied up to the rest of Argyll at the narrow Tarbert neck, where once King Magnus (promised all the lands of Scotland that he could sail his galley round) had himself and his boat with her sails set dragged across on rollers, and all so that he could claim the grand, green farm-lands of Kintyre.

For the way Kintyre is, there is a rough ridge of mountains almost all the length of the land, some forty miles, except that, at the level of Campbeltown, there is a wide, low-lying stretch, the laggan of Kintyre, reaching from sea to sea. Here, on the good land, incoming Ayrshire farmers used in the main to grow barley for distilling, but now concentrate on dairy production.

South again, the laggan rises to another mountain block, ending in steep cliffs facing out onto seas so wild and dangerous that most smaller boats would rather go west by the slow Crinan canal route, across mid Argyll, than risk rounding the Mull of Kintyre. From any of these heights, with their thick heather and black bog, one can see wide waters on both sides, to the east the steep, fantastic line of the Arran heights and to the west the islands, Gigha, Jura and Islay, far and lovely, and to the south Rathlin island and the remote Irish coast line.

But these Kintyre hills of ours drop on both sides to a fringe of cultivated land. There is local lime-stone and many farmers gather the heavy sea tangle for a potash-rich field dressing as their fathers did before them. Wherever there is enough space, and especially where the sheltering valleys wind down towards the sea, each with its salmon-rich river, there are small villages, some of which used to live partly by fishing. One of them – Carradale, at the foot of Carradale glen – is still a fishing village, with a new harbour and some sixty men and boys actively pursuing their old job, but with modern methods.

Kintyre has been long populated. There are burial places and the remains of forts everywhere, vaguely dated back a good two millennia, though probably in use for longer. The gold-braceleted raiders came and went. The Norsemen left place names, Skipness, Torrisdale, Sanda, Smerby, and probably a good few descendants as well.

Meanwhile Kintyre had become Christian, and in the twelfth century Reginald (which, of course, is the respectable form of Rognvald), Lord of Islay, founded the Cistercian Abbey of Saddell. By now most of the great square of Abbey building is ploughed over, the traces lost to any but the keen archaeological eye, but the graveyard and the ruins of the church itself are still there; the tombs have little hunting scenes carved round them, while the effigied abbots seem to have kept their chain mail and two-handed swords. No doubt they were needed.

For in those days there was plenty of fighting, indeed it might have been a dull life without it. Sometimes the King's writ ran in Kintyre, but often enough people looked instead to the Lords of the Isles, or to their powerful local vassals, MacDonalds mostly. Yet gradually the power of the kings grew; castles were set up; Dunaverty in the south, the old castle of Carradale, of which only the base of the walls can be seen now – and that at the back of the golf course – as well as a castle at Kilkerran, the modern Campbeltown.

By the sixteenth century, there were a number of powerful families, not only MacDonalds, but MacAllasters, MacEachrans, MacNeills and MacMurchys; there are plenty of the same name still. But the Campbells were beginning to look south from their stronghold at the head of Loch Fyne, and when that clan want something it is not rare that they get it! They had, by the beginning of the seventeenth century, constituted themselves the guardians of law and order, agents of the King against the rebellious Highlands. The first step was the founding of a Lowland-type burgh – Campbeltown. From there, Campbells and their loyal supporters could keep an eye on the rest of Kintyre.

Then, in mid-seventeenth century, came the backwash of the Scottish civil war, with feelings on both sides running desperately high, the name of God invoked at the hangings, houses burnt down and cattle driven. In 1645 General Leslie, who had defeated Montrose at Philiphaugh, massacring all too many prisoners, was anxious to get things finished. There were still MacDonalds holding out in Kintyre, in a wet and stormy May. They were commanded by the old left-handed tough, Coll Ciotach, the MacDonald of Colonsay, and his son Alexander. Among the officers was MacDonald of Largie, the house of the Brounie, on the west side of Kintyre, and one wonders what warning the Brounie may have given before he set out. For the Brounie was active with warnings and the granting of reasonable wishes until quite lately, when Largie Castle was unroofed in order not to have to pay rates, and the poor Brounie no doubt skipped over to the other MacDonald house on tiny Cara island.

The MacDonalds tried to hold the invading army at Rhunahaorine, opposite Gigha, but Leslie won the battle at little loss to his own men, and then marched south after the rest of the flying MacDonalds. It was at the castle, just outside the new Campbeltown settlement, that Leslie, resting and feeding his soldiers, heard that most of the Kintyre men, under the command of Big Archie MacDonald of Sanda, were in the old fort south of the Mull, Dunaverty, preparing for a siege.

Dunaverty was on an ancient rock site, very high and strong, but without water except for one branch of the Coniglen Water, protected by a trench which was held by a strong party of the besieged. But it was here that Leslie's army attacked, and cut off the water. A few hot summer days and surrender was inevitable. Three hundred men came out of Dunaverty; all but one were killed, most hacked to pieces, a few hanged or shot. Others, smoked out of a cave, were handed over to the Scots regiment in France, to serve there for fifteen years, with no possibility of getting word back to their folk.

Even in that state of religious anger and suspicion, many people were shocked. Much harm was done to the Covenanting cause, both then and in later opinion. A few other murders decorated Leslie's return, yet perhaps the worst thing he did was to bring the plague with his army into Kintyre. At the end of the epidemic some parishes had half their land waste; holdings which had once been cultivated gone back to rushes and brambles, heather and bracken. And indeed it was after this that so many Lowland families came to Kintyre and changed the look and speech of it, though there were Campbells as well, mostly from other parts of Argyll.

A later Earl of Argyll started from Campbeltown on his attempt to overthrow the government of James II. Things ended soon and disastrously for him and for his men, some of whom were Kintyre folk who had been pressed into his service. They were banished to the Americas, and bad times followed with reprisal raids, theft and violence. It was not until the eighteenth century that things settled down. Kintyre, in common with the rest of Scotland, was tired of enthusiasms and desperate loyalties, wars and death. It was in this condition of exhaustion and spiritual drowsiness when my great-grandfather and his brother, Robert and James Haldane, came sailing over, landed somewhere about Skipness, breakfasted at the Clonnaig [Claonaig] inn, and proceeded to the conversion of what they called heathen Kintyre, much to their own edification, at least.[1]

During the last century or so, Kintyre has declined in numbers, like all outlying parts of all European countries; for the islands and peninsulas of Greece depopulate themselves as fast as the remote Highlands do, and Athens, absorbing the migrants, begins to be sadly like Glasgow. The old statistics show four times the present population. There are ruins of clachans and single houses all through the glens and the remains of old lazy-bed cultivation now gone back entirely to waste, as it did after the plague. Old legal remains stay too; a single farm may still be in theory a croft, holding all the old common grazing, on which, nowadays, no neighbour puts his cow or sheep. Parts of this, no doubt, was due to wars elsewhere; the Highlanders, always on the edge of the poverty line, were very easily tempted off into the Army, even when their lairds did not offer them like cattle.

Earlier this century agriculture was in a bad way; nothing paid. And, of the twenty-four distilleries working in and around Campbeltown, only two are still in use; the pure Campbeltown malt whisky is soft and deep-toned, but not easy to come by. Again, there is less demand for salt herring, either at home or abroad, and surprisingly little for delicious fresh herrings. Bad years on the Clyde have brought down the number of boats, but things are looking better this year and a fresh mackerel beats even a fresh herring. The Forestry Commission has been a great help, and those who are always nagging at the Commission for planting solid stretches of a single conifer, should be pleased at the modern diversification of planting, though I am sorry to say that when flowering or foliage trees are planted along the edge of forests, they are only too often a prey to the modern raider.

Above all, farming is looking up; there are herds of pedigree Ayrshires and Galloways, and almost every farmer has a hirsel of blackfaced sheep on the hill above his steading. The Milk Marketing Board has been a boon, and the Kintyre Farmers' co-operative collect and market eggs, as well as dealing in seeds, fertilisers and so on; almost everyone has electricity; the days of hand milking are over. And the young farmers are good at keeping the dance going all night!

For the visitor, Kintyre holds extraordinary visual beauty, both from the east and west roads. Even a hardened old native like myself will be unable not to stop and look: the ever-changing seas and skies, the seasons sweeping over the cultivated land, with a scatter of white lambs and woolly calves in spring, summer goldening the green oats, and then the pattern of ripening stooks and the small ricks of hay standing in the fields before they are brought into the stackyards. Sometimes there are seals playing close inshore, or a whole field settled on by a great flock of pink-footed geese. Fallow and Jap deer are fairly common, and there are only too many foxes. There are several pairs of golden eagles, and plenty of rarish sea birds. An old farmer neighbour of mine used to go down to the shore and feed the eider ducks with bread.

Kintyre people are increasingly keen gardeners; in Campbeltown palm trees pop their heads over grey stone walls. Rhododendrons of one kind or another are in flower from January to early July, though it is in June that the wild rhodies which have spread over so many hillsides, burst into magnificent bloom, so that, for the time being, one forgives them for being pests. Come to Kintyre any time of the year. There is always beauty.

Scotland's Magazine, v. 56, June 1960, pp. 32-5

[1] See 'The Haldanes in Kintyre', later in this volume.

In Sight of the Sea

(1964)

Kintyre is always in sight and sound of the sea. The long West Loch almost cuts the isthmus at Tarbert, where King Magnus of the Danes pulled his longships across, full rigged, on rollers.

To the east are the jagged Arran mountains, to the west the low islands – Gigha, haunted Cara, Islay, and Colonsay [1] – and beyond, the soft evening rise of the Paps of Jura.

There is a road all round, often within spindrift distance of the sea. On a strong west wind great gobbets of yellow foam blow across the west road. On the east side the road is narrower, and one is apt to meet a Highland or a shorthorn bull taking his ease on it. In spring the lambs are a hazard, but in a few months they have become traffic-conscious and skip out of the way.

Almost everywhere there is some low-lying land between sea and hill, and all is used by small farmers, partly for cattle and also for the black-faced sheep that spend most of their lives on the hills. Crops are mostly for winter keep: oats, turnips, kale, and potatoes, and good hay.

In the old days I always had a sack or two of oats ground for porridge meal at one of the mills, but now, sadly, it no longer functions. On the broad laggan of Kintyre you will see fine herds of Ayrshire cows; they're mostly polled these days, which spoils their looks, but makes them much easier in the byre or travelling to sales.

For wildlife there is the occasional red deer as well as fallow, Japanese, and roe deer. There are badgers, foxes, and otters, and, of course, the charming red squirrels. These are shy fellows, all of them, but with luck one gets a sudden sight. There is a splendid profusion of birds, from the tiniest finches, the gay flocks of brambling, and the delightful eider duck to the big predators, including golden eagles, as well as the gannets whose bomb diving shows the fisherman where the herring lie.

There are harbour seals and grey seals; they lie out on the rocks and sometimes one can hear them singing and wonder whether they may not be about to shed their sealskin coats, come ashore, and play havoc with local hearts. Porpoises and basking sharks cruise around, and the bigger whales, which, like gannets, show the fishermen where to shoot their nets.

Campbeltown has bus and aeroplane connections to Glasgow, and in summer there is a steamer, but this is usually crowded, and if the town could be joined to the mainland by a car ferry to the Ayrshire coast it would be a help. There are still a few fishing boats here, and the nets still dry on the railings round the harbour, but some of this is due to the rise in the prawn fishing.

Campbeltown and Carradale both have prawn boats as well as ring-net boats, and some crews working during the season with clam dredges. The fishermen's co-operative in Oban collect shellfish, keep lobsters and such in good condition in tanks, and market the rest, to the great satisfaction and profit of the fishermen. Though that isn't to say that you can't buy a local lobster, or for that matter the excellent Campbeltown kippers.

This is oddly beautiful country at all times of the year; in winter, with a light powder of snow on the dark central uplands; in spring as the flowers begin, backed by the light green of larch or beech or the blue-green of pine and fir; in autumn glowing with the orange blaze of bracken and rowan and sometimes the colouring trees, which the Forestry Commission have imaginatively planted along their edges. Don't miss the rhododendrons, the rare and lovely in gardens open to the public, and the ordinary ponticum which covers whole hillsides with purple a month before the heather.

For those who like golf there's a famous course at Machrihanish, a smaller one at Carradale. There are plenty of safe and beautiful bathing beaches. I've never found that the famous Gulf Stream warms the water, but my grandchildren spend hours in it.

And then there are many relics of older times, from Campbeltown Cross itself and the armed abbots on the gravestones at Saddell away back to more ancient burials. Today's campers may well find themselves on a site where earlier campers, shellfish and root gatherers, once lived. But the ghosts, like most of today's fishermen and farmers, are kindly to the stranger.

The Glasgow Herald, 14 November 1964, p. 11

[1] Colonsay does lie to the west of Kintyre, but, unlike the other islands mentioned, does not form part of the view, since it is hidden by Islay.

Wartime at Carradale

(1991)

In 1937, my husband, Dick Mitchison, not yet the Labour MP he became, and my cousin, Archie Haldane, who had not yet written his charming fishing books[1] but worked in the family office in Edinburgh, bought a house and estate of about two hundred acres on the Kintyre peninsula, all of which had gone a bit back and was cheap as such things go. There was a garden, a great square of summer beauty, and there were various people involved, from the head keeper and head gardener down.

I was not at all enamoured with this, having enjoyed summer holidays most when we went off to other bits of Europe. We had to disentangle a lot of things on our buy, including people. I had no wish to run a farm, and the older employees disappeared with pensions. In the end there were five men, including Lachlan whom I asked for, knowing that he deeply wished to come away from his west coast island to somewhere which at that time had a good and easy boat journey to Glasgow. We did not then realise that the big motto in the Islands and Highlands was: Never trust MacBrayne.[2]

There were some happy times, making friends with the fishermen and many of the village, which was still mostly in small cottages, let all summer, with the owners moving into outhouses. We were the Big House and well thought of because we never shut the gate, and made things easier both for fishermen and summer visitors. Lots of friends came and there were all sorts of goings-on. I found it a good place for writing. Then came the war. We sat there listening to the radio. It had happened; one of my eldest son's Cambridge friends said: 'Now everything we ever said is pre-war.' The same applied to the estate and all the rest of Carradale.

The same old enemy, but for different reasons; fortunately, not the same old war. Fewer of our friends were killed. But those of us who remembered 1914 were struck to the heart. However, we were deeply occupied with the arrival of Glasgow [evacuee] children and I found myself suddenly having to take on a farm. We had let a neighbour browse cattle on fields which were never given any help and whose fences were wobbly. I had to make the basics of a farm which meant, to start with, fences and ploughing. One of the men on the estate had some farming knowledge and I was told to keep him while the others went off to war. All returned, cheerfully and intact.

We started with a borrowed plough and a few essential tools, but we had half a year ahead of us and, almost at once, the Kintyre War Agricultural Committee, quite happy to give a lot of help to eager newcomers, began to look after me. The field just in front of the house – the cricket-field it was called – was to be ploughed and sown, and the broken old fence newly put up.

I remember harrowing there with the big horse Jo, and his companion, the riding pony. The Navy in the bay was doing some [gunnery] practice, all too like the real thing. One shell went so close to our heads that the two horses bolted. I still had the reins but could I turn in time? Would they jump the fence? Would I fall into the spokes of the big harrow? At the last moment they saw the fence and stopped, sweating.

I remember, too, that Lachlan, ploughing a more difficult field, went aside so as not to go over a lapwing's nest. Other pictures from then are still in my mind. Sowing seed with both hands from a sowing-sheet strapped over my shoulder. Oats were not difficult, but meadow grass was, for it was so light. One had to choose a calm day and it was as well to have inside of one a solid verse, such as the Scottish church psalms, to keep a good measure going and not waste expensive seed.

Harvest itself started with Lachlan scything and me binding. It was several years before we had a proper binder. However we had borrowings and help from friends and neighbours and tried to return it. Some things were regularly done by the group of local farmers and there was much help, too, from neighbours who had been on farms but who were now on the old side. They still, I think, enjoyed giving a hand. For a time we winnowed the oats in the big barn with the help of the squeaky old water-wheel, always slowing to a halt just when everything was going well. Many friends came to help, and sometimes during the war it was hard enough to get extras for hungry work-guests. There was no extra sugar for jam-making – only what one could somehow squeeze out of the ration. How splendid when, occasionally, there was a military guest with extra rations, which I grabbed. Our only electricity lighted a few lamps from a small engine, nothing like enough for a freezer.

There was a lot of fun, especially in the building of ricks and then the roofing of them. Now and then the agricultural committee turned up, or one member of it did, quite helpfully, but after the beginning they rather lost interest. There was one very lazy farm a bit further along the sea edge, but most of us got decent harvests and above all potatoes, which were a boring lifeline.

Things changed a lot in, I think, 1943, when I got a tractor second-hand from my uncle in Perthshire, and what an excitement driving it! On the whole it was a faithful steed and if it went wrong, one could give it a big knock or else put a hairpin through the pipe. But most of the work was done by hands and feet. We got extra rations in the potato harvest and I tried to provide a decent, heavy sandwich. Schools were closed and children keen enough to help. In some curious way coffee was never difficult to buy – had there been a big order for it just before the war? Most of my family were coffee-drinkers, so there was often tea to spare. But there was no way of keeping fruit or green vegetables, and winter eating was mostly tatties and salt herring. How I regretted not taking an offer from a friend in Campbeltown, a few miles down the road, who was doing Army jobs, to get me some of the most attractive rations. Most farms made butter and, after a while, we managed some, but it wasn't easy to do all the things one hoped to do.

Of course I wanted milk to start with, but my first buy of Dumfries cattle went down when the tests began. I had to start again with one milk cow and fewer happy hopes. The seagulls came ramping over and went off with my chickens. One of the fields seemed hopelessly wet all over: I got a team of Irish drain-diggers, but it didn't work. It was another year before it stopped flooding. I put a shuck³ through my boot when I was cutting the tops off turnips and walked back sploshing blood. In fact I did every possible silly thing. But by the end it did look more like a farm.

We had a relatively small flock of very ordinary sheep, but there was a lot of get-together over dipping. We sheared them ourselves; I was slow but at least I never made a cut. I remember Lachlan throwing me the big tup (well tied!) to get on with. This tup was in the habit of coming to the house and shouting till I found a bit of bread or turnip for him. The time came for a change and I felt he would miss me. I said to the buyer that he had been quite a pet and I thought he might miss me. The buyer winked and took a bit of something out of his pocket, held it out and away went my ram, not even saying goodbye.[4]

Gradually we acquired more of the essential gear. Our sheep and cattle got reasonable prices. But I had a lot more things to do, including looking after some of De Gaulle's army, men who had been tortured by their French fellow citizens, and getting in touch with Glasgow socialists – and of course communists. Some turned out to be quite helpful at harvest. Lachlan and I went together to the sales. In one of these one of my own beasts turned on me (and who can blame a frightened young cow in the ring?) and I was only saved by Lachlan at the last moment.

After my first borrowed reaper I got a new reaper-and-binder. Every year the big thresher which wandered round all Kintyre used to come and we all got together, for it needed a small team to work properly, forking off the stacks, binding the corn bags, trotting them off and of course killing the large rat families from the bottom of each stack. One year I was driving the bags back to the house and a rat suddenly jumped in beside me out of the killing scene. We looked at one another and I took off saying nothing while he sat on the seat. A little way back I opened the door on his side. That showed I was never a real farmer.

The Countryman, v. 96, October/November 1991, pp. 40-5

[1] *The Path by the Water* (1944), *By Many Waters* (1946), and *By River, Stream and Loch* (1973).

[2] The direct steamer service from Campbeltown to Glasgow, calling at Carradale, was discontinued at the outbreak of World War II and never reinstated.

[3] This may represent 'heuk' (pronounced 'hyuck'), the Scots word for a sickle (not very suitable for the job, and likely to lead to an accident), or possibly 'shuch', a specialised knife for snedding turnips.

[4] See 'Philip Ram' and 'I'll Never Forget', later in this volume.

PART II

THE VILLAGE AND THE BIG HOUSE

The cast of the Carradale play 'A Matter Between Macdonalds'
The programme and cast list for the play is on page 34

Village Play-Making

(1941)

This was our second New Year play at Carradale, but since our first the Village Hall has been finished, with curtains and a stage – not deep enough, only ten feet – with inadequate wing space and no dressing-rooms; all that, nicely provided for on the pre-war plan, had to be left out. We were lucky to get it finished at all. But we had electric light, enthusiasm, ingenuity, and an author old and experienced enough not to mind any amount of collaboration: that at least I can say for myself.

I thought I knew from last year more or less who could learn a part and who could act. Many of what ultimately decided to call itself the Carradale Dramatic Club were members of the Gaelic choir, with singing and speaking voices far more full of colour and warmth and rhythm than any you get in the south. The feeling was that we should do a Highland play. I had lately been reading *The Lyon in Mourning*, a contemporary collection of Jacobite documents; I kept it out of the London Library for six months, excusing myself with the thought that so valuable a book should not be allowed to return to the blitz! Jennie at the paper shop had the high cheekbones and dark eyes, the daring but gentle look of Flora MacDonald. Chrissie and Denny must obviously be in; Willie must have a part where he could play the pipes. Among these dark or red Highlanders, one fair one, whose memory and acting I knew could be first-rate, had to be the Prince; I stopped him on his way back from work, in his torn and patched forestry clothes, to tell him so.

Almost all our young men were gone, to patrol boats and minesweepers mostly, including my chief collaborator from last year, and blackbird-voiced, blackbird-haired Jemima had gone to nurse in Glasgow. Most of the cast were well over thirty; one or two had passed fifty easily. Apart from last year's play, which was a kind of Nativity pageant, involving little movement, only one had ever had any experience of acting before, though some had sung in the Mod competitions. Last year we'd had no make-up, but it was essential on the real stage; several jibbed at that at first, felt, I think,

Programme.

THE CARRADALE DRAMATIC CLUB

PRESENTS

A MATTER BETWEEN MACDONALDS,

A ROMANTIC PLAY

by

NAOMI MITCHISON

The action of this play takes place on Sunday June 29th and Monday June 30th 1746, in the Island of Skye.

Characters in the order of their appearance

Angus MacDonald, shepherd to Sir Alexander
      MacDonald of Mougstot, ... Dennis MacIntosh
Eilidh MacDonald, serving woman to Mrs MacDonald
      of ~~Mougstot~~ Kingsburgh. ... ... Betty Mackenzie
Wounded Man, ... Robert Paterson
Neil MacKechan MacDonald, ... ~~Willie Galbraith~~ D. Campbell.
Prince Charles Edward Stewart, as Betty
      Burke, ... Duncan Munro
Lachlan, a servant to Kingsburgh, ... Lachlan MacLean
MacDonald of Kingsburgh, ... Donald Jackson
Mrs MacDonald of Kingsburgh, his wife, ... Chrissie Paterson
Nannie MacDonald, her daughter, ... Margaret MacDougall
Katie, a serving woman, ... Kirstie MacConnachie
Flora MacDonald, ... ~~Jennie Galbraith~~ Jemima Maclean
Sandy MacDonald, ... Willie ~~Alexander~~ Galbraith
Ishbel of the Smithy, ... Margaret Paterson
Lieutenant MacLeod, ... Duncan Semple
Men and Maids at Kingsburgh:—Sarah MacKinnon, Lilla MacIntosh, Effie Fisher, ~~Jim McKinven~~, Kathleen MacDougall, Nan Galbraith, Minnie Paterson, Peggy Mitchell, Ella MacMillan, Mairi Buchanan, ~~Ian MacDonald~~, Valentine Mitchison. Dorothy Melville, Ilts Meugo.

Characters in the Epilogue

The Child, ... Valentine Mitchison
The Woman, ... Naomi Mitchison

Scene I.

An open place, a few miles north of Kingsburgh.

Scene II

Mrs MacDonald of Kingsburgh's room.

Scene III.

Hall at MacDonald of Kingsburgh's house.

Scene IV.

A short way from the house.

EPILOGUE.

that it was slightly ungodly, explained to me that in those days no Highlander painted his face. ... But after a few private séances we got round this. It was difficult for R., in charge of the sewing-basket and the make-up box, and who had done it for schoolboys, to know how to deal with these rope-scarred hands and sea-and-wind-beaten faces. But there was a strength and nobility there which needed no disguising.

I got my story roughed out. It became clear that, to establish immediate local colour, and also for the sake of historical probability, the opening must be in Gaelic. My own being fragmentary, I invoked Donald J., the schoolmaster, another dark, six-foot Highlander, who walked over with my small daughter after Latin, seized on the script of the first scene, put in the Gaelic, and read the rest aloud with such conviction that it became obvious that he could and must do the difficult part of MacDonald of Kingsburgh, largely using the actual words of the reported conversations in my source books. Apart from his dozen lines in the Nativity play, he had never acted, but he was a real gift to the producer! He could learn a long part, had no stage difficulties, stood still or moved with a swing, remembered his stage placing, and, when other people got into a muddle, he 'gagged' in the Gaelic.

The next three-quarters of the play was written with my mind easy about one actor at least; but the first scene wasn't finished with. Chrissie P., one of my stand-bys, wondered if there was a small part for her husband. I had never associated the skipper of the *Rolling Wave* with anything so frivolous as acting, but I know now that both Chrissie and Rob will be two I shall be depending on for our next play. We discussed what he should be, and finally put him into the first scene, heightening its dramatic effect, as a wounded man from Culloden. Nor was that all; several others were seized with a desire to act, including even an elder of the kirk. Lachlan, who has to be put down as half an agricultural worker on each of the two buff forms which, for its own reasons, the Department of Agriculture likes to divide my farm into, thought he would like his part mostly in Gaelic. We sat down to it. He was to be MacDonald of Kingsburgh's groom, who has a mare requisitioned by the Hanoverians. What was the mare to be called? After some thought, Lachlan asked: 'What colour would the mare be?' We went deep into the facts of a situation!

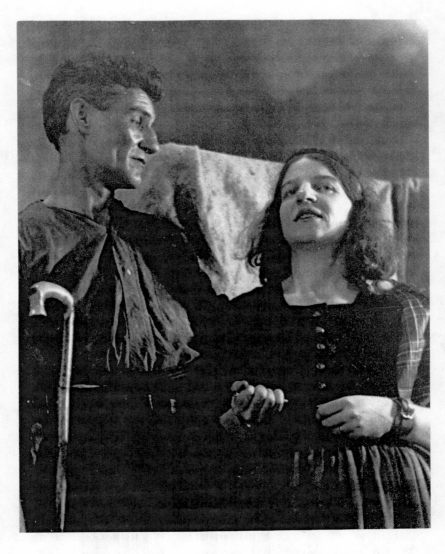

Denis Macintosh and Mitchison in costume for the play

We began our first rehearsals more than two months before the production date, but it was none too soon. We could only have them on Saturdays, when the fishermen were in – Sunday rehearsals were unthinkable. When the boats were doing well, peculiar difficulties arose. We Scots are a hospitable race; it had been real pain to the men of the fishing fleet during the bad years when they could not afford to offer so much as a glass of whisky to a friend. Now, assuaging their hurt pride, they tended to overdo it, and there were times when rehearsals became a little complicated. But they worked during the week: two boats would get together somewhere up Loch Fyne and rehearse their parts. I made up my mind to start, even when the rehearsals were only at the house – for the Games Committee couldn't bear us to steal their Saturday night! – to get the entrances, exits, and stage planning right from the beginning, but to allow and encourage suggestions and alterations from the cast. These came, shyly perhaps, but steadily; in general they were dramatically sound. Sometimes there were verbal alterations, for instance where I had used an east coast Scotticism, dating from my own childhood, but wrong for west coast speech rhythm. Songs and action were introduced. By the end half the Gaelic choir were in for one scene. Would it be all right if we did or said this or that? It would come easier so. I altered my script as the words altered themselves.

When it came to dressing, we borrowed from far and near; lovely MacDonald kilts and plaids, soft from vegetable dyes and much wearing; claymores and plaids; lace and jewels – these hardly seen from the audience but giving the wearers a sense of period and change that helped them over stage shyness. The claymores suggested a sword dance for my ten-year-old; we wanted them drawn and flung down in grand steel arcs; she cut her bare foot at one rehearsal in the small space we could give her, but not on the great day. Scenery was kept very simple: for the indoor scenes the ordinary curtains of the hall, with a trophy of arms wired on; silver candlesticks and bowls that lit up well – silver which is a nuisance to clean and which I, at least, find over ostentatious for private use, so that I had it put away, now at last coming into its own for a communal use and pleasure. Outdoor scenes were harder; we had to have a back-cloth. We sewed lengths of hessian all one afternoon;

Mitchison's daughter Val performing the sword dance.

it was eyeleted for cords and sized, but nobody felt competent to paint a romantic background. However, the sword-dancer's slightly older brother came back from school and set to work, after a walk round 'to see what shape the hills were'. Unfortunately he painted the sky last and it ran a bit, but that didn't show from in front! Our wings were screens borrowed from the first-aid class, covered loosely with canvas given by one of the boats.

All sorts of things came in useful. Duncan S., whose farm land marches with mine, and who is now lending me his tractor and disc plough for a hard piece of ground, was my one Hanoverian. At first I thought his uniform would have to be hired and would take from our earnings. But an old hunting-coat that had belonged to some Edwardian laird, filled in with a jabot of lace, a felt hat of my own looped into three corners, lightish breeches, and the black rubber thigh boots that are so useful round the midden, combined with excellent acting to produce the right military impression. In historical plays the men's clothes are much harder to get right: even our kilts and plaids were historically inaccurate, but our audience was not too critical. We decided against the historically accurate wig, as well, partly because of the expense of hiring and still more because one needs to get accustomed to wearing them, and the ordinary theatrical wig, at least, would not have gone with these faces. Duncan S. had given a fine sheepskin for the kilted shepherd, but Denny, who was playing it, refused to have anything to do with the skin: nets and herring, yes; but no' sheep! And indeed it was a bit raw in parts! We cut strips off it for leggings, pinning them over stockings. I found, rather to my shame, that my own summer sandals, with a plain strap across, were none too small for these men. Most of the girls gallantly went barefoot; short hair was a difficulty, but the matrons wore caps, and much was done with tartan scarves and handkerchiefs. Skirts were stiffened with wire; my waiting-maid heroine, Eilidh, even unearthed an old crinoline frame, but we discarded it finally, having discovered for ourselves that there is more difference than appears between the Victorian and the Georgian dress skeleton. She was a comparative newcomer to the village, her husband away in the army; she hardly knew a soul at the beginning of the rehearsals, but by New Year she was part of us.

On one thing I held out against the cast. They all wanted to bring in Jacobite songs, but, as I told them, it was highly unlikely that 'Speed, Bonny Boat' should have been sung the evening of the landing on Skye! Yet the idea kept cropping up; we finally compromised on having it sung between scenes. I didn't fuss about the pipe music and the Gaelic songs, so long as they were not obviously modern; one song was put in because – so they told me, and no doubt they knew – it was written about a girl of the same house as the MacDonalds in the play.

The play ended by having a verse epilogue; this was no part of the original scheme; I had thought the short play would put fully as much strain on the memories of unaccustomed actors as they could bear. But they kept on asking me: What happened afterwards? As most of the characters were historical, I could find out by digging around in various books. That started me on a process of historical thinking, some of which I put into the epilogue, speaking it partly myself. I had not meant to mix my southern voice (though perhaps not so tonelessly highbrow as it was two years ago!) with the lovely Highland voices, let alone that a producer can't also be actor. But this seemed indicated, and the rest wanted me in. Another reason for the epilogue was to give the forester-prince, a fine verse speaker, the final curtain, where the whole thing was brought up to date – on my theory of history – and put directly across to the audience on their own terms. All this might have bored a more sophisticated audience or one without that sense of continuity with the past which Scots country people have. They liked it.

We got the prince hastily into kilt and shirt for this, with a drawn sword; during the play, when he was in disguise, he wore an Italian officer's cloak – anyone capturing any more and wanting to dispose of them, please let me know! – and yards and yards of the cheapest striped cotton (very cheap stuffs often don't date). It was amazing how much he took even when we had induced him to remove coat, waistcoat, and a whole collection of jerseys!

The dress rehearsal was discouraging; they usually are. But on the evening, all went well. The second-sight scene was startlingly impressive, instead of funny; the lovers, who had tended to rehearse at arm's length, now acted with fire and romance and even held their final embrace until the curtain went down, without giggling! Those who had been stiff and shy suddenly came to life. The singing was grand. It was a difficult audience to act to; some of it had never seen any kind of play before; many had only come to see their parents or uncles and aunts make fools of themselves. But next time we do a play I think more of them will come, and more seriously.

Of course there were bad moments: while I crouched in the wings with the prompt copy, keeping my head out of the way of the floodlight and trying to stop the characters in the wings from talking, I promised myself that I at least would never do this kind of thing again. But, if Hitler doesn't interrupt us, we are going on tour with it next month, to various halls round about Kintyre. And most of us, I expect, suppose we shall be doing it again, and gathering in more actors and helpers. Sometimes we shall act already written plays, though I shall be surprised if they don't get altered in the acting. But we shall produce our own as well.

P.S. – Since writing this we have taken the play on tour, as far as petrol restrictions would allow us, collecting solid sums for Red Cross, and so on; it was all quite strenuous – the producer walked sixteen miles across the hills once,[1] to measure her stage! Both cast and play have altered slightly; songs were put in or taken out; once one of the Gaelic choir came back on leave and was immediately roped in to sing in the ceilidh scene. We have had all kinds of quarrels and misadventures, but we have got over them and now we are beginning to wonder what we shall try next!

SMT Magazine, v. 28, November 1941, pp. 23-5

[1] See *Among You Taking Notes* (1985), pp. 148-50.

What to Do with the Big House

(1943)

The Wednesday class has just left. Dougie doesn't get spare petrol for his bike any longer, so the perilous journeys – though they always got back safe, somehow – with himself, Chrissie, and Christine, and maybe the box for the bagpipes if they were wanted elsewhere, never happen now. They are all off together, a wee glisten of light on the oilskins before the black-out shuts it fast again. Duncan has said something funny and there's Margaret's deep laugh and Edda's light one. The washing-up has been done with competence and dispatch; Christine, Lois and Val have finished off the odd bits of sandwiches. Rosemary and I push back the library chairs, and see that the gramophone records are back; Duncan and Ian have been playing the romantic Gaelic love songs which seem to me to be overcharged with sentiment. They say it's because I don't understand them. But if the fishing is slack next week, Denny may be over, and we'll try and get him to sing. Lilla will come if he does, and then she and Margaret can sing 'Afton Water'. Willie, if we coax him, will sing his own song about his own fishing boat, the *Cluaran*, that Ishbel wrote the words to and that he put the tune to himself.

Jean, our teacher, has left early, with her lasses; they must be up for the milking to-morrow morning, while the rest of us are still asleep; Jean's neat feet, that take so easily to the intricate, varied steps of the country dances, will splash through the dawn-wet yard to the byres. Her forebears, also dancing 'The Mucking of Geordie's Byre', no doubt went the same way barefoot.

The Wednesday class is a more or less serious country-dancing class, started by some of us who were bored by the glooms and bottom-waggling of 'modern' dancing, as interpreted locally. A fox-trot or tango can be beautiful and satisfying to dancers and onlookers when really well done, but the unskilled are an inelegant sight and usually look worried! However, we all agreed that it was no use doing the country dances as badly as they are often done in the Hall, and that we would like to learn to do them properly, and to do others. Sometimes in summer there is a sudden influx to the class

– visitors, and others – once a dozen boy scouts, some so small one tripped over them, others so large that they tripped over everyone else – and then we just do the easy ones, but the regulars like to learn new ones. I am clumsy-footed by comparison with the rest, but I love the patterns of the dances, the concentration they need at first, the finish that can be put on to them. We all have our favourites.

As often as not some of the class will come over on a Saturday, though not if it's a cinema Saturday, for then we are all over at the Hall, and I am taking the money at the door, getting into a muddle over the change, and probably being turfed out into the meaner position of tearing the tickets and keeping one-half in case the Excise should call in person. There will then be some who are not actually in the class, but who like that kind of thing. The fishermen will be in. Red Rob and Johnnie will likely be over. If Nurse hasn't been called out for a case, she may be over. Sometimes Peter brings his melodeon, and Dougie will play the pipes for a reel or two, but mostly we depend on the gramophone. Any of them will pick up the easier country dances – Bob of Fettercairn, Cumberland reel, and the like; it's there in the blood. The waltz country dance is another that everyone takes to, and we usually have a set of quadrilles. Between times we have relatively 'soft' dances like Pride of Erin, St Bernard, and some of the barn dances and two-steps. It all has to end before midnight and the Sabbath except during double summer time, when only the very strict feel that it is really twelve o'clock when the clock says so. Indeed, I have known the clock to be put back, and that not by myself.

So much for the dancing. In winter there are more classes and practices. Once a week we have a girls' choir practising Scots and Gaelic songs. Lilla conducts it and Ishbel supervises the Gaelic, thinking ill of our Kintyre pronunciation compared with that on her native Uist. Before the war Carradale had one of the best of the Gaelic choirs that used to compete at the Mods; for the time being, this has had to dissolve, so many are called up or doing war work; but these younger girls, mostly between fourteen and eighteen, are perhaps the makings of a new choir. Then the children had a concert for the Red Cross and that meant practising songs, plays, and dances almost every evening after school – and where, if not here? I gave them much advice, most of which they didn't take, and helped with the clothes; I was much flattered when one of them asked me to teach her to dance the hornpipe! There are rumours of a bagpipe class; if that comes to anything, we hope to see the Home Guard with a full pipe band yet.

If the village hall had been built according to our pre-war plan, with a couple of committee rooms and a library, the Big House wouldn't have been used so much. As it is, the cinema committee will meet here sometimes instead of at the hall, or one of the other committees. As a village, we tend to go into committee, thus providing ourselves with fine opportunities for gossip and back chat. Nor, if there had been a local library of any kind, would our own be so much borrowed from. But Argyll, a poor and backward area, alone of all Scottish counties, never went in for the Carnegie County Library scheme.[1] So now children and grown-ups alike come and borrow books, mostly adventure stories, but quite a lot of travel, history – above all Scottish history – economics, and so on. My Neil Gunns are practically always on the wander, above all his *Silver Darlings*, the epic of herring fishing, which the men here know for the good thing it is.

Most of the houses within reach of Campbeltown have parties of sailors out for tea from time to time. This has usually to be on a Sunday, and the unfortunate English find themselves unable to appreciate the Scottish Sabbath! Nothing can be more depressing than a Highland small town on a Sunday, with the self-righteous only too much in evidence. From time to time a lorry-load of sailors comes out to us on a Sunday afternoon, but by no means all my friends in the village are prepared to come and entertain them, especially if it means dancing, as it usually does – and oh, what a passion they have for the worst kind of jazz music! Food isn't too easy, but they usually bring butter and sugar, and we give them an enormous rabbit pie and baked potatoes and salad. One harvest Sunday I mobilised them to help me shift the stooks in a field, but few of them had ever handled a sheaf, and none of them would let it be explained to them, so the result wasn't a great success. This year we have gone on with the harvest work on fine Sundays, but an elder observed quite seriously that whenever the farmers took in their corn on a Sunday it always rained on the Monday just to show them.

We had some manoeuvres here in spring, and the men were mostly billeted in the village hall. We managed to get up a concert for them one night, and it was suggested that some of them would like a 'sacred concert' on the Sunday – this to happen, of course, over at the Big House. A couple of dozen men turned up and the front rows joined in, but the rest curled up comfortably and played cards or read the *New Yorker*, while we sang Moody and Sankey hymns at them! I wish I knew what they thought of us, or, indeed, what the many English soldiers who are quartered in remote parts of the Highlands, which they approach with distrust and whose beauties they tend not to appreciate, think of their northern neighbours. I know they think ill of our squalid public-houses, and English country boys long for a decent country pub, where you can have a game of darts and a glass of cider or shandy, and nobody any the worse for drink. I hope the Scots boys who are quartered in England will demand such places when they come back.

The Sabbath is a difficult question; there is little to be said for merely turning it into a play-day, just the same as any other, which has been the main alternative. We want to be able to re-focus our ideas somehow; but the Church is not the only place where that can be done – nor do people always do it there. I should like, for instance, to see a Sunday debating society and much Sunday reading; the alternative for the young people is mooching around, cat-calling between boys and girls, or worse mischief. And there is altogether too much regard for a Sabbath by the clock. I have known someone refuse to go out poaching on a Saturday night, for fear the ploy might go on into the sacred hours! His poaching, of course, like most, perhaps, in the Highlands, would have been for sport only, never for profit; an infringement of legal rights, perhaps, but never of moral law.

Game preserving is a sore subject, and keepers may make trouble which it takes years to wipe out. Drink is another sore subject. The price of whisky has upped, but so have most wages, not to speak of the fishermen's share-outs. At New Year, our neighbours bring us bottles which have to be sampled, and for myself, I can't bear the smell of the stuff! A pleasanter New Year present is the rare shortbread, or the lump of coal in a bag: 'warmth from me to you'. When our eldest son was married, we introduced champagne, erroneously thought to be a temperance drink; as one of our guests, minding pleasantly on it later on, observed: 'It slipped down the like of lemonade'. That was a grand wedding party, though some strange rites were practised on the bridal pair – and there were some which I heard of in time and stopped! The wedding cake was a present from the baker, and such a cake as we shan't see again until peace-time.

One of the few pleasures of the war, though, is this matter of presents. We are always passing things about; I will find a net of herring at the door, or maybe a skate, for it is known I like these odd creatures. Many of our business transactions, indeed, will be in kind. I bought my circular saw with the summer feeding of some young rams! Such transactions induce a feeling of satisfaction : I had grazing to spare, Duncan had a saw to spare. It all fitted in nicely, whereas, if there had been money to pay – well, nobody ever has money to spare!

All this is part of neighbourly life. But the Big House has seldom been genuinely neighbourly. It has been in a different layer of culture, centred, as often as not, on London. And – it has had that money to spare which its neighbours didn't have. Things are different now, and the folk in the Big House have come to understand that, not everywhere, but wherever they have any roots, native or acquired. Yet, to be neighbourly, they have to overcome the fear and distrust of two hundred years.[2] Reasonableness alone will not do that. Nor even endless patience, though that is needed too. How many times I have seen something start so well! – a class or a practice or some attempt at education – and then break down. The West Coast depression had been too much for it. I think this will go on happening; yet I must be patient; every time a thing starts is like the false start of an engine – disappointing enough, but warming the thing up until the real start comes and the engine can be put into gear and go ahead.

Until the engine starts, until Scotland comes alive again, as I believe she will, the Big Houses must help. The only alternative is to walk out, to leave the buildings and the gardens to become schools, convalescent homes, small hotels, or – during the war – even to meet their final degradation as Government offices. Yet that seems rather a pity. Schools and hospitals should be built as such, not made to adapt themselves to all too solid masonry. Is there anything else that can be done, which will be for the good of the community?

I think there is, but it is none too easy. If the Big House is to become part of the life of the surrounding countryside, its standards must not be too different; it must not overawe. And its stock must be common stock. I think, because I am a writer, that it can be allowed and excused in Carradale that this house should have shelves of books; they are not so much property as tools. Besides, we are a fundamentally literate nation; books are thought well of here by manual workers who might laugh at them in the south. But there are certain quite unimportant forms of class difference in manners and customs which do count. Perhaps they shouldn't; perhaps it is illogical of the ones outside the Big House to care about them, but none of us are reasonable that way. I remember when I stopped having meals at upper-class urban times, taking to the high tea, which is the sensible meal for people whose working day ends at five or six, somebody coming in and nodding, saying with warm approval that it was 'like folks'.

Yet the main thing is the personal attitude. If I consider myself superior, at once I cut myself off. Even if I consider myself different. Honestly, I know I am more intelligent than most of my neighbours, but what is that intelligence for if not to be at their service, to be used by those whose native intelligence has been crushed and stunted by poverty and anxiety? I can write an official letter easily; and I can type and duplicate it; surely I should do so for them! And so they are beginning to know. To some extent, already; more, I hope, later on, the Big House is a kind of bureau for semi-social, semi-legal advice (the more so when my husband is at home), a place where typewriter and telephone are at the service of those who want them, where officialese can be translated, where doctors' jargon, which perhaps they were afraid to think about or ask about, can be explained. A few children come here for help, on and off, with their school French and so on, or for stray facts that they cannot run down elsewhere. All this is only beginning. I know that there are immense hang-overs, plenty of people who will never be friends, who will never feel at ease here, nor want to come. There are those who think the old ways were better – they would rather have the gates shut in their own faces, even, so long as they were slammed still harder in the faces of some of their acquaintances!

Yet, while I think myself more intelligent and far-sighted than most of my neighbours, equally honestly I don't think I am morally better than they are. Where they can be good, kind, and brave, and in general just, simply and warmly and from the heart, I must twist and double-cross, mixing my motives. Artistically, again, I am more educated, have wider tastes, but I am no more sensitive, no more delicately adjusted to fine shades. If I am more skilled in some ways – rare ones, perhaps – they are more skilled in other ways. We can, and do, learn from one another.

This, then, is what one thinks after the class. And during the class – what then? Dancing Glasgow Highlanders, admiring Margaret's footwork, trying to copy it, caught up by the tune, the randy words that sing themselves into it: The elders of the kirk were there and quite surprised to see ... Dancing Fettercairn, one's hair brushing back against one's partner's arm in the allemande. Dancing the breathless schottische, close and wild, close to the wild remote eyes and mouth of the wild partner, the fisherman, the forester, the farmer – what then? Are we anything but equals in the great pleasure, the heightened living of the dance? Have there not been ceilidhs and dancing all over the Highlands? People dance still where the Highlands have trickled down into the Clyde valley; there is dancing and singing and the spoken Gaelic in Glasgow workers' living-rooms. There is story-telling and great laughter, and thousands of songs. How should that be killed by the wireless and the newspapers and the unneighbourliness of cities? How would it not happen again in the Big House?

There, I suppose, the thing is. It is simple enough. It costs very little. We give people some of those peculiar drinks that go round just now, which look like orange; in winter there is tea. Just now we have tomatoes in the garden, so we make cheese and tomato sandwiches; earlier, there were gooseberries. Sometimes someone will bring a basket of scones or a quarter-pound of sugar. I remember, two years back, how people sat on the edges of their chairs, how it took all one's patience and efforts to get them going. Now there are only moments of that. People used to ring the bell, or wait, standing on one foot in the hall; now they walk in. Angus was angry at me the other day for knocking at his door instead of coming in. 'How at all would you knock?' he said; it was a bad, modern custom. In the good days when everyone was poor together there was none of this knocking. Nor was the Big House part of that friendliness. It could be now.

SMT Magazine, v. 31, February 1943, pp. 30-4

[1] Argyll County Library service was eventually set up in 1947.

[2] Mitchison expands on this theme in her children's novel *The Big House* (1950).

Garden Fete

(1950)

The campers and I were furiously picking raspberries. The two mathematicians were working out the odds in a penny-throwing game. Val was making some rather nasty sweets with golden syrup and cocoa and what-not. Janet was cutting up the slab cake and swiss rolls which had come from Glasgow two days before. The urn and cups which we borrow every year from the Village Hall duly appeared. And we were all looking at the weather.

The morning before we had turned the cut hay which had been rained on for days and had to be tugged out from the growing grass. I had two blisters from raking and yet another from picking sweet peas in the evening. To pick them with the quick finger movement that breaks the stem clean without tugging, the juice always comes on a certain part of one's middle finger. However, I had some ten shillings' worth picked and in water overnight.

It had rained again in the morning, and the rasps were soft, but eatable. We had skimmed the milk and there should be enough for quite a lot of saucers of raspberries and cream at a shilling each. The rest would go by the pound. The red currants were not ripe and the late Scotch strawberries were melting into pulp under the rain, but there were some white currants ripe and sweet.

In the old days, when there was a District Nursing Association, and people felt they had to keep it going, I would have had a lot more local help, from the committee and their friends. But now the nurse's salary is guaranteed under the Health Scheme; the proceeds of the garden fete would go to tidy up the Pensions Scheme. This means that the districts which could not afford a nurse – and there were quite a number of them – now get one, and the anxiety and worry, and 'Can we afford to let her have a car or must she go all up the glen on her bicycle?' are over. But the local interest has gone too.

A few faithful members of the old Association turned up in the afternoon. Nan always does the fruit-stall, at which there is a huge queue. Lilla always leaves her paper shop in charge of a very small assistant and does the flower-stall. But we would never manage without our annual camp.

The summer visitors, who are our main source of profit, began, as usual, to come about 2.15. The Fete is supposed to be from three to six to suit the Campbeltown buses, but that doesn't stop them. I hadn't got my collectors on the gates quite in time, and an ingenious small boy had stationed himself there and took the shillings from the first two or three old ladies, no doubt having in mind that there would be a travelling fair at Carradale at the end of the week!

However, the weather was keeping up, we had moved out the trestle-tables and all the garden chairs and set up sideshows. The two mathematicians had put the finishing touches to their money game. The shilling was in the bucket. The beans were in the bottle. I rushed up to change out of my raspberry-stained working clothes into something suitable for the lady of the house.

I came down, ducking under the No Admittance placard I had put at the foot of the stairs. Last year visitors had wandered all over the house, had opened drawers and commented loudly on the untidiness of my bedroom. This year I was prepared to tell them that we had a case of plague upstairs.

Already a party was gathering to be taken round. We had done a frantic tidy-up in the drawing-room, but even so there was a sewing-machine, sundry bits of material, the remains of the mathematicians' calculations and my desk in its usual state of chaos. The gramophone records on the library floor had been gathered up, and the dining-room, for a wonder, was quite respectable. I took a deep breath and intimated that there was a bowl for those viewing the house who cared to contribute. It is supposed to be a silver collection, but there are many silver threepenny bits in Scotland and I do no better than the churches.

The drawing-room is full of bits and pieces of various ages and places. I gave my usual little lecture on the Greek and Peruvian pottery, the Jacobite wine-glass, the Swedish straw toys, the books, the pictures and the view. I have a turn about abstract art, illustrated from Wyndham Lewis[1] and Gertrude Hermes.[2] By now I am quite good at that and forestall the question: 'But what is it *of*?' I realise that most people are much more interested in things to use than things to look at. But I was not quite prepared for the old lady who asked if anyone lived here. I ought to have said, No, it is the family ghost who uses the sewing-machine.

By now there were quite a number of children chewing happily at Val's sweets. The mathematicians were raking in the halfpennies. The raffle tickets were getting sold. The raspberries and gooseberries had all gone, but nobody wanted the delicious white currants. And so far the rain had kept off.

At last I had taken round everyone who wanted to be taken. I had made my last joke for the afternoon. Perhaps half a dozen people had really liked the pictures, but I am almost sure most of them thought they were not only crazy, but downright ugly. Yet, if any one of them had been willing to make a slight change of focus, I am sure I could have made them see what it was all about. But for the vast majority of people in Great Britain there is no attempt made at education in any form of artistic appreciation. So the gap grows between people who like two quite different kinds of surroundings, and are uncomfortable in one another's.

We piled our takings together, weighty with pennies and halfpennies. With expenses off, it will work out round about £20. The house does not need quite so much cleaning as it did when people walked all over the bedrooms, too, but still there is an accumulation of mud and sweet-papers and dropped flower petals. Washing up began. And so did the rain.

Scotland 44, October 1950, pp. 10-12

[1] Percy Wyndham Lewis (1882-1957), artist and writer, collaborated with Mitchison on the novella *Beyond This Limit* (1935) and painted her portrait in 1938.

[2] Gertrude Hermes (1901-83), printmaker, sculptor and designer, a friend of Mitchison.

Christmas at the Big House

(1951)

I gird up my brawny thighs. I roll up the sleeves from my work-grimed fists. The Christmas holidays are beginning. Have we asked more people than there are beds for? Yes, yes, but some of them probably will end by not managing to hitch-hike this far; if they do it will no doubt be a pleasure for them to sleep in the coal hole. I shan't bother anyway. Everything will be all right. Last year we still had our old electric lighting plant, and of course a large supply of candles and paraffin, not to speak of the possibility of borrowing the Tilley lamps from the school. This year we are grandly on the mains. We have put in various electrical gadgets. How sinister it is when an electric clock starts going round the wrong way after a power cut!

Various animals have been slaughtered, or are about to be. The bacon is back from curing, the oatmeal back from the mill. I have painted a number of fir cones with silver and gold paint to go in among the greenery; I have a horrid feeling that they look rather revolting. Inexorably the day of the children's party approaches; I suppose the ones who aren't asked – or their parents – get more pain from not being asked than the ones who are asked get pleasure. But this non-Benthamite situation seems to be inevitable; I can't manage more than fifty-six, even borrowing spoons.

Here we have to cut our Christmas holly a month ahead and keep it in water; otherwise the fieldfares descend and in one day the berries are all stripped. There is any amount of pernettya, though, in all shades of pink and red; in summer we try to keep it in bounds by hard scything. The extraordinary thing is that some people even pay for plants of it! Goodness, they even pay for plants of the ordinary rhododendron that ramps through our woods like something out of astounding science fiction. I have been cutting evergreens of all colours from the grey-silver of abies or Atlantic cedar down to the golden green of the great cypresses; I tie them rapidly into swags to hang about the house. I find that my stepladder is broken – the plumber dancing round a cistern no doubt – so I rush down the village asking anyone I meet if he can give me the loan of a stepladder. The hotel is sorry, but it

Christmas card, drawn by Gertrude Hermes, depicting Carradale House

is already borrowed. However, nice Robert Lochpark (there are so many Roberts, so many Patersons, so many Colins, so many Campbells and Galbraiths, that everyone gets nicknamed for his house – as John Bungalow, or for his mother, as Colin Effie) finds me a stepladder. I dash back with it and begin hanging up garlands and decorating the tree, carefully putting all the nicest glass balls, hoarded year after year, out of reach of small clutching hands.

Doris comes in to help me with the jellies. Suddenly I remember the leak and climb on to the roof. There don't seem to be any tiles loose, so it is either a crack in the lead guttering or else the top of the chimney stack, but perhaps it won't rain quite so hard for a day or two. Meanwhile I go round with a spanner and a granddaughter, Sally, easing the cold taps, which are all stuck but make a magnificent fountain when I unstick them.

After the children's party there will be a breathing space. The family will arrive together, but several of it will cook. We shall pluck the goose, carefully keeping the down. I do this every year and then always lose the down – it takes several geese to produce enough down for even a small pillow. People will go out and shoot; I can bear it if they shoot large things, but plucking snipe is just not worth it. We shall probably do a communal deer shoot and bits will be distributed round the village. I have little sympathy with the deer, who mess up my potatoes.

Then comes New Year. It is much more important than Christmas up here – indeed, there are those who feel very strongly that Christmas is Popish – and normally we work on Christmas Day. But instead there is a long New Year holiday. On Hogmanay itself we have a dance. I invite a good many people, but even more turn up. Many of them bring small, secret flasks of whisky or what is known as a cocktail – usually a mixture of port and gin – and take one into a corner to share the pleasure. I have become adept at accepting a glass with enthusiasm, talking in such a way that the donor is looking at my face rather than at the glass, removing myself from the corner and passing the glass on to someone else! The dance breaks up in the small hours and then we all go out first-footing. The village is all awake and ready to receive visitors, unless, as sometimes happens, it is occupied, as one of our hosts explained, when apologising for a somewhat tardy welcome, 'wenching on the sofa'.

We come back, take an aspirin, and go to bed. One year, I remember, I was doing the milking and it didn't seem worth while going to bed. But the next day we go on first-footing. Sally will be old enough to come with me this time; three isn't too young to start the joys of ginger wine and cake. Besides, it is part of the duties of the Big House, part of a social pattern. It may be a pattern which is out of date; it is certainly a very old one. But it is an enduring pattern; it gives a sense of continuity, of security. One anchors on to the past. It was a different past; it was a past in which the Big House ones never dreamt of cooking and washing up and doing odd jobs of plumbing. But, if one can take that in one's stride – and why shouldn't one? – the continuity and the security last. And that, I think, is rather important for Sally.

The Manchester Guardian, 31 December 1951, p. 3

THIS IS A GARDEN of cared-for flowers,
Sweet fruits and salads, the great and small,
Paths for walking in sun or showers;
But what lies over the garden wall?

I ask it once and I ask it nine times,
I cannot love my garden at all,
The moneyed garden of ancient fine times,
I must climb over the garden wall.

Over the wall the fierce winds blow,
Cold, cold, and I can't go back.
Rattle of hail and beat of snow,
Flying slates as the branches crack.

Behind the winds, back of the snow,
Something is waiting,
Something resting.
How do I know?
By no clear stating,
By no fine testing,
By no one answer.
Behind the garden, back of the wall,
In the first hard question,
The leap and struggle
Of the fully human, demanding all,
Is thought or being I cannot know
And I will not fear
But push my way through the blinding snow
To the turn of the year.

Christmas card with a poem by Mitchison

Highland Funeral

(1953)

It was a shock to find that my old friend had died so suddenly – and yet not altogether, since, when he came to me a month before, he had spoken to me about his will. I had said to him that he had ten good years to look forward to. But he had shaken his head and smiled a little. Then, at the tup sale, he had taken a cold, and suddenly it was all over. No more to see his tall shape, black-raincoated, on the hillside, a cromag of his own making in his hand; no more to hear him tell the meanings of Gaelic place names or speak of old days; no more to have him point to the wild birds which he knew almost as well as he knew his own sheep and hill cattle. The blue eyes, the friendly face at market or sale or harvest dance: no more.

His was a namely family, and there were many relations as well as many friends, so it was an honour for me when the undertaker, himself a far-out cousin, asked if I would 'take a cord'. It was the wish of his sister, knowing so well of our old affection. Twenty-five years ago I had helped to carry my grandmother's coffin across the streets of Edinburgh to the family burying-place, but it is very rare for a woman to be asked to do this in country districts. The womenfolk come to the service in the house, as I had often been, but not to the grave.

The service was partly in Gaelic, the beautiful correct South Argyll Gaelic, now dying out. The kitchen was packed with the chief mourners. Others waited outside. Most of them were men of his own age, farmers and fishermen; but the two head foresters were there, and three of the local schoolmasters, Gaelic speakers all of them.

The little old farmhouse, grey stone and grey slates, stands half way down between the road and the sea, Kilbrannan Sound, blue flecked with white on a chill south-easterly wind. We stood at the door, watching as the coffin was lashed cross-wise to the pony-cart, strongly with fishermen's knots. Then it led off up the steep little brae and along the road, over moorland where his cross-Highlanders or cross-Galloways moved and grazed, dropping through a thin wood to a wider fertile strath and the old churchyard at the near side of the burn, headstones clustered round the old walls of Saddell Abbey.

We walked behind, hearing the pony's hoofs and the blowing of the dead leaves, myself the only woman in a long procession of dark-coated men with their black ties and old ceremonial bowlers. The parents of the man I was walking with had been married from Whitestone. It had been a cheery place in the last century; there had been dancing and piping. Earlier yet there had been a still up one of the burns and many a good drop of the stuff coming from it. But now it was more than patching that the place needed.

There was a longish carry for the coffin up the path to the churchyard and then to the grave dug by the headstone of his father in the very middle of the old Abbey ground, just beside the stones of the first abbots who were also armoured warriors, carrying their swords. We held our cords and lowered, each throwing in a small handful of earth after the service was read. Then we watched while he was covered in, not going away as one does in towns, but accepting the forthrightness of death and burial, and the old bones going back again into the soil and the strips of green turf laid back over. All was being done by his friends, while we spoke of our daily life, of sheep and crops and herring, and of the man who had been our neighbour.

We spoke of him, too, at the harvest dance, during Strip the Willow or between the figures of a quadrille set. He would have liked that. He had been a fine dancer himself and had liked to see folk cheerfully together. He would not have us sad. But he would want to be remembered, as remembered he will be.

The Countryman, v. 49, Spring 1953, pp. 44-5

Platform Party

(1953)

Campbeltown was full of excitements, an extra plane, a funeral, a great hire of buses, a tup and lamb sale. I dragged myself away from this, leaving Lachlan to bid for half a load of wedders, and boarded one of the bus fleet, full of everyone who was anyone – all the Town Councillors and ex-Town Councillors, County and District Councillors, all the officials, all those with whom one sits on committees and their wives with them, as dreary a collection of hats as you ever saw. In a community the size of ours we all know one another, indeed yes: we know one another's virtues, and O how well we know one another's vices, filling up from the imagination if any wee bit of evidence is missing. We edged through the buses, eyeing one another and wondering how in all the world this one should sit next to that one, considering what would be said, and has he no shame?

This was no merely local occasion, and indeed we had all received magnificently, almost regally embossed cards. We were off to see the opening of the Lussa Hydro Electric scheme. Of course, this was only the official opening; for eighteen months we have been enjoying Hydro Board electricity. Oil lamps are unsaleable; we have forgotten the smell of polish and paraffin; there are no more candle drips on the stairs and I am sure the ghost population is considerably reduced. Unregretfully I had said good-bye to my engine which used to produce a few wobbly volts for the house, but went wrong, towards the end, at least twice a week; when I have nightmares about it now I can wake up and switch on the light. Every house in the village is on; the farms use new electric gadgets; and innocent fishermen have been seduced into buying sham log fires and pink plastic lamp shades.

The buses turned off the east road and up Glen Lussa. It is my own electoral division and I feel maternal towards it. Nice to see the foundations of the four new council houses and thank goodness the glen road isn't my responsibility. Higher up the glen the silvery great pipes came wriggling round the bends like a rather unusual type of burrowing dragon. The power-house, roughcast and stone, is a handsome building which fits beautifully into the greys and browns of the glen. I thought of my poor council houses, economy-axed into flimsy little boxes. And again, of the remarkable ugliness of Scottish seaside resorts. Praise be for Hydro Board architects! The approach to the power-house was, however, somewhat surprisingly bordered with pink and mauve primulas and coleus plants. Inside it was light and pleasant and the generators and switchboards fashionable in grey and dark red with pale blue trimmings. They had all the functionalism which is so satisfying to us moderns, but all tastes were catered for by draping them here and there with fuchsias and trailing smilax. Which were ever so pretty.

We sat and gossiped for some time. The local farmers were there in Sunday suits but uncompromising boots. Those who wear the kilt proclaim themselves as being one social stage up, an odd thing when one remembers that the kilt used to be worn by the poor and oppressed. To wear a kilt and carry a cromag is definitely one-uppish and few of the decorative cromags are much use as real shepherd's crooks. I had one once, but the handle broke on the horn of a ewe I'd hooked. Then the Platform Party turned up and for forty minutes there were speeches. I was wondering how the lamb prices had been and I also wondered if these occasions were exactly the same in Soviet Russia, where water power is as important as it is for us in the Highlands. There would at least have been some genuine Stakhanovites[1] and the respectable element would have been, wouldn't it, a bit less confident, after Councillor X and our highly respected fellow citizen Mr Y had been sent to dig a canal between Forth and Clyde. Or rather to re-dig the present one which sorely needs it. And they would have red cannas instead of mauve primulas. But now the generator was turned on; the soft giant noise drowned us.

We had all of us noticed, on going in, a promising marquee, and there we all flocked, saying to one another how *sincere* the speeches had been. I suppose brilliant oratory is really very undemocratic and might draw us towards the *Führerprinzip.*[2] All the best people plumped themselves down in front of the food and were promptly given tea. I am not a passionate tea-drinker and hesitated; my reward was Platform Party champagne, quite a surprise after so much talk about water. Then there was great gossip, and the generator purring itself along and the current flowing out and everyone taking it for granted and ready to grumble passionately if the least thing goes wrong. When we re-embussed the atmosphere was vastly mellower; we slapped one another on the back. Temporary reconciliations took place across the aisle of the bus; a snatch of song appeared here and there, to be hastily shushed down in the interests of respectability. At the foot of the glen road the bus stopped for me to get out. And there – look! – was the lorry with my wedder lambs looking out from between the bars with their dirty fleeces and little black noses like so many common, ordinary people who had not been sent an invitation by the Hydro Board, who had never been among a Platform Party.

The New Statesman and Nation, v. 46, 31 October 1953, pp. 516-7

[1] Elite workers in Soviet Russia, honoured for exceptional hard work and increased production.

[2] German, 'leader principle'; Hitler's principle that ultimate authority rested with him.

Living in Scotland Today

(1955)

Here am I, in Kintyre, living the same kind of life that my aunt, Elizabeth Haldane, used to lead at Cloan on the northern slopes of the Ochils, when I was a girl. How annoyed I used to get then with her endless good works, committees, County and village affairs, visiting the sick and the aged, dealing with people's troubles and such-like serious and boring goings-on! Somehow my life has flowed into these same lines. It is bound to happen when the chief woman of the 'Big House', whether Highland or Lowland, has an acute – perhaps a guilty – sense of duty, or, for that matter, if she just can't bear seeing anyone else doing things less competently than she thinks she can do them!

My aunt was the first woman JP in Scotland and one of the Carnegie trustees. I am a County Councillor and member of the Highland Panel. I have stood for Parliament but never if there was any danger of my getting in. Of course, if we had a Parliament in Edinburgh – but that is another story. Both the administrative and advisory jobs are interesting, or can be made so. But they mean a lot of travelling, tiring enough, as so much of it means driving oneself over the kind of road where one can't take it easy. Poor Argyll has no administrative capital, so we meet in any of the small towns, and occasionally a County Councillor tumbles into a snow drift or misses the ferry. We're used to it.

On the Highland Panel I have made long and fascinating journeys. When the Fisheries group was working we went to practically every tiny fishing harbour on the mainland or in the islands. This way I have landed on the Out Skerries and in distant Shetland voes; I have walked plenty of rough and wet island roads, seeing more than the mere fisheries problem. I have waited alone in scaring darkness for the sudden appearance of the North Ford ferry boat, the welcome light and voices across the waves. One gets to know the Highlands in a deeper way than anyone living in any single place or, for that matter, interested in any single thing – fishing, climbing, engineering, archaeology or what-have-you – can never [sic] know them.

I was born in Edinburgh. Much of my childhood was spent there or in Perthshire. But I have lived at Carradale on the west coast for seventeen years. That feels like a long time, although for most of the oldest inhabitants I'm still a newcomer for whom wool can be pulled over the eyes – though not perhaps as successfully as some of them think. Carradale isn't really Highland. It is mixed in blood and in feeling. In summer it is full of visitors, mostly from Glasgow and thereabouts, so it is their standards of taste – or what are popularly considered to be their standards – which are aimed at. The boarding houses feel they ought to open a nice tin rather than give people an ordinary, common herring.

When I first came here there was still some ceilidhing, the small gatherings round the fire with home-made songs and music. But the wireless killed that. Who would want to be listening to their cousins and neighbours singing the old stuff when you can have all the top singers on the wireless? It is only among the older folk that there is a different point of view, though they sometimes hide it. But maybe it will need to come back, re-made – as ideas do come back with the ever shortening swing of the pendulum of taste. Our Village Hall dances tend to be mostly what are called 'modern', long after reels and country dances have become madly fashionable in London and Edinburgh! The girls do learn some country dancing, but the young men don't bother. Instead, they go in for the kind of horse play which landed me with a couple of cracked ribs after an eightsome suddenly disintegrated. But our harvest home dance, run by all the farmers of Carradale Glen, always has a fine quadrille set properly danced, mostly by the older farmers – and me.

The Village Hall management committee, on which I serve, is only one of the many committees and groups in the village, which, like all villages, is rent with bitter feuds.[1] Indeed, feuding is one of the main pleasures of village life – so long as one doesn't take it too seriously. Unfortunately many people do and quite a lot of unhappiness results. I'm afraid the women are worse than the men, mostly because their horizons are even narrower. But the men are bad enough!

Apart from the few family farms, the men used to be almost all at the fishing – herring fishing with ring-nets in Kilbrannan Sound and beyond. I am part owner of a ring-net boat, so I know the ups and downs as directly as anyone else in the place, and many a night I have been out with the boats, and sometimes steered home with the tired men asleep below and myself in the wheel-house trying to keep her bows on one star out of many. As the boats became bigger and the methods of fishing more efficient, fewer men were needed to catch the same amount of herring. Unhappily, too, fewer people seem to like a herring for their breakfast or tea, and at present there are not even the same amount of shoals as there used to be in our waters. We don't know, yet, whether this is just a succession of 'bad years' such as we have had before, in this century and last, or whether it is possibly the result of over efficiency in our methods.

It remains that fishing will not keep the same population, especially on modern standards, and we are lucky at Carradale to have a big State forest and steady employment on it for a good many men and women with the Forestry Commission, which has built houses which are really nicer than most of my County Council ones. If there is one thing more than another which has checked the drift from the Highlands, it is the Forestry Commission.

At present our own forest is still very young, though we can begin to see how handsome some of the mixed planting is going to be, with all the colours of larch and Scotch and the various spruces and cypresses, with the bright green of beech and gean and maple through them here and there. We have a saw-mill and hope later on to have some kind of forest industry. Already we have a craft centre, with weaving and good solid baskets made by some of the tinker families who have settled down to be ordinary householders without losing their old skills.

My own dealings with the Forestry Commission have always been of the friendliest. I have planted a 'small woodland' under their supervision and am getting a grant for it. Once it was planted up with sitka I went round the edge with a spade and a basket of tree and shrub seedlings which had sown themselves round the house, as they do so easily on the west coast when rabbits are kept at bay. When the Forestry Commission wants cones of the less common trees, I am only too happy for them to take mine; it makes me feel like a kind of forest grandmother.

Tree planting is for winter. With spring and summer the farm work becomes more insistent. I run my own farm, 45 acres of arable and some 300 of rough grazing, and there is little that I haven't turned my hand to from milking to building a stack. I am lucky with the folk who work for me, and maybe they are a bit lucky too, for these relationships are never all one way. My land girls have married young fishermen and come over to help at harvest with a fine crop of babies. Indeed there is plenty of help at these times, and I keep to the old custom of giving people a drill of potatoes in my field in exchange for help in planting and lifting.

My main 'cash crop' is Galloway cattle, which stay out all winter, though they have a big open-ended shelter, which we built out of our own blown timber. I buy in very little feeding. We have usually had a good hay crop, though sometimes my mind turns to silage. But I almost always start cutting a fortnight before my neighbours, and what I may lose in quantity I gain in quality, and have a lovely aftermath for the beasts when the ricks are moved out of the fields. Turnips and kale do reasonably well, but sometimes I feel very strongly that I'd like to have just one reasonably good field! My land is very light, reclaimed machair with occasional streaks of peat; it is always hungry for fertilisers. After a storm from the south we get sea tangle piled on the beach and one of my favourite jobs is collecting this with a Land Rover and trailer – and usually a grandchild or so, to help ... and hinder. It is grand for the young grass and clover, and also for potatoes.

If one has a big house it seems a waste not to fill it. People don't mind helping to wash up or giving a hand with fruit picking or harvest. So a lot of the time our house is as full as ever it was in the old days, sometimes with six or eight under-twelves. One gives them picnics and hopes they won't come back in an hour with all the sandwiches eaten and asking if it isn't tea-time yet! For them there's a safe beach and climbing trees, especially the big macrocarpa behind the house where one can climb up and up through the branches and out at the top into a new world; there are eggs to find, wood to bring in, messages from the village shop. All this means a bit of organising, though we grow a great deal of our food. I try to keep the deep-freeze, which we got just as soon as the Hydro Board electricity came our way, well topped up with raspberries and herring and deer and cream and broad beans and the many and various bits of the pigs, some of them smoked by the Campbeltown kipperer who sometimes, too, smokes us a salmon.

My husband, who is Labour Member for Parliament for Kettering – and with it Corby where so many Scots folk go when there is no work at home – is a keen fisherman, but I think little of orthodox methods which doubtless give lots of pleasure but don't always produce the fish. Whereas, when I go out with a net ... And that is just as exciting, in a different way, when one sees through the clear water the great silver salmon half caught in the bag of the net. Once I was so excited that I jumped right out of the boat on to the top of the salmon. We do our netting along the beach, and on a summer night our footsteps in the sand are bright and strange with phosphorescence.

Most of the children turn up, with their children in turn, and friends from all over the world. Two of my sons are scientists at Edinburgh University and that's not so far. One of them is as keen on gardening as I am and we get together and talk shrubs in what must be a maddening way to everyone else. These holiday times don't leave much space for writing, though cooking worries were taken off my back the day my neighbour, Mrs Campbell, came over and asked if I would care for her to give me a hand. Little did I know what delicious meals we were going to get from then on!

You might think a writer would like to be on her own, un-bothered, part of the time at least, but the house is no elegant ivory tower. On the contrary, it develops massive and unexpected leaks; the slates blow off – usually through the old conservatory roof; the chimneys smoke; the boiler cracks; the window cords break; the dry rot crawls busily about, providing one with an exciting kind of domestic warfare; and there are far too many ghosts. Also the rats think it is their house and appear to thrive on all types of poison. In the evening, when one thinks one can settle down with a typewriter, constituents come in to complain about the state of the roads or to try and find out how they stand on the housing list. But between times, maybe, I'll get an odd bit of writing done. The County Library is good and very helpful. If I go round with my mouth shut and my ears open I hear plenty. I find the west coast version of Scots very lovely, based as it is on a Gaelic grammatical structure; and here in Kintyre there are fascinating local words and idioms to salt it up. Often, when I am in the middle of something, I take a note book out with me. There is nothing like a fairly monotonous and rhythmical farm job – as Robbie Burns knew well – to set one's imagination going.

Sometimes, of course, I get fed up. I long to go right away and live in just one room. But then, I've learnt all these jobs, with difficulty and pain sometimes. I've got to know all these people. It would be a pity to throw it away, wouldn't it? And, even if other places have the sun and warmth that I sometimes miss so much, this is Scotland, my own country. And that's where I belong.

Scottish Field, v. 103, May 1955, pp. 18-20

[1] Like the village in Mitchison's novel *Lobsters on the Agenda* (1952).

Pigeon Shoot

(1955)

Rats and pigeons, which have made us such profitable hosts, know a great deal too much about us. Rats know we will attack them with every nasty weapon short of the hydrogen bomb, and the Royal Society for the Prevention of Cruelty to Animals will say nothing. Pigeons will be sitting among our sown corn having a good guzzle and if we come along with a gun they'll be off well out of shot. If we are just ourselves they'll hardly move out of the way.

The pigeons have been extra bad in the glen this year. I thought it was time to organise a general pigeon shoot, and wrote in for permission to the Agricultural Executive Committee; they will, for this, give a grant on the cost of the cartridges, which are a lot dearer than they used to be. The pigeons, however, have their spies in the Ministry and doubtless the pigeon post was working as efficiently as ever.

Eddie went up the glen and made his plan of campaign with all the neighbours. Carradale Glen is about half a mile across of flat alluvial fields, good land though not easily drained. The middle farm, Auchnasavil, used to be a dozen crofts[1] and it was said in the old days that there was always food there for any traveller and his horse as well. It means 'the field of the barn' but as usual the difficult Gaelic spelling has been anglicised. That must have been done at the time the Ayrshire farmers came in during the nineteenth century,[2] making prosperous sheep and dairy farms instead of the small crofts – but, of course, dropping the population, so that now the whole parish carries less than half of what it had in 1821.

In the glen itself the lower slopes are arable, but as the sides steepen there are a few old plantations of spruce and fir, mixed with rhododendrons, with the newer Forestry Commission plantations above and between them. This makes good shelter and should help to conserve the soil, which so easily gets eroded away in our West Highland valleys of heavy rainfall. It promises years of employment and perhaps even some kind of forest industry, but it certainly does suit the pigeons. It suits the foxes too, and, with the scarcity of rabbits, the foxes attack the lambs – not to speak of my geese. The whole ecology of the peninsula is likely to change. We have seen capercailzie half-way between here and Tarbert. I would like to think we would get back the pine martens, which, as Fraser Darling so wisely reminds us in his 'West Highland Survey',[3] keep down the squirrels, of which we have far too many for the good of the young trees, and would also help over the pigeons, whose eggs and nestlings are a special treat for pine martens.

Failing pine martens, we have to try to shoot the pigeons, so off we set after tea. It had seemed an average kind of West Coast day, a bit soft but not too bad, but as the evening went on the wind went back from south through west to north-west. In the western phase a lot of heavy cloud came hurrying eagerly in from the Atlantic, crawling down the hills opposite where I was standing and breaking in a great drench over everything, especially me. We had hoped for a fair wind which would have put the pigeons down, but it was not nearly enough, and when the pigeons began flying it was from all directions and very high.

I was at the corner of an old wood and the young plantations, a son and a husband – both good shots – higher up. They fired occasional shots, but for a long time I didn't fire. It was about as much use as firing at aeroplanes. When at last I did try a few shots, the flying birds jumped as though one had pushed them in the tail, with really remarkable acceleration but no great result. On the other hand one could warm one's fingers on the gun-barrel, and they were beginning to need it. In the worst of the rain I retired ignobly to the trunk of a big tree. Close to me a grey tree creeper was running up another dry trunk in an enviable way – it's difficult to see quite how they do it. Of course it was when I was there with branches above me that a pigeon did come in flying fairly low. One or two settled in treetops farther into the wind, but when I tried to get near enough to shoot they moved off disdainfully.

Occasionally there was a shot from away up the glen: the Strangs from Auchnabreck or Rory from Auchenfraoch. Dunkie and Eddie were over at the far side, the foresters scattered, Colin and Lachie down the glen. There was no knowing where the pigeons might be coming from. Below me there was the big flat field with what remained of the Auchnasavil turnips, getting a final eating off from the sheep; there was a great streak of flood-water across it, and as the evening wore on it widened and joined up with other wet patches.

My duffle-coat was not letting in the rain, but I had a woollen square on my head which was now soaked; my hair was still keeping it off but it was beginning to trickle into my ears. My son had set off in ski-ing clothes, but after a time came down, saying they could stand up to Alpine snow but not to West Coast rain. For a time he stopped in one of the clearings and I signalled to him when a bird was coming over; but somehow the bird always seemed to swerve at the last moment, though I was fairly sure it hadn't seen him. He went off; but my husband, being made of sterner stuff, stayed on. As it began to get darker and wetter I could have wished the stuff hadn't been quite so stern!

The colour faded out of spruces and bracken tops. One could no longer see the birds against the hillside, but they were still wheeling about, high up. I tried another shot or two, but they were really too high. And at last my husband turned up, carrying some birds, and not apparently wet, because he was wearing the kind of massive tweed which is virtually a sheep. We sploshed down through a field that, two hours earlier, had certainly not been mud over the ankles. Gradually we got news of the others. It wasn't very impressive: 150 cartridges fired and only twenty pigeons shot, of which some had fallen into thick rhododendron and couldn't be found. I don't know what the Agricultural Executive will say, but I suppose it wasn't too bad for the kind of evening it had turned out. At any rate the shooters are keen to try it again. I expect the pigeons know and are already making their counter-plan; possibly some of them are peeping in through the window of the Agricultural Executive's area office to see what they say to my letter.

The Manchester Guardian, 11 May 1955, p. 5

[1] More likely, in Kintyre, a multiple-tenancy farm; see Angus Martin's *Kintyre Country Life* (John Donald, 1987).

[2] Or earlier; many Ayrshire names in Kintyre date from the seventeenth and eighteenth centuries.

[3] F. Fraser Darling, *West Highland Survey* (1955).

The Garden Opening

(1955)

On the coldest evening in February I hear the telephone and stumble into the icy telephone room, so as to be asked to give a date in July for my garden opening. After last year I had fully intended not to have it again this year. Just as I also intended the year before. 'All right,' I say gloomily, 'the last Wednesday in July, and let's hope it isn't the same day as the Women's Guild sale in Campbeltown *this* time.' Shall I have a stall with flowers and vegetables? I can't really imagine that there will ever be any flowers again out of the frost-locked ground, but I agree, and to have a dance in the house that evening. And forty per cent for the village hall? Yes, certainly, I say. We have at last built the extension to the village hall which we weren't able to build during the war, and of course we are in debt again. The main thing, however, is that some of the village hall management committee will come and help. I couldn't do without them!

July. Oh well, lots of time till July, I think, hurrying back to my log fire. But only too soon July will come.

Scotland's gardens are opened throughout the summer for the District Nurses' pension fund, the National Trust, and any local charity or good object that the owner may like to name. Shoals of people come along. The owner is all dressed up, madly trying to be polite to everyone. Only those who have done it themselves know the work and worry that's gone into it. One has teas, of course, and one must arrange to have them indoors if it is wet. Numbers are as unpredictable as weather. It may be fifty teas or a hundred and fifty, but usually there are depressing slabs and sponges left over and piles of sandwiches curling at the edges which one tries to palm off on one's helpers.

The flowers should be picked the evening before, once the sun is off them. One dives into the damp, midgy backs of borders and brings in armfuls which those who don't like midges can then make up into shilling bunches and put into jam jars. People like flowers they know, and will avoid the branch of some interesting rare shrub in favour of a bunch of sweet peas as like as possible to what might be found in a shop. The soft fruit must be picked, wet or fine, the same morning. Fruit and cream is always popular. I borrow cups and saucers from the village hall, as well as one of those monumental urns which take hours to heat. Our village hall is an important part of Carradale life. We had a lovely plan, but it had to be cut owing to war-time restrictions. That meant there was no way from the stage to any kind of green room; play acting lagged. But now we have two handy committee rooms, a door, and an amateur dramatics group. The district nurse holds a mother's clinic in one room, distributes orange juice and weighs babies. In the other the County Library books will be housed as soon as the new shelves are up. There isn't a family in the village which doesn't borrow books, and we don't need to worry about comics when the school children can and do borrow books, sometimes as many as three a week. They start with the sillier school and adventure stories, but soon get on to natural history, crafts, Kon-Tiki and Everest.[1] It is not so long since Argyll had no County Library, and there were those who considered it unnecessary extravagance: the Bible and the daily newspaper were surely enough for anyone? But, with an enthusiastic County Librarian at Dunoon and plenty of interested, unpaid help, it has forged ahead.

Some of the hall committee's daughters and nieces come and help to gather raspberries and currants, and top and tail the little yellow gooseberries, sweet as honey, not to be bought in shops and growing on the prickliest of bushes. There will be some organising of penny traps – treasure hunts, crowning the shilling and so on. But most important of all, someone firm must be at each entrance before the visitors begin to come, as they are sure to come, a good hour before the appointed time. One year an enterprising small boy collected for himself quite a few shillings before the official gate minders turned up. The earliest comers all bring hungry children and empty baskets in case there is a bargain to be snapped up.

For of course there are a few bargains, especially among the raffles. Did I say raffles? No, no indeed, the polisman will be after hearing us! They are tests of skill, but nothing so easy as the weight of a cake, since there are housewives who can do that to an ounce, but how many strawberries in a basket (which has been partly stuffed with moss), how many currants in a currant loaf, and the like. Come on, come on, you may win that very exciting embroidered tea cosy which was last seen being a prize at the Lifeboat dance in Tobermory. You may win that box of rather nasty chocolates. Or of course you may win a salmon. Because, the night before, I shall have been out with a net.

It was the poachers who taught me how to use a net, and some of the magic is out of it now we are all so old and respectable. But still one must move cautiously and quietly, for salmon, like keepers, are quick to hear a footstep crunching on gravel or a raised voice. Sometimes we use the net as a drag and sometimes as a plash net; the methods are rather different, and one must use one's judgment according to the state of the tide and the direction of the wind.

In June and July the salmon come into the bay, crowding round into the mouth of the river, waiting for a spate when they can get up into the pools. If one rows across here on a still night they turn and flash below one, glowing with phosphorescence and looking even bigger than they are. But a still night is bad for netting; one needs a ripple at least on the surface to cover what one is doing. Usually one person waits on the beach with the end of the net, while the others row out, shooting the net over the stern of the boat, trying to make as little noise as possible on the gunwale with the corks. The one on the beach walks on a little in the direction of the boat, his feet – or hers! – momentarily marked out by the same phosphorescent glitter that lies on the fish. The boat makes a wide circle out and then comes back to land. If the net is used as a drag, they jump out with the end of their rope and both sides of the net are pulled in quickly and evenly, trying to keep the sole of the net, with the weights on it, close to the ground, so that the salmon will not be able to dart underneath and escape. The net has to be well in before you can tell whether there is anything in the bag. But then there are startling pulls and jerks and in a minute you will see a heave up and the surface broken by a netted fish trying to get away. Pull out the bag of the net with a rush and well up the shore, keeping the struggling silver rolled in it!

There may be one or two good-sized fish, as well as grilse and sea trout, but the smallest will have got away, since we use the wide – and legal! – salmon mesh. Often there are little flatties, dabs and soles and bright-spotted plaice. If they are really small, throw them back. They will recover and you can watch them wavering and rippling their way back into safe waters. The big salmon leap and struggle in one's hands, and often enough, if one leaves them a moment on the beach, they will get away into the sea again. But we need a good basketful for the sale.

If the net is to be used as a plash, the object is to scare the salmon into it so that they will be meshed. Once a big loop of net has been made between boat and shore, the ones in the boat beat on the surface of the water with the oars and those on shore throw stones, trying to drive the fish into charging the net. Then the boat rows back along the inner side of the curve of the net, hauling in, disentangling the fish and throwing them back into the boat. This way you get mostly big fish, and no flatties.

Of course, you may strike a blank. The fish have moved. They may have heard you, or there may be something about the temperature or feeding conditions, which has taken them elsewhere. We have two or three bits of the beach which seem best. It does not spoil the river at all when done with discretion. Nor, of course, does discreet poaching, as every keeper knows. The difficulty is that poachers aren't always discreet. Those who want a fish for tea are one thing, and they get it, all over Scotland, and everyone the best of friends. But when you have the thing on a big scale, with money coming into it, then it's different – as every decent poacher knows!

But here are the salmon, which we are about to raffle – no, to offer as prizes for competitions of skill. Any that are over will be auctioned. No, the second prize is a set of hand-painted doilies. ...

In the evening we dance. With luck I shall be able to get hold of an accordionist, in fact I have a plan for inveigling an accordionist on to the village hall committee. We also try and sell off whatever cakes and lemonade have been left over. And sometimes of course we raffle a salmon. It is getting late for anyone to notice.

Throughout the day we have had a variety of helpers, young and old. They will all manage to be there for the time when we count our takings and try to remember what the flower stall made last year and whether it was Mrs Campbell's or Mrs Macintosh's cake which did so extra well. The summer visitors are taken with decorations, but we, the locals, know who our best bakers are. The children who have been in charge of the side-shows bring in a staggering weight of pennies. And as often as not there will be a donation from someone. For the garden opening is a social event. Everyone would miss it if, one year, I lived up to my determination not to have it again. And I suppose I might even miss it myself.

The Scottish Companion, ed. by Rhoda Spence (Edinburgh: Richard Paterson, 1955), pp. 127-31

[1] Best-sellers of the time: Thor Heyerdahl's *The Kon-Tiki Expedition* (1950) and Sir John Hunt's *The Ascent of Everest* (1953).

Weather

(1955)

The most peculiar things happen when the Western Highlands dry out. Our houses, ceasing to be damp for the first time in a century or so, begin to shed their plaster. Victorian ceiling-papers come down with a mighty rumble on guests in bed. Cracks open in woodwork. I suppose it is the damp which holds together most Scots houses; one gets quite alarmed when the slight familiar smell of mould fades right away. Oddly enough, the dry rot has chosen this summer to invade us in a big way, sending eager growth systems careering through the rubble of which our thick walls are made.

The old lead pipes have been cracking here and there. Perhaps they were cracked all the time, but an odd leak made no difference in normally soaked ground. It was only when water got scarce that we noticed. Our water supplies come from an excellent spring, but also from one or two roses in a small burn; at some time before anyone bothered with making or leaving plans a great proliferation of pipes took place. When we dig them up, hacking through tree roots to get at them, we cannot tell if the water bubbling up through the split is coming or going. Hopefully we turn one of the many stopcocks; probably nothing at all happens.

The new county council water supply for the village has held out magnificently. But the Department of Health has insisted on treating it in a kind of science-fiction contraption up near the source, with the result that nobody likes it for tea-making. 'Does it taste the tea?' I ask. 'No,' they say, 'but it's a kind of a funny colour.' So they take their kettles along to the various old springs.

One pleasure of the drought was the comparative absence of midges. They breed in marshy ground, and much of that had dried up. One could even do harvesting in the evenings without being eaten alive. There were clegs early on, but we who are used to being bitten by clegs seem to develop the antibodies which stop the bite from poisoning us. A cleg will go on sucking away for several minutes; they have beautiful eyes. They cannot lay their eggs until after they have had a drink, so I suppose our blood is their great need. The salmon, waiting in the bay for the river to rise enough for them to

Dry rot, Carradale House

swim up, must feel the same kind of need. They jump impatiently in the sea. At night, if one is rowing across, they streak away in a thin blaze of phosphorescence. The few that have got a certain way up the river swim uneasily round in their pool as though it were an aquarium, trying to find a way out and up. But in some places the river has completely disappeared in a dreary bed of stones.

The spell of dry weather has meant light crops and poor pasture. We shall have difficulty in feeding the beasts over next winter – unless, that is, we have another warm spell and some growth after a few days' rain. But almost everywhere the harvest is in, in record time. Last year it was still out in November in many places and people still struggling to save part of it.

Every now and then there were forecasts of local rain, including our area. Sometimes, even, the barometer would start going down. But we do not put much faith in barometers here, though they are nice to tap. In general the weather happens before the barometer gets to know about it – or else just passes over. It is much better, anyway, to look at the real signs: first up at the weathercock and then, beyond him, at the carry – the true direction of the high clouds; to see if Ailsa Craig is showing, away to the south; to listen for the sound of the waves; to feel from the air if there is a haar from the east or a touch of salt from the south-west. It is always round one, this weather, whispering messages, telling one to do this or that on land or sea. It is queer – driving into Glasgow, say – the way the weather drops away from one as the houses begin to close round. One does not see the stars any longer; one does not know if the dew has fallen light or heavy; one has no need of full moon for walking at night.

Naturally we are used to rain, to damp patches in the walls, moulds on the plants, rheumatism in the joints. We are used to the steady drumming at night, the corn laid and tangled. I never expected to want rain, nor to go out gladly into the first smirr of it so as to smell the scent of the relieved plants and the laid dust: something that reminded me of the weather break at Delphi after the long dry months of the Attic summer.

The rain is on now and the ground at last beginning to soften. As it softens the worms come up. The runner ducks which have become such expert fly-catchers will now be able to set their beaks to the ground on worm level instead of eight inches up on fly level. But the first to get his beak into the lawn was a young woodcock; he walked about just outside the kitchen window, having a lovely time, going dab, dab, dab with his long bill. I expect he was one of a brood hatched in the woods just beside the house. One year I saw a mother woodcock taking her family across from the lawn to the soft garden border, which was easier digging. They had to cross a gravel path and then a little hedge of clipped heather, easy enough for mother, but the babies did not want to jump over and all ran up and down till they could find a hole to go through.

A few days ago there was a whole crowd of house martins flying round and playing. I thought they might be going to make late nests under our eaves. But the next day they shifted on. I wish they would build; it would be a change from the messy sparrows and the starlings that make as much din as a house full of grandchildren.

The Manchester Guardian, 8 September 1955, p. 5

Hogmanay in a Fishing Village

(1955)

Our village has no licence. You would think that would spoil New Year for them. Not at all! For a long while back we have been making preparations. The respectable folk of Carradale have been coming back from expeditions to Campbeltown, Tarbert or even farther afield, with a bottle of the hard stuff in a pocket where it won't be showing. Cakes have been baked, too, and such things as biscuits and lemonade laid in, for the weaker brethren.

Nowadays we keep Christmas in a way which would have shocked our righteous forefathers. There are parties in the Village Hall for the children, with high Christmas trees out of the Forestry Commission plantations. The forester always gives me a little one, to stick in my old German Christmas tree stand that can be wound up and plays tinkly tunes. But we grown-ups are thinking a week ahead to Hogmanay.

The awkward thing is when Hogmanay, the eve of New Year, falls on a Saturday – as it does this year – in which case any dancing we do after midnight is strictly unofficial and first-footing is much cut down, or on a Sunday, which takes the heart out of things. Yet, if it comes in the middle of a week the fishermen may be away; even for Hogmanay you can't afford, in these days, to miss a good fishing.

I concentrate on food and the accordion player. You may think you have a good player all set to come, but suddenly there is a wedding in the family and off he has to go to it. I wouldn't choose New Year for a wedding myself, but it's a popular time with some. Then the indignant grandchildren have to be cleared out of the library, the table tennis tables folded up and as many breakable things as possible put away. The room looks nice with the green garlands slung about it, all the mixed evergreen of a Highland garden, from the shining silver of the under-side of some of the abies to the gold-green of the golden cypress, the dark shine of escallonia and the blue of the Atlantic cedar. We don't have much holly, but there are bright berries of pernettya, crimson and pink. I pick fat buds of the rhododendron Christmas Cheer before Christmas, and expect it to be out for the New Year. In a mild year there may still be roses, and last year the tassels of the lobster claw were beginning to dangle scarlet, though the frosts a fortnight later finished them and, alas, the whole plant, which was well spread over a south wall.

The village shops won't open for several days, depending really on the inclinations of the baker, so I have to get in lots of bread. So does everyone else, and there isn't always enough to go round. I try to get everyone to have an early supper, but if any of the men have gone out shooting and then had a big tea they sometimes refuse to be driven! Most of us don't change till after supper because of the washing up, but those who have been cutting sandwiches ought to be allowed off that. Then we get the table set with jellies, trifle, cakes, sandwiches and fruit salad. There are piles of saucers but never enough spoons. However, one trusts, as the evening goes on, that one's guests will stop being fussy about little things like clean glasses and spoons.

I make huge jugs of orangeade: anything more important is my husband's worry! But quite a number of the younger men will prefer my tipple or at most a glass of beer.

If I'm lucky I get changed into a long dress before the guests begin to come. The earlier ones wait in the passage room – I can hear them giggling – until there are enough of them to make a break-through. But the accordionist and Willie, who always plays the piano, are there already and probably demonstrating the accordion to the grandchildren. Susan has reluctantly been got out of her slacks and into a party frock. Sally, on the other hand, can't wait to get dressed up. Graeme is unbelievably clean and tidy. The rest are in bed and asleep. But next year Neil may decide to stay up.

The dancing begins rather stickily. Everyone waits for everyone else. It isn't until after the first eightsome that things begin to go with a swing. We dance almost nothing but old-fashioned dances, the pattern waltzes, Pride of Erin and St Bernard and Hesitation, the two-steps and barn dances, Gay Gordons and Dashing White Sergeant. Sometimes we get enough tolerably good dancers for Duke of Perth or Scottish Reform, but usually we don't rise beyond Petronella and Strip the Willow. Quite a lot of the girls know the more interesting dances, but the boys won't bother to learn.

A good many of the dancers have a hard day's work at the back of them; they've been pulling turnips, putting out hay, mending nets – some of them were out at the herring the previous night and have barely had a snatch of sleep – or clearing and burning on the Forestry Commission ground. The women have been baking or cleaning up the house ready for the first-footers. But you wouldn't guess it from the way they go at the dancing once it gets going. They go at the food, too, clearing off the full plates. There are a few children among them, for it's hard if the mother always has to stay at home. But they are wearing their party manners. Some people like a cup of tea and know their way to the kitchen, and there's usually a party of washers-up.

In the party there is always a hard core of people I have definitely asked, but a great many more come, especially later on. Towards midnight old feuds are being made up, eternal friendships are being sworn, sentiment flows like champagne. People bring their own bottles, some with the hard stuff, others with a pretty revolting mixture of port and whisky, which is supposed to be almost temperance. I am expert at accepting drinks from my supporters – for, after all, a county councillor has a reputation to keep up – but not actually drinking them.

Now, with any luck, we have a set of quadrilles, danced mostly by the older people. We remind one another of the figures: 'scoosh' or 'soldiers'. And then we begin to look at our watches, which never say the same thing. A collective compromise is rapidly reached and we all get into a ragged circle and sing that singularly gloomy song, *A Guid New Year to Yin and A'*, of which few of us know more than the first two lines. Then my husband makes a very small speech; it doesn't matter if it is the same as last year. And then everyone kisses everyone else.

My own theory is that, because everyone has the Cold, it is essential to have a disinfectant; presumably alcohol is one of the best. At any rate the Cold doesn't seem to spread any further after New Year. Young and old wolves prowl rapidly; there is an occasional slap, but for the most part it's simpler just to carry on.

From midnight on, the party comes and goes, or rather it goes and comes. One says good-bye to a guest, gives him firmly to his wife to take home, but look, there he is back again by the other door! The real after-midnight first-footers come in and are duly given their glass and their bit of cake. At last, in the small hours, we think that everyone has probably gone and adjourn to the kitchen for bacon and eggs. It was while we were at this one New Year that we heard a very peculiar noise; this turned out to be the bottled gas turned full on, while round the cylinder one of our guests was curled up and snoring. We pulled him up, woke him and explained that his friends were looking for him. He wavered away into the night. Later, it appeared that he had mistaken the screw of the gas cylinder for the handle of the front door, and merely turned it.

First-footing goes on from midnight until a few days later. I pay my next morning visits with an assortment of the younger grandchildren, guaranteed to eat cake and drink ginger ale and fizzy orange. Nobody works; I do the afternoon milking and feed the hens. One year I had an Egyptian friend staying who, as a 'dark stranger', was very popular. Occasionally the old gifts are brought, especially the lump of coal for warmth in the heart and the house. But mostly one is welcomed in with 'What will you take for your New Year?'

By the end of the short afternoon I am driving very slowly and carefully, coming back from the harbour or up the Glen. It is the mixture of whisky, sherry, gingerade and rich cake – and, of course, kisses. The best thing to work this off is a brisk game of kickapegs, our family version of continuous hide-and-seek in the dark, with much running violently up and down stairs, jumping over sofas and suchlike.

The next day is much the same, but people's faces are redder and their walk heavier. And then – well, that depends on the fishing. If there are plenty of herring and the boats have had good share-outs for a few weeks back, then they can afford an extra day's holiday in honour of Hogmanay. But it doesn't look like that this year. The bottles will soon be empty, the cake soon finished. The fishermen must go back to work, and the shop must open to let them take their bread and meat for the week on board. And when the fishermen are away then the holiday must stop.

But for quite a while afterwards I find myself saying 'Happy New Year' to anyone I meet on the road who happens not to have come our way at Hogmanay or Ne'erday. It comes naturally and one goes on saying it in places like London if by any chance one has to hurry down there early in January. It may seem silly there, but to us it does mean something very real: it means that there has been an actual break in time, in the day-to-day turnover; one has come round a corner and the new stretch ahead may be in some way different, genuinely happy, a New Year worth speaking about.

Country Life, 1 December 1955, pp. 1250-1

The Farmers' Dance

(1955)

Everyone knows that the Farmers' Dance is the best dance of the year and everyone wants to be there. But it is by invitation only. There is some rather naughty swapping of cards, which we all deplore at the next meeting of the National Farmers' Union, but by and large those who come have something to do with the farming part of the community. We each have our own list, but there are some invitations from the committee: our young minister and his pretty wife, the banker, the two vets, and the team from the threshing mill. We leave all the arrangements to Duncan, who is secretary of our NFU branch, probably for life, as none of the rest of us can be bothered with the work.

I had shoved all sorts of other dates aside to be up north for the dance, yet, when the evening came, I found myself oddly encased in an icy highbrow identity. I duly put on my best evening dress, but the reluctance to go was black and hard inside me: why couldn't I stay at home and write a book? Towards the end of the year most of us have The Cold, but it was more than that: it was the deeply chilly feeling of being apart from the rest.

After the customary speech of welcome everyone settled down round the thirty-eight whist tables, the biggest whist there has been in the hall for years. I can't play and have never felt I wanted to. The intellectual freeze-up continued. Then came the tea and the enthusiastic whisking away of the whist tables. All the women duly sat down in a row on the chairs along the edges of the hall. The men gathered in a black knot round the door and eyed us. The first two or three dances have to be danced with wives and sisters-in-law. The rest of us waited, making suitable remarks to one another. An eightsome reel started up. How nice it would be to be danced, but doubtless there were others with a better claim. No – Rory from Auchnareoch put a large, strong hand on mine and we sailed off into a set. In the old days when every farm had its own harvest home the reels were danced on a barn floor, much more appropriate for our style than the polished wood of the Village Hall, but our partners are well up to turning recalcitrant

Neighbour and farmer Alec Mackinven playing the accordion for
dancing in the library

cows or dipping headstrong ewes. Rory never let me slip. As we set, picking up rhythm and delight from one another's faces, the ice began to crack.

But indeed we were all warmed up by the eightsome, which settled our tea well. We got down to a programme of the hard dances, with a wonderful accordionist who flung himself about, sweating like a waterfall, filling the hall with his leaping dance time, that shook the low shouts out of our throats at each recurring climax of the short pattern of steps. Yet I was still not completely unmelted, when one of the mill team took me up for a Hesitation. Anyone who can give me the feeling of being eighteen and floating round a dance floor must be a good dancer himself. Nor did that half-forgotten sensation leave me for the rest of the evening; the defrosting was complete.

One needs no verbal or intellectual encounter with a good dance partner; within the embrace of the music contact is easy and adequate without words, unless the formal words that express the beautiful swaying of the cornfield under the hand of the wind: 'Grand evening. Aye, grand evening. A great player, the man. Aye, great altogether.' Nor is the interval between dances long enough for one to rediscover any critical identity.

It is a curious thing, but although a great many intellectual (to use a not entirely satisfactory word) women enjoy dancing, hardly any intellectual men are any good at it. Let me add, very firmly, that liking to look at ballet is not the same thing. That is not to say that all the men at the farmers' dance were good dancers; and, indeed, one or two who are quite good at it never got on to the floor at all, so intent were they on the pleasures which lay beyond the door. For our village hall is strictly dry – inside. Nobody was drunk, but there was a certain amiable vagueness about some later partnering.

The younger men and boys tend to kick up and even to bring a jivish pull and swing into a sedate Pride of Erin. But watch Lachlan dancing a schottische. He is bolt upright, his shoulders unmoving, his knees seeming to move little, but his feet skilled and light, feathering the floor with dance steps. The men almost all wear the traditional blue serge suit, about as inappropriate as anything one could imagine to their dancing bodies, though no more un-Highland than the stiff shirts and black ties, occasionally topped by a tweed cap, which one sees at the grander farmers' dances in Campbeltown.

But the women and girls look all the better in their bright colours. Nylons for all, with cheap and pretty dance frocks, have done a lot towards a classless society. But wide skirts fly and have to be severely beaten down during the twirling of the Gay Gordons.

All too soon it is the last waltz, but, after all, in another four hours the cows are due to be milked. My partner says with a certain surprise: 'Here's me standing up still for the last dance!' Either his head has improved or the whisky has weakened sadly. So back under the brilliant moonlight past the door of the byre which we always lock carefully on dance nights, since courting couples are apt to disturb the cows. Not only was my cold away, but the deeper cold, in the heart, that was gone, too, as if it had never been.

The Manchester Guardian, 28 December 1955, p. 3

Mistress Jean and I

(1956)

I am not a good cook. How I'd like to be able to say I am! But all my daughters and daughters-in-law would laugh so loud if they heard me that I'd never be able to set spoon in saucepan again. All the same, I'm past the dunce stage when one stands helplessly in front of an egg wondering which way up to boil it. I can gut or fillet a fish with no bother, skin a deer or a sheep, and my butter is as good as you'll find anywhere. Also, I'm willing to read a recipe and have some idea of what I can substitute, when, as so often happens, one or two of the ingredients are just not in the cupboard. But I'm terribly bad at knowing when an oven is the right heat, and I've left things in till they were burnt black more times than I like to think of. Also I get dough and little bits of cabbage inextricably mixed up with the innards of my typewriter, which, stupid thing, never quite manages to digest them.

But there are lots of things which I find much more fascinating than cooking, and which have to be done. After all, I am doing very much what a Scots bonnet-laird's wife might have been doing in much the same kind of house a century-and-a-half ago. In the old song, *The Laird of Cockpen*:

Mistress Jean she was making the elder flo'er wine:
And what brings the laird at sic a like time?
She offed wi' her apron and on her silk goun ...

No doubt she had also in the intervals of being interrupted – lucky woman, no telephone! – been brewing, baking, preserving, drying herbs, making lotions, balms and, I'm quite sure, the opening medicines which our poor forefathers couldn't do without. She probably had quite a lot of ill-paid, inefficient and probably dirty domestic help; kitchen lassies sleeping in straw under the stairs. I have shockingly little help by her standards, but mine are clean, properly paid and relatively skilled, as well as being pleasant kitchen companions. But also I have a deep freeze, a fridge and other bits of modern equipment.

Yet my basic problem is the same as hers: to run a big house where there may be anything from ten to twenty guests of all ages and tastes, as far as possible economically and on local products, and to appear with clean finger-nails and intelligent conversation 'in my silk goun' on appropriate occasions. I also run my own small farm, a great deal more directly than Mistress Jean, who probably didn't herself muck the byre or fork sheaves, still less drive a tractor, though she may well have done the milking, and that without a neat little milking machine. This farm means, if I am organising things properly, that I have plenty of milk all the year round with a higher butter-fat content than is demanded for commercial milk, so that it sets for cream and the skim milk is about what one normally gets in one's town tea. I have eggs all the year round: the deep-litter hens start in late summer when the others have gone off: the eggs I sell pay for their meal and pellets. I fatten two pigs, almost entirely on small potatoes, household waste, skim milk and whey. One of them is smoked by the local kipperer for bacon and ham, the other goes into the deep freeze as pork, brawn and so on. Equally, I have my own mutton and poultry, including magnificent geese, which also provide delicious pillows and cushions. A few sweeps of the net on the right evening, and we have enough salmon for winter: this, again, sometimes smoked by the kipperer. The deer that come down off the hills to eat my potatoes finish up in the deep freeze, so do any game birds we don't eat at once.

This is a fishing village, with no lack of seasonable fish, but herring don't do in a domestic deep freeze; they have to be sharp frozen with a much greater temperature drop. Indeed, no fish is completely satisfactory, though as good as much one gets elsewhere. The salmon are basic material for delicious pies and quite good plain boiled when hot, but not up to standard when cold.

Then there are cheeses, made when milk is plentiful and guests scarce, and of course fruit and vegetables. But these are rather more trouble, for we get far more fruit than I have storage space for in the deep freeze. That means quite a lot of bottling, especially of the pie fruits, gooseberries, which always seem to harden in a deep freeze, raspberries and currants, as well as tomatoes, either whole or in purée. The few weeks of summer fruit really demand whole-time work from two or three people, especially as one can't pick late in the evening or one is eaten alive by midges. Everything comes on at once, including the peas and beans which have to be blanched before freezing.

Last year I tried mushrooms which were very plentiful. We used to come staggering back from the fields with huge baskets – I wonder if the price ever dropped to the poor city consumer! These I blanched and froze, packed tightly. I have used them all up, and they were certainly wonderful for soup or stuffings, and, in fact, lost little of their delicious texture. We made some mushroom ketchup, too, and some were dried. I meant to dry some of the little yellow chanterelles which are such fun to pick from the mossy hollows in the pine woods which they favour and where one can smell the delicious slight apricot scent of them. But one can't do everything! They are oddly tough and need to be stewed slowly and served with a fairly rich sauce.

I grow as many different types of vegetables as I can, though some, like turnips and carrots, are better grown in the fields than in the garden. The only garden potato I grow is a delicious little salad potato, which cannot be field grown as it is not immune to the potato mould disease. We are too far north for maize or butter beans. I have tried both, but we don't have the sun to ripen them. Nor can we grow chicory without a lot of trouble. But it is nice to have a few cheap treats off the Soho barrows when one comes down to London! The worst of a garden is that, in our uncertain climate, one can never quite time the crops. Cauliflowers never space themselves out nicely, and lettuces bolt when one's back is turned. Last year was a wonderful tomato year, but in a wet and cloudy summer they are apt not to ripen till late August or September, leaving one with baskets full of small green tomatoes to make into chutney. I still have jars of 1954 chutney to finish up.

The fields produce my porridge oatmeal, too, so much nicer than bought meal. We take over half-a-dozen sacks to the water mill down south of Campbeltown, and pick up the meal a week or two later. Sometimes I take a grandson down with me, for not all children have ever seen a mill working. It is unlike anything else they are likely to see: the heavy, simple machinery, all so pre-atomic, so un-streamlined, going back so far into history, the rustle and smell of the corn and the enormous families of cats which, again so very simply, live on the equally enormous families of rats. This meal is rich and nutty, though not as dry as shop meal; one has to store it off the floor so it won't 'go foosty'. It makes the best oat-cakes and porridge which is insulted by any English addition of sugar.

Sugar, alas, is one of the things I have to buy, though it is a lot cheaper than it was in Mistress Jean's day. She must have had big sugar loaves, off which the housekeeper would chip lumps as she needed them. But I expect she depended a great deal on honey. Last year my bees did their stuff. I am terrified of bees, though I couldn't do without them in the garden. They come into the cold greenhouses when the peach trees are in blossom in early spring and save me from having to go round every branch with a rabbit's foot to fertilise the flowers. But the Forestry Commission trapper, who is also a first-class musician and a man of great charm, has a way with bees. He took the honey and put in new sections, so that at least I know what ought to be done even if I'm scared to do it. I have put a lot of the sections into polythene bags, to stop the honey from crystallising hard, as it does when fully exposed to the air. But it would take a lot of honey to sweeten things for modern tastes. What a terrible wartime problem the sugar for jam-making used to be, made up out of the spoonfuls that one didn't put into one's tea or coffee! I can hardly accustom myself to being able to use as much as I need.

It's not easy to organise jam-making so that it doesn't overlap into the evening, that's to say jam-making on the scale that will fill enough seven-pound jars to do us for the year. Yet an evening session with two or three stirrers and tasters may be very pleasant. Nothing so stimulates gossip as the swirl and bubble of the strawberries, with perhaps another lot in a basin, soaking up sugar overnight, so as to be jammed tomorrow, and adding a higher chord to the symphony of smell. There may be jelly dripping, too, the jelly bag slung between two chairs. From its second pressing we get delicious fruit drinks all summer. I remember so well my nervousness when I first made jam on a large scale during the war. I kept on looking at the book, with no confidence on how it would turn out. One of the old WRI hands came over and told me never to bother with books: 'Just throw them in, my dear, they'll do fine.' And that seemed to be the way she always won the prizes in the rural competitions. But then, she had what corresponds to green fingers in the cookery world.

I suppose really it's all a matter of confidence. My younger daughter went for a year to a progressive school, where the children were encouraged to do what they liked and not forced to go to any lessons. It was a stimulating change after the strict discipline of the village school and, being a kind-hearted child, she spent a lot of time helping the overworked cook. She came back perfectly confident of being able to bake a batch of scones for twenty people – and taught me. No fussing with weights and measures! But I like some of the less conventional measures, to rub in one's fat, for instance, for the length of time it takes to sing the complete metrical version of Psalm XLII. I'm sure Mistress Jean did that, too.

My family are rather unsympathetic about some of the local delicacies, especially carrageen moss jelly. Yes, it is a peculiar greenish colour, and, yes again, there was an unfortunate incident when I didn't wash it enough and a lot of gritty little shells got into the jelly. But does that slight irritation compare with the pleasure one gets from plucking the lovely deep port-coloured carrageen off the low-tide rocks? Dulse is another seaweed that tastes nice when one picks it up and chews it, but less nice as part of a meal.

It is the same with some of my milk products. Town dwellers don't, on the whole, like buttermilk, nor the bowls of sour milk that I make in summer, though there is nothing like this for bucking one up after a hot afternoon in the harvest field. Most country people drink milk; our standard midday meal used to be milk, potatoes boiled in their jackets – preferably Golden Wonders – and salt herring from the barrel which every farmhouse had. That's a good meal when one comes in hungry, but few town folk like salt herring and we can't bear their pasteurised, homogenised milk which may even turn out to be flavoured with orange! But most people like crowdie – the sour milk cheese made quite simply by hanging up the sour curd to drip for two or three days, with as much cream in it as possible. It can be enlivened with onion or garlic, salt and paprika or, indeed, anything else one happens to think of. Mistress Jean quite certainly made crowdie, and probably syllabub which I long to make. One milks into a bowl of white wine, automatically frothing it up and presumably not bothering about an occasional cow hair in the syllabub.

I wonder if Jean made her butter much saltier than I make mine? I'm inclined to think it went rancid rather quicker, possibly because the pails and churns were not efficiently scoured, but more likely because of dirty milking conditions, unscrubbed hands and unwashed byres. It wasn't so long ago, after all, that butter mixed with tar was used for dressing sheep against the fly, instead of our modern dips.

I wish I could grow coffee. For my own part I wouldn't mind a bit not having tea! But no home-grown substitute is anything like the same, and our coffee bill is the thing I avert my eyes from as quickly as possible. We have also, of course, to buy bread or wheat flour; I can't grow wheat and nobody would thank me for barley bread, which used to be the staple in the west of Scotland. We can't grow citrus fruits or olives. Nor is it really sensible, as far north as we are, to try to make our own wine, though such good wine has been made by the skilful in the south. Some of my neighbours make bramble wine, parsnip wine and so on, with a view to New Year. I can't say I really like it. Elderberry wine can be nice, but we don't find we have many berries. The elder flowers, though, transmute gooseberry jam into something with a lovely muscat flavour and should always be used. Yes, I have thought of brewing. For that matter I've thought seriously about distilling. There are any amount of old stills about, and the old sites where they used to work. The customs officer has a car, true, but one could hope for warning. The sensible thing would be to have a Village Hall distilling committee. The Hall is built over a stream which runs through a concrete conduit below it, apparently a natural for distilling. And if all the committee were involved, the penalties might be easily shared out ... and what a revenue earner!

You see, in the middle of all one's activities, one is being rung up about the Hall sale, or the secretary is coming in and asking if one will answer a letter for him. After all, one has the typewriter. Nor is being a county councillor merely a matter of attending meetings. And sometimes, of course, one squeezes in a bit of writing. Many a promising manuscript has got grease-spots all over it or been used for wrapping things. Still, the kitchen is often a good place to escape to, not exactly an ivory tower, but something of a castle. I've an idea that Mistress Jean may have felt something the same about hers.

Good Housekeeping, September 1956, pp. 58-9, 188, 190, 192

Life Begins at Balloch

(1957)

I didn't quite get there all the same. I left the bus at the fountain of Alexandria, which is, alas, so little like what it sounds as if it ought to be like. I knew I would need to get on to the Luss road before I would get a lift, and that might only be as far as Tarbet. So my journey was only beginning.

I had missed the Campbeltown 'plane because the County Council meeting had gone on longer than I had expected. The only 'public transport' – blissful word that we are all getting to know so well! – meant hours of sitting in a bus, in which it is almost impossible to read after dark, and a very late arrival in Campbeltown, with another fifteen miles back to Carradale after that. It was a lovely day, just right for hitch-hiking. The fact that one is a mere female of – well – a good wee bit beyond 50, need not stop one. But it is a far cry from Alexandria, or even Tarbet, Loch Lomond, to Campbeltown at the far end of Kintyre.

I discussed this with an interested bus queue, who gave me good advice and Horrible Warnings. The bus arrived. But when I gave the conductress my threepence she indicated that the gentleman at the end had paid for me. The days of chivalry are not over. The gentleman at the end was a postman and no doubt felt – and rightly – that both county councillors and postmen were valuable public servants and should stand by one another.

Then I got out and strolled along towards the Luss Road with a rather silly looking but light canvas bag and a briefcase full of County Council papers which was heavier, but not too heavy. Now two strong men leaped out of a car saying 'Mrs Mitchison, I presume?' Feeling like an explorer found out in a jungle, I admitted it. They were the *Daily Echo*, had heard from some other councillor that I was hitch-hiking, wanted to photograph me doing so. Yes, they would take me along to a lonely looking stretch of the road with a nice background where I would be sure to get a lift.

I didn't quite like to ask them why they had spent so much petrol on this Quest for Councillor Mitchison, so we went on and found a nice broken-down fence – no, I didn't break it myself – and a view of Ben Lomond. The photographs were taken while I ate my bun.

There were not many cars on the road, but plenty of lorries. Like many hitch-hikers, I think lorries are in some ways preferable. This one stopped amiably and I got in. It was going to the Strachur road contract and would take me over the Rest[1] and as far as the road off to Dunoon. I have driven that Lomond-side road often enough, and many a hiker I have picked up. One of the last times I did that, two young mountaineers got into such an argument – about modern poetry, I think – in the back that they could hardly bear to get out when we got to the Youth Hostel. But one sees the road far better from the high cab of a lorry.

It was early afternoon by now, the loch pale blue, streaked with shimmering violet, and the orange of reflected sun on bracken. The driver was obviously getting as much pleasure out of it as I was, though he put it less into words. I had never realised before quite what a job it is steering a heavy lorry round these curves; however slowly you drive, it can't quite keep inside the lines. He was a courteous and careful driver, signalling clearly to passing cars, using his driving mirror. But he had to watch the road and perhaps did not notice one charming sight: a bus driver and a conductress, hand in hand, looking out at the loch.

The big lorry took the Rest easily. Different in the old days, before the new road! As a member of the Argyll Road Board, I couldn't help feeling proud of the road there, though there are some bumpy bits on the long stretch down Loch Fyne. I got off, with good-byes and good wishes, at the turn down to Strachur and Dunoon. The great U-shaped glen, a typical glacial valley of ancient time, was in shadow, though when we passed under the shadow of the Cobbler[2] it had been brilliant with sun on a dapple of snow.

I walked down into the sunshine which filled the hollow of Loch Fyne. It was all wonderfully peaceful in the cold, golden light. There was a buzzard flying out of the tree-tops below, and at the side of the road a flourishing plant of cotoneaster horizontalis, grown perhaps from a chance bird-dropped seed and naturalising itself very happily. Nothing at all came by on the road and when I got down on to the level road beside the loch the herons humped along the edge turned grave yellow eyes on me and concluded I was harmless.

A large brick lorry came by, driven by some descendant of John Knox; he gave me a menacing look and lumbered on. A car came; it looked friendly enough, but made the kind of gestures which meant either 'I don't like your hat' or, more probably, 'I am going to stop for a drink at the nearest pub'. I was beginning to find my briefcase a bit heavy when a small lorry stopped for me, driven by a shy and gentle Kintyre driver, who said sadly that petrol-rationing was spoiling the ceilidhs.

He, too, was enjoying the scenery as we drove on, but it was the kind of lorry which goes splendidly downhill, reasonably well on the flat, but not at all well uphill. So we progressed slowly and darkness came before the turn to Lochgilphead, where one drives along the edge of the loch opposite what seems to be the innumerable city lights of Ardrishaig, so much more impressive than the daylight view.

He had to go some messages (as we say hereabouts) in Tarbert, and then was going no farther than Tayinloan. I said I would risk getting a lift after that, but should I get some one going directly to Campbeltown I would take the chance. The Tarbert District Councillor, who knows everyone, said encouragingly that I would have no difficulty at all, and was about to organise things, when I saw a likely looking car go by and signalled to it. Yes, it was going to Campbeltown, and turned out to be an acquaintance, the manager of an electrical firm on his rounds. In the course of a fascinating discussion about lampshades, refrigerators, and a new kind of electric grill, the miles whizzed by, and in no time we were in Campbeltown.

I was home in time to cook the supper. And why not? If one is in a fairly simple difficulty, that people can understand, they will always be eager to help one. It is only the very complicated difficulties that one has to solve for oneself. In fact, I really can't think why I ever want to travel anywhere except in this simple, cheap, and practical way.

The Glasgow Herald, 19 January 1957, p. 3

[1] Rest-and-be-Thankful, a section of the A83 road through Glen Croe.

[2] Ben Arthur in the Arrochar Alps.

On the Council

(1957)

In August the Kintyre District Council always meets in the Tarbert junior secondary school, which is having its summer holiday cleaning, so that access to our committee room is somewhat complicated by sudden areas of soapsuds and buckets half-way up the stern stone stairs. When we get there, it is, as usual, the science room and we sit round a table decorated with curls of Bunsen tubing and the scars of decades of hot beakers and acid spills. As usual, we have to sit on high wooden stools; as usual, I suggest that Tarbert might lend us cushions, and, as usual, I get a wry smile from the Tarbert representative who is an ex-schoolmaster and perhaps believes in this type of corporal discipline.

On most of the committees, boards and what-have-you which I attend from time to time, one finds that ministers – who abound in Scotland with our profusion of churches – doctors and ex-teachers talk most; then come the owners of small businesses and contractors. The farmers for the most part only talk of what they know; the lairds tend to be reserved and rather deprecating as befits the dethroned boss class. If there are any representatives of the artistic professions, they are apt to be silent and then suddenly burst into sometimes chaotic blazes of irritation.

It is not at all easy to get people to take on local authority work. With us, any meeting means a day off work and a long journey, anything from fifteen to a hundred miles, to take my own case, or even, in winter, to Glasgow, which is sometimes easier for everyone to get to than anywhere within the county. Expenses are paid and an allowance for those who lose a wage, but not for the self-employed. Nor can an employer, however willing, always let a man off. The quarterly committee meetings, for instance, take three days. A conscientious councillor will have to spend time and money on letters and phone calls, as well as personal visits and inspections.

My own inspections have recently been centring round our old sewer. The new council houses have a lovely new sewer, whose outflow was carefully checked for drift in the sea. But most of the houses are still on the old estate sewer. There is a plan for a replacement, but it has rather fallen behind the places which have no drains at all.

The old sewer always prefers to burst in the middle of the tourist season and in hot weather; this has something to do with the tourists using our sanitary facilities with such reckless abandon. It is not easy to mend, and the end which goes down on to the beach looks as though it had been nibbled by sharks. I ring up helplessly, bleating to the county engineer or the road surveyor or both; they rush to my rescue. There is also the little matter of the slope off the main road down to the village hall, past my byre. The water from the road runs into the byre drain and chokes it. 'You should tell them to put it right,' says Lachlan. I say that I don't see how I can complain, seeing I'm the councillor myself, but if he should see the road foreman, well ...

Our road foreman is a round and twinkling man, who has an agricultural smallholding on the Department of Agriculture estate at Moy where he does a number of highly sensible things, including being the first to practise strip grazing, improving both his pasture and his milk yield. He tells me the gossip from the far end of my division, and once gave me a tow from his lorry when my car stuck on a hill. The Moy tenants are a fine lot of people, progressive and intelligent; I wish I could see a land settlement policy and more of these holdings, for there are plenty of people who want them.

Tarbert, though, where the August meeting is being held, is at the further end of Kintyre. Not all of us are there. But we dig firmly into our problems, half of which are about roads. One is the Dunaverty road, trodden, one would think, by plenty of ghosts from the old massacre, but a special complication for us because it goes down to the tiny harbour from which one takes off for Sanda lighthouse; this means that we get a contribution towards it from the Lighthouse Board. And then, of course, there are the public conveniences; the one which is owned by the Tarbert Harbour Board is a real shocker. What is a bit worrying is that, whatever cleaning and replacing is done, in a few weeks it is just as bad, fittings are broken, walls scrawled on. It is a pity that our level of civilisation is so low that we can't have such things without having caretakers to stop all this mess being made.

We discuss water supplies too, and the letters which are to go from ourselves to the county, including a recommendation for a compulsory purchase order. Then we diverge on to litter and decide that we could spend a little money on litter baskets. We are one of the district councils which have a little money, as we impose a small rate – and, of course, get equalisation grant on it as well. One of the councillors tells how he suggested to someone that they put an empty cigarette carton into a litter basket instead of on to the road 'and got dogs' abuse for it'. I did the same thing at Kyleakin in Skye, waiting for the ferry, when the people in the car ahead of me threw out paper on to the road instead of taking the trouble to get out of a stationary car and walk a few yards to the basket. I suppose they consider themselves to be in a higher social class than the defacers of lavatories, but they have the same attitude.

After a glance at cemeteries, we end up, as always, with housing, including the usual letters from dissatisfied applicants who see no reason why the undeserving Mrs X should have got a house and not themselves. A council house is worth scheming for. People move in with relations in order to become more overcrowded. Thank goodness I have no local allocation to do this time!

Could everything be done just as well by a few officials? I'm never quite sure. I suppose we councillors do keep them on their toes, though I can't see our district clerk ever being inactive. And a meeting is, in its way, a pleasing social occasion, though a lot easier on the behind in Campbeltown. Perhaps one day Tarbert will get around to giving us cushions!

New Statesman, v. 54, 31 August 1957, pp. 245-6

Does this make sense?

(1963)

Some places are rather a long way from the main centres – the Great Wens of western culture. Though it seems a bit heretical to say so, some people like living there. Campbeltown, for example, at the very end of the Kintyre peninsula, is 134 miles from Glasgow. The nearest railway station is Arrochar, 98 miles away. No railway goes down to the Mull of Kintyre; the Dukes of Argyll did not hold with them and anyhow if the Dukes had let us have one, Beeching[1] would no doubt be about to close it. Campbeltown has a population of around 6000 most of whom were very badly housed up to the end of the war, so it has a biggish slum clearance and rebuilding programme. There is a lot of reasonably good quality brick clay a few miles from Campbeltown near the Machrihanish coal pits. Some of us thought that this would mean a brick making concern near Campbeltown which would employ some of our many unemployed men in making bricks for houses and also for use in the pit, where brick has almost replaced timber in the workings. How wrong we were! If a brickworks had been started near Campbeltown it would have made too many bricks. It is only economic sense that modern high cost plant should be completely utilised.

So what happened? Load after load of bricks came down from the large modern brickworks beyond Glasgow. They came down the Lomond-side road, this winding, beautiful, fantastically overcrowded road which is, crazily enough, the only way from Glasgow to the West of Scotland. They then came down to Lochgilphead on a trunk road, that is to say a road which is paid for entirely by the general public through grants. After Lochgilphead they were on a class 1 road ranking only for a 75 per cent grant from public funds, the rest from the County Council. It is no longer a trunk road because – and you should hear us laugh about this in the Highlands – it ends in a harbour and people continuing their journeys go on by boat.

These brick lorries have caused considerable wear and tear. But this does not go on to the price of bricks. Two lorries passing on a highland road will do hundreds of pounds of damage in as many seconds, crushing down the verges. But they don't have to pay. Of course if Campbeltown had got its modern brick kilns it would have had to export with the wear and tear the other way.

No doubt there was a time when there were small brick plants spread about the country as, curiously enough, one sees them in Denmark still, where to some extent they specialise in different kinds of bricks. In this country they have been rationalised away. So were most of the Campbeltown distilleries, but I regret these less as they caused many worthy Campbeltownians [sic] to live in an almost permanent alcoholic daze. Though after all, why not?

The Campbeltown clothing factory is doing well and employs quite a number of girls, but that is because the owners were genuinely interested in coming to a remote place: that is to say, their motivation was not entirely economic. Apart from that, men are presently employed in taking the entire face off a rather beautiful hillside in order to put in Nato oil tanks. Nobody in their senses thinks this kind of employment will last.

Gradually Campbeltown people are streaming away, some to Glasgow, many to Corby where Stewarts and Lloyds employs them, and they say, yes, it is fine and the wages are good, but they miss going down to the harbour, they miss the sound of the seagulls. So much for Campbeltown and a dozen other Highland towns.

Now let us look at Bechuanaland, the country of the Batswana. I am now tribal adviser to the Bakgatla, a job which has its similarities with being County Councillor for Kintyre East. Certain things jump to the eye. At present from a quarter to half of the younger men go to the mines of the Republic of South Africa on nine months' contracts which tend to spread to a year; this, it is increasingly realised, is socially and morally bad. This employment for obvious reasons makes the country extremely vulnerable. But you have to have some money to pay even your small tribal tax and to set up house. So I say to myself what we need is local industries; I'll find some! Our main product is cattle; cattle have hides. Our people get bilharzia from going barefoot in infected mud; also one cannot use a spade without shoes. I thought too that in the shoe industry where fashion replaces fashion so rapidly it should be possible to get old shoe-making machinery – shoe factories hire their machines and send back what they do not want – of a fairly simple kind, low cost machinery which could be operated by men who are only semi-skilled and would produce not very fashionable shoes, but shoes that ought to be low cost as there would be little transport and a low wage bill. Again No. Shoe companies go to the Great Wen – in this case probably Johannesburg: wages there, profits to Europe, the Batswana only do the paying. It doesn't make sense – not to the Batswana, nor to me.

I asked around in one industry after another but always there are these enormously ingenious high cost machines turning out products cheaper and cheaper because they use so little labour. And the people who would like to work and buy these cheap things have no wages and even if they had there are not enough of them to make a market for the output which a modern machine would inexorably produce.

Of course in countries with Welfare State Organisations everyone has enough money for necessities, or almost everyone, and perhaps old age pensioners don't wear out so much shoe leather? The unemployed in Campbeltown don't starve. Nor do the Bakgatla since it is a moral tenet of the tribe, as of other Bantu peoples, that one shares what one has, food or blankets, with those who for the time being are worse off than oneself. But they do not have money and some things, including shoes, can only be got for money. So they are forced into the cities, which for them probably means the mine compounds, just as the Campbeltownians are forced into Glasgow or Corby.

Now I am only a poor weak woman constitutionally incapable of understanding economics, trying to advise some thousands of savages whom I love and respect, but I also write science fiction and I see that we are giving up the struggle against the machines which are nibbling us up and forcing us into their patterns. Some people get away from this struggle by insisting on very short working hours so that the machines can't damage them for more than, say, 40 hours a week; and if they have cars they can live a reasonable distance away from their masters. I keep wondering what is happening now in Russia; when I was there last they were so pleased with their machines that one was still taken to admire them. It was even odder when I was there in the early 1930s and the mere possession of a typewriter entitled one to a room in a hotel not, I suspect, for oneself but for the Malinko Machina, the little darling.

This is, of course, an economic pattern, though it might have come about less if we had not loved and admired machines so much in the nineteenth century. In a society which gives lip service to social equalitarianism (even among the 'young' conservatives, who at the same time feel that the only really admirable thing is to make money – a rather different concept from just 'being rich') the lower paid people demand more wages, while those at the top become increasingly ingenious in not being caught up with, and in fact are becoming richer in spite of taxation. Machines and the scientist inventors put a good spanking pace on all this, as do the export drive boys, pointing out how we must keep up with the low wage, long hour economies if we are to survive as one of the Top Countries.

It is no use arguing with the efficiency boys. They can always produce figures to show they are right, and we must go on producing with bigger and bigger units and as far as possible in uniform products. It is only when some other factor comes in that one's argument begins to carry weight. This must be either a quality factor when people will pay more for a thing made less economically: clothes or chocolate or delicate machinery; or the social factor which is much less measurable and may include things like the desirability of Campbeltown people being able to stay in Campbeltown, as well as the undesirability of breaking up the Argyll County Council roads. There can also be sudden extras like a defence factor which comes into the need for Bechuanaland factories, as it did in the Forestry Commission plans before and during World War II.

The extra factor is very clear when one thinks about land and its ownership. In a great many parts of the world very large estates are the most economical way of farming. This does not mean they have the heaviest crops or the best milk yields, although we are sometimes apt to think so. It means that the relationship between costs, including labour costs and product, is at its optimum. If the same land is broken up into smaller units run and worked by tenants or owners the result is probably less economically satisfactory if they count themselves as labour in their costings. But suppose they don't?

I make a good deal of butter in summer from my spare cream; the skim milk meanwhile goes to the pig. If I counted in my own labour either as dairy worker or as writer or, goodness knows, as skilled professional typist, the butter would be madly expensive to make. But if instead I count the time spent as occupational therapy, then the butter is quite economically eatable and of course infinitely nicer than shop butter.

This kind of thing taken over a population is a social factor; it is counting in what people genuinely want – human happiness. But of course happiness is much harder to measure than efficiency so it is ignored or denigrated as much as possible.

Luckily there is a certain mystique about land which is so obvious that it has reluctantly to be allowed for. It is realised that in many countries people want to work on and have security with a special piece of land whether as tenants or owners. It is less easily realised that in some other countries they want to have a communal tribal security based on land.

It may be, to go back to Kintyre, that Carradale Glen might be more economically farmed as one large estate, clearing away boundaries and using modern machinery. But that would so minimise the happiness of owners and tenants that the social factors might outweigh the economic ones. Yet there are many large landowners in the Highlands and Islands of Scotland (I am thinking of actual people) who claim that they are making splendid economic use of the land they are farming. The tenant farmers who have been removed might say that the social factor has been entirely omitted from the calculation; what they actually say is more monosyllabic.

This does mean that sometimes the social factor counts. In the Highlands and in various other special areas in the United Kingdom, inducements are offered to new industries. Luckily a few do come. But nobody is interested like that in Bechuanaland. And very, very few Batswana have any capital. What about the Treasury then? What about these lovely subsidies of grants and loans that come the way of the intelligent seeker in the Highlands? Here I think one must consider the attitude of the Treasury which doesn't hold with allowing much for the social factor. I asked, for example, whether a water supply could be brought from a dam to a large tribal town some thirty miles off; it would no doubt be a fairly high capital cost but one which wouldn't make us blink in this country; and there would be some upkeep because of pumping, etc. I was told that the Treasury wouldn't dream of countenancing such uneconomic spending; the people in the town would only drink the water or even wash with it, a most uneconomic thing to do. Conceivably the Treasury might be induced to bring water to a factory site if they were sure the factory was going to come; and the poor thirsty tribesmen would be cheap labour.

Now I want to know, is this making sense? Isn't it driving us into a position where almost everyone will have to live in or very near large factories and these factories will have to be grouped in larger and larger cities so as to get the maximum benefit from power, transport, etc? The amusement industries will follow the workers who will be living in a way which will make them want quite elaborate amusements in order to appear to themselves to be happy. And of course they will be able to buy more and more things, so the wheel will go round.

If I say this isn't good enough, if I say it is uncivilised – that it is because of this encroachment of high cost machines that people in European streets look so oddly unhappy – am I being a Luddite? I don't think so; I only think that the ingenious chaps who use the utmost technological skill to design machines, which are more and more automatic, using less and less labour, might try instead to think up cheap machines which use labour not too dangerously or unpleasantly and which because of small overheads should be able to produce cheap goods. An interesting problem of design surely. But I am worried. In asking for this am I against progress and us being Top Nation? Or am I just sensible and saying something which more and more people are beginning to think?

New Society 50, 12 September 1963, pp. 21-2

[1] Dr Richard Beeching's report *The Reshaping of British Railways* led to the closure of many railway lines in the 1960s.

Planning a Kitchen Complex

(1972)

At five-thirty in the dark of the early summer morning I stumbled out of bed in London to a 'phone call: the house is on fire, we don't know if we can save it.

Archie Paterson, skipper of the *Harvest Queen*, had seen the flames as they came back across the bay at the end of the night's fishing and made full speed for the harbour. One of the crew 'phoned the Campbeltown fire brigade, another got the local brigade out of their beds and all the fishermen who were about, while Archie dashed up to the house, woke Lachie at the farm, Ant and Percy in the garden cottage. All started pouring on buckets – by now not much use – and getting things out of the main part of the house.

What had gone up was the long kitchen wing with pantry, three bedrooms, one of which I had just dolled up from being a corn store, and all the clutter of scullery, storerooms, gun room and the place where possibly the fire started – the stone flagged room with the deep-freeze, the only piece of electrical equipment which was in use. But of course nowadays an electrical fault is always the culprit!

The local fire brigade, with splendid insouciance, stood on top of the oil tank hosing as much as they could. The fishermen started in on pictures, books and china. Then the Campbeltown brigade arrived 'flat out in twenty minutes' and luckily nothing and nobody left squashed in their wake on the narrow winding road! Percy wheeled the pictures off in his garden trolley to get them out of the way of the hoses. When I got there the fire brigade were finishing off, seeing that no hot ash was left and making jokes about the salmon from the river getting up the hoses. I asked after the cellar, was told that it was knee-deep but they'd saved the whisky, so we and the fire brigade had a picnic too. In the main house two bedrooms were gutted, there was a huge hole in the roof and water had brought down various ceilings, but it was all so much less bad than it might have been.

There was now rather a lot to do. Among us we got the house into some kind of order and I didn't look too often at the old wing.

The local tradesmen were marvellously helpful and ingenious. All my china had gone but luckily not the silver; the joiners reconstructing a floor really enjoyed having their cuppa from an eighteenth-century teapot. But what was to happen?

We needed a new kitchen and pantry but also bedrooms to replace the three which had gone, a replacement sewing room and a gun room and lavatory. All these would be smaller than the originals but I wanted a rather bigger drying space, a washing room and if possible another bathroom, however tiny. It all had to be keyed on to the levels of the existing house. The other problem was that my husband had been having heart trouble and even before that I had been trying to install a lift, very difficult in the original house. Now a small lift shaft could be incorporated. In the event he died before the actual building was even begun but the shaft was an integral part of the structure and remains as cupboards and an alcove with the possibility of reverting to its original use, supposing there was ever need.

Naturally one always supposes that building a comparatively simple bit of house would be something one could do oneself. That mood doesn't last long. How does one choose an architect? Through friends, through asking, through seeing something he has designed. Too young, he may leave out the plumbing; too old, it will just be a small bit of a large office machine. I had a talk with Bill Cadell; when he came over he got together not only with me but with my daughter, Val, who is head cook in the holidays, and with the family in general. He soon realised that the kitchen was to be central to the house, that sometimes we might be just a couple of the family who would prefer to eat in the kitchen, but then suddenly, we might be thirty or even more, probably having to organise meals both for grown-ups and for the younger children. In fact, it had to be a room which was both a living kitchen and a catering establishment. It had to open into the dining room, but also to allow people to funnel off through another room if, for instance, they were coming to stay and wanted to put their suitcases down. This meant a preparation, cooking and gossiping area, from which one can see down to the back door and if necessary take avoiding action from unwelcome visitors, an area close to the dining room, for serving and washing up, where there would be china rather than pots and pans, and a way through to the other room. The lift-shaft cupboard acts as a kind of central axis round which these three spaces revolve.

The door into the dining room and the door into the other room, which is something of a passage way but has a big desk, a good deal of storage space and is used largely for business, both had to pass through the outer walls of the old house, between three and four feet thick. On the way to the dining room there is a slight slope up, but none the other way. However, the levels of the old house are quite crazy. All this was, so to speak, organised and made possible by a splendid staircase that goes up through the kitchen, with a great Scandinavian type window – something I have always wanted – going right up behind it to the top landing from which one has a gorgeous view.

This means that the kitchen is genuinely central, the room where everyone stops – and sometimes helps. It is made cosy by a wooden roof, port-holed with lights and gently coved over the area of the pantry and the china shelves which thus gets a character of its own. This is emphasised by the tiles round the sinks: in the pantry area there are bogles from the deeps of the Highland dream or perhaps kelpies out of the tap water from the spring at the top of Sheneval field; but in the kitchen area pterodactylish birds, some two-headed and not one the same, fly on their own business. All are the brain children of Chuck Mitchell from the Glasgow School of Art.

Cooking can be pleasurable, but one needs plenty of space, varying degrees of heat and two ovens if one is likely, as we are, to be working at the same time with large joints and large cakes. And one may as well avert back-ache by having one at shoulder height. At the moment I have one large deep-freeze, in a room which also has ample shelves for dry goods, on the landing half way up to the next floor.

Country problems are far from town ones; the deep-freeze may have our own venison, lamb, pork, salmon or trout, cod or haddock, or vegetables or fruit from the garden. I also buy some deep frozen foods in bulk, including things one may suddenly want for the children, sausages, for instance, or ice cream in gallon tins. The top trays usually have tidbits or left-overs I can quickly pull out. Game freezes perfectly if it is left till it is really ready before being packed away, but one must be quick with fish. Most soft fruit does better frozen on trays and then packed into bags, though strawberries and nectarines are best in syrup. It will be no bother to prepare at the kitchen table and then hand up.

Washing up is less pleasurable, but most people can be lured into helping by a nice dishwasher. Below the pantry sink working tops there are two Colston dishwashers, so that a small party need only use one. They have the great merit that almost everyone knows how to work them.

One spends a lot of one's life in the kitchen, but that is only one floor of the new block. Below there is a replacement gun room, much smaller than the original one, with a sink for a big catch of fish; a washing room with drying racks on pulleys, a hot room big enough to take dozens of wet macs and shoes, and a small sewing and ironing room. This opens from a wide passage which narrows to a door into the old house and the way to boiler room and cellar. Just inside the front door there is a neat little loo, with such a gorgeous view that we decided that as it is slightly above ground level and can't really be seen into, we shan't have any curtains or ground glass!

But in some ways the nicest part of the house is above the kitchen where the easy stair, going up past a shelf of flowerpots, ends on a wide passage and a rail on which everyone wants to lean and look out over the garden and hills to the west. Here there are three bedrooms, with built-in cupboards, which take one person luxuriously and two if necessary. There is a tiny bathroom, a separate loo, a brush and linen cupboard, and a small alcove formed by the top of the lift shaft.

Here there is a splendidly solid shelf able to take a typewriter, which makes it into a tiny writing room. This was the idea of the foreman joiner, Mr Scally, who didn't want to waste a piece which was over from the beautiful beam which one sees finishing and supporting the kitchen floor. It is already a favourite place. The sisal matting which will go onto the landing will continue into this; the white – or rather 'magnolia' – walls in most of the rooms and passages have been replaced by a warm mustard colour. All this joins onto the main house by way of a fire door and a passage

The new extension to Carradale House

Drawing-room mantelshelf with Hermes' bronze head of a young Denny,
Carradale House

sliced off one of the big old bedrooms, which has in consequence become a much nicer shape. Bill clearly knew it would be, but I couldn't believe it till I saw it.

Working with local tradesmen in the Western Highlands is very different from the distances of such relationships elsewhere. Mr Scally, the joiner who created my little upstairs writing room, has worked on the staircase and made the kitchen cupboards; they are plain wood with Formica tops in a pleasant faint grey-blue stripe. You might think the drawers unnecessarily heavy but I doubt it. They will last for generations and they run like mice. Mr Cochrane, head of the painting firm, had his first job as an apprentice on my blue drawing room which is still in reasonably good trim after more than thirty years. When it came to choosing the colour for the outside paint work, we went round with two or three pots, trying them out.

The roof, however, had to be done by an outside firm. I was fed up with constantly replacing my old Ballachulish slates, good as these are, after a few months of Highland weather, though the main house must stay slated with the old lead ridges and gutters that gently wear into holes. I didn't want a roof of asbestos or something of that kind; I wanted to be able to have the house in good shape and with the copper colouring nicely before I was too old to enjoy it. So copper it is.

The new building is a storey higher than the old one and takes less than a quarter of the ground space. But I have kept part of the old walls to three feet. Percy and I are planning irises which have never been very happy in my acid soiled garden but will like the lime from the walls. Inside will be a car park. One of our problems was to key on the outside of the new part to the old whitewashed harling of the main house. Bill and I went round various houses, hoping that Skye marble chips would solve our problem but alas they had no marble brightness. Finally the walls are harled with Swedish quartz pebbles on a white sand cement. I tried my hand at this, it looked so easy. But I never could get the flick of the wrist which must take years of practice.

We had a topping out party for the locals; I suggested wives and girl friends, feeling – and rightly – that they'd be interested in the kitchen and must have heard quite a bit about it. But there was also a contingent from the Campbeltown Pipe Band, three pipers, a drummer and accordionist, so there was plenty of music for the dancing.

Some of my silver says *Stet Fortuna Domus*: May the luck of the house hold. With all the friendliness that has gone into it it should be a lucky house.

Scottish Field, v. 119, April 1972, pp. 50-52

Drawing-room facing West. Murdoch in chair facing out to terrace. Prof. Mo Bedawi talking to Val on the sofa

Caravans to Carradale

(1979)

Carradale Bay is a beauty spot on the west coast of Scotland. But in the hot summer of 1976 it was anything but that. Legally, a landowner can have only three caravans on a piece of land, however large; this law asks to be broken and usually is. Caravanning families came to Carradale for a week or fortnight, as they had always done, and surely I could fit in one or two more – other places did! And could their sisters and aunties come and join them just for a few days? Or else they would turn up late at night, Mum exhausted, the children crying.

What was I to do? I tried to keep within the law, but it is broken increasingly as more and more people, unable or unwilling to pay hotel or boarding house prices, take to the roads. The caravans spread along the line of the beach, nice for them but increasingly unsightly; not yet a health hazard, but that might be the next step. The only answer seemed to be a proper caravan site, keeping the caravans clear of the beach.

The first thing I was told was that I should apply for at least two hundred caravans to make it 'economic'. But I did not think that the Carradale community should be asked to stand the influx of several times its own village population. I was also worried about the water supply which is liable to run out in a dry summer. Forty to fifty caravans and a few tents would work, though unfortunately I would no longer be able to take in the big Scouts and Boys' Brigade camps, nor yet the more friendly and interesting Woodcraft Folk,[1] with their splendid camp-fire parties.

In the summer of 1976 I put in my first planning application. Letters, forms and plans floated between me and Lochgilphead, where the Argyll and Bute District Council has its innumerable offices. Various officials called, including a somewhat inexperienced young man from the Highlands and Islands Development Board. Nobody had anything but praise for the site, which today has the blessing of the AA and the RAC. I made laborious and messy plans, not being very skilled with tracing paper, from the somewhat out-of-date OS map. It became plain that more would be needed.

However, most fortunately for me, I had sold my old byre and outbuildings to working jewellers, Mike and Trish Hurst, who had set up house and workshop, doing everything themselves, down to the drains and up to the slates. Mike took over not only the essential working drawings for which otherwise I would have needed a land surveyor, but all business dealings, not merely with the local authorities but also with the various contractors, most of whom were local. Trish designed our very handsome logo. I had wanted to give it a Gaelic name but was advised not, as it would only confuse the tourists from the south!

When the application for planning permission was put up to the public there were several objectors, all of them fairly recent incomers who had settled at Carradale and did not want to see any changes. The Carradale natives were on the whole pleased, realising that it would mean more money spent in the place, more tickets bought for village hall concerts and dances and more contacts for the younger people. But the objections held things up, though meanwhile Mike Hurst (who trades as Wallis Hunter Design) was pricing ready-made ablutions blocks and I was arranging with the Crown Commissioners a royalty for lifting road gravel from the bar in the bay. This has also to be cleared with the harbour authorities.

The Clyde River Purification Board had to know about drainage. But the main problem that worried the district council was the new entrance. There were already two, but they entered the main road at corners, and, although they were perfectly all right for normal traffic and used for decades without accident, they would clearly be difficult for heavy caravans turning. There was only one straight bit of main road with sufficient view both ways; the entrance had to be there, but it meant building a new road across a field which is, rather awkwardly, partly mine and partly farmed by my tenant whose sheep are extraordinarily adept at jumping cattle grids.

Would I have started if I had realised how complicated it was all going to be? Or how expensive, especially with prices going up month after month while we waited for the relevant committees to decide our fate? The Highland Board was very sympathetic and I trust will look favourably on our grant application – which cannot be considered until all the bills are paid and receipted. But the district council wanted more and more plans – what can it possibly do with them all? – and made tiny alterations of no consequence but something of a nuisance for us. However, planners must be seen to plan.

Comparing prices, it was better to buy a ready-made ablutions block with showers, designed for easy cleaning, heating and lighting, and not impossible to move if a new one is needed in ten years' time. Caravanners must surely prefer an all-in ablutions tariff, including ample hot water. On arrival they get a key to the block for £5, refunded when they give it back on leaving. Electricity was decided on largely for safety reasons; there have been too many accidents recently with gas cylinders.

1977 saw a constant, though leisurely, coming and going of forms, documents, letters and phone calls. District and regional councillors must have got sick of being rung up by one or the other of us asking if it was not possible for the authorities to get a move on. Finally a phone call from Lochgilphead told us it was through the Planning Committee though there might be some small further provisions asked for by Health. Yes, we could go ahead, and so we did, especially on the new entrance, which meant felling some nice trees, bulldozing an old stone wall, putting in the cattle grids, bottoming and gravelling the road.

Then came the blow from the Health Committee, almost a knock-out. We had to double the number of loos, which meant frantic telephoning and re-ordering, with corresponding alterations to septic tanks and soakaways. They asked for a fence along the ridge between the site and the three acres of machair along the beach, meant as a general play area, with one access instead of the present several winding paths through bracken and whin. Luckily Mike was able to convince them of the unwisdom of this. He also persuaded them – when somebody actually came down to look – that we did not need hard standings on the sandy ground, practically unscarred at the end of the season.

They also demanded more water points; these are well and originally designed, with timber wings separating water from refuse; for the latter we chose paper bags, more expensive than plastic but biodegradable. We have to take at least two tractor loads a week up to the main road for collection.

We managed to get it going by June last year, charging £1.50 a night for caravans. Our main season is only six weeks, starting from mid-July, though we hope it will grow. Some caravans unfurl into holiday villas with a set of awnings, so this year we must charge per person. We must do the same for camping and only hope that another summer will not see a repetition of the ghastly and very expensive mess that a few drunken campers made of the ablutions block, pulling out fittings and breaking what they could.

We managed quite successfully with a part-time caretaker, who, in wet October with all the caravans leaving, began planting the shelter belts envisaged by planning with whatever shrubs I thought would stand the poor soil and the winter gales: mostly the common rhododendron, seedling brooms which may come out in various colours, pernettya, heath and an arundo that seems to enjoy sand. However, I have put in one seedling Monterey cypress; if it can stand Pacific gales in California, it might stand Atlantic gales here.

We have plans for plenty of other improvements during the next few years, but the main expense is clearly over. In the end I had to find some £16,000 of capital (excluding the value of the land, which comes from the estate). But I think it will be well spent, not only for myself, but for the general pleasure and for the local prosperity of one part of the Highlands.

The Countryman, v. 84, Summer 1979, pp. 170-55

[1] A progressive educational movement for children and young people, established 1925.

Carradale catch

(1987)

Carradale River has had a good many adventures. My husband, Dick, was a keen fly-fisherman and others in the family enjoyed the river too; there seemed to be so much more time for such things fifty years ago! There were of course the usual poachers, wanting a fish for their tea and a bit of sport; they got away with it and we got herring and mackerel in return, not to speak of having the house saved from a raging fire, mostly by the village with bucket-chains. We all got on with one another.

When at last the river was formidably poached by two local lads who emptied cyanide into it, they got no sympathy from the village. It killed three-quarters of the stock; dozens of the poor things floated up, dead or dying, all along the banks. We asked the family doctor if we could eat them. He rang up the Chief Medical Officer in Glasgow who said it was all right if they were properly cleaned, but added, 'Let me know if there are any incidents.'

Everyone was really upset; it wasn't proper poaching. They did it for money – and did they warn the folk they sold the fish to that it had been poisoned? No, no, and they hadn't used any skills, it was pure murder. The village was all for a hard sentence when the culprits were caught. But that was long ago. Gradually the river built up, the sea trout came back; here the salmon are always late, never before the end of August.

After my husband's death – and he had landed a nice fish in the autumn before – there was less fly-fishing. There were shorter holidays, other interests. We tried ticket fishing, but it never seemed to work and tended to make quarrels. Myself, I was only interested in fish for eating, rather than catching – or not catching. I could fill a good bit of my deep-freeze by going out along the bay with a net and a few friends on a lovely June night when the sea trout were gathering. And indeed it is perhaps a less cruel death for the fish.

Meanwhile the river was deteriorating. Trees fell in, banks crumbled. All of us got older, less able to cope, with plenty of other problems on hand. And now it wasn't the old story of our old acquaintance the poacher wanting a fish for his tea; money was the thing, and when that's what you are after, anything goes. A new approach was needed. One of my grandsons began to sound out Public Opinion. This is easier for a male, as Public Opinion mostly happens in the bar, to which females are not very welcome, at least in Scotland. He introduced the possibility of an angling club.

It appeared that the idea might be cautiously accepted. We all met very amicably. Everything was properly drawn up, put onto paper. I was allowed to keep six rods, though I have never used more than two. I could also go down to the bay and net six times during the season. In practice I have never taken the net out more than three times, but, if it was a bad year or the river so high that the fish could all crowd in on any tide, it might be nice to be able to have another go.

Nothing was laid down or actually put into words, but I never net the mouth of the river, always keeping to the far side of the bar of stones and gravel that shifts every year, but follows the final course of the river into deep water. I always ask one of the committee to come down and they usually do and enjoy it, though half-regretting that some really good fish hasn't been given the chance of going up and being caught *their* way.

The club pays me £250 a year and pays the rates. I pay a small rent to the Forestry Commission, through whose land part of the river goes. The charges which the club takes from outsiders are £3 for a day's fishing or £12 for a week. I have a caravan park – carefully placed between sea and woodland, so that it is no disadvantage to the landscape – and people who come there are often keen to fish. But it is the village which really uses it and who have been steadily improving the river. The fishermen will go out at weekends and deal with obnoxious trees. There are visitors who have come to Carradale year after year; one of them brought his wet-suit and did some clearing of the deep reaches. It seems to be giving enormous pleasure to a good few people.

We did have a poaching incident last year – local, even related – and the club would have liked a sharper penalty. We have to see how the next season turns out, but I doubt if the answer lies with the police force. Or, indeed, with any kind of outside body. The pressure towards good behaviour must always come, as historically it should, from the community.

The Countryman, v. 92, Spring 1987, pp. 93-8

Drawing-room mentelshelf with Hermes' soapstone heart and seagull
sculpture in centre above fireplace

PART III

THE FARM

A Small Farmer Looks at her Farm

(1942)

Considering my own and my neighbours' farms, I am bound to see that small farming in Scotland now is very much like it was two hundred years ago. Rough land often rents for nearly the same in sterling, though the money does not buy what it did then in home-grown produce or in labour. In fact, most of the obvious differences can be put down to the increased value of labour – and its increased skill. One thing goes with another; when land was worked by a tail of unskilled, ill-fed, uneducated cottars and small tenants, farm implements were rough, home-made with clumsy tools. But, as 'improvements', mostly meant in the first place to put up the value of the land, demanded more intelligent workers, and fewer of them, and as the displaced country workers went to the factories, so factory-made agricultural implements began to be used – all in their turn to displace labour but to raise the mechanical intelligence of those that stayed on, and with it earning power; though seldom enough to keep up with increasing prices and a reasonable demand for better standards.

So the main differences we see between now and then are chiefly the methods of cropping and stocking made possible by fairly complicated machinery, and by the imports which an increasingly prosperous country could afford, but also wire fencing instead of earth or stone dykes, ditches, and hedges. I think perhaps one might see a change in the farm workers' faces too, a certain lightening, a quickness, an ability to take a new point, which was hidden earlier on under heaviness and anxiety and superstition.

Yet certain sorts of skill have mostly gone. Take one of the old, elaborate dykes, such as Macintosh of Borlum[1] described in the times when we Scots first began to take heart again after our civil and religious wars, and to think of our country's salvation through the land. If it was to be made at any pace it would need two skilled men and several more unskilled, and the hedges – new to Scotland then – would have needed careful looking after. Now we run a wire and stob fence along in no time. Angus and I pace it out, counting the number of stobs and straining posts we shall need, and, when I am obviously wool-gathering, back in the past, perhaps, he catches me up: What number did I say now, Mistress Mitchison? We made one nice-looking fence, much admired locally, out of stobs and slabs – waste wood from the sawmill, yon slabs. But the question we are asking ourselves is, how long will they last? The slabs are only outside wood, softer and quicker rotting; some people give these fences three years, some fifteen – it remains to be seen – and creosote is dear in such quantities, and takes time to put on. Angus and Rosemary have their hands full, as it is. There are some beech or mixed hedges which need yearly trimming with a fierce weapon called a scoocher,[2] but few quickset hedges. I am not sure, even, if there is any local knowledge or practice of quick-setting. When I think that in the 1845 Statistical Account of Argyll they explain that rabbits have been tried, but don't do! When, I wonder, was it that the rabbits got such a hold on Scotland?

The fences, then, are different from the old ones, but Galloway cattle are an old breed. Our crops will be better in quality; but the rotation is much the same as it has been since the end of the ancient runrig, with its cropping to death of the outfield, and the beginning of long tenancies which allowed the farmer to think ahead and began modern farming. We all of us practise the three-year cereal – green crop – cereal and sow-down; then hay and pasture until the next plough-up. Sometimes we take a second oat crop after ploughing lea: I had meant to this year in one field, but the urgent national need is for potatoes, so they are going in instead. I doubt if anyone in this part of the world had heard of turnips or potatoes two hundred years ago, but they were beginning to grow them in the Lothians and the Merse; when it came to the '45, there were plenty of good lairds who were so thoroughly interested in agricultural changes that they had no mind to try the political ones. We used to grow barley up here, it was the best of land for it; there were distilleries working up and down Kintyre, legally and illegally. But the whisky monopolists forced rationalisation, or, as we would say more succinctly, closing down, on the Campbeltown distilleries.

We drain much as our forefathers did, though we no longer seem to stop the drains and flood before a hay crop. We use lime much as they did, though we don't practise the marling that was common in eighteenth-century Scotland. Indeed the whole theory and practice of top-dressing has altered in the last hundred years, and will alter yet. We have not come to the bottom of soil chemistry. My own land had not been seriously farmed for some time; liming was overdue, as one could see by the fine crops of sourocks that grew everywhere. Last year I did a little liming and this year I am doing a good deal more. Johnnie M. speaks of it with an almost greedy pleasure; I shall be putting heart into the land, and he feels for the land as I, a newcomer, can never do.

We gather as much seaweed as possible after the storms and bring it in, as people have done along the coast from times out of mind. It smells delicious and I love scaling it, whereas I haven't got a proper farmer's feeling about scaling dung, however well rotted and full of admirable properties! To most farmers, a storm brings little good, but I know that when the sleet has stopped beating on the windows, as it is now, when the seuch in the bay no longer sounds through everything, a background to my typing, even, we will go out with the cart and get what is yet needed for the lower end of the meadow.

But we use artificials as well, even for potatoes which take most of the seaweed, and get a crop several times as heavy as our ancestors', partly on fertilisers, partly on research work in crop genetics in this country and elsewhere. The bush fruit in the garden are getting nothing but seaweed; they thrive on it, though it becomes entangled oddly with the lower branches of the gooseberry bushes, reminding one, during the midgy days of summer picking, of a dried and alien potash content.

Whether my relations with my workers are ancient or modern, I don't know. But I think they are good; we trust one another a good deal. They start as anti-feminists; Rosemary had to make herself well thought of by sheer hard work and ability to bear pain and cold. How far I myself being a woman matters, and in what way, I don't know: not yet, not with Highlanders. We certainly get good fun, and a certain warmth and light-heartedness from working together. We all worked after hours at harvest, in the tension and excitement of the fields, binding and stooking, shouting to one another, watching the weather. This year we are likely to work harder yet, and at the potato planting and lifting, too. People must have done the same for hundreds of years, violent spurts of work, and between times enough dancing and singing, not to speak of the daffing and gabbing and gossiping, to make life tolerable. I believe the rest of the small farmers think well of me for tackling what is, after all, a difficult job; they watch what I'm doing, come and give me advice, lend me things. I expect they see that my hands are getting torn and rough and almost perpetually dirty, as a working farmer's hands should be.

Yet, can I take myself and my farm seriously? My job, I suppose, is writing; above all, historical writing. There, perhaps, I have an excuse. Historical writing means historical research. I am trying to see what was really happening in eighteenth-century Scotland, to see below the surface of romanticism and politics and anecdotes. Unless I stand where I do, how at all will I see into the mind of the man and woman in my own position, the intelligent ones who thought that the land mattered: people, often enough, with city education and city contacts, closely related to traders and merchants, aware of the urban problems and the urban solutions? For in Scotland we were too poor to stand aloof, and boys from the oldest families were duly apprenticed to skilled trades, or went in for banking or oversea trading, or simply sold silks and linens behind a counter. For that matter, your mantua-maker might have a title, and the Paisley thread industry was started by the daughter of a small laird.[3] England was moneyed and class-ridden, but our class divisions were odd and fluctuating; only the richest and most anglicised could afford to stand on class dignity. Anyone who wants to assess eighteenth-century Scotland must look to the Society of Improvers in Agriculture in Edinburgh, and with the same kind of spirit as their own. Macintosh of Borlum, the one competent Jacobite leader in the '15, spent his last twenty years in prison – a decent prison, no doubt, by modern standards; no State nowadays allows its political opponents so much contact either with books and newspapers or with friends, and Borlum's pamphlets were published in London. He seems to have spent most of his prison years reading and writing and talking things over with his fellow agriculturists; and much he recommends has happened since: Agricultural Colleges, County Agricultural Executive Committees, and research of all kinds.

When I think of him, or of Saltoun or Belhaven, or for that matter of Cockburn of Ormiston,[4] one of the first of the Lowland lairds to experiment with crops and inclosing – not at that time inclosing for sheep or deer or anything which would turn men and women off the land, but so as to give a few fields a rest from the fierce winter grazing of the half-starved common herd – and also to give his tenants long leases on good terms, I know that such men would go round at this time of year, planning as I myself am doing. They were on a larger scale, of course. I have no tenants – thank goodness! – but I have plenty of neighbours, working farmers, either renting or owning their farms. We meet at farm sales, where everyone seems to forgather, mostly, just now, to see what they can pick up in the way of farm implements. At the last one, everything mechanical went at a fantastically high price; as one of them said 'If the cows had been on wheels, instead of legs, they'd have been double the price!'

When any of us tries anything new, then all the rest prick up their ears. I am going to see what can be done with electric fencing this year. Nobody has tried it yet, hereabouts, and we don't know whether it will cope with the rabbits; if it works with me, then others no doubt will give it a try. Since 1939, I have duly ploughed up lea, and thought I had done pretty well. But this year the County Agricultural Executive asked me to try and plough part of the bay, a sandy warren, half grown over with bracken – this we have been trying to crush, a few acres at a time, but leaving plenty for the children and courting couples who stray about the bay all summer! – and full of rabbits, though not quite so many as in former years, as we have been trapping and eating them steadily.

I wanted to do what I could, but didn't see how I could manage the fencing, even if I could get a permit for the wire and stobs; fencing three or four acres takes time, and most of our fences are having to be re-done this winter. At first they wanted me to grow potatoes the first year, but I didn't see how I was going to get the ground sufficiently cultivated for drilling; whereas, a once-over with the Government tractor would do for an oat crop, and as things are, I'm afraid we may want our own potato crop in Scotland and in England quite as much next year as this. So I made up my mind to try an oat crop with an electric fence round it at one side of the bay; next year I shall plough the same acreage at the other side of the bay, while this first side is under potatoes. And I shall move the light electric fence over. The potatoes will not need fencing, as I can keep stock off the bay during summer, and neither rabbits, hens, nor deer will want to eat potato shaws. The year after that again, when my first side will be oats, sown down with hay seed from the barn, the fence can be moved again. That is, if it works! I feel about it just as my forebears did two hundred years ago, trying out something new, some crop perhaps that had done well in the south. They were often over-hopeful, certain that an English method, or for that matter a French one, would work, insisting on Suffolk or Essex ploughs, hoping for the same crops that the market-gardeners round London produced – vegetable crops, it might be, that the Scots members of the English Parliament had met at dinner tables and taken to. Perhaps I am over-hopeful about my fence. I shall know in six months.

None of this is done without much consultation, arguing with Angus, talk of a crop there was on that same piece of bay thirty years ago, or maybe nearer forty. The field where I had meant to have a second crop of oats will be potatoes instead; Lachlan and I prowl round looking for a good place, free of rats, to put the seed potatoes; fortunately there are occasional rats in the drawing-room, otherwise they might go there! Our constant trouble is shortage of sacks; we used to have plenty, but I rashly let some go with sphagnum moss, others with waste paper. But my potato customers are very thoughtful about keeping them; they tell me my potatoes are extra good. I try to say to myself that this is merely Highland good manners, but all the same I find it ridiculously pleasing.

I am going back this year to an old custom. There are plenty of families here with no gardens, or inadequate ones, where they cannot grow these American roots which, so oddly, have been a main staple food here for the last hundred and fifty years. So I am offering a drill or two of cultivated potato land to anyone who will find their own seed potatoes and give us a hand with planting and lifting. That will suit everyone; the crop will be eaten, and I shall get the potato grant, if, as we all suppose, it is continued this year. Potato-lifting, like harvesting, can be great fun. Last year flocks of children turned up, the difficulty being to dissuade very small brothers and sisters and stop them from getting spiked by the obviously fascinating digger or walking under Jo's careful hooves. I'm sure it is a bad precedent to shut down schools for 'potato holidays', and of course it includes stopping the education of the smaller children as well; it means that they cannot settle down for the short August to September term, or get the good of it that they should. Yet most of the children enjoy field work up to a point. If farming is ever again to become a dignified and honourable job, some children will want to learn it, as part of a technical course; then things like potato-lifting might be thought of and treated as part of education, not a break in it. But it should not be allowed to break the courses of those who are doing some other kind of technical course, or the few, rich or poor, who are academically minded.

This year we have managed to induce one of the riding ponies, the rough Highland garrons, to go in the plough; I think our nice respectable Irish cart-horse, Jo, found it a little disconcerting at first because Echran, in a state of nervous affection, insisted on biting his neck. The first furrow they made wriggled like a snake between the ploughing marks. But soon Echran began to understand what he was needed to do, or perhaps Jo explained over the oats in the evening, and now they plough beautifully together, and the seagulls sweep and scream round Lachlan's head, and the lovely smell of the new furrows with the seaweed ploughed into them, drifts up as soon as the sun is at all warm.

It takes a little time to get into the habit of long-term planning that one needs on a farm. To think how this will fit into that. To see below the surface, among roots, the hunger and crowding of plants. To consider the possibilities of the seasons, for there is nothing certain about west-coast weather. I cannot do it yet. I have to write things down in a notebook, with queries after every plan, where a lifelong farmer would keep it all in his head. But it is amazingly reassuring, those days most of all, when everything seems to be in flux, when there is no security. This at least goes on, taking its own time. Our personal time is in a bad way, as all the poets witness, Eliot and Auden alike painfully aware of it every moment, as Yeats was too. But a farm forces one away from that dithering and uncertainty, into five- and seven-year planning periods, giving one a time-standard to steady oneself against. Farm workers get that steadiness; they cannot be panicked by the winged chariot, any more than the farm seasons themselves can be hurried. That is one reason why they are so good to work with. Watching my farm, as my folk watched theirs two hundred years back, I see crops and beasts; but, before all, the lives of men and women, with whom I work and live.

SMT Magazine, v. 29, March 1942, pp. 23-5

[1] Macintosh of Borlum is a subsidiary character in *The Bull Calves*, published in 1947, which Mitchison was researching at this time; see also the notes to the novel.

[2] Probably represents the Carradale pronunciation of 'scutcher', a hedge-trimming knife.

[3] Christian Shaw of Bargarran, perhaps better known as the central figure in the Paisley witch trials of 1697; she is also a character in *The Bull Calves*.

[4] Andrew Fletcher of Saltoun (1653-1716); John Hamilton, 2nd Lord Belhaven and Stenton (1656-1708); John Cockburn of Ormiston (1679-1758).

The End is the Beginning

(1942)

It was a bad, late harvest in the north-west; we had scarcely two days together fine from the beginning of August until on into November. How we envied the accounts of the grand harvest in the south! Most of us lost a good part of our oat crop; it was a wretched, wearing business, turning the heavy sheaves on a day that had cleared up, hoping that they might dry out at last, and then seeing them wet through again the next day, sprouting green blades and masses of soft white rootlets like worms where the wet lay worst, under the bands. Dry sheaves are easily managed, but these soaked ones were heavy and smelt bad; it was all one could do to lift them about, and they left a nasty slime on one's hands.

Potatoes are a sun crop too, and they had little sun this year; my own yielded badly, masses of tiny Kerr's Pink, fit only for hen's meat. Arran Victory from the new seed did better, but they are a dark potato, rather difficult to see against the ground. For the potato harvest too we had to make use of every fine day. I am not keen on Sunday work as a general thing; one is tired out of all measure at the end of the week as it is, and agricultural work cannot be done automatically by a tired-out person. But this year we needed to do what we could. One Sunday afternoon we did seventeen drills, with two of the fishermen and the district nurse, herself a farmer's daughter, coming out to help. The digger was borrowed from my neighbour at Dippen – for, indeed, we are all on the friendliest borrowing terms, and I am usually the borrower, as I started with so little gear of my own.

In a good year one has a few weeks of comparative rest between the back-end, the tail of harvest, and the preparations for next season. It is golden weather, rich with rowan berries and brambles; one has the feeling of the crop won, an armistice between oneself and fierce old Nature. But this year we had no time to sit back, no time to take the guns out. It had been a bad year for game too, the wet summer killing off the young birds, and I have seen few enough of the bonny, outlandish pheasants that were so plentiful last year. Even the black game that come down the wind like express trains are few and far between. This year we shall have to take any shooting very seriously; I shall have every reason to be ashamed of myself if I duck when a blackcock charges me instead of shooting it!

We have been spreading dung in the stubble field that will be turnips next year. I like that much better than I ever thought I should. Nowadays I feel completely like a farmer about it, admiring the good, well-rotted stuff, feeling as though it were pudding; good food for turnips anyway! The smell is really not at all unpleasant once one is in the right frame of mind, and it is very necessary to feel this way, because one gets the stuff all over oneself, forking it up from the midden into the back of the trailer. It is heavy, though, and a full load is sore on the light trailer wheels. The trailer is a good deal broader than any cart, and solid. There is scarcely one of the old gateposts that hasn't been pushed half over, one time or another, and now the coping-stone is off the low enclosing wall of the midden. Goodness knows when we shall get it on again or do any of the other small jobs that need doing about a farm. Not yet, anyway; there is too much immediate field work to be done.

I broke away from custom, saying we shouldn't dump the dung into little heaps all over the field, but scale it out from the tractor as we went. This was partly because I find it intolerably heavy to go on scaling with a fork all the time, but I can quite well do it for half the time if I am also climbing in and out of the seat and driving the tractor on. And as I go slowly forward Lachlan pulls out a forkful and scatters it with a turn of the wrist over the bare patch where the trailer has been standing.

Only a few farms have started their ploughing so far; we mostly have fairly open weather until after New Year. But there is no time to be lost. We have to order our fertilisers too, our seeds and seed potatoes. Those who want the Government ploughing outfit should apply for it. But I am not sure how many will this year; last year the boys who were doing it were good tractor-drivers and mechanics but knew very little about good ploughing. I think this is a general difficulty about mechanised outfits; one feels that the moral should be rather more agricultural training for the drivers. We have, most of us, asked for the Government thresher, all the same; threshing with a big machine is more of a mechanic's job. We only hope it will come at some reasonably convenient time.

So far I have done my threshing with a water-wheel and an old mill that is gradually falling into a state of hopeless senility, though various people have tried their hands at mending it. The millpool is small too and takes a long time to fill up, especially in weather dry enough for one to be able to put the sheaves into the threshing barn. It is exciting, though, to wait with the sheaves opened out and ready to be put between the rollers; through the thick stone wall one hears the nearing rush of the water in the great iron pipe, then the first creakings of the wheel as it begins to turn. One waits till the mill is going full strength and then feeds in the stuff. I am not yet good at feeding it thinly and evenly; the rollers seem to snatch great lumps out of my hands and then protest about them with an alarming series of jerks and clanks before they settle down again.

During harvest I felt so depressed I could not bear the thought of ploughing, starting another crop year. Yet here we all are again, starting off, full of energy and plans, not to be deterred even by the many forms we have to fill in.

The Manchester Guardian, 17 December 1942, p. 4

Down on the Farm

(1943)

All farms are short of labour all the time. At least that's my feeling now, for I can't so much as sit down and write an article, let alone a book, without feeling that, if it is dry, I ought to be at the hay or the turnips or the corn, or whatever it happens to be in the season, and if it is wet I ought to be mending something or painting something, or maybe potato-sorting, which is the worst of all! But these last years we have all been trying to grow more, and if we haven't tried on our own, the County Agricultural Executives have been down on us.

Increasing mechanisation is some help, but it hasn't made so much difference on the small farms, and won't until we are in much closer co-operation. The really labour-saving things are very expensive and don't pay their way unless they are worked on a large acreage. And some kinds of machines need a team of people – often unskilled – to keep up with them. For instance, there are (though for me they are still in fairyland) beautiful potato-lifters that sort and bag, and for all I know have a chip-making and cellophane-wrapper attachment as well. But we work with a tractor digger that grunts along the drills, scattering the potatoes, often with such force that they dive back again into our sandy soil. The gatherers have to line up and scramble like terriers, and end the day with aching backs.

We had two camps helping with our early potatoes: one lot were local schoolboys, and the other Glasgow boys and girls, factory workers mostly, and quite unused to country things. They set to gallantly, but found it rather tough and unaccustomed; they couldn't see the scattered potatoes as easily as the rest of us could, and they didn't realise at first that new potatoes have to be handled gently because they bruise and then don't keep. When I explained to them all the processes which the field had gone through before the crop was ready, from the first gathering of sea-wrack after the storms to give it the necessary potash, down to the last setting-up, they were extremely surprised and got a new light on potatoes, and even wondered how they could be sold so cheap.

Both camps helped me with the hay harvest. It was wonderful weather, and the Glasgow boys and girls were badly sunburnt, not realising that it isn't safe to start by taking off one's shirt for an afternoon. I think that must have happened to a good many city helpers this summer, as well as cleg bites by day and midge bites in the evening. Also they found the forks and rakes rather difficult to handle, but one or two of the local boys had done this sort of thing often and were quite expert. I'm sure the technical terms must muddle the town visitor badly – they muddle me quite enough, with their difference from the similar English ones that I was used to as a child. All the things the hay may go into – coils and windrows, and huts and ricks! The heartening; ah, it's in grand order the day! By now I am used to speaking of the graips where I once used to use the English word, fork; but none of the Glasgow ones knew the word.

Nor are most farmers very good at explaining exactly what they want done, to some one who doesn't know the ordinary way of it; I know they sometimes get impatient with what appears to be the town-folks' stupidity, but which is merely a lack of comprehension of something they have never seen or done before. Nor do all districts do things the same – from binding a sheaf to building a stack – yet each is convinced that their own way is the right, and the only right, one.

Town visitors don't like early rising. But indeed we cannot start work as early as we would like on the farms because of daylight saving. That means that everything is supposed to start two hours before the natural time, but the dew doesn't dry any faster because of an Act of Parliament. One cannot do much with hay or corn before ten in the morning, here in the west anyway. Potatoes, however, could be started round about eight. My campers tended to sleep in, and the fire to cook breakfast didn't always start, but Robert, a sheet-metal worker, down here for his annual holiday, was there on time. 'My day starts at 6.30,' he had said a little reproachfully when I apologised for getting him over so early. Potatoes were new to him, but, as he said, 'It's a change'.

I had a Major in the Guards with me for the sheep-dipping. He started with illusions about sheep, the same kind I used to have before I bought a flock of wedder lambs. He thought sheep were gentle, amenable, sweet-natured animals. A day of them settled that; but at least he got great satisfaction out of the dipping pole. One would not enjoy dipping sheep nearly so much if one had not already dragged them by the horns, angry and reluctant mutton, or seen one or two escape and make a dash for wherever they oughtn't to go. He seemed to feel that sheep-dipping should form part of any Commando training!

Two of my own children are off at school camps, one doing forestry, the other potato lifting; I gather the pay is an attraction, but also the fact that it's a school do and they'll be with friends. My youngest – a good berry-picker! – has been allowed back and is at it already, though not so deep in farm work as my neighbour's two small girls who help their father with his milk round. At fourteen and sixteen, the others were extremely useful last holidays, when we were liming and sowing. But they, by this time, know how to harness a horse, lift a sack, or whatever it may be. Most town-folk have to be taught everything and usually begin wrong. In hedging, they almost always strike downward with the scoocher, instead of upward, which is dangerous as well as less effective. If they are thinning turnips, they hesitate, unable to make up their minds which of the eager young seedlings is to be allowed to survive, or leave two, one to help the other, which is the worst thing to do; one has to suppress one's imagination over this kind of thing, just as one must over so much of one's dealings with farm stock. Obviously the cows do mind when the calves are separated, but not as much as one thinks if one starts picturing them as people.

Town people have a habit of rushing jobs, too; the slow tempo of a farm, which can be speeded up into tremendous energy at a crisis, is necessary. One cannot do very heavy work too quickly, or one gets tired out. And the slow look round the field is often full of purpose.

It is only very rarely that an office worker is much good on a farm. If you have any kind of manual skill, you will get into the swing of another kind quickly enough. Scientists who have worked in a laboratory can always pick up the method of using some farm implement, and are ingenious at thinking of ways round natural obstacles. Doctors are good, too, and there is often something for them to do in the professional line before the day's out. They don't worry over farmyard sights and smells so much as some folk do. But I am afraid writers are apt to be rather bad. They have preconceived ideas about the good earth and back to Nature, and all that, and when they bump up against Nature they are likely to get a shock.

For it is all harder work than the visitor supposes, and you can't just stop; if you do, just because you are very tired, you may lose your crop or your beasts. And it's no good for the town-dweller to suppose he can turn up in the middle of the afternoon and be just as welcome. The farm folk have been working since the end of the midday break; and the visitors may think it stupid to knock off at five, they aren't aching as we are. Besides, there's the question of overtime for the skilled man to whom the unskilled townsman is probably working as feeder.

I often ask the town people how they'd like to live in the country and work here; they all say it would be marvellous, they'd chuck their jobs in a moment, if they could, to come here. And quite often it *is* marvellous, the way they're doing it; for they have to sit about in the hay a lot of the time while the rest of us are at it, doing the skilled work.

Yet all the same, one *is* pleased when anyone offers to lend a hand, even if it's not a very strong one, even if it is only for an hour or two. But most people walk slowly along the road and stare at us working in the field. Possibly one looks odd – I know I dress for comfort rather than photo-appeal. Probably they need a real holiday. Certainly any one who is working on a wartime job does. But not all of them are doing that. And some are bored, looking for a way of 'passing the time', as they put it. A day on the hay passes the time quick enough! And it's immensely useful to have some one about to do the odd jobs. While my Glasgow doctor dug out potatoes as though they were appendixes or psychoses, his wife sewed up the holes in the potato bags, one of the jobs which I might have done, but somehow never did. I'm sure she has more sewing than she knows how to deal with at home, but this kind in the middle of a field, with a blue Riviera-ish sea to edge the picture of fern and earth and black Galloways grazing, was somehow different. Nor does one grudge a good picker as many raspberries as they feel like eating.

When I was a child I was brought up to help with farm work whenever I could, just as I would have helped in my father's laboratory. I can't have been more than three when I went out first to glean with the old ladies from the Auchterarder poorhouse. Sometimes for years, during my London life, we never spent a holiday near enough to farm work for me to do anything, yet I never quite lost the knack of binding a sheaf. But so many city dwellers have an utter unfamiliarity with country things: how can this not be bad for the balance of national life? We have had an urban policy in the past, from a ruling class of manufacturers. It has taken a war to put farming on the map for most people. But we shall need to go on producing food, for ourselves – a poorer country, surely – and for Europe. Will city people feel that a peace plan as well as a war plan makes their co-operation worth while? My feeling is that nobody will be able to afford fancy holidays after the war, and, for that matter, that nobody will feel quite comfortable to sit about and be amused. We shall all have got into the habit of lending one another a hand. As farming becomes more mechanised the town worker feels more comfortable with it; my boy helpers always brightened up if it was a question of tightening nuts on the tractor, but a townsman tends to keep at a cautious distance from even the most amiable cart-horse or cow.

In England part of the harvest is in already, and from one place and another one hears of the help from the town visitors. But it is usually a simpler business there, and often more mechanised. Here in the west our oats have to be cut comparatively soft; they ripen and harden in the stooks. It is doubtful whether we could ever use a combine harvester. Last year, with the weeks of wet weather from August to October, it was difficult enough to use an ordinary reaper and binder. The tractor was bogging half the time. Day after day would we spend turning the sheaves and putting up the blown stooks. None of my town friends realised what a tough job it was: the aching back and torn hands, from handling wet, heavy, rotten-smelling sheaves, opening them out where the corn was sprouting and re-binding. It was difficult for them to get the idea of making a right stook, knocking together the reluctant blond heads of two oat sheaves, standing up the six like tired dowagers – by the end of harvest I always thought of the sheaves as old ladies! One day we had a party of sailors over. I tried to explain to them about turning the sheaves in a field. A few of them listened, but most of them rushed at it with whoops and complete incomprehension of what it was all about, turned half the sheaves upside down and remade the stooks so badly that most of them were down by the next day.

But this year – so far! – the harvest prospects look good: the fields are whitening already. Glasgow Fair will be over and the local summer tourist season half finished, but I shall have friends from the south staying, and men or girls on leave, and all liking to help on a different job. The Free French who come here make me jealous, telling me about unlimited sunshine, vines, and olives, and the incredible fertility of the corn-growing parts of North Africa. They feel, I think, that it's hardly worth taking all this trouble over such poor land, though they like cutting down trees (and, these days, if one is thinking of making a new gate or henhouse or fence, the first thing to do is to fell a larch or Scots fir), partly perhaps because of the satisfactory feel of the axe in the hands – and there goes Laval's head![1]

Harvest is grand when all goes well, when there are enough on it not to make the work too hard, when you need not be looking over your shoulder at the weather half the time, when you can linger a little in the field. One gets extra rations for harvest workers, and needs them. A basket full of pieces with jam and cheese, and maybe lettuce and tomatoes, goes in no time. My own men like their tea, but there is much more of a kick to be got for the town-folk out of unlimited milk. Harvest rations don't include milk, and every one wants extra proteins. I have just got a licence to kill a sheep, after filling up one of these fine fruity forms, not so difficult as most, really, because the answer usually was 'not a pig'. I am wondering if I shall be able to make a winter coat out of the skin!

If we have the weather, I hope for a good mixed team for harvest. There will be town helpers, my own friends, and perhaps one of the summer visitors if it occurs to them, the children – immensely tough no doubt after their forestry and potato-lifting – and perhaps one or two of the fishermen, and, when she's out of school, small Ebby, who comes with me on the tractor and struggles gallantly to open even the stiffest gates.

SMT Magazine, v. 32, September 1943, pp. 29-35

[1] Pierre Laval (1883-1945), a member of the Vichy government in France which collaborated with Nazi Germany during World War II; executed for high treason after the war.

Marginal Land (1)

(1944)

But for the war we should never have tried to crop the meadow, for all that folk here say there used to be a fine puckle of hay off it in the old days. Since then, in all the long bad years for farming, when it was worth no one's while to keep the land in heart, rushes got a hold of the meadow; they got worse every year, and thick moss between them choked out the grass. But if I did not plough here, and if I am to keep up my acreage, as we are all pressed to do by the War Agricultural Executive Committees, I should have had to plough Sheneval, my one good pasture field, or else take in another piece of the bay, ground that is almost pure sand.

Thus it was that 'J.T.', the county adviser, came over at the back-end and walked with me over the meadow and took levels and fished up soil samples with a kind of enormous corkscrew, very joke-provoking in Scotland. The first thing was to get it drained; there were old open ditches and some stone drains. In the old days there had been an open ditch across the top, filling up from the midden, which was let loose by a series of small sluices to fertilise the ground for a crop of meadow hay every year. But now we had to get out a proper drainage scheme. Half the cost, which is considerable, comes from the Department of Agriculture when the thing has been passed – or so I hope: so far I have had only a series of depressing little buff slips. The first thing was to collect the tiles and the drainers, and while one or the other eluded me, in spite of increasingly furious telephone calls and letters, the months slipped by. At last one load of tiles came, and we unloaded them eagerly on a cold winter day, taking them out of the lorry two at a time and piling them at the roadside. A big lorry could not get across the ford and through the narrow gate into the field, nor could it have turned in the field without sticking. So the tiles had to be reloaded on to the cart and taken along to the ditches as they were dug. They were sore on the hands. Several times Joan, my smiling, orange-headed land girl, and I slipped in the mud and rolled over our tiles, chipping them and ourselves.

Drainers are rare birds and can command their price. Neil and his mate had all the charm of Irishmen, but – well, I was the boss, but I knew nothing about draining and they were keen to get on to the next job. And yes, it was terrible bad weather and there would be whiles it was hard to get down as far as good drains should be, and the bottoms running with water, and, indeed, they were decent, quiet men to have in the house. But when 'J.T.' came over and took the situation firmly in hand I don't think they were altogether surprised at having to re-dig and deepen most of their drains. Only the whole thing took time, and it was March and the good frosts all over before the meadow was ready for ploughing.

As the drains were so newly laid the ploughing had to be done by a caterpillar tractor; the rush roots would be tough, beyond what horses could do, and would need the department's single-furrow plough. The caterpillar does not put the same pressure on any one place as an ordinary tractor, and negotiates mud well. It arrived on Sunday, and the churchgoers looked askance at it and me. On Monday there were great consultations between 'J.T.', whom I had known so far as a respectable Government official, but who was now in overalls, and the Government tractor-drivers. The first break had to be made along the line of the old open ditch, and we were all at it, shoving over the first furrows with boots and forks and hands into the hollow. Then came day after day of Peter's ploughing. We were at work ourselves, planting the early potatoes, lambing, then liming and sowing our first oats; I would take Peter over his tea and pieces – one gets a very useful small extra ration for a man coming in to work like this – and then he would go on working till dark.

Then it was finished at last, and the plough going the long way round for the head rigg, meeting great tree roots and doing its best with them. We had cold nights and sunny days; the furrows began to dry out. But before the discs could be put on it we had to move the stones which were out on the surface from the old drains. It has not been easy working with the horse lately, as the Navy has been doing considerable [gunnery] practice and poor Jo is desperately nervous and has bolted with the cart several times. But he was good with the stones. Many of them were too big for any one person to handle; some were still half-buried and had to be levered up with the punch. Angus would be grubbing away at them, muttering about the old days of cheap labour when men had quarried and laid these stones, maybe a century or more ago. Joan and I would be collecting the smaller ones, getting them into the front of the cart. Then Lachie and Angus, between them, would get the big fellows on, and then Jo would get the cart moving along the furrows, Lachie at his head to encourage him and keep him from falling on the difficult, slippy ground. And one more load to the growing dumps at the corners of the field. We took some eighteen loads off the meadow.

I still find it hard to believe that there is the makings of a seed-bed in all this roughness, but 'J.T.' says so. I know he is unbiased; he is experienced and loves the land; I believe he is really happy when he gets down to overalls and mud. And, indeed, while one is working one feels that something is going to come of it. It is less than half a year to harvest. We shall see.

The Manchester Guardian, 21 April 1944, p. 4

My Farming and My Neighbours

(1944)

Here farming is one continual struggle against bad weather. In wartime we are all short of labour; hill farms cannot get much help from official school camps, though some of the Campbeltown boys camping on the Bay help, as does my land girl's sister during her holiday.

I started farming on land which had been neglected for years; the fences were all broken, there was no farm gear at all; we had turned most of the old Mains farm buildings and byres into a village hall and a couple of modern cottages, badly needed – and I never expected then to regret the old barn or the big stone-slabbed dairy! I had practically no farm experience; it was thirty years since I had milked a cow. Lachlan, my farm hand, who was under-keeper, had some experience of very rough farming in the Hebrides, but he too was a learner.

I have also to look after a large house, where I may, from time to time, have to deal with rations or even cook for twenty people, some of them tired out from war jobs or on leave, others back from school, all hungry. I have to do all the village odd jobs which fall to the woman in the big house – anything from collecting rose hips, seaweed and old rubber boots from the seashore to visiting the sick or distressed, writing to Government Departments on behalf of the ring-net fishermen, helping people to fill in forms about this, that and the other, or wangling spare valves for the village hall cinema.

Even after the fields have been properly looked after, they are not good land, nor ever will be. There are between fifty and sixty acres of arable, some two hundred of rough grazing and two acres of walled garden which is now run as market garden. There is at least no lack of customers, but, since the Ministry of Supply cut down the neighbouring woods, we have been plagued with bullfinches; last year they left me no black currants or gooseberries and few early apples or plums.

I put the worst side of it first. Against all this, we are practically never short of water. One year we had a bad dry spell immediately after sowing, but it is never serious. Anything grows – including weeds. Our winters are not desperately cold, in fact we could sometimes do with heavier frosts after ploughing. There is little bad disease, either of crops or stock. Above all, one can count on a measure of practical goodwill.

Until I lived in the country I did not know what neighbours were, or what they can mean in the way of help – or irritation! When Duncan came over with his tractor and mowed the Mains field, which would have taken me four days with the little one-horse mower, I felt, 'This is being neighbours, this is how life should be.' It becomes unthinkable that we should in any future time compete instead of co-operating. For the first time the big Government thresher came round Carradale last year – we had asked for it the winter before, but it somehow didn't materialise. That meant a team of two or three from each farm, all working together because the machine forced us to, and enjoying it – the feel of the icy water on our chaff-stung eyes and straw-cut hands; the good meat; the fresh scones and delicious farm butter; the serious, lined, kindly faces; the wild orange hair of Duncan the tinker – there would mostly be three Duncans and three Willies; and the pleasure of the filled grain sacks behind us in the forenoon and ahead of us till evening. I believe that mechanisation will come this way to the small farms, an enforced working together and breaking of barriers of suspicion, and maybe a return to a way of life which was there long before and which is natural to the soil.

Something new has come to the countryside with the various Government outfits. The tractor-men bring the news and pass it round – how else would I learn that the High Ugadale shepherd had a dog for sale, and I needing one so badly? One of them caught his first salmon here, on a fly I recommended, after a tough day on the harvest. He told Lachlan that he always fished, but this was the first time he had been offered the use of a river! Some of the men are good enough mechanics but unskilled with the instruments, especially perhaps the plough. Much of the ploughing here has to be very shallow by south country standards, as there is little but sand or rock below the top skin of turf. I did my first tractor ploughing two seasons ago, finding it none too easy. The first bit was shamefully crooked; I had a wild feminine impulse to unpick it. I couldn't manage the ley at all; the ground was full of rabbit holes and the tractor forever plunging into them and digging itself in. Even on the stubble, soft patches persisted where the burrows used to be. This is the kind of soil that has to be made with turf and dung and the sea tangle that comes in after the November storms, but it needs two rotations at least before it looks as it should.

This is essentially dairy country, and my neighbours on both sides have attested herds. I didn't want to go in for the business of milk selling, profitable though it might be. As far as I'm concerned, nothing makes it worth while to get up in the dark for milking! But my rough grazing is perfect for Galloways, and I wanted milk for the house. The business of becoming an attested herd is most complicated; at one moment there was nothing for it but to throw a temperament. But the various officials concerned have been – well, as good as neighbours. I am second to none in my annoyance with Government by impersonal civil servants in distant offices, but the kind of civil servant who actually comes round and knows what he's talking about and wants, not just to collect statistics, but to help one to farm decently, he's fine! If land nationalisation means the State as a good landlord, everyone who cares for the land must be for it.

My Galloways are pedigree stock and look it. Linda and Daisy, the milkers, are comparatively *bourgeoise*, but respectable. Jo, the Irish cart-horse, is sensible, strong and nice to work with. He used to try to intimidate me by making snapping noises, but now that we have got to know one another there is none of that. The Highland garron is wilder, but a clever and willing little beast. But my farm instruments are anything but respectable – almost all second-hand, some on semi-permanent loan. I always borrow the turnip drill, and I never use anything but Archie the Baker's roller. Bits drop off the tractor. But it usually goes, and sometimes with Duncan's splendid new discs.

So far, we have made quite a good job of hand-sowing, and it's a thing I enjoy doing. I mind one Saturday afternoon and four acres sowed and harrowed by two neighbours, a fisherman and an engineer from the sawmill, and myself. Others help with hay, harvest or potato lifting. Even the Forestry Commission and the Ministry of Supply, not usually neighbourly bodies, have come into the game, loading a cut of my own Scots fir or larch with theirs, and sawing it at the mill, helping me out in my many difficulties about wood. Yet should I say it was these impersonal creations? Surely it was rather Duncan – yet another one! – and Ian, my actual, living neighbours, with whom I have the neighbourly relations.

The farm can't be said to have paid yet, even counting the tons of potatoes we have eaten in the house, trying out all Lord Woolton's recipes.[1] Starting from scratch, that was perhaps inevitable, though a better farmer might have avoided my worst mistakes. But the sheep, for instance, have been quite a success, and here it was the first Duncan who persuaded me to try sheep of my own instead of merely wintering his, and then bought me a flock of wedder lambs – in pouring rain just where the road widens a bit at the foot of the brae before you get to the pier – and gave me good advice on dipping and liver-fluke pills and lessons from his shepherd, and generally encouraged me to tackle something which was so far from my pre-war life that I could do nothing easily. No doubt my neighbours often find me silly and annoying and difficult to understand; sometimes they are bound to wonder what I'm after at all – and I expect this stands for those who work for me and who are even more closely my neighbours – yet on the whole they probably like having me about. And I get annoyed and frightened and depressed, and sometimes angry with them; yet I depend on them. The relationship is at the bottom one of deep affection, of working together, of being neighbours in a small place and in the Highlands.

The Countryman, v. 30, Autumn 1944, pp. 23-6

[1] Frederick Marquis, 1st Earl of Woolton (1883-1964), was Minister of Food during World War II. The Ministry issued booklets of austerity recipes with which Lord Woolton's name became associated, such as the Woolton (vegetable) pie.

Marginal land harvest

(1944)

We got a fifty per cent grant on everything – except our own work. On ploughing, discing, drilling, and on fertilisers and seed; but not on carting off stones, hedging, and fencing, or broadcasting the compounds and potash with smarting eyes and sore hands. The field had been going down worse and worse to rushes and bog year after year. I put what little lime I had left over on to the peatiest part. It was still soft, for the drains were late in going in. All summer I was nervous about it, for there were plenty who had said it would never do; but I had the idea that if I got a crop off it I should almost be able to call myself a farmer.

I had the Government reaper-binder ordered in good time. It did the ripe fields first, battering all down in fine style, with hardly a break of the twine. Then it went on to Archie the baker's ripe fields. I thought between his and one or two others round about it might give time for the meadow to ripen. But by the time the travtor was back half the field was still green with only a tinge of yellow. Part was badly laid with the heavy August rain that makes corn such a chancy matter in the West. Another storm might lay the whole field.

Lois, back on a week's leave from the ATS, came in for stooking. It ws all right where the corn was standing and the sheaves even and dry, but where it was laid the things just wouldn't stand anyhow, and between that and the midges we got rather annoyed with folk going by on the road above and staring at us. But it was clear enough that it was great corn, as such things go in this part of the country. Peter, the Government tractor driver, who had ploughed it, was very complimentary.

Then came another time of anxiety. Hereabouts we have to wait anything from a week to three weeks for the corn to ripen properly in the stooks, for grain and straw to dry and harden; the greener it is cut the longer it takes. Yet if one waits till the corn is plumb ripe one risks losing it by the seed dropping – or, if it is laid when it is ripe, there is far less hope of winning it. From time to time we restooked the sheaves. Probably none of us stooked really well to start with – I doubt if the girls or I have quite got the strength to give the sheaves a hard enough dump and knock their silly, shaggy heads properly together.

The weather was broken and often cloudy in the mornings, not clearing right till late afternoon. We farmers shouldn't grumble at double summer time when it is so good for the town workers, but it has made things very difficult these last weeks. Finally there was a Saturday morning with an east wind and we decided to put in, starting with the front fields, which had been cut first and were in grand order. I half-wanted to go on to the meadow that evening, but it was the night for the village cinema and I had to take tickets at the door, Angus had to deal with the projector, and Lachie was acting hall-keeper. I suppose I might have worked on by moonlight, but we were tired and I thought the weather would hold. It held over Sunday forenoon, but broke in the afternoon before anyone could get yoked up. Then there was a week of rain.

Again we put up fallen stooks and turned wet sheaves and shifted the bindings where the oats were beginning to grow. It began to clear on Friday. On Saturday we turned all the sheaves, shifting them in their bindings so that they were opened up to the weather. On Sunday afternoon we started putting in, though it began badly for me, because Jo, the carthorse, trod on my foot. This is bad enough when one is wearing a solid shoe, but shoes are seven coupons and I was wearing sandals.

Then came three days of struggle, turning the tails of the sheaves up to whatever sun and wind there was, moving them out from the hedge into the open, constantly sticking one's hands down to feel under the bindings, so that one's fingers were always jagged round the nails and bleeding from the sharp straw.

The field was rough still; another ploughing will settle it better and it should be smooth before it goes down to grass again. But we had to be careful. One time I thought I was going to have a trailer-load over. But the stacks went up slowly and steadily, with Fred throwing out any wet sheaf; I think it is always rather fun for the men when a sheaf happens to land on me. We were putting in at the same time from another small and late field, trying to keep most of the stacks separate, but having to work it as best we could with an eye always on the weather and clouds coming up suddenly from behind the hills. My sixteen-year-old son, having learned to load and work the horse, graduated to the tractor, only breaking a couple of stobs and a gatepost! – as indeed one always does at first. And then we were taking in the worst of the sheaves for the head of the last stack. At the end there was a trailer-load over, covered with a tarpaulin, in the stackyard. It was 7.30 and we were all desperately hungry. Almost everything was in. I had won the crop from my marginal land. I should like, rather vaguely, to have some idea of what its money value is, but I shan't really know till the threshing. They say it will thresh well. But what it means to me and what, I think, it means to Angus and Lachie and Joan, who helped to make a field out of an old bog, and the stray friends who helped me is not to be measured in money.

The Manchester Guardian, 22 September 1944, p. 4

Marginal land crop

(1945)

The Government thresher, promised in December, never came till January. It had broken a shaft. But meanwhile we had come to the end of our straw and were needing to feed the beasts on hay, which is apt to mean that they won't eat the straw afterwards. They had promised also to let me know before it came, as I should have to gather help; but it did come at dusk, too late to get any message to outlying farms. So first thing in the morning, while they were getting the tarpaulins off, I drove up the glen to Brackley to find Johnnie MacLean. Snow on the ground lightened the grey dawn, and soon the hill-tops grew plumes of pink and gold. Johnnie was out in the fields, and I waited with Jemima in the dark kitchen, and by and by she blew out the lamp that was standing in the window and it was morning and warm light spilled over the eastern hills and poured down the far slope as we drove back.

I always want to be up top, cutting the bindings on the sheaves and feeding in, but somehow I never am. My own Joan and Jennie from Dippen, old pals, were there, and the rest, pitching up, tugging the bound-up battels of straw out of the tail of the thresher, and loading it on to the trailer. There is always less to do at first, but when the sacks begin to mount up and when you are pitching from one stack to another, so as to finish the ones farthest from the thresher first, then you need all the labour. It is remarkable how much more room the straw takes up when it has been threshed. We filled the small barn and the loft and began to restack it. But as I was going to move my stackyard next year and to plough over most of it we couldn't build at the nearest point, and there was a lot of argument.

The corn seemed to be threshing well as things go up here. Angus from the baker's stood by, tying and changing the sacks. That is rather a nice job too, but I am not strong enough to move the sacks or help to get them on to the cart. It was all I could do to empty them. We hadn't nearly enough sacks, nor have we a granary, and the big corn-bin over the stables is a rat's paradise. But there is one small room at the house, used mostly for storing apples – now, alas, finished. We moved out the fruit racks and began emptying the sacks. After a time there was a lovely knee-deep Sahara spread across the floor, each emptying making new mountain ranges; Valentine, helping me, found herself impelled to roll in it, so attractive it was in feel and colour.

It is extremely difficult, unless one has a lot of men at it and everything going slowly, to know exactly how much one is getting from each stack. We had used the stack of mixed corn from that field and the wee field by the Carradale Water, and also the stack which had been made of the last stuff to dry and which was certainly not so good, for the cattle earlier on. But there were five stacks from the marginal field which I thought would be all right. I judge that they will have threshed between seven and ten hundredweight each. It was mostly good, heavy grain, not the small stuff. But of course it isn't worth nearly as much as the Castleton seed oats (12 cwt) which I sowed.

Of course, for me with my Galloway cattle the straw is invaluable. The Ayrshires eat it too, and I need it in the stables. We are perennially short of dung for this poor land, and I have made a kind of cattle court and shed which has to be kept filled with straw, which is partly tramped and partly eaten. We shall get through it all, and I hope the hay can be all kept for the dairy cows and the horses. We were constantly throwing out wet sheaves from the tops or bottoms of the stacks to the cattle, who pranced round; the Leicester ram came up too and got his share.

I found myself rather depressed because I seemed less able to pitch sheaves or move sacks than I had been two years ago even, and if one has neither brute strength nor years of skill and judgment behind one to give one confidence, one isn't much use as boss. Actually I expect I worked harder than anyone there almost, and with it all achieved far less. We had tea and pieces at four. It was almost dark by the time we had finished the last two stacks and quite dark before we could start up the cold car to take back the others to Dippen and Brackley, and the road skiddy with new freezing.

Meanwhile I am waiting for the Agricultural Executive Committee to come round and tell me what I am to do next with the marginal field. My own idea is potatoes in the dry part, but not more than two acres; we put all the sea tangle that came into the bay this year on to that, and it is spread, though not all the dung is, so far. The wetter part could be turnips and kale for the cows, and there is a steep little brae that would be very difficult to drill where I should like to have a broadcast crop, to cut green; as the land had some potash it might be possible to grow vetches. But possibly that's all wrong for this part of the world, and I want to ask about it. We've been expecting 'them' for at least three months! I am almost sure they will want me to 'keep up my acreage' of potatoes. This would make sense if potatoes did well or if they could be sold. But it doesn't make sense to grow bad potatoes which are fit only for cattle or poultry food. However, we shall see. But at any rate the marginal land looks so far as though it had almost been worth taking so much trouble over. Though no doubt I must wait ten years to get the real result.

The Manchester Guardian, 30 January 1945, p. 4

Philip Ram

(1945)

With cross lambs the price they are, it seemed only sense to get a Leicester tup to go with the blackface ewes. But as every other farmer thought the same, the prices were twice what I had in mind to pay. The shearlings were going up to £20 and I fell out of the bidding. But the two prize-winners were yet to come and, once you were on to those figures, I thought it might be worth giving an extra £5 for the second-prize fellow. Personally, I preferred his looks to the second prize, and I'm sure sheep prices are very much a matter of the ring's fancy, once you are away from the worst and the very best. It was just as well I did bid, as he was the last Leicester in the sale, though by that time I was in such a state of flurry that I didn't realise it! It was such a very male gathering, what with the farmers, the shepherds, the auctioneer and the rams themselves. But at least my chap with the square-cut fleece and noble upright head didn't have the wild horns and expression of the blackface tups. We bundled him into the back of the car, where he folded up and lay down like a kitten, and I called him Philip.

Well, we put him into the small park in front of the house, for it was a bit early for him to go with the ewes. He chummed up with the Ayrshire cows, Linda and Daisy, and the calf Avril, who came through to graze in the daytime. There was the aftermath of a good crop of sown hay with extra clover. As Mr Black of Tangy, his breeder, had advised me, I gave him some cattle-cake every day and sometimes oats, so he got to know well what it meant when someone came to the field. But he was a little dubious about Susan, who is nearly two and afraid of nothing on four legs. She used to rush at him, shouting 'Meh!' When he got used to her he was apt to try to eat her coat buttons, with no success. I believe he thought the Bedlington was an unsatisfactory kind of sheep, a natural error; when poor Clym cowered with his tail between his legs – having in his youth being much beaten for chasing sheep – Philip would smell him several times, then stalk away.

His marriage had to wait for the dipping of his wives and their recovery from a very natural surprise and depression. The ewes were at the far end of the field into which we took him, but when he came to the top of the brae and sighted or smelt them, he gave one shout and went for them. They gathered in a bunch, facing him; I followed discreetly. He lowered his head and began to bite them: or perhaps kiss them. Anyhow they liked it.

The next morning I came to the field with the cake, calling Philip. He was surrounded by his harem but at once looked up and came trotting over; a small spotty-faced ewe came timorously after him. The next day two wives came. The third day I had to walk across the field, call and shake the basket for some time before he would attend. Finally he came and took a piece and let me stroke his ears and under his chin as usual. But there were three wives in attendance and he was *distrait*. Since then I have been to the field and called and, though he looks round, he finds his duties as a husband will not allow him to attend. I have to dump the cake in his box and hope he does not share it with all his spotty-faced blondes. His proud and noble head is bent earthward to the level of his wives. He never, never thinks of me.

The Countryman, v. 31, Spring 1945, pp. 107-8

Marginal land: second year

(1945)

When the ploughing goes wrong nothing makes up for it. Neither we ourselves nor the Government tractor managed to make anything of the piece in the middle which was still wet. The acre that was hopelessly rough was sowed down to oats and did quite well. If our summer weather had been like last year's we might have had to scythe it and bind by hand, and indeed I was dreading that, but the dry spell in August gave us a wonderful harvest everywhere on the West Coast. None of my own oats was laid, and though this acre stood out in stooks for some while we carried it in the end, and there was a good head of corn on it.

The potatoes were good, the best crop I have had yet. My last year's potatoes, grown in very sandy soil, were almost all diseased, either with scab or with what we call sprain, small spots through the white. So I decided not to use any of my old seed, but to get new. I had fifteen drills of Sutton's Perfection, a second early, and most of the rest Kerr's Pinks. I had two or three drills of an old-fashioned potato, Great Scot; the seed was given me by one of the farmers up the glen who thought I might like to try it. It did well, not cropping as heavily as the Kerr's Pinks, but nice round creamy potatoes, easy to see when one was gathering. We had helped Archie the Baker with his potatoes. I have never had a spinner, but have always borrowed either his or Duncan's. Earlier this year I went to a farm sale thinking I might get one, but what is the use of paying maybe £30 for something you are only going to use for two days in the year? Archie's mare had foaled, so we lent him Jo to go with his Bobby, and my people went over and worked with his. He also had a whole squad of tinkers, who all wanted to come on to me. I said I only wanted four, which annoyed them, and on the Saturday morning, when we started, none of them turned up. However, we had ourselves and various children, and my undergraduate daughter, who worked with immense conscientiousness but said feelingly at the end that she hoped next year the potatoes wouldn't be lifted until after the beginning of term.

Then came the awkward question of Saturday afternoon. It was a bit difficult to know what to do, with the men from the other farm working. One of my own men was a church officer and had to go to do one of those peculiar pre-Sabbath things one does with churches. And I don't like working weekends unless one absolutely has to. We are all so tired. And I desperately wanted to go on tidying up a book of mine[1] that is nearly finished. I dithered, consulted the glass, which was very high, looked at the wind, and wondered if the anti-cyclone that the BBC was talking about would come our way, and finally decided to do the rest on Monday.

Sunday morning was brilliant, hot and coloured, the sea Mediterranean blue. But the afternoon clouded over ominously. One of the herring fishermen said it would rain for sure, because of the spiders' webs in the grass. Another fishing friend, his thoughts on a spate and salmon, looked happy. I went to bed badly fidgeted and woke to hear the wind rising and a sudden rattle of rain. It was grey in the morning, but there had been no more rain beyond the one small storm-burst.

I had fixed up a quarter to nine for the work to start, but hardly anyone was there except two of the tinkers, who, indeed, had been in the field for an hour, not having realised that the clocks had changed. They were nice, strong girls, with the grand, glowing, wheat-coloured tinker hair. I find the older generation rather terrifying, but the younger ones are decent enough and manage to keep wonderfully clean, considering that they all have to pile into the tents.

The first few drills were hard going, but during the next hour everyone else turned up. I tried to distribute the boys to work with grown-ups, as when they were together there was more talk and chucking potatoes about than gathering. I worked with two small ones, one of whom declared himself a farmer, the other a fisherman. There was a kind of kindergarten of small brothers who picked up a potato now and then and got under our feet, and occasionally got hit by a flying potato and wept loudly. My two weren't very old, but were very willing and rather bright specimens. I asked one of them what he liked doing at school, to which he answered with a sweet smile, 'Nothing'.

Later in the day I worked with the Baker's youngest hand, who gathered at a tremendous pace, whistling 'Let Him Go'[2] all the time.

The Kerr's Pinks were really lovely to look at, bouncing out from the spinner, rosy as apples. We had planted them in rather strawy dung spread along the drills, and I had been afraid it was not rotted enough, but obviously it was just what they had wanted; they had burrowed into it and made themselves nests for their big pink eggs.

Everything was going well when suddenly there was a crack. The spinner had stuck on a stone, and the old wood of the breast-pole and swingle-trees had broken. We had to stop and rush off to Dippen to borrow others from Duncan. Luckily he had them – his spinner worked from the tractor – and we also got the sawmill to cut us new ones from the turkey oak that had come down across the drive in the September storm to replace the Baker's old ones. I thought at first we should never finish that day, especially as Lachie and I had to go off and keel the lambs that were going to the grading market early the next morning, but the drills were getting fewer, and by the time we got back from the sheep there were only four to do, and we managed them before dark.

Now the long pits have their rush coverings and a light cover of earth; before we put on the heavy frost-proof cover we shall lift a load of each kind, perhaps more of the Suttons. Already several folk have asked me for bags, and I know that these will be in demand when it comes to a bag to raffle for any of the many good causes which we raffle for on and off all winter.

The Manchester Guardian, 29 October 1945, p. 4

[1] Probably *The Bull Calves*, published 1947.

[2] 'Let him go, let him tarry', an Irish traditional song, popular in the 1940s in a version by Gracie Fields.

Marginal land: sowing out

(1946)

For the last eight months the weather has been kind to us in the West of Scotland. We have done our best to repay it by getting ahead with everything. The easy harvest and easy gathering of our potatoes meant earlier ploughing; we have had more time for hedging and draining. The ground was dry and warm for sowing, easy to get into order for the drill plough. Now the corn is brairding everywhere; Fred tells me that the great golden fire on the whins means a heavy ear on the oats.

The marginal field had its troubles this winter, all the same. It became apparent that the main leader drain was not big enough when the sudden rush of water off the road came sweeping in. There is a box for cleaning where the new drains meet the old one and the ground was always wet round it, so we decided to open another drain to take off the surplus water. When I lifted the iron lid of the box a large eel gave me a dirty look and rushed up the drain. We used up our old drain tiles and a few new ones, laid down with wet straw round them so that they should draw better, and it certainly seems to have done the trick. In time I shall get a fifty per cent draining grant on this. But the middle of the field is still dark, peaty ground with no bottom, and I am afraid we shall see rushes coming again there in a year or two. Perhaps after the second rotation it may do better, but that is looking ten years ahead, which is an uneasy thing to do nowadays.

This year most of us used the Government tractor outfit for some at least of our fields. Here we had their powerful plough for the difficult bit; again it turned up old stone drains, and the heap at the side grows. Then the meadow was disced and sown with a seeder, from my own seed oats.

After that we turned to the other fields, got our potatoes in earlier than we have ever done since I started here, and had a great rodeo rounding up the Galloways before we could separate out the young stirks for market. Meanwhile the oats brairded and it was time for the under-sowing with grass seed. Grass seed is always expensive, and I think it is worth getting a really good mixture, with some extra clover in it, which should appreciate the potash left over from the rotted sea tangle. My big bag cost over twenty-two pounds for the five and a half acres. Before this I have always sown by hand, a lovely job, broadcasting it with both hands from the sowing sheet with just enough of a light air to catch and scatter it. But this year Duncan lent me his seed barrow, which does eighteen feet of a swathe, and the whole field took less than an afternoon. It isn't altogether easy, all the same, to see where one is going. I had a couple of old tiles tied on to one end of the barrow to scrape along as a mark, but I couldn't always see it, especially if the tiles had happened to fall off! I only hope it will come out evenly, not in stripes.

It was nice to do; these jobs are sufficiently skilled to keep one's mind occupied, and yet one can also notice the colour of the budding trees and hear the cuckoo. One's horse may always decide that he is bored. Jo made one attempt to bolt, but between the heavy ground and me on the reins he didn't go far. Lachie had the pony with the grass harrows – borrowed from Duncan, of course! On the road above the fishermen were going by to the boats.

There seemed to be one really bad wet patch, all the same, and I couldn't quite account for it, though I knew that water had lain there in winter. I made a wide cast round it with the seeder or Jo would have been floundering. At the end I thought I must do something about one corner where I had obviously gone off the track, so I went over the bits I had missed with a skirt full of hay seed. These are the times when a full and fairly long skirt comes into its own, and who is to be shocked at one's bare knees at the far end of a field?

The next thing that has to be done is to get on the artificial manure, again sowing it broadcast from heavy sowing sheets. But this year I left it to Lachie and my new land-girl trainee – I hope it hasn't discouraged her too much! I am stiffer in the back than I was when I first spread the stuff; it is sore on one's hands and eyes too, though not nearly so much so as ammonium sulphate. And the next thing will be to roll it with the heavy roller – borrowed from Archie, my other neighbour. This is always rather fun to do, because of the up-and-down pattern it makes, like some textile. I hope to get some of the docks up; there are still too many, which have cheerfully survived both ploughing and hoeing.

The wet patch was worrying me; at last I asked Angus to dig it up. And there was our main water supply pipe quietly dripping away. 'It must have got a wrax from the couter of the plough [a wrench from the blade of the plough],' he said, and, indeed, it is horribly near the surface in this one place and, of course, can't be altered. Once the field is laid down to grass for five or six years it will be safe, but we must try to remember it at the end of that time. How long it will be in grass depends on this year's harvest. If we get a good year the grass will flourish and the clover will take. But if the corn is laid, then the grass under it may be rotted and killed out. That is just one of the chances we have to take. Meanwhile the seed potatoes which we grew there last year have been planted in the Mains field and should be rooting and sprouting now. On a farm one year is always preparing for the next.

The Manchester Guardian, 9 May 1946, p. 4

My weeds

(1946)

Up north we have three main weeds – bracken, common rush and ragwort, or, as we call it here, bennyweed. Bracken creeps in off the hills wherever it gets a chance. If a farm is deserted, as so many farms were in the bad years, it comes down into the arable and, in a season or two, has everything smothered. Then it is enough to daunt anyone who may think of taking the farm over.

A small farmer can do little about it by himself, though an increasing number are hiring the bracken-cutting outfits. I had one of those clanking contraptions that half break and half bruise, and towed it around hopefully for a year or two. It took a long time with the horse to get through even a few acres and, when I tried it on the tractor, all went well for about five minutes, and then the tractor went into a rabbit hole. Unlike the horse, the tractor made no effort to get out, and it took a couple of fishermen with poles and spades to free it. Where I cut the bracken two years running, it is definitely thinner, and the Galloway cattle get about in it and trample it down a bit. They certainly discourage it more than sheep do, but they do not go into it unless it is thin to start with.

Sometimes we cut it for bedding, especially if we are short of straw, but that needs a spell of fine weather in the late summer or autumn, and such spells are usually overfull of other necessary farm work, so it often doesn't get done. One year I cut some young green bracken to make bracken compost, which seemed to me to have some effect on my potatoes, but not enough to bother with it again, for a great deal of scythed bracken sank down into a very small compost heap.

The only thing to be said for it is that it is rather magnificent-looking stuff, turning a grand tawny colour in the back-end. It has other social uses, of course. When I started cutting the bracken in the bay, there was some dismay, I believe, among the young couples; but they still have some fifty acres left for their own sports.

Rushes have nothing to be said for them. The Galloways, again, eat them when they are young and fairly tender, but not if there is anything else to eat. And how they come! We have a high rainfall, and the ground, in spite of drainage, is often waterlogged for weeks or months. Yet I do feel aggrieved when they begin spreading in a field on a slope where I know the drains are running. Once they are there, of course, they creep around on their exceedingly tough roots. I hoped that liming would deter them. Perhaps they would have been worse without it.

As for the bennyweed – which looks extremely handsome when it is in flower, though I never like to say so – even the Galloways won't touch it, though the sheep give it an occasional nibble. There is nothing for it but to root it up before it seeds. In one place we cut it over last year with the mower, after we had cut the hay in the next field, but by September, when most of it was over elsewhere, this patch had gaily sprouted quantities of healthy branches from the bases of the cut stems, and they were all golden with flowers. Perhaps we would do better to introduce the caterpillars that eat it in the south! It comes up whenever there is a gap.

I suppose, if we could deal with these three, we might be able to pay some attention to yare (spurrey), and to the polygonum *P. persicaria* which is bad among the potatoes, and seems to escape hoeing, or, perhaps, takes a delight in re-rooting itself after one thinks it is safely out. Scotch thistles do seem to die out if one scythes them at the right time, and docks can be pulled. Liming does at least have a marked effect on sorrel – sourdocks [sourocks] here – and we don't have so many buttercups as there are in the south.

I suppose the wild hyacinths are a weed in their own way, but I cannot bring myself to regard them as that. One ploughs up their white bulbs in any field near a wood. But, though the cows have no liking for them, I have. When a plant is sufficiently beautiful, one gets the maximum satisfaction by ceasing to regard it as a weed.

The Countryman, v. 33, Summer 1946, pp.282-3

Marginal Land (2)

(1946)

Well, we got it in at last. Between storms we managed to carry about a third of the Meadow, from the end where it got most breeze – for wind matters far more than sun. Some of our neighbours hung their sheaves over wires put up in the fields; indeed some northern farmers have permanent trestles and wires ready for this emergency. But we had not, so we had to shift every sheaf from the Meadow into the Mains field, which we had carried, and where the ground was reasonably dry and there was an open sweep for the wind. After a dry night and day we managed to get the most of it in, yet there were obstinate sheaves which would not dry out at all which were all matted with roots and shoots.

We must have lost several loads, though some went to the hens and others to the cows. But a good deal of grain must have been shaken out with all the handling it got. There was some very poor stuff in the last stack, and I wondered how long it would stay without heating. But luckily the big thresher came, working at one farm after another; we all helped one another and everywhere the worst of the stacks were put through. It saved the labour of thatching and the anxiety of watching to see if they would heat. I put through four stacks, which threshed well, and we sent off fifteen bags for a start to a registered dealer. These will give me useful cereal coupons for cattle or poultry feed.

We had all got our crop in about the same time. Then came a few more fine days, to thatch the stacks that were to stand over winter with the rushes cut earlier and to dig the potatoes. There are only a couple of diggers in the whole glen and these none too new, so we pass them round, trying to be as quick as we can. I got through my two and a half acres in two days, and it was an astonishingly good crop, clean and dry and bulking well for such light soil. It is tiring work, but we were cheered up in the afternoon by a piper – a relation of one of the gatherers – turning up and playing to us.

Early in the year the Carradale branch of the National Farmers' Union, of which I am president, had decided to hold a joint harvest

home if it were any way possible. We had hopefully visualised a
dinner, but rations would not run to that. So we decided on a whist
drive and dance for all our friends and helpers in the Village Hall.
I was going south and was deputed to get the whist prizes. Duncan
got invitations printed and sent out some to a few of the farmers'
friends in the community, representatives of the other branch, the
bankers, the Animal Health Officer, and our young vet, back from
five years in a German prison camp. Most of us had been grateful
for odd help during corn or potato harvest, from one or another of
the fishermen, for instance, and our schoolboy potato pickers were
represented by their elder sisters.

We realised that there would not be enough whist tables to go
round and hastily collected as many others as we could, also packs
of cards; one of mine, used for lowbrow games of family grab,
had five aces, but what about it! Duncan kept wonderful order,
disentangled the players and, when it came to tea, sent them off
in an orderly way for their trays. As president I made the speech
of welcome. I wanted people to feel that all this was a deep and
important thing, part of a way of life; I wanted to say what I think
is in the minds of most people who work their own land: that the
thing is a way of living, that it frees you from the personal time
of a single life, and gives you instead a time scale of seasons and
rotations stretching far beyond the frail mortality of the individual;
I tried to show how we were one with our forefathers and our
successors, for I think that was what we were all feeling. And then
we started off on the dancing!

We had all agreed that there was to be no modern dancing;
that was not in the spirit of the farming community. And our band
– two accordions, piano, and drum – helped us by never giving
the dancers time to cool down between dances. I say 'cool down'
advisedly; in a short time we were all shining! Almost everyone
got up for the dances, with the nice look of the kilts here and
there, and some of the couples grey-haired and some very young,
slim dark girls and the big boys who were for ever trying to whirl
their partners off their feet. Indeed it was no use at all trying to
keep one's feet in the quadrilles; one had just to resign oneself and
hope to come down safe – there is something to be said for a fairly
long skirt too! It was fine to see the wives, who had worked almost

harder than their husbands, year after year, looking after houses and children and hungry men, and on top of that cows and churns and sterilisers and poultry, and maybe an odd bit of garden. They deserved a good time more than anybody.

There was a full moon outside the Hall and possibly other things; as the evening went on one's partners tended increasingly to smell of peppermint. But this too is surely part of the tradition. We still had a full floor for quadrilles at one o'clock in the morning, but those who had far to go and maybe milking again at six o'clock were beginning to drift off. The last dance is traditionally a waltz, with the lights out and one's partner's cheek kindly against one's own. The waltzes are mostly to the Scots tunes everyone knows and sings, but the two-steps and barn-dances are too breathless for singing. But there is the sharp cry from the base of the throat, all of us together on the main beat of the dance, this queer clamour that I miss so much in English dancing. It goes on in one's head walking back under the full moon which shows up Molly and Avril and Victory, our V-Day[1] heifer, a lovely little Ayrshire, grazing in the Marginal field. And, behind the continuing glow of the dancing, I suppose most of us farmers were also thinking of the next things: dung-spreading and ploughing, the year already turning towards the harvest of the next.

The Manchester Guardian, 19 November 1946, p. 3

[1] Probably VE (Victory in Europe) Day, 8 May 1945, though there was also a VJ (Victory in Japan) Day, 15 August 1945.

Marginal field: hay crop

(1947)

When I sowed the field out with grass seed last year there were no 'misses', but a clean over-all braird of grass. But after our bad harvest, with the corn lying before cutting and then the stooks out – although we changed their position – for weeks, there were bald patches all over the Meadow. We raked up what straw we could in spring and reseeded the worst of the patches; when the hay was high and green they were all hidden, but when it was cut they showed again, with nothing on them but weeds, some of them. And below the trees there was more corn than grass.

It was a difficult season right up through July; we cut half with our own tractor and the mower which started as Duncan's but is gradually becoming mine. Then the tractor began to bog. I have no proper land wheels and though I am in the queue for them I am afraid it will be long enough before I get them. Lachlan worked late that evening at the cutting, with Jean up on the seat of the mower and myself doing a bit of raking at the corners. Then it rained again and the field got worse. But luckily Peter was over with the tractor and did the top half for us. We got it up in fair order, the Scottish way, into small ricks or huts in rows along the field. If one is not too sure of the grass one puts it up into small ricks, not tramped, and with poles for ventilation. It is best, of course, if one gets it up with the least handling of the hay; every time it is turned it loses some of its goodness. My other hayfield, sown with a better mixture with more red clover in it, took longer to dry, had to be turned several times and never made properly. But the last cut of the Meadow came at the beginning of the weather break – these wonderful days of sun and light wind which we have been having for a fortnight. It went up well and we tramped the ricks and put up some without the poles. It has been up for a week and the earlier half for a fortnight, when we decided to carry.

I had one small stack from last year still in the stackyard, with perhaps two and a half tons of hay in it. We built this year's hay crop into rather bigger stacks, four of them and a full barn, perhaps fourteen tons. The mutton-shed field, where we had the crop with the red clover through it, was rather a disappointment. When we opened the ricks only the tops were in order; the rest was heating and mouldy. I got half a bag of coarse salt, and Fred, who was building the stacks, sprinkled it through the musty hay, so that it will be eaten all right this winter. I think we all felt a certain urgency; it was just after Attlee's speech.[1] We know we shall need all the food we can grow, for man or beast.

We put in with the tractor and the cart, and a general muster of friends helping to fork or build the loads. It was good enough fun for everyone, for the weather looked like holding and there was not the desperate urgency which makes one ache. I like working with a pitchfork: there is something very satisfactory in getting a good forkful and swinging it up. I like shoving the top of a rick into the cart. I like loading a rick I have built myself, remembering the care with which one tried to get it symmetrical – one must use some fraction of the art of a stack-builder even for a small rick which will only stay for perhaps a fortnight in the field – the fuss over the last forkfuls, and the tight reeving down of the stack ropes. I like loading, filling up the corners, keeping it wide. I like driving the tractor, even driving with one hand and holding on to small Su, who is not quite sure about it, with the other. I suppose Su will remember her grandmother tractor-driving or sliding down the ropes from the top of a load.

I had my qualms about bringing the ricks from the field after they had only been standing for a week. But, after all, in England they bring the hay straight in from the windrows or coils to the stackyard, and it was English weather we had been having. Fred said it was in great order and there was a lovely smell from it when the ricks were opened. It was two days' work bringing it in; thank goodness double summer time was over, so we could start at a reasonable hour and did not work beyond seven.

Folk tell me that in the old days the Meadow was great for hay. But I doubt if they got a better crop than we did this year. I had dressed it with nitro-chalk, following Fraser Darling's last book,[2] and I think this suited it well. At the present price of hay I suppose I got about a hundred pounds' worth out of the five acres, and I hope for another crop nearly as good next year. Meanwhile there is grand aftermath for the milk cows, now that the other fields are eaten down. The Meadow will have to be turned over again and go down to a second rotation before it is a real farm field instead of a piece of ex-marginal land. It should stay out for four years first, I think, and then we shall plough again.

Meanwhile we cut the hedge along the top which was spindly and useless this winter and put up a fence. This is not as easy as it sounds, because the wood for the fence stobs has to come from somewhere. Most of these came from a fallen turkey oak, and I hope they will last for oak-ages: they are not as straight as larch, but what is a wiggle here or there? Sharpening stobs on a circular saw is great fun, too! But the straining posts are larch. Hedges are nice enough when they are well tended every year or in the south, where the old quickset hedges go on thickening from one decade to another. But spindly, neglected beech and thorn is no use and not beautiful.

Four years ago, when we first put the field under the plough, I thought perhaps it would have to be sown out for permanent pasture and not cultivated again. But it is plain by now that we shall go on cultivating, getting back into production the fields, like my Meadow, that had once been farmed but had dropped away to nothing in the days of our commercial pride, but now, in the days of our struggle, will help us to win.

The Manchester Guardian, 21 August 1947, p. 3

[1] Clement Attlee (1883-1967), Labour Prime Minister 1945-51, concerned with steering Britain through a time of 'austerity'; food supplies had not yet recovered from World War II shortages.

[2] Frank Fraser Darling (1903-79), ecologist and writer; the book is possibly *Crofting Agriculture: its practice in the West Highlands and Islands* (1945).

Marginal Field

(1947)

When we took the hay in from the meadow, into the big stacks, ten days after it had been put up, the aftermath had grown up beautifully, and I had visions of a second crop. But then came the six weeks of sunshine, and even in the wet meadow all growth stopped. It was good stuff, all the same, and the milk cows had a great time with it. We had rather a mixture of cows: big white Molly, who is amiable and slow-witted, the two little black cows who still remember their first owner from whom I bought them two years ago and go to meet him when he calls to them, and a pure Ayrshire heifer of my own breeding, due to calve just before Christmas. Then there was one of the black Galloways who had lost a calf early on in the hard winter and was bringing up a red-and-white cross shorthorn bullock called Pre-Fab. There was yet another Galloway – appropriately enough, Cassandra; she had broken into the bull's field six months too early, but had produced a successful heifer calf, curly and dun like its pedigree father. If she was kept back from the bull for a year now she would grow to her full size, so we had her in with the milk cows and the yearling Galloway heifers. And there was a blue-grey, a cross between the Galloway bull and mainly shorthorn Molly. They looked nice moving about in the green meadow.

The west did not dry up so badly as the rest of the country. And I carried my corn with no trouble at all, never shifting the stooks from the day we put them up to the day we lifted them. It had seemed rather a risk taking them in after only a week in the fields, but the grain had hardened and I felt we should do it. This week we had the big thresher round and threshed three of the stacks. The sheaves were in lovely order, right down to the bottom, and the straw will be good eating for the cows; the grain was not as heavy as last year but drier and cleaner.

However, there could be no second cutting of hay anywhere, and the aftermath has not lasted so long into winter as it usually does. We grazed little Munch, daughter of Punch and Molly, on the drying green between the poles, so as to use all the odd bits of grass.

In the unfenced Hebrides most cows are used to being tethered; why not here when we want to make the most of our grazing?

At the moment Punch is on loan to one of the neighbours, and we see him looking very magnificent among the bracken, now colouring to his own warm dun, when we go in to Campbeltown. He is an amiable creature. One evening I went over to the byre and found Jean milking with Punch standing beside her, leaning his curly head on her shoulder. She was calling him her wee lamb and he was behaving in a most lamb-like way. But he looks enormous and alarms the summer visitors, who cannot believe that he is really only interested in their queer human doings.

At this time of the year one has to decide what is to be done next with all the fields. I have nothing sown out, so must get hay from last year's hay fields, including the meadow. The cattle have eaten it short, tearing at the delicious grasses, while they turn up their noses at coarse stuff in the fields which have been out for five years and are due for ploughing. I have been wondering how to dress the fields, and got a soil analysis from the agricultural advisory officer. In spite of all the liming which I have been doing for the last seven years, all the fields are lime deficient. In fact, most of them are deficient in almost everything, though some had got up to normal in 'organic matter' since the first year I had a soil analysis.

The meadow has 'acidity very strong' on its soil analysis. This was rather surprising. Two years ago it had a dressing of two tons to the acre of ground limestone, and last year it had a lighter dressing of nitro-chalk. But the field must have had the acidity of years of swampy, almost peaty conditions, moss and roots rotting in stagnant water. It would take yet more limestone to get it into a reasonable state.

I am feeling a bit depressed about my artificials. We had a fire which burnt out the garage, stables and engine-room; luckily nobody was hurt – the horses were out, and the big car, as usual, was away being mended. But the artificials which I had over as well as some which had just arrived were all turned into so much mud by the activities of the fire brigade. We were lucky that the stacks did not catch; they would have done with our ordinary west wind, but it was a still night. We lost all the harness and a lot of things which are difficult to replace – for instance, the wood which we had cut ourselves for gateposts and rails and for next season's potato boxes. It is discouraging now to have to go back and start all over again with a fallen tree!

I cannot even order the ground lime until I have somewhere watertight to put it. There are slates off the roof of the barn, and they cannot be put on by the slater till the mason gets round to doing something with the skews and the joiner puts in two or three new bits of sarking. And while I am about it I had better cut two or three branches off the big beech tree which overlaps the roof. The slater would like me to cut it right down, but I do not want to; it is a beautiful tree and the red squirrels run up and down it.

At any rate the drains are running splendidly now. Fred tells me that the eels which frightened me so when I lifted the lid at the drain junction are the best thing in it for cleaning drains. I suppose it would be better still if they had huge bristly whiskers, but perhaps it's just as well they haven't!

The Manchester Guardian, 17 November 1947, p. 3

Threshing

(1949)

Up here in Kintyre, the same as everywhere else, the drought last summer spoiled the corn. It was so short that the reaper-binder hardly caught it, especially where it grew on sandy soil like my own. But at the same time we all felt that the continuous sun had ripened and hardened the grain well, and we believed that it would thresh not too badly. Most of us had about half the number of stacks we usually have; we said to one another that we would save on the threshing surely! I myself had four and a half, as against some fourteen last year. And one of these had heated. That was what was happening all over Argyll. It had been still, warmish weather when the stacks were actually being put up and for a while afterwards. And we count on a breeze to blow through and dry the stacks; a rainy breeze does no harm, for the rain is caught on the outside, while the drouth from the breeze penetrates and cools the centre of the stack. My sown-out field, where the sheaves had heavy bottoms with clover and soft grass, had been none too easy to harvest; there were a few damp sheaves, which, with ordinary, windy West Coast weather, would have done no harm. But this year they heated. One morning the top of the rush-thatched stack was smoking like a chimney. We watched it anxiously, and at last decided to pull the stack apart. By the time we did this some of the sheaves were already almost too hot to touch; but they cooled down quickly and we rebuilt the stack.

Now it was November and the threshing mill coming round. It arrived with the two men, who are now old friends, on a wild, rough day of rainstorms. They put it in place in the stackyard so as to start as soon as the weather was possible. It seemed to be clearing in the evening, but I woke in the middle of the night to a terrific thunder-clap and rattle of hail. In common with everyone in Carradale, I put my head under the bedclothes and tried to get to sleep again. In the morning the main ridge of the roof was blocked with solid hailstones and the staircase running with water. Outside the ground was white with snowy hail.

But it cleared and the neighbours started coming, for the threshing means team work. The moment I knew the threshing mill was due we had to get ready to feed an extra dozen hungry men; they like traditional food, a good solid soup, 'mince with an onion through it', masses of boiled potatoes – our own were extra good this year – and a solid pudding to follow. And in the afternoon, tea in the stackyard.

It was apparent at once that the corn was threshing well; the good corn was pouring out like a small river, clean and even and dry; there was less tail corn than usual. Bag after bag was tied up and thrown on to the bogie of the tractor, to be poured out on to the floor of the girnal and brought back – for bags are scarce nowadays. Before the war there were any amount to be had for the asking from the shops, but now we have to pay for them.

The men who come round with the mill bring a roll of fine netting with them and spread it outside the stacks so that the rats can't get away. As we get to the bottom of the stacks, the three dogs get excited; Lachie's charming idiot of a woolly sheepdog pretending to be competent, Monty, the spaniel, making a great fuss, and the little terrier, who always gets the rats, regarding it as her normal job. I can't say I have much sympathy with rats; they might so easily supersede us as the main inhabitants of earth if we go on behaving as rattishly as we do in so many field of activity. On the other hand, what could be nicer than the harvest mice – I never grudge them their few ears of corn – or the little elephant shrews that wobble their tiny, intent way through the grass?

Meanwhile the bundles of straw, each tied in two places – except when the knotter fails to work, as it does quite often! – are made into a separate stack. We shall have to use it sparingly this year, probably not feeding it to the cattle until after the New Year. But we had an extra good hay crop, and good turnips, so we should manage all right. The bundles are forked up to the top of the straw stack, which is made long, with the bundles across it; the builder may be at the far end, so there should be two people on the top. Part of the time I was one of them, catching the bundles and throwing them over to skilful, kindly Duncan MacAlister, who was saying that he had started building stacks as a small boy. He seemed to need no guiding from below, but, at a certain point, began to draw in his bundles, so that the two outer rows overlapped more and more on to the middle row, and gradually made the ridge of the stack. Up there we had a wonderful view of snow-capped Arran across fields and woods. Now and then there was a wee skliff of rain wandering about; first there was a short, fat rainbow quite close to us, and later there was a thin elegant one. But the afternoon sun was hot.

We finished in good time, and the mill moved on to the Baker's; from there it would go up the glen to Brackley, and then on to Rory's farm, Auchanrioch, across the new Bailey Bridge which the Forestry Commission put up across the river, and above that to Auchnabreck. In some places it will thresh half the stacks, in others – where there is no room to store the corn – it will thresh them all. It seems to me, judging by eye, that we have as much corn from four good stacks and a small one as we had from seven stacks last year – perhaps more.

I shall have a bill from the Department of Agriculture for about £5, less than half of what I paid them last year: indeed it will work out at less than half, considering the extra food, and board and lodging for the tractor men. I shall use some of the oats myself, bruised for the horses and dairy cows, milled for our own porridge, as it is for the poultry. Some I shall sell; it is worth round about twenty pounds a ton. We shall use every scrap of the straw. But what I like, and what, I believe, we all like, is the feeling that we have been producing food, the basic thing, food for man and beast, without which no country can flourish.

The Manchester Guardian, 17 November 1949, p. 3

The Year of the Late Harvest

(1950)

In the old days the years would be labelled by the men and women in the primary industry of agriculture. There was, for instance, the Year of the Short Corn,[1] worse even than last year, where on my light soil the corn was often too short to be caught by the string of the binder, however low it was set. This same sandy soil stood me in good stead this year, letting the rain run away through it – no doubt taking lime and good minerals with it at the same time. But we at least have our harvest in, while some of the farmers, on the West Coast as elsewhere, still have their corn lying out, sometimes even uncut, in the beginning of November.

It has meant hard work though, overtime, and putting in on a Sunday. It also meant that at a certain moment I decided that the sodden and sprouting sheaves had better be fed to the cows or the hens before the sparrows had eaten the grain and the straw had become too unpalatable for even the Galloways.

In August we still had hay in the fields, cut weeks before and steadily losing its fodder value. It had been a great crop, and our June cut, in the first field to be ready, had gone up at once and was sweet and good. But some of it had never even dried enough to go into coils. What we could we made into small stacks, with probably not more than two tons in each, liberally sprinkled with salt between the layers. The thatching rushes were cut, but there was never a day fit for thatching. Then we reaped our first field, the seed oats, Ayrshire Bounty, a heavy crop with a great head to it.

The second field was lighter; we cut it on a fine afternoon between two wet nights. The third field was next to a wood and scarcely ripe. Rashly we let the Government binder go on to someone else, thinking it could come back to us in ten days or so. In an ordinary season, the binder can usually get round all right, but this year, with so few cutting days, everyone was grabbing at it and there was considerable ill-feeling, with the poor drivers trying to calm down irate farmers, each of whom said his own need was greatest!

It ended with my not getting the binder in time for my third field. The oat crop, which had looked increasingly lovely all summer as it grew and shot and ripened, was beaten down by one storm after another, first in strips, then all over. The ground was waterlogged; the tractor, which could just cut it the one way only, bogged and slipped and dug deep mud skids all over the field. At last we had to cut what was left by hand, scything and bunching in the old way.

It was not the only field to be down. One of my neighbours had a splendid oat crop which went down suddenly and ripened to gold in a great mat. He managed to cut it, but it was difficult to dry; our normal course is to leave the stooked sheaves out in the field for ten days or a fortnight to dry and ripen thoroughly. He got part of it in, but there was still a lot out. Then came one of the few fine days. He cut another field. Was he right to do that or should he have put in from the cut field? As it turned out, that might possibly have been better, but how was he to know that there would not be another fine day for a fortnight and by that time the sheaves would be growing green and wet to the heart? This is the type of decision – big or little – which a farmer has to make.

We got ours in, but not in any very good shape. I suppose we must have lost about an eighth. The fields were strewn with fallen grain, but we moved in the hens. And the geese had an excellent time too! There was not much pleasure to it and hardly a stalk good enough to make a harvest plait. There was one thing to be thankful for all the same; as it happened, most unusually, I had none of my fields sown out with grass. If they had been, and the way it was this year, with the tractors – the Government one with the binder and my own with the trailer – churning everything to mud, next year's hay would have been ruined. I am afraid that happened often enough.

The light soil which dried reasonably quickly made it possible for us to lift our potatoes where it would have been hopeless on a heavy soil. There was one peaty patch, but here we bagged them. Our old-fashioned way of having other people who need it taking a drill or two in our field in return for help at the lifting works well enough, and all were pleased with the yield. One's first day at lifting is always amazingly sore on the back, but it is wonderful how quickly one gets into it, and an evening of hard dancing with the Campbeltown Young Farmers' Club put me right!

Last year my turnips all had brown heart. This year, with a dressing of Nordan, they are small but firm. The kale is a green forest. The grass in the pastures and on the rough grazing in the Bay is still growing. And on one or two of the wet days we gathered the tangle from the beach. For the south-west gales that laid the crops also left quantities of seaweed, rich in potash, as well as a large ship, which broke her tow rope on the way to the Clyde for breaking up and which came almost into someone's field with the high tide, and now sits three-quarters out of the water looking like some rather silly person's bright idea for solving the rural housing problem.

The Manchester Guardian, 6 December 1950, p. 3

[1] Various years are referred to thus, most often perhaps 1826.

A Binder of One's Own

(1951)

Year after year, as the oats have turned colour, Lachlan and Jean and I have begun fussing about the Government binder. What farm was Peter on now? Surely he was due to come to us? What – he had gone to the Glen first? Monstrous! Messages were sent, the telephone wires buzzed, unless, in their usual autumnal mood (we get branches across them rather often), they had broken down. And duly, towards Christmas, I would pay from £8 to £10 for 'hire of binder'.

Last year it all came to a head. I had sent in my order for the binder first, but … It was suggested we should toss up; I lost the toss and half my crop. It was a very bad season, with only occasional gaps in the rain, much the same kind of weather as we are having now, in fact. The binder did not get round to me until a fortnight later, and in one field the oats were down and sprouting on the ground, so that relations between us and the other tosser-up were extremely strained for a while. I began, in the rather roundabout way which West Highland life induces in otherwise respectable people, to inquire for a binder of my own.

Such profits as the farm makes are ploughed back. Last year I bought a new potato spinner, which meant that, instead of borrowing one and rushing at it with hired labour and anxiety and an eye on the lowering clouds, I could do a half-day's digging any time that suited. There was also the rebuilding and slating of the old hay barn. I couldn't afford a new binder; besides, my acreage under oats didn't justify it. But a second-hand binder, reconditioned – ah, that was possible! It came from Perthshire, my old home, and arrived just as we had finished opening the roads in the riper of the two fields. It is an old four-foot-six horse-drawn binder adapted for a tractor; it isn't pretty, but perhaps when winter comes we may touch it up with a spot of paint.

What a relief it was not to be worrying about the Government binder! Peter was said to be down on the Laggan somewhere. Little we cared; he might have been in the moon. Now our own binder, with Lachie on the tractor and Jean up behind, was going steadily round the field, taking longer, no doubt, than the six-foot Government binder but it was our own time. The knotter worked beautifully, with no loose sheaves to pick up and bind. We smeared ourselves with anti-midge cream and decided to work on till late. There were four of us stooking, with some very well-meant but faintly amateur help from two members of Parliament. Sometimes I would walk behind the binder for a few yards, watching it work and thinking how nice it was.

Then it dropped a nut, and a second nut. We rushed back along its track like squirrels but only found one of them. And then we found that a connecting rod had broken, and another one, with the extra strain on it, was twisted. By now it was late, but next morning saw me sending telegrams and putting through telephone calls in an attempt to get spare parts for what was after all rather an old machine. We have up here a very sympathetic telephone exchange which helps one to chase spares all over Scotland – as well as being genuinely pleased about happy telephonic events such as new grandchildren! But one's temper frays: at least when the Government binder broke down, as it did often enough, it was their responsibility, not mine.

Then Lachlan decided that he and the smith could make a connecting rod. It was raining again and we couldn't have been cutting anyhow. He went off with the bits and came back triumphantly. The next day we finished that field and made a start on the next.

The second field is the Meadow, marginal land which I drained some ten years ago. This is its second rotation. The draining had never been very satisfactory; the leader should have been a six-inch pipe instead of a four-inch. And some of the side drains had been badly bedded and had sunk or broken. The water from the road and the field above, drained this spring, poured in after heavy rain until a young loch used to spread over it. But this year the County Council put in a short length of drain to take off the road water. There is something to be said for being off the County Council. If I had been a member still I should never have had the face to clamour for this drain; when they turned me out I felt free to make demands!

Our August storms had laid the corn badly, while the wet weather earlier on had encouraged the weeds, especially the red-flowered polygonum, which is one of our worst enemies up here. We wondered how the binder would manage. It has done wonderfully well, cutting one way only, getting underneath the matted oats and making some kind of a sheaf. They will be ill to dry out, with the amount of weed there is in them, but still the stooks are standing up and there is a remarkably good head on the oats. It is a light crop everywhere, probably because the ground was still heavy even in April and not all the seed germinated. But a heavier crop might have laid worse, and the good head will make up for it in the threshing.

We were working at this field yesterday, cutting it in blocks, when the rain came on, hard and suddenly, so that we all got under the tarpaulin, wondering if it would put the oats down even worse. There was not much more than an hour's work on the block we were cutting, but it was no use after the rain. This morning, though, Lachlan and Jean went out between showers and finished it. We would never have managed it at all with the hired binder; it would not have been worth while for Peter to come out for an odd hour or two.

Clearly it is going to be like that for the rest of the season. It will be a case of working whenever we see a chance, even if it is only for the time between one rain cloud dying away over Arran and the next coming shouldering up over the hills that stand between us and the Atlantic. A difficult harvest with the hired binder and poor Peter torn between all the farmers who want him at once. But – so long as it doesn't break down again, and here we touch wood – no bother at all with a binder of our own!

The Manchester Guardian, 10 September 1951, p. 3

I'll Never Forget

(1952)

That was the year we had the blackface ewes – and Philip. I have given up sheep now; most of the Highlands are the worse for too many sheep, forever tearing away at the fine grasses. My own rough grazing is far and away better since I have had the Galloway cattle on it. But that year I had only started the Galloways, and there was room for a small herd of sheep.

Philip was a Border Leicester with an aristocratic Roman nose and a tremendous sense of his own importance. I had a little grey dog at the time, which Philip thought was an inferior sheep and used to bully. He bullied me too. When I was alone he considered himself the man of the house; I would suddenly hear his bleat, not at all meek and sheeplike, but loud and demanding. Then he walked in and insisted on a large feed of oats or bread – he wasn't above cake, for that matter! And he didn't at all mind walking upstairs for it.

His wives were an anonymous lot, who stood around gloomily in their old dirty coats among the clean bouncing lambs. Time and again one would be struck – it was a bad summer – and we would have to dig out the maggots, swab with disinfectant, and keep watching. And at last we came to the clipping.

There are certain physical sensations that one can't ever forget; the June heat, the smell of sheep and dip that clings to one for days, unexorcised by soap and water, the tickle of sweat and the worse tickle of flies, the disconsolate baaing of the sheep, the sharp steel of the clippers and the strain on one's thumb muscle. When one of these sensations returns, all the rest come with it. There was a tin of midge cream that we passed across to one another; I think it kept the mosquitoes off, but the small flies thought it delicious, and it stung when the sweat carried it into our eyes.

We were up in the corner of Sheneval, hot and windless under a great green chestnut, with the temporary sheep fank, where Philip and his wives milled around and barged into the stobs and wires and were almost away time and again. I was wearing canvas shoes and no stockings, and at first I tried not to get too much muck on my bare legs, but as the afternoon wore on, I stopped caring. Lachlan was a lot quicker than I was, but neither of us were real experts, like the shepherds with the big neighbouring herds. I took about three times as long over each sheep as a good clipper would have done. One started along their bellies, clipped up the sides and throat, and worked steadily to the back, pulling away the loose fleece.

Blackface sheep are almost always hand-clipped. When June comes and the old fleece has lifted, there is a strong coarse undercoat that one works through with the hand clippers, keeping half an inch or more away from the skin. As the fleece comes away it lies in a pool of grey, outworn stuff all round the sheep, and she lifts her head out of it, looking surprised and new and clean, almost beautiful. I kept on thinking they looked like new ideas coming clear out of the old words. There are ticks and keds in the old fleece; I remember how I hated them at first, but after a bit I stopped noticing them; they were just part of what one was doing. The old fleeces were warm and rough inside, still very close to being part of a living creature.

One sheep had the beginnings of maggots, not through the skin yet, but you could smell them, a sweetish, sickening smell. We marked her with an extra dab of keel before letting her go. The sheep never seemed to notice being cut – not that we cut them much, but every now and then there was a little red mark on them where the shears had gone too close – nor being hit or nibbled at by maggots. But they hated being tied. One had to be tough with them – tougher than I like being with any animal. The only satisfactory thing was when one untied them and they struggled up from the ground and bounded away, jumping off the ground with all four feet together, racing like lambs. They would give a wonderfully expressive wriggle of satisfaction, and one felt if only it had been possible to explain beforehand!

As each fleece was done we cut away the daggs and rolled up the main thing into a bundle, and stuffed it into one of the sacks, counting to ourselves how many more there were to be done. We got dirtier and dirtier and there were clouds of midges. One longed for a breeze to take them away. Our hands slipped on the greasy sheep as we caught them, and the others knocked into us, getting more and more panicky as there were fewer of them left in the fank. Then we got hold of Philip and threw him; Lachlan tied his legs and then shoved him over to me, half teasing and half, I think, feeling that it was appropriate for me to shear him … it was the right way the story should go.

He bleated like a foghorn with anger and resentment, and, I think, surprise, that I – that part of his world which gave him bits of bread and carrots – should have turned on him. I sheared him carefully, taking nearly half an hour. It was a different thing altogether from shearing the blackfaces. His was beautiful wool, much finer and springier than the others. I opened the fleece up along the belly. Sometimes rams are sheared standing, but that was beyond me. I clipped up one side while he breathed at me hotly and fiercely. Once that was done and the fleece pulled back from his side and neck, I turned him – or rather I asked Lachlan to help me. Poor Philip, he had lost all his male dignity – he and I both seemed to know it. The shears went snip-snip, close to his skin, as he panted and sometimes struggled, but I never once cut him. The eye in his smooth, curved, heraldic face was like a great jewel. The tongue flicked in his half-open mouth.

We untied him and he heaved himself up and rushed away, then, before he got back to the others, turned and stamped. We folded his fleece separately – it was much more valuable than the blackface fleeces. I wiped my overall sleeve over my face, rubbing off flies and dirt and sweat. We went on with the sheep. Sometimes one of us said something, but the remarks would have long intervals of work between them. The sun was coming lower through the chestnut branches. At last they were done.

We were in the field again next day, looking at the sheep. They looked clean and fresh now against the green summer pasture, but the ewes were an ugly, awkward shape. There was a dressing of dip to be put on to the one that had the maggots. She seemed all right. But Philip walked away. He was having nothing to do with me. I called him, I held out bread. It was no use. I felt like a traitor.

It was a week before he would talk to me again, and at first he was suspicious, wouldn't let me stroke behind his ears. But in time he forgot. Later on I made up my mind not to have any breeding-stock; one either has to have a hirsel of sheep or none. So the day came when we had to take Philip in the back of the car to the ram sale at Lochgilphead. I shall always remember him walking in a puzzled way round the auction ring. I was standing at his side, and when I called to him, he came trotting up to me. He didn't, of course, fetch as good a price as the shearling rams, and we hadn't managed to give him the fancy square clip that is fashionable among Border Leicesters. His new owner was sympathetic. 'Ah,' he said, 'I keep apples for mine.' And he began feeding Philip with bits of apples. The last I saw of my ram, he was dancing round his purchaser, trying to get his nose into the pocket where the apples were, intent, as usual, on having his own way, forgetting me.

Scotland 65, July 1952, pp. 10-13

Sheneval

(1952)

This was the first year we took a crop off Sheneval. The name perhaps means the old village – corrupted, like most Gaelic place names. That might account for all the stones in it. In 1937 it was in a rather bad state, not having recovered properly from its last rotation. The grass which was under-sown with the last corn crop had not taken well, perhaps because the corn had lodged. But gradually it got better. A dressing of slag some five years ago cheered it up a good deal, and clover took well. Later it had some ground limestone. Last year I got the drains cleaned out and a few new ones put in.

This spring we ploughed and gave it a dressing of superphosphates. One little bit was steep and still very wet in spite of the draining; the tractor tilted dangerously and we had to leave it. I hoped we had seen the last of the big patch of thistles which seemed to come up year after year in greater profusion, even when we cut them over before seeding. How wrong I was!

It was time for me to get some new oat seed, though my own Ayr Bounty seed, already used two years, has done very well in the third year in the other oat fields. I asked for something new, stipulating a stiff stem and a good head. So often our oats get broken down by heavy rain and wind just when they are ripening, and this is particularly bad when grass is sown out with the crop. We need our straw for feeding out-wintered cattle, and a stiff stem is probably not so good as a long fleshy stem, but, of course, no oats ever have the same feeding value as hay. Anyhow, I consulted MacFarlan Shearer, who are a very old-established firm in the world of seeds, fertilisers, feeding stuffs, and all those fascinating things like tarred roofing felt and sheep dip. They live in Bogle Street, presumably with an old-established Brownie guarding them with a bowl of cream set at the door, and they seem to bear with me when I write them letters saying 'Did I remember to order my turnip seed? If I did I want twice as much.' They recommended an oat called Minor.

We drilled it in just before a cold spell, and it took some time coming through. Then all at once the whole field was brairded, the lovely tender green of the young shoots that makes our April fields so lovely. In May we had our usual dry spell, which we always grumble about because it means danger to the turnip seedlings unless they are well rooted before it comes. There was also a sudden late frost which withered the potato shoots so completely that I thought it was blight. So did half the farmers in Kintyre. If we had gone to bed early and not got up until after the sun we would never have guessed at three degrees of frost. It put the potatoes back but did not kill them, though no doubt it helped the weeds which might otherwise have been suppressed by the potato haulms. They came later on, in a wet June and July.

This wet weather suited most of my fields, including the very sandy one in front of the house where four years ago, in a drier year, the corn was so short that it would not bind at all but fell all ways at once off the canvas of the binder. And the Sheneval corn grew too. Going down to the village for messages or committee meetings, I would eye it. As it grew tall it was very pleasing to see other people leaning on the gate looking at it – even to watch them go into the field and examine a head or two, for it was beginning to carry a handsome, heavy head.

We got the hay up in the fields, but during the second half of July and on into August there was no getting it into the stackyard, for rain or drizzle fell almost every day. It was beginning to darken, and at the same time the corn was ripening. This happens often enough in Scotland, and this time we had the extra work of trying to clear some of the rampant weeds out of the turnips.

Then suddenly the weather cleared. We went hard at it, on both hay and corn, working overtime in the evenings and on Sunday afternoons. Until the roads were cut I had not realised what a good crop it was in Sheneval. I had been worried in case it was down in the middle where we could not see – it had stood wonderfully all round the edges and even under the overhanging tree branches. It was stiff to bind and very golden.

After three rounds the binder stopped. We had had a little trouble with the canvases; then a knife had broken. But this was worse. An old break which we had not known about and which had been painted over had sprung, and the two pieces of metal were lying apart. It was part of the main framework, taking the whole weight. Lachlan and Colin worked at it patiently, loosening nuts and prising away at the metal; they managed to put in a piece of metal over the top, a kind of rough splice. We all wondered if it would hold, but it did.

We went on till eight that evening, finishing three-quarters of the field. The sheaves were extraordinarily difficult to stook, just because they were so ripe and stiff and light on the ground, so light that they felt like sheaves ready to put in. And where the old patch of thistles had been, there they were again, bound in with the corn; up to a point one had to disregard them, but all our hands were jagged and sore. Looking into the half-cut corn was, to me, something very beautiful; it stood up straight and even in the drills, clean straw, the heads all on the same level, with an almost architectural precision; I had never seen anything quite like it in my own oats.

We were all very tired and the breeze was coming from the east, which always means fine weather here, a clear sky too. I took the risk of leaving half the sheaves unstooked. And the next morning was fine again. We finished the quarter of the field that was left and stooked everything, restooking a good many sheaves which had fallen. Ordinarily we on the West Coast leave our oats in stook for at least a fortnight so that they should ripen and harden fully and the damp dry out of the stems. But if the weather holds – and of course it probably won't! – we may bring Sheneval in after only a few days in the stook. I have a feeling that some of my neighbours will be asking for seed from it. So long as all goes well up to the threshing!

The Manchester Guardian, 15 September 1952, p. 5

Harvesting in Kintyre

(1952)

Harvesting in the Highlands is never straightforward. By now I have seen most of my fields through four corn crops; I know what weather suits them, both for growth and for winning the harvest. The cricket field in front of the house – though it must be a generation since anyone played cricket there – is the easiest to harvest. It gets all the wind, more than ever since the Hydro Board cut a great swathe through the trees at each side. But it needs rain in May and June to get a good growth of straw, and even in a wet year like this there are short patches, for the soil is reclaimed machair, little better than sand.

It is very seldom that we can get the corn straight in from the stooks. I thought we should manage it this year from one field, for the corn was beautifully clean and stiff, the ley crop with no difficult bottom of hay and weeds to dry out. We did about a third of the field straight from the stooks. Then of course the rain came. It never seems to be dry for more than two days at the outside since we got past mid August. And it is seldom that we have all the hay into the stackyard before we are on to the corn.

It is the same thing all over the Highlands, and maybe part of the answer is silage – silage and a great deal of co-operation, for a silage pit on a small farm is just nonsense.

Sunday work is no longer frowned on, and on a Sunday afternoon there is no shortage of workers, as so many friends turn up – fishermen or foresters, perhaps, but none so far from the land that they have forgotten how to pitch up a sheaf or load a cart. Our guests are a more doubtful blessing. It was, I think, the Dutch professor who was so very vigorous and managed to stick his pitchfork into so many tender spots on other people; he had to be diverted to cutting down trees. But nowadays quite a lot of people have some farm experience.

When we speak of winning a crop we really mean, etymologically, getting the wind through it, and hay is put into wind-rows. But to me harvest is always like a battle which one tries to win with as few casualties as possible – though I myself am in favour of throwing

Harvest at Carradale

the most difficult sheaves at once to the cows or the hens instead of waiting for the wild birds to eat all the grain.

When it is over we are all battle scarred; our backs ache with stooping over the swathes and bunching after the scythe goes round to open the roads, and there are few reaper-binders where the knotter mechanism always works.

When you can chuck the sheaves straight up from the stook it isn't so bad, but once the corn is thoroughly wetted and the stooks must be cowped, one has to shove one's hand up under the binding of the sheaf to see if it will do. After an hour or so of that one's fingers are all bleeding at the nail, let alone the tiny thistle jags that one doesn't notice at the time but that can be gey sore the next day.

Yet even when things go far from well, there is something oddly soothing and satisfying about the steady progress of harvest, the clearing of the fields, the continual smell of the corn. It seems to have an importance which is not measurable in cash terms, for a Highland oat crop is not particularly valuable. One may sell a ton or two, but most of it is for one's own farm and kitchen use: nothing like Kintyre ground oatmeal for good porridge! We take a bag or two down to the mill at Southend after the threshing.

But that is not what we are thinking about. The sense of worthwhileness is in being a part of something which has gone on from the very first tentative beginnings of civilisation; and which will go on so long as we do not batter ourselves off the face of the earth.

That is perhaps why we cling to mixed farming when perhaps it would be more sensible to go in for cattle, fed on silage – perhaps grown as a special silage crop in the rotation place of corn – and turnips. For that matter; much of our land here is doubtfully worth farming if there is any other alternative – for instance, trees. Yet we go on, helped by some of the modern, quick-maturing, stiff-stemmed oats which stand up to our weather.

If I were twenty years younger and had a field or two of rather better soil I think I would try barley. Kintyre used to be barley-growing country in the days of the Campbeltown distilleries, and we could do with more barley meal for pigs. The modern still is so large and complex that it has to have completely evenly ripened barley – which has to be imported from the East Coast, or even (crowning irony!) from Holland.

These triumphs of modern invention produce a whisky which is quite unlike the old Highland malt whisky, but which has an enormous organisation behind it. The one Highland thing left is the name on the label. Yet for hundreds of years Highland barley was used for making Highland whisky in pot stills, apparently to the satisfaction of whisky lovers – of whom I am not one.

Wouldn't small-scale distilling from home-grown barley be an appropriate Highland industry? Again, if I was twenty years younger ... and let me hasten to add, legal distilling. Or do I really mean that?

Meanwhile harvest remains a weather lottery and a test of capacity. I can make a shape with the beginning of a hay stack, though not when it gets far up.

But I am no good on a corn stack. And harvest cannot go faster than the stack builder. The most skilled person must build the stack, but someone who knows what he is about must watch it, knocking in a sheaf which sticks out too far and telling the builder if he begins to go out of shape.

As the stack goes up there is an outward pressure and a tendency for the whole thing to bulge. One knocks in the butt-ends of the sheaves either with a spade or with a piece of flat wood on the end of a pole, consolidating it all the time. But the head of the stack must be entirely the builder's responsibility. With us it is complicated by the power lines, which not only must not touch but must be well out of reach of anyone forking down to the threshing machine later on.

There is a distinct skill, too, in building a load on a trailer. If the sheaves are mixed, there is skill again in waling them out; someone on the field has to make decisions. If one is driving the main thing is to drive slowly enough when one has a heavy load on the trailer, and also to keep the children in order, especially on Saturday and Sunday when they are out of school.

Sally, who is three and three-quarters, has enjoyed her first harvest, especially going in the tractor, safely cushioned by Big Colin. I remember when I was her age – and it is about the first thing I remember clearly – going out from Cloan to help the old women from the poorhouse to glean, in the field beyond the burn. There is no gleaning now – or rather, the hens do it when the henhouse on sleds is pulled over into the stubble. And the old don't any longer have to break their stiff old rheumaticky backs for a few pennies.

But Sally knows how the corn turns into porridge, just as I knew, and just as small children helping and hindering at harvest have known for so many hundreds and thousands of years.

The Glasgow Herald, 18 October 1952, p. 3

Trials and Rewards of Becoming Attested

(1953)

When part of Scotland becomes an 'Attested Area,' what happens? It means to the country in general that healthy milk is being produced and tuberculosis is being cut down; this applies above all to the tuberculosis in children, the chief milk drinkers. In practice, not only is the milk cleaner and better, but there is more of it, for a healthy cow gives more milk over a longer period. That's the national point of view. But what about the farmer?

My own area, Kintyre, was about half attested when I started farming. That is to say, the cows had passed the tests showing they were free of tuberculosis and the byres and dairies were up to standard. This was all voluntary at first – and indeed I had been brought up with it, for my mother's Jerseys were the first attested herd in the south of England. And that, in turn, may have been partly because as a child I developed tuberculosis from a bovine source, in the days when the only safe milk for children was something which had been boiled and boiled until it ceased to taste like milk.

I had intended to have only beef cattle, because of the general bother of milking and also because there was no byre and dairy. Nobody had kept cows here for some time and we had turned the old dairy building into a cottage. But that didn't alter the fact that, if I wanted to have an attested herd, I would have to produce a byre and dairy which were up to the required sanitary standards. That was because, under the temporary wartime restrictions, only dairy herds holding a licence to produce TT milk would be considered for becoming attested, so I had to be at least a notional dairy herd!

This meant great practical difficulties; I scratched my head and hesitated. But that wasn't all. If I didn't have an attested herd I involved my neighbours on both sides in double fencing. As the boundary on one side is a tidal river, that presented problems for a start – when the river is low any beast can – and does – wade over, but if we fence anywhere near the water, a high tide and spate leaves nothing but a few broken stobs and a trail of wire draped in seaweed.

So my first beasts were at least tuberculin tested, but I was still not able to register as an Attested Herd. Disaster came quickly, all the same. First one, and then another, developed contagious abortion. This is something which has taken its toll of herds for many years but which has only been recognised as dangerous to human health in the last decade or so. Milk from an infected cow can produce undulant fever in those who drink it and may well be responsible for undiagnosed illness. And it can be stamped out. They have done so completely in Denmark and have taken steps to do it here. At present there is a voluntary scheme of vaccination and more and more of the cattle breed societies will only take vaccinated stock. Soon there will only be a few stubborn and stupid people who do not go in for the voluntary scheme; then it can be made compulsory. That is a good democratic way of doing things!

But when my beasts went down vaccination had not started. Now it is against the law to sell infected beasts in the open market, but some of them were apparently all right. Still, they had been in contact and might have been infected. I sent them all to be graded – the meat is perfectly all right for human consumption – and emerged from the transaction a sadder and slightly wiser woman. Then I left the farm without cattle at all for some nine months, only keeping sheep, which do not carry the infection.

Meanwhile I began to plan for a real attested herd. I had any amount of help and advice from everyone concerned, the local veterinary practitioner, and particularly the Ministry of Agriculture officials. My own feeling is that if you really want to do the right thing, Government officials will take infinite trouble to help, but if you are trying to dodge your duty towards the rest of the country, they will certainly catch you out.

The main thing was that I had to get some kind of buildings up to standard. At that time one could not spend more than £100 without a special licence, for all civil building was being clamped down on. However, what with getting second-hand rooflights, finding old bits of marble for dairy shelves, and doing quite a lot of the work myself, I just managed to scrape through. We turned part of an old piggery into a small byre, putting in a concrete floor and more ventilation. There was no building anywhere near that would do for a dairy, but finally we made a tiny but adequate one out of an old game larder.

And, of course, once I had the byre and the dairy, I had to start with a milking cow so as to use one at least of the lovely new stalls and fill a couple of the new dairy dishes! And once you have one cow, you soon have two, or indeed three, and some nice young stock coming on, and in fact you are thoroughly involved.

The main things I had to do were most reasonable; the object was cleanliness, light and ventilation. Before the alterations were over I had got to know quite a lot about plumbing, masonry, and slater work. When the Hydro Board brought us electricity I had, first, a light and then a milking machine installed; but neither of these was a necessity for attestation, and at first all the winter milking was done by the uncertain light of a swinging oil lamp.

The herd had to pass two clear private veterinary tests as well as one free official one. Then it reached attestation status. Now the tests have dropped to one in eighteen months, and the whole of Kintyre is an attested area free from bovine tuberculosis. As there is no sign of any breakdowns in the herds, probably we shall be able to go even longer without herd tests. In the old days, with two tests a year, it used to be a real rodeo with my half wild Galloways. The bull was usually no trouble, but the young stirks would leap over any fence and kick in any direction; I was thankful if the thing ended without any severe damage to any of those involved. If only one could have explained to them! At first I used to get very worried over apparent reactors, but this was always a bird-carried type of infection, quite harmless from the bovine or human point of view, and inevitable when a grazing can be affected by large birds like seagulls. I have never had any real reactors.

It was the same with most of my neighbours. Their stock was healthy enough, but the buildings were old and low and not up to standard. But gradually the whole glen came in. Most of them sell TT milk, either on a milk round or in the creamery. Farmers with attested herds get a bonus, either on the milk or per head of the herd. It was obviously worth all our whiles to take the extra trouble, although a healthy herd is worth it for its own sake, not merely as a bit of 'subsidy farming'. We were all rather proud when our whole area became attested.

Our standards are kept up by the milk officers, who are paid partly by the Ministry and partly by the county. It is very easy to become a bit sloppy in our methods; that is perhaps especially so with a milking machine, which must be kept very clean. Every year there are more machines and fewer hand milkers; but, even with a machine, it is essential to keep a personal relationship with the cows which are being milked. After all, we take away their calves at birth and yet expect them to go on giving milk. They must be provided with a substitute calf, someone to love and lick. A milking cow must be constantly handled and petted. That is one reason why there is normally a better milk production where a big farm is broken up into smaller agricultural holdings.

While we were still a mixed area, with some unattested herds, there was always the danger of infection at sales and markets, in spite of the fact that there were always two separate sets of cattle stalls. But the Ministry officials were on the spot; if any infection occurred it could be traced back, with all the excitement of a set of clues in a detective story. But now that particular complication is over. Supposing by some horrid chance we were to get an outbreak of foot-and-mouth here, we know the detective story would start in a matter of hours, all contacts would be found and isolated, and the whole thing brought under immediate control. When that happens one sees the reason for the form filling, the cleaning of lorries and so on, all the things which seem so irksome at safe and ordinary times.

Some people in an attested area have always had difficulties. A few have reactors which must be got rid of. Few buildings of any age will pass without alteration, but the bothers finish and the good honest face of cleanliness and higher milk production is there to stay.

The Glasgow Herald, 28 September 1953, p. 2

Mild Winter

(1954)

The rowan berries always go early and the fieldfares come regularly in early December, just before I have decided to cut the Christmas holly, and strip the two or three trees in half a day. The bright red sorbus berries are usually gone too by New Year, but this year they are still there. After our two frosty days there were perceptibly fewer, but now the birds have left them again. There are any amount of peewit and curlew in, and wherever the farms have been able to get ahead with ploughing they are having a good time in the soft turned ground. But most of us have not had a chance of ploughing even our ley land. Everything is soaking with the perpetual rain. The fields are wet and green.

Last year I sowed out the meadow in permanent grass. It has been through two rotations since I rescued it from marshland, but it is always difficult. The drains are all running hard, but still it is waterlogged down the middle. I worried as to whether the permanent grass would take; the seed is dearer than ordinary five-year ley seed. I was careful not to graze it too hard earlier, to let the cattle poach it about with their hooves or the sheep tear it up. But now it is so thick and green that I have turned the sheep on to it, with a scatter of turnips which they can take or leave. These were autumn-bought lambs, little wedder hoggs, the cheapest I could get. Some of them are fattening up nicely and I plan to sell off a dozen or so towards the end of the month. It may well be cold enough soon to check grass growth and I do not want to have too many to carry through the difficult time.

The two bull calves are looking well too on the good young grass. I am waiting for the 'man from the Department' to come round and license them. Then I can advertise them for sale. As they are children of Mint I have called them New Penny and New Shilling, leaving the culinary names for the heifers. The cattle in the Bay, too, are not bothering to eat their straw and are making little use of the shelter I have put up for them. In a hard winter they would all have been crowding in.

In all the older gardens all up and down this western sea coast there is a dotting of bright red, a rather watered crimson on dark leaves, where the rhododendrons are out, great trees of them; a few of the rest are coming now, nobleanum with the scarlet, translucent flowers that are so often frost-blackened in March, and other early spring flowerers beginning to show colour. There are tinies, of course, witch hazel, and the elegant little azara, whose dark green leaves are dotted with powdery yellow flowers at the back of the axils. The camellias are budding heavily, including one which has not deigned to flower for fifteen years. But can we hope that the buds will stay, not blacken at the base and fall?

The snowdrops have come firmly out, masses of them, and it will take more than a few degrees of frost to worry that crowd! There are primroses and heaths and yellow barberries. A pear tree came into flower just after New Year, but the blossom did not last more than a morning. It is all having an excellent effect on the hens and a correspondingly disastrous one on egg prices.

Most days up here have a fine hour or two. Behind a sheet of glass the sun is so warm that peach trees in an unheated house are on the point of flowering. But sooner or later it always seems to rain. Plough socks wear out in two or three seasons, and my ley socks have come from Greenock; but there seems to be no chance of using them. On the laggan of Kintyre some fields have been under flood water for months. The whole Atlantic seems to be softly shedding itself on to us from the west winds.

Most farmers say gloomily that we shall pay for it later. Perhaps we shall. If the grass which has already made so much growth is to be checked and then come away again, we shall probably have to feed it well with artificials, or sea tangle if it comes in to the beach. It may be that we shall have an increase in certain kinds of insect pest, but, equally, more birds may survive to eat them. I hope at least the pheasants will stay out of the garden. They have a horrid passion for tulip bulbs.

In a really cold winter my hamster, which must be a nonagenarian by hamster standards, hibernates in such a chilly way that several times I have nearly buried him. But now he is lolloping about my desk in the liveliest fashion, reaching up a slippery little flower jug and trying out the various petals; he likes primroses best. However, he prefers to go around with a brussels sprout nearly as big as he is. I wish I knew among which of my papers he had hidden it. I suppose it will turn up some time. But it is quite clear that he does not think it is winter at all.

The Manchester Guardian, 18 January 1954, p. 3

Wet July

(1954)

In the ordinary way we cut rather before most of our neighbours, thinking that our hay will make up in quality for what it loses in bulk. Hay in the Highlands is usually left to July, but we try to cut in what is often a dry fortnight, the second half of June. I went gadding off to the PEN conference, telling the men that I expected the hay would be up by the time I got back. I came back to find acres of sodden, cut hay but only three ricks up; no fault of the men, but day after day of rain.

It was as well they had managed to cut, for the grass would all have lain under the heavy drip, and it was coming to no great harm where it was, unturned. But there was still a field to cut. Most of my neighbours had barely started; it had been difficult enough getting a dry day for the shearing.

One gets the best hay when the cut swathe of grass is wind-blown and sun-scorched right through, so that it does not even need turning, but can be raked straight up into the rick. Then it is green and sweet; one could almost eat it oneself. But this year the wet, cut stuff had all to be turned by hand. I have about six acres of first-year hay and not quite as much second year. We had also cut a small field of third year, which was easily won as there was very little red clover in it. The field that interested me most was the second-year hay in the Cricket Field, as we call it, though it must be a generation since anyone played cricket there. It is reclaimed machair – sandy pastures along the sea; where the rabbits have scraped in it, pure sand is scattered from below. On a southerly gale salt spray blows over it. I am trying to build it up and hope, this time, to leave it out for as long a ley as possible. Corn grows there well enough, especially in a wet year; in a dry year it is apt to be very short. But it is no good for any green crop. We put sea tangle on to the young grass in one quarter of it the first year, but hardly any tangle came in this winter, so we could not go on with the treatment. But it had a dressing of slag this spring. It was a cold, late spring, though, and then a dry April, and the grass was not very long or thick, though there was a good enough sole and plenty of clover.

We cut one half of this field and then left it to put up the hay in the Mutton Shed Field, so called because it holds the shed where the mutton used to be kept, and that too was a long time back! There is something lovely about mowing; the texture of the sward is so varied and behind the flickering teeth of the mower the sole is so fresh and brilliant a green; above all there is the smell that one walks in like a deep sea, the smell of coumarin from the flowering grass and the distinct sharper smell of crushed clover stems bleeding sap.

We cut the second half and it did not rain, but the weather was chilly and still. We turned the first cutting but, looking at the heavy sky and the weather vane going from north to west, thought it best to leave the second cutting in the swathe, where it would come to no harm if the rain came. We might get the first cutting up before the clouds broke. But the rain came, a great downpour over it, soaking everything. Yet, when it cleared it was a perfect day with a sharp breeze and bright sun. We turned the second cutting and by the time we were finished the first was dry enough to put up in fairly small ricks.

Several people together work at this rick-building, which is quite skilled, in careful harmony but without saying anything unless towards the end it seems to be leaning one way or the other; once it is over the top of the sticks – three light poles tied together – I crawl round, pulling out the hay from the base, so that the rick sits square and weathertight, while the men fork over my back. Sometimes I drive the old horse, Jo, in the hay rake, gathering in, leaving a lovely clean track of erased green behind the rake and tipping the hay out with a great clatter. We have tea in the field – tea nowadays with cake, buttered scones, any amount of sugar, and none of the bother of writing away for permits! Then we work till late. Today we finished the second cut and went on to rake up the stuff from the old orchard, poor hay with never a spark of clover to warm it. We finished everything half an hour before the rain.

Year after year I say to myself that really we ought to make silage; year after year I do nothing about it, saying as an excuse that So-and-so had a failure with his silage, that one ought to grow a special silage crop, and so on. Perhaps the main reason is the aesthetic one, the beauty and rhythm of haymaking, the smell of the cut grass, the equally delicious smell of the hay itself. Such reasons should not affect a proper farmer. Next year I really must make silage! But shall I?

The Manchester Guardian, 26 July 1954, p. 3

Visitor

(1954)

'I think it's horrible,' she said firmly, 'to treat deer as vermin.'

I said: 'They aren't exactly vermin. We eat every bit.'

That didn't make it any better. What was wrong, I'm afraid, was that I was *thinking* of the deer as vermin. And it made no difference when I showed her the patch of oats where the deer had trampled and rolled. They had come out of the forestry plantation, where they are rather a nuisance as they eat the young trees when they feel like it. These are fallow and Japanese deer, introduced by a sporting landlord a generation or two back, and now flourishing. There are a few roe as well, but no red deer.

'Deer only eat corn when they are starving,' she said. I gathered that the authority for this was a debate in the House of Lords.

'There's plenty for them on the hill just now,' I said. But it was no good. Deer were noble animals and should be so treated. Horses were noble animals too. She had been giving my best apples to old Jo in the field. We don't grow apples easily up here and my Beauty of Bath is a tree I always pick very specially. Various grandchildren were eating them, but the grandchildren were definitely not noble animals. I gave her some green windfalls for Jo; but she disdained them, saying they would give him a tummy-ache. I ate them myself.

Meanwhile the binder was sweeping round the field. We had cut the roads round the edge the day before, and I was still very stiff from stooping and bunching after the scythers. There is still a nasty patch of thistles in the top corner of that field, and one has to bunch with circumspection. Bunching is a very primitive, feminine occupation. The men in front go upright with the scythes, stopping now and then to sharpen them on the stones they carry in their overall pockets. I go steadily on behind, making up the oats into solid sheaves, about as heavy as the sheaves the binder will make, then twisting a band of straw round them, making it tight and shoving the ear-end under with an increasingly sore thumb. But one doesn't notice one's back-ache until the end of the field. It is worse than potato gathering, for there you are always standing straight again and carrying the baskets.

The binder had made three rounds which, with the hand-bound sheaves from the road, made four rows – enough for the first row of stooks. It is best to leave four rounds of the binder at least before stooking. There is a shorter carry with the sheaves, and the end result is better, leaving plenty of room between the rows for cart or tractor. I was trying to show her how to stook. Some people get the knack quite quickly. It looks easy enough, but stooks must be made so that they won't come down with the first wind. In the other fields it had been very marked that the amateur stooks had come down first, sometimes even before we had left the field. I had been restooking there, and wondering what Lachie and Colin, behind their Highland politeness, really thought of their would-be helpers.

It was difficult to get her to see that one must take two sheaves at a time and dump them hard down so that their butt ends sloped and their heads locked in with the other sheaf heads. She was working in gloves, because of the midges. Certainly there are midges, but not, as I kept on saying, mosquitoes. She would pick up a sheaf and look round vaguely; once she stopped and picked off a large black slug which she put back tenderly on the grass edge. I suppose it was a noble animal too. But not, perhaps, the midges.

There is a certain rhythm in stooking, as in most farm work; Eddie and I could work together for hours without getting too tired, he mostly picking up two pairs of sheaves to my one pair, but each fitting in to what the other is doing. But she could not get the rhythm. Perhaps it all seemed barbarous. Perhaps she felt the whole farm was savage and unfeeling, that we shot and ate the beautiful deer without regard for their individuality. Farming is savage, of course. One separates the calves from the cows; the cows moan and the calves bleat, for the first few hours anyway. The poor little Ayrshire bull calves are bundled off in sacks to the slaughterhouse. If one dared to think of it with anthropomorphic kindliness one's milk production would go rapidly down. Perhaps if we were kinder to animals we might be less unkind to other humans. Or perhaps more so: one can't be sure.

But the midges were getting too much for her. One puts on anti-midge cream, and they walk round in it looking for a gap; at least they don't raise large blisters like the July clegs. She went in. No, the Highland midge is not a noble animal.

The Manchester Guardian, 7 October 1954

Leaning on a Gate

(1955)

Lachlan and I are leaning on a gate. The gate will need renewing soon. However much one creosotes or paints, wood doesn't stand up indefinitely to eighty inches of rain in the year. It is not the season for straws but I am chewing a hawthorn twig. What is a farmer doing when he leans on a gate? Well, we are not saying much, but our eyes and ears and noses are feeding in facts just as though we were calculating machines. The clicking goes on inside just as though we had electronic valves, and in a while the sum has been totted up and comes back into consciousness.

We look slowly across a field. Under it we know – we can almost see – the pattern of field drains that lie under almost all arable fields in Great Britain. A century ago there were stone drains – we ran into them in the course of re-draining. Later, some of them were replaced by tile hoops over slates. Now there is a predominantly arrow pattern of three-inch tiles running into a main drain of four- or five-inch tiles, which discharges into a ditch. All is on a slight slope and anything from two to five feet down; if a tile gets out of place you may have to dig down to replace it.

Looking at the field, we remember what crops and what manures it has had in the last ten years. We think back to the look of the soil two rotations ago. Certainly it is richer than it was then, though I'm afraid a soil analysis will still show it poorer than it should be in almost everything. The turnips round our feet are surprisingly good; but they had one of those compounds that make up for the boron deficiency that causes brown heart, that maddening disease of hollowness and smell. Yet they didn't get much chance at the thinning and cleaning. It was so wet that the weeds took root again after they were pulled. But that was better than drought, though it was bad for the potatoes. Never have they been such a poor crop – except of course that time we had them in the bottom of the Meadow.

'Did the earlies come yet?' I ask. Lachlan and I perhaps both see the same picture of early potatoes in the sprouting boxes in the warmth over the stables. 'No' yet,' he says, and I think how nice it would be if anything ever happened without one having to send a reminder. Yet as like as not they've been sent off and the sacks are just lying around somewhere between Ayr and here. 'They'd no Sutton's Abundance,' I say, 'and it's a nice-tasting potato.'

'Dunkie would maybe give us a bag,' says Lachlan, adding that he and Eddie had a bushel or so off him last year and they did great. The men have their own drills in the field and so does anyone who cares to give us a hand with planting and gathering in return. Lachlan puts in tags, but he would probably know the rows anyhow, just as he knows which are which of the Black Galloways. I only know a few of them, though one knows the milk cows well enough.

The field beyond the road, Sheneval, is beginning to look green. 'Was there any tangle in?' I ask, thinking partly of the young grass – for now is the time to put on the sea tangle, rich in potash, which brings on the young clover – and partly of the potato ground.

'It should be,' he says; and we turn our faces a little towards the south from which the weather comes that throws up the broken tangle – and often takes it away on the next tide. He knows that one of my favourite ploys on the farm is going down with the Land Rover and trailer and bringing up the strange, many-shaped sea stuff. He would like me to do my special things. In the days when we still sowed by hand I had a straight eye and could take a sowing sheet – the same shape of slung basket that Demeter had – and sow with alternate hand strokes, either oats or the more difficult grass seed, on marks I had set myself at the far end of the field. I liked doing that. But now we almost always borrow or hire a mechanical seeder for our sowing.

His own favourite things, I suspect, are building a corn stack and ploughing with the new Ferguson tractor: skilled jobs. Once I did a bit of ploughing and the further I went the crookeder got the furrows. After a while he came and watched. The time came when he grunted with disapproval, took over and put it right. Another thing I am bad at and he is good at, is backing the Land Rover with a loaded trailer. This used to be a shaming business at harvest, which is anyway a time of laughter and mockery between men and women; but last year I had the bright idea of opening the fence at the far end of the stackyard so that one could drive straight through without any backing and turning. So I was one up!

We chew over a good many other problems while we lean on the gate, thinking out what needs doing. There are the fences and the fallen limb of the oak. There is the question of hay for the Galloways; I am wondering how it will last out. My neighbour Duncan is going to come over and spread the dung for us with his mechanical spreader. When any of the farms gets a new mechanical device, it always gets lent around. The threshing mill, which is owned and operated by a smallholder down by Campbeltown, goes round all the farms, a day or half a day at each. A team of fourteen or fifteen comes to work it from all the farms, a social event and a huge dinner or tea at whichever place the mill is in use. I doubt if closer co-operation is possible; and the configuration of the land makes little, odd-shaped fields which could scarcely be worked with bigger implements than those we have. Probably these small, family farms are as good land use as one is likely to get. But, though the fields in the Carradale valley are alluvial and crop well, my own are raised beach with only a few inches of decent soil above the sand, except where there are streaks of peat. Onto these I try to put an extra share of lime; but it always seems to me possible that the best use for my land, and some more of the marginal land along the coast, would really be as an extension of the forest.

Above Sheneval the young forest, mixed spruces, with Jap and European larch in different shades of pinky-grey, climbs well up onto Tor Mor. Lachlan and I both see the wood as beautiful. But could we ever give up to trees these fields we have worked on, that are ours by right of knowledge and labour? I doubt if this kind of feeling of ownership is a bad thing; and I doubt, also, if it is different in kind for him and me, who have been workmates for fifteen years.

The New Statesman and Nation, v. 49, 26 February 1955, p. 276

Maggots and Potatoes

(1955)

Most years we end the winter with at least one stack of hay over. But this spring there wasn't a wisp left. The Galloways were finding nothing to eat in the hundred acres or so of rough, sandy ground between the house and the sea. The calves were beginning to come, and their mothers needed food to keep up their milk. The last of the turnips had gone, and the dairy cows had had the last stalks of kale. The only grass that was coming on was the young hay sown last year under a nurse crop of oats. But one can't put a crowd of hungry beasts on to that.

Some years we have the 'early bite' by mid-March, the first young grass that puts cream into the milk. But now, ever since the snow melted, we have had dry, cold east winds and sharp night frosts which have killed off the young shrubs in my garden which normally stand the winter, clianthus and embothrium, veronicas, the tender olearias, and even the hypericums. The flower buds are nipped on the early rhodies, including the nobleanum which was coming into scarlet flower at New Year. The only creatures that benefit from this are the bees, which usually die in crowds about now, probably through taking poisonous honey from the heavily blooming rhododendron barbatum. They have had a lovely time with the peach blossom in the old, unheated glass houses, though I have gone round pollinating with a rabbit's foot on the end of a stick, just in case the bees were being stupid.

Our ley field of oats is sown, my neighbour Duncan lending his sower. I have sown this field with my own seed, keeping the bought oats to sow as a nurse crop over the hay grass in the third year of my rotation. It is an extra early oat, and if I can get it off a fortnight sooner it will give a better chance to the grass below. Our early and second early potatoes are in too.

My old horse Jo no longer has to strain himself opening and closing potato drills, though it was wonderful how well he knew just where to tread. Now I have a Ferguson tractor, and I have borrowed a three-bladed drill plough from yet another neighbour. It works beautifully, and with great power. Tomorrow I am borrowing the big grubber from the Forestry Commission – who haven't yet got me a new wire rope for my winch to replace the one they broke last year. In the evening Lachlan is taking the discs up the Glen to Dunkie, who won't risk driving down all the way on his tractor which he has just got and which he still finds rather scaring! At present I have the newest potato digger in the Glen, and it goes the rounds in October, but fairly soon it will be my turn to get some other implement to go into the pool.

I wonder if this general borrowing is the beginning of a formal co-operative or whether it works better as it is? The great thing is that, the present way, we've all got to be on good terms with one another or the thing won't work. But it is certainly the only way for small farmers to get the benefit of these ingenious and efficient modern farm implements.

We have all had postcards from the Ministry about dressing the cattle against warble fly. The dairy cows were done at once, but our suppliers ran out of stuff, there was such a rush on it. We are a TT area here, and obviously bovine tuberculosis will soon be a thing of the past. Most of us are in the scheme for inoculation against brucella – contagious abortion – and get our queys done during their second year at a nominal rate. If warble fly can be knocked out too, we shall have done a great deal towards healthy cattle, though it seems probable that milking by machine is not the best for mastitis.

The derris powder came at last, and we drove the Galloways into their shelter and then into the narrow passageway we have made which is so handy for all the many unpleasant things we have to do to cattle, inoculating, testing and marking their ears being the least nasty. Then we soaked their backs with the derris dressing. The maggots of the warble fly make great lumps on each side of the spine. These open, and if one presses with one's thumbs, out hop the enormous maggots on which one puts a foot. The dressing is to kill them before they come out, so that they never turn into horrible warble flies. Some of the young beasts were badly affected, with twenty or thirty swellings, which, I must say, they didn't seem to mind. But the old cows never had so many. Perhaps they are a bit tough for the flies to get through. Lachlan and I stood on the rail and soused them all with the stuff and rubbed it in. But it will have to be done again in a month.

It gave me a chance of seeing how they had stood the winter – always rather difficult to tell with these Galloways who dress themselves in black hearth rugs. They had a good bit of flesh on them, but it is difficult to tell with the old girls who have lost their figure, whether they are in calf or not. So far I have six calves out of eleven possible mothers, but only two are queys. It is probably not worth my while rearing bull calves. They have to be very specially looked after, though if one of these turns out really well, I might try again. But if one is going to prepare a bull, one has to give him quite a lot of artificial feeding over his first winter after weaning, and unless one is fairly sure he is going to pass the inspectors at the end of it, the thing is doubtfully worth while. I rather prefer the duns; it seems to me that they are even slightly heavier and better doing. But they never make such good prices. At the last sale I put in two in-calf heifers; the black made £60-odd, but the dun, which I thought was the better of the two, only £37. But perhaps duns will come back into fashion.

The young Ayrshire quey stirks run with the Galloways in winter when the bull is not with them; they develop very thick coats too. I use AI entirely for the Ayrshires, but it would be a brave man who did it to these wild Galloways. I bought a very large bull, middle-aged as bulls go, at the Castle Douglas sale in November; he is low-slung and short-legged, and my feeling was that my beasts were getting a bit long in the leg. On the other hand I have really no reason to suppose that a short-legged bull will pass on this characteristic to his progeny. So here am I, brought up as a geneticist, behaving in practice like any old farmer from the back of beyond. But, as so little genuine knowledge exists about the inheritance of cattle characteristics, I suppose there is nothing else I can do. The bull has a long pedigree and his progenitors seem to have come from respectable farms. Also, he is a nice, well mannered bull, who takes his cabbage leaf like an old Etonian.

The New Statesman and Nation, v. 49, 7 May 1955, pp. 642, 644

Thoughts on Growing Grass

(1955)

What I need is more grass. My cash-crop is the traditionally Highland one of cattle, though, as the centuries go by, one has reluctantly to give up raiding one's neighbours. Besides, grass is the obvious thing to grow in a district of heavy rainfall, round about eighty inches a year. Other crops may fail or be intolerably hard to win, but the grass grows green and long and lush. Some people cut for silage, but good hay is as valuable or better, and we have usually managed to make good hay, partly because we can count on a reasonably large labour force in haytime. I look speculatively at my innocent visitors: even an MP can be made to do useful work!

But grass needs looking after, like any other crop. Lachlan and I go round the fields, discussing the problem of each one. Sheneval, the field which was sown out last year, has a beautiful, wind-rippling, thick hay crop, but not as tall or as ripe as the grass has been at this time in most other years. It did not come away at all until the end of the cold weather. We shall probably cut a fortnight later than usual, well into July. The meadow below the road is a different problem. This is second-year grass, and has suffered because we had a job getting the corn off it the first year, while last year patches of the grass were lying after our wet June, and killed the layer below. It is a very wet field, in spite of all our draining, and the steady outpour that shows these drains are working. So I decided, after two rotations, in one of which we lost almost all the green crop owing to the wet, that it had better go back to permanent pasture. But this spring there were patches with no grass on them, only horrible creeping buttercups and the other weeds of sour land. It had lime not so long ago, and phosphates last year, but probably most of it has washed away down the drains. I thought the best thing would be a light dressing of nitro-chalk; this is less drastic than sulphate of ammonia which brings on the young grass leaf at the expense of the clover. The sourest looking bits could have some lime as well. Lachlan sowed some seed we had over – and how madly expensive grass seed is! – on the bald patches. He sowed the nitro-chalk by hand – two hundredweights to the acre. But it wasn't easy to see just how far the flung handfuls were falling, so now the field has some peculiar pinkish yellow stripes of untreated grass between the green stripes that have lapped up the nitro-chalk and are growing strongly.

The grazing fields are looking well, though they will be bare enough by the end of summer. One of them will get some ground limestone: hereabouts we need two lime dressings in each rotation, somewhere in the middle of the grass ley. The old cricket field in front of the house is very light soil. It improved the year we put some seaweed on to the young grass, but there was no tangle drifted into the bay this year; we had the wrong winds for it. The sole of clover is not persisting, and a lot of the grass is rather dry cocksfoot which the beasts don't like much. I have some young stock there, Ayrshires and Galloways, and they have left the cocksfoot and pulled up the fine grasses almost as badly as if they were sheep. Lachlan is going to give it a run with the mower high off the ground, to cut off the grass heads before they seed, so that the plants will have a chance to leaf again.

But between the cricket field – and it must be many, many years since anyone played cricket there, though the name persists – and the sea there is a hundred acres or more of rough grazing. It is old raised beach, very poor land. We ploughed some of it during the war, but it wasn't worth doing; there were only a few inches of soil above the sand. When we first came it was heavily over-grazed by rabbits and sheep. I changed to cattle, though I still have a very small wether flock, lambs I buy in at the back-end and sell through the year – or eat. We also ate enough of the rabbits to have made a big difference. The grass is very much better now. But what grows even better than grass is bracken. The best way to get my extra grazing that I so much need, is to clear some of the bracken.

Lachlan and I read in one another's minds the magic word: Grant. This is up to fifty per cent of the cost of cutting, but it must be done to the Department's satisfaction, and over a period of three years. Deaf to urgent Labour Party election workers, I filled up the bracken-cutting form in a committee room and sent it off, in a typically Highland way, on the last possible day. The ground was looked over while I was away electioneering and I don't even know for certain if it will qualify, but all the same I am cutting and shall make my second cut in late July or August. Next year I shall probably only need to do one cut. I hope to cut ten acres, still leaving plenty of good thick stuff for Carradale's summer courtships. The bracken is now two to three fronds in leaf and makes excellent garden compost, though a trailer load melts down into a few forkfuls.

We are using the old mower and tackling the levellest bits of ground first. When Lachlan goes for his dinner I take on. The smell of the cut bracken is as strong and exciting as Bond Street; the sun blazes on one's arms and neck. I watch to see that the snicking blades don't jam on whin stalks or hummocks of earth. If they do I must stop and clear them. If the snickering gets uneven and jumpy, that means that one of the teeth has fallen out and must be found and the rivets hammered back. But mostly it goes well, about half an acre to the hour, the old Fordson – she was second-hand in 1940 – rocking lumpishly over the uneven ground. I steer clear of bad rabbit holes and watch for peewits' nests, but so far have found none. There are far fewer peewits than there used to be, ever since, I think, the bad winter of 1947.

On most of the cleared land there is soft grass growing underneath, but I am not sure how it will go on through the year. There is some trefoil, but no clover; and it may be that once the bracken is away we may have to do some re-establishment of grass, or rather of sward, because on this kind of land there are probably a number of valuable herby plants which the cattle will like as much or more than coarse grass. A lot of grass research is going on, but not much on the kind of sward which can easily be established and kept up in West Highland conditions. This sort of research takes time and doesn't produce immediately impressive results, but it ought to be done and money ought to be found for it.

Of course, this isn't the only way to increase grass production. I could put on a lot more fertiliser and divide the fields up into small strips with electric fences so as to have intensive controlled grazing. But this would mean expenditure both in capital and labour which the farm can't stand. In Denmark a farm this size would certainly use controlled grazing, probably on fodder crops, lucerne or clover, either with electric fencing or by tethering. But nobody is used to working that way here, though in the Islands the crofters' cattle are tethered. Ayrshires are touchy anyway. They'd probably stage a sit-down strike.

The New Statesman and Nation, v. 49, 11 June 1955, p. 809

The Year of the Good Hay

(1955)

This week we have been doing something which is almost unheard of on the west coast of Scotland: we have been cutting the grass one morning and putting up the hay the next afternoon. The blazing sun has dried and the light wind has ruffled through it. There has been no turning and wetting, nothing to take the good out of it. The thick red clover of the seeds mixture withers into sweetness. The most scientific drier wouldn't have done it better. The colour is a lovely, gentle grey-green, the smell goes softly through one's body. The only thing is, it is slippery to work with, just because it has never been tossed and twisted.

We put it up on tall, narrow pikes, on wooden tripods, and tie it down with crossed ropes. Mostly it is the four of us working, as we have done so often through the summers, but this time finding it lighter than usual to do, though we are running with sweat all the time, clean body sweat that smells rather like hay. Sometimes the Boy Scouts come and help us, turning up, like the parable of the vineyard, just before tea in the field. Few of them have done any farm work and they find it awkward to handle fork or rake. I am not so young as I was, but don't feel it tiring to work with a pitchfork, getting the tines into the hay rather like eating spaghetti, and twisting the fork so that the hay slides off the tines when it goes on to the rick. One doesn't think about how one does it.

Raking strikes me as an essentially feminine occupation, and again, it is easy if one does it the right way, sliding the smooth handle effortlessly through the supporting hand, moving in rhythm. Yet how few women one sees working in the field in this country compared with France or Denmark. In an ordinary year, with fair weather but nothing outstanding, we have to rake the first swathe once, cocking it up so as to catch the wind. In a bad year, especially when it may lie for days and the new growth of grass begins to shoot through it, one may have to rake two or three times. Then one longs for a silo. But not this year. I remember saying to Lachlan in the middle of wet March: 'Maybe we should try silage after all,' and he said: 'Ach, surely we'll get some good weather for once!' And so we have.

Building the pikes is an art. Watch Lachlan or Eddie looking just where the next forkful is to go and putting it there unerringly, keeping the width of the stack even round the tripod – otherwise it may topple over – and seeing that there are no hollows left; then, as it begins to mount and draw inward to the top, stroking it even with the tines of the fork. When we come to lift the pikes, in a fortnight's time, to take them into the stackyard, these forkfuls will come up separately. A knowledgeable forker will pick them up like that and chuck them easily into the trailer. But then the loose hay will be compacted and flattened into layers, a few inches thick.

I am less certain about how to put up the hay, and I can't reach to the top where a final wisp is laid with a kind of dainty certainty. But I know without words when to help with my own fork to steady what has been put on. Often I am the one to go round the base of the pike on hands and knees, pulling out the loose hay from the bottom and getting an overhang. This keeps it drier and to some extent shapes the whole thing. We use our old stack ropes for the cross-over, fastening them down by pulling out a wisp of hay inside, twisting it as we do so, as though making the beginnings of a hay rope. That twisting stops it from just pulling out, and the hard held stack rope is itself twisted round the hay and then the double twist is tucked in at the back of itself, so that it can't get loose. All so easy once you know how!

Lachlan is cutting with the new Ferguson mower, which has done very well. To bring in the hay, we have old Jo the horse with the horse-rake. He can't work for very long at a time, and he is getting past pulling even a horse-rake uphill. Next year, I suppose I shall have to buy another horse. Don't tell me a tractor can do everything! But at least Jo makes the rows, and then we have a home-made tumbling-tom, a wooden bar with pointed spars on it and two handles to hold it down with. It rakes along the windrows, collecting more hay than the rake could manage. I drive it in to the place where the pike is to go up, the man on the handles lets go, and it tumbles over most satisfactorily, delivering the load and then righting itself.

Originally the pony pulled this while the horse was raking, but it goes equally well on the Land Rover, on chains. It saves a lot of work and doesn't go out of order. No doubt the men would find it very enjoyable to have various much more elaborate instruments, such as those one sees looking all glorious at the agricultural shows; but an implement has to be very useful indeed if one is only going to use it for a few days every year. Nor can one do much passing round or lending of haysel or harvest instruments, at any rate up here, where everyone is trying to make the most of the few good days. My neighbour Duncan, though, has just rung up to ask if I will consider chipping in on a hay-baler! Yet there are various things we would very much like to have, a Ferguson cultivator for instance. Some of the old government ones were being sold the other day. I sent Lachlan over, but we had looked up the catalogue price of new ones beforehand, and he stopped bidding before they went right up – as they did – to the new price. Some people get carried away by an auction, and any kind of old junk will make something.

A cultivator doesn't take up much room, but some things do, and we are having to think about a new instrument shed. We are going to build at the end of the village hall, which has swopped me the site where an old roof had fallen in, in exchange for some ground where cars can park. I wish I could build a really handsome shed, to go with the village hall, but I am afraid it is going to be corrugated iron, though I might find something less nasty than bright green for painting over it. One has to think very much in terms of sheds when one gets instruments; some farmers don't get round to it, and their nice new things lie out in the rain and the rust gets at them in spite of the new paint.

In the country, people name the years, not by numbers which don't mean so much, but by what happens in them. It means less now, maybe, than it did in the years when a full meal chest meant life itself. But here in the west, at least, I think this will be The Year of the Good Hay.

The New Statesman and Nation, v. 50, 30 July 1955, pp. 130-1

Cautionary Story

(1955)

Everything had gone almost too easily to be true. By early August the oats were ripening, pale gold in the windy centres of the drying fields or on a southern slope. The edges were still very green and would never have done for combining, but this isn't combine country. It was a case of making up our minds whether we would cut part of the harvest rather too green for the sake of getting the rest in good order. The drought was bound to break fairly soon, and once the change came the corn might go down under the first rain and we'd have the usual lengthy and tiring business of cutting out by hand the bits that were laid. As it was, every stalk was standing beautifully. We decided to cut, though some of the corn which Lachlan scythed in the first field was green enough.

Cutting and stooking went easily – too easily, because a dry summer means a light crop and a half empty stackyard. As we finished the first field we were already deciding to go straight on to the second. Instead of cutting roads we would take the binder straight through the standing corn, with a final cut going round the opposite way to pick up the stalks which had been squashed down by the tractor. I doubt if this would work with heavy corn, but with our light, clean straw – this was the ley field – it worked perfectly. By five o'clock there was not much of the field left. I came back from milking and asked the men what they'd like to do. All wanted to carry on, and no farmer grudges a couple of hours overtime in a summer like this. It was eight o'clock and the midges beginning when the binder finished and we were doing the last of the stooking. Duncan came walking over the field to ask could we lend him a spare for his own binder? It was grand to be able to say: 'Borrow the binder itself!'

The corn was light to handle, almost dry already, and I felt we might risk putting it in the next week if the weather held. Yet all of us, even in the middle of our harvest, half hoped for rain. The grass is mostly eaten down, even the aftermath from the hay fields which usually lasts well into September. The sown out field had hardly a blade of grass in it, for the sandy soil scorches quickly. The turnips were small, the kale floppy from lack of water.

But two or three days later the clouds began to pile and drift; it looked like the weather break coming. We went out to the fields, weighing sheaves in our hands, plunging our arms in to feel them under the tie. Most years the stooks are left standing for a fortnight or more, at the very least over two Sundays. Neither Lachlan nor I had any experience of this new kind of dry weather, but it was thought that some of the farms were putting in already and surely these sheaves were dry! We decided to break with custom and make a start with oats which had only been standing three days. Mostly we have to re-stook once or twice, then to overset the stooks into the wind and often to wale out the dry sheaves, leaving one or two that are too wet to bring in. Instead of that we were scooping out the whole field, two rows at a time, the tractor with one load, the Land Rover with another. Lachlan was building quickly with these good sheaves that kept their shape and went straight on to the stack. How well we remembered the bedraggled, shapeless things that had to be built in at the end of last year's harvest – ten months ago. The corn never dried out properly. Colin has to wash it before the hens will touch it, so black with mildew the last of it is.

We got all but the outside row in some places, and one corner of the field which had been shadowed by trees. Here the corn was still greenish and soft: no use of putting it in, even though the stalks seemed dry. We switched to the other field and, again, took out all the middle. The next day we took some more, but I had to stop over-eager helpers from putting on sheaves that looked right but were really not fit to take in. By now the clouds had come low, driving between us and the slope of Tor Mor, on a level with the higher Forestry Commission planting, blotting it out. But still the ground was hard and cracked. We put on the tarpaulins and waited for the rain. There was a day and night of it, enough to help the water supply and stiffen up the drooping kale. Then the wind that had brought it went round and dropped. It was still and hot when we took off the tarpaulins again. Too still, too hot, and my own stackyard is sheltered by trees; well enough during threshing when a hard breeze can blow the chaff into one's eyes, but not so good for drying corn. I drove back and saw Lachlan on top of the half-made stack, lying on his face with his arm down the centre feeling in.

All the stacks were heating. The first one looked all right, but the straw we pulled out was hot in the ear. There was nothing to be done but take it all out again into the fields and re-stook. It was a depressing bit of work, the sheaves were limp and squashed, difficult to prop upright; some were coming loose from the binding. We knew we were bound to lose a good bit of corn this year. We blamed ourselves for bad judgment. And it was all going the wrong way round: the same feeling a herring fisherman must have, throwing back into the sea a hold-full of dead herring when the markets aren't taking them.

There was not even any breeze in the fields to dry out the sheaves. It was queer how damp and clammy they felt now, though they had seemed so dry at the beginning. There must have been more sap in the stalks than I had guessed and the fuzzy, blackened yarr in the bottom of some of the sheaves was like a nasty sponge, soaking up damp out of the still air. I have known stacks to heat and then to dry out completely, but that was in late September when a frosty night and a cold wind would kill the heating organisms in the grain. A few props, skilfully put in, would lift the sheaves enough for a draught to blow through. At worst one might have to take off the top of a stack. But these ones had to be taken down to the last sheaf and dried off for two days. One field was new seed I had bought this year – and seed corn isn't cheap. I hadn't meant to buy in any seed for next year. But how is this heated corn going to germinate? I don't know. I can do a germination test. But I don't like to depend on it. The worst heated corn will have a queer taste in porridge and to the beasts themselves.

It is all in now. But it meant an extra three days, working late, waling out and re-stooking, losing grain all the time. Some of it had been stooked the second time in a field where my bull was lying in the shed with a badly cut knee, not coming out much. But this was too much for him, he came out and started on the sheaves. I went over and got him by his nose-ring. He is the friendliest bull, but too big to notice a mere woman pulling at his nose. His long rough tongue came out and licked all up my arm but he wouldn't move from his dinner. The sheep didn't bother much with the stooks, but we had to chase the geese off. And of course the pigeons came down in clouds.

It was all up the glen that my stacks had heated, and I had plenty of sympathy from my neighbours. They know what it feels like when this sort of thing goes wrong. I hear that it has been the same at some of the farms down Campbeltown way. We may never get the same kind of summer again, but, if we do, we shall be slower to go against custom. We shall be that much more careful and less confident. Perhaps next time we shall leave out the stooks too long.

The New Statesman and Nation, v. 50, 10 September 1955, pp. 294-5

A Year's Work Done

(1955)

Potatoes are the last of the harvest. We have all been at them, whenever the weather was good. Most of us with fairly small acreages manage with our own labour, but it is different for the big growers. The older ones, for instance, from a tinker family who are respectably settled in a council house at Carradale, have gone over to Arran to work on the potato lifting there for a fortnight; that should help with the rent. But it suits us to follow the old custom and have several families taking drills in our potato field in exchange for help in planting and lifting, so we have a mixed crowd helping us. I hope the deer won't be a nuisance this year. The fallow and Jap deer often come at night, digging down with their knife-sharp hooves through the covering rushes and earth into the potato pits and making a terrible mess.

I milk on potato lifting afternoons, to give Lachlan a bit more time. Usually the cows behave perfectly, coming slowly along to the gate when I call them, old Vicky going out first and swiping with her horns at Primrose if she tries to push. The two calves, who are still being pail fed, sometimes dodge out, but if they do I don't bother. They'll go back soon enough when I clank the pails with their milk. However, the open gate of the potato field is too much for them. Clover makes for it, even Vicky turns and goes lumbering in, her heavy udder flopping. The potato pickers all shout at the cows and I am furious with them for behaving so badly in front of company. But I get them out at last and on their way to the byre, though with digressions for delicious nettles – do they understand that I don't like going into the nettles after them? They know their places perfectly, of course, and settle down, waiting for me to start up the milking machine. I never tie them up at this time of year, though later, when they are in at night, they have to be tied. One of the water bowls got broken not long ago, and it was some weeks before we got it brazed. Now, whenever Clover comes in, she takes a drink, just to be sure it is there. I only have three milking just now – and Primrose, who calved last Christmas, is going off. Catherine, one of the heifers, is due to calve in a fortnight. I like to calve the heifers myself and sell them with the second calf; they have then had their milk recorded for one lactation and one can say something about butter-fat. They are at their best then and prices should correspond.

I wash them and take the fore-milk and slip on the rubbers. The cows pay no attention. None of them seems to mind machine milking, though I'm never so sure about AI, which can't be much satisfaction to a cow. However, it does mean we don't have people getting gored by Ayrshire bulls, which are notoriously fierce. Last year my cousins up by Connel gave me a cross Jersey-Highland calf; Barbara Castle[1] and I brought her home in the back of the car. This can be a very good cross, especially for butter making, but one can't tell just how the genes are going to work out. Highland constitution with Jersey milk is grand, but, of course, it may be the other way round. I don't know that Lachlan approves of Sonas, who has the typical Jersey build, with light hindquarters and a little dip in the back. She has an almost Highland coat and should stand the climate, but is still small. Perhaps she is slower maturing than a pure Jersey and shouldn't be put into calf until next year.

While the milking goes on the potato pickers come past the door of the byre and we exchange gossip while they wait for the bus. Lachlan and Colin take back the trailer with a load of small potatoes for the pig and the hens, not to speak of the geese. Once we have plenty of small potatoes we can cut down on other feed. It hasn't been a bad crop, and the kale and turnips better than we had ever thought they would be, considering the drought and the light soil they were growing in. Up in the outer Islands, the crops grown on heavy peat have been extra good, though not the corn from the machair – the wonderful sandy strip along the western edge of the Hebrides, which is sixty per cent shell-sand and dries out very quickly.

Our under-sown grass, which was hardly visible when the nurse crop of corn was cut, came up beautifully through the stubble once it got a good soaking, but it is still soft and we shall have to look after it if there is to be a good hay crop next year. Part of the dung is out already and a few days will finish the job off. The young cattle are on the ley field which Lachlan will plough this winter; we chuck over a few turnips and heads of kale, which will all go to dung it. The milking cows have been on Sheneval and are now in the Meadow, giving Sheneval a few weeks' rest and a chance to come away again in this weather which is still warm enough for growth.

So long as there was plenty of cheap women's labour, nobody bothered to invent electric milking machines and churns. Now there are very few hand milkers anywhere but in the semi-subsistence areas. Most crofters' wives will milk except, I suppose, in Lewis, where all the family is too busy weaving to bother with cows! Here the smallholdings run by the Department of Agriculture – County Councils have nothing to do with them in Scotland, though the TUC don't seem to have grasped this – all have milking machines.

I like churning, now that I don't have to churn a handle for half an hour as one did with the old churn. Jemima taught me to work butter, raven-haired Jemima of Brackley Farm, whose mother was one of the best butter makers in the Glen. What matters is to wash it thoroughly, with fresh cold water, then with briny water, then with fresh water again, working it with cold hands each time. Then one leaves it in cold water to firm, before making half-pound prints. I wish I had a nice wooden butter print, but I expect they've all been collected by arty people, just like horse-brasses, which are so difficult to get if one wants them for an actual horse.

It seems strange to us to have got through the year's work by now. Mostly we are still struggling with the harvest in October, getting more and more tired and fed up. 'This year we'll have some time to ourselves,' said Duncan. There are so many jobs on a farm that never get done, mending and trimming, replacing gates, painting, putting on loose slates. I hope to get some sea tangle up from the shore. At the moment I am having an irate correspondence with the Commissioners for Crown Lands about this. Indignant letters fly between us at the rate of at least two a year. Why should I pay them for taking their nasty, messy seaweed away – a whole half-crown a year, imagine! Just wait till a whale gets stranded on the beach, then they'll *ask* me to clear it away!

The New Statesman and Nation, v. 50, 22 October 1955, p. 504

[1] Barbara Castle (1910-2002), Labour MP; cabinet minister in 1950s and 1960s.

The Big Mill

(1955)

The big mill arrived on Saturday. We have been watching for it, hearing rumours of its movements farther down Kintyre. Towards the end of last week it began to rumble up the Campbeltown road on its way to Carradale. On Saturday it was at High Ugadale, threshed three stacks in a long morning of brilliant sunshine and came on here, settling down like a couple of elephants under its green tarpaulins in the middle of the stackyard. Then the rain came.

A threshing mill needs a team to work it: three on top feeding in, two forking up to them, two on the sacks where the grain comes out, two or three to build the new straw stack and maybe one to drive away the sacks to the girnal where the corn is to be stored. So somebody comes from every farm that is anywhere near. In return one of you goes to his farm when the time comes. Which means that some woman is worrying about the dinner for the threshers; for one has to make plans ahead for a dinner for twelve hungry men.

Sunday seemed fairly promising, so when I went to milk I took over the joint to Doris, who said she would also see to the soup. Then she gave me a kettle of water to make hot meal for the cow which had just calved. But Catherine wouldn't touch it; she seemed more interested in trying to eat my socks. I wonder how much mental and physical pain cows go through in the process of being useful to us. I hate seeing the little Ayrshire bull calves being tied into sacks and sent off to the butchers: most vegetarianism is built on that.

Monday looked unpromising but the mill men were here at eight. The mill belongs to one of them, and I'm afraid it is much more efficient than the government one ever was! The rain hung off and they opened up the top of the mill, while Lachlan took the thatch off one of the stacks. Joan, who used to be my land girl, had said she wouldn't see me stuck, so in a while she was over with her youngest, a tough young man keen on rocking horses. We put on potatoes, cabbage and stewing apples and I made a rather complex milk pudding, doubling everything in the recipe, putting on my spectacles to read it and taking them off to stir, because they are the kind that keep on dropping into things.

When I went out, the first bags of oats were coming through, nice dry corn, but small. The stack was threshing well, but when we came to the part which had heated at harvest time the grain was discoloured. When things are going well, a sack takes about three minutes to fill, then you drop one shutter and lift another so that corn pours out of a different spout. This gives you time to pleat the mouth of the first sack, tie it with twine and heave it into the trailer. At the other end Eddie and Colin were building the straw stack, catching the bundles of straw as they came off the teeth of the mill. We shall need all that straw for the beasts this winter.

A threshing mill is a very pre-atomic piece of machinery. It is driven off a wobbly belt from a tractor's power drive and is full of moving trays and forks: simple components worked by simple rods and cranks. No bit of it can be said to be streamlined; there is no stainless steel, and, for that matter, very little paint. But it does its job, though the trays are apt to get clogged with damp stuff. Once the rain came on so hard that we fetched the tarpaulin and put it back on the stack. Then it eased off and Lachlan finished pitching off that stack. There are very few rats so far. They come in winter and the February threshing is enlivened – for those who like it – by rat massacres.

MacKinnon from Ugadale had come, brother to our MacKinnons at Auchnasavil, who are renowned for their beautiful ploughing. There was one of the Patersons, a Strang boy and Johnnie MacLean; but with the weather the way it was, it didn't seem worth while getting the rest of the Glen. We went in to our dinner, talking about Princess Margaret and how hardly the poor lassie had been done by and maybe she would scarcely have the heart to eat her own dinner.[1] My pudding was like an English débutante: nice texture but no particular taste. Still, they finished it. Then the rain really came on; there was nothing doing in the afternoon. All night it was battering round the house. But the morning came with the clouds clearing raggedly, and by nine the Glen had come down in force, with Rory handsome in his red jersey, Dunkie with his aged pipe, and another MacKinnon; and the mill started up. We got through two stacks and a small one, the odds and ends that had been left over from the last field. All went without a hitch. Clouds hung among the hills, but not a drop came our way. Would I have the dinner early and then they would move on to the Baker's for the afternoon? They would get his past and be away up to Auchnasavil by the evening.

I rushed on another pudding and Joan set-to on the potatoes. By mid-morning the beautiful golden straw stack was towering eight feet above the mill. It will settle down, though, to half its height, and we shall feed it all out before the next threshing of the last two stacks. These small, northern stacks thresh at about a ton-and-a-quarter each, say four tons altogether for the three-and-a-bit stacks. It looks like good feeding oats. We shall bruise some for the milk cows, use some for the old horse and the hens – but the deep litter hens need their own special feed – and get some ground at the water-mill out beyond Campbeltown[2] for our own porridge. Sowing oats will be from the next threshing. But I don't see us having any to sell this year, unless the odd bag for some of our hen-keeping neighbours.

Not long after eleven the driving belt slowed down and the mill men started shutting up the flaps, pulling out the trays, for all the world like big kitchen sieves, and shaking out the chaff. The tractor pulled it slowly out of the stackyard and we took in the last of the corn sacks. I'd be glad if, at Dunkie's age, I could still carry a hundredweight of corn on my shoulders. At dinner there was much amiable wrangling about where the mill was to go next, Rory and Johnnie each saying their own potatoes were the best. It struck me that this was exactly what the Chinese call a 'mutual aid team'. Funny, how embarrassing we should find it to call ourselves anything of the kind! But that was just what we were. In the end they all went off cheerily to an afternoon at the Baker's, Lachlan going from here with our tractor, which is always a great help for carrying the corn sacks. The weather is coming from a clear sky now. If it stays in the same airt we shall get the whole of the threshing through this week.

The New Statesman and Nation, v. 50, 26 November 1955, p. 700

---

1 Princess Margaret had just announced that she would not, as strongly rumoured, marry the divorced Group Captain Peter Townsend.
   There was a popular perception, evidently held in Carradale, that she had been persuaded or pressured into the decision.

2 Probably at Machrimore, near Southend, though there was also a water-mill at Tangy, north of Campbeltown.

Think of a Number

(1956)

I meant to write about the turn of the year in mud and frost, the tractor bogging at the gate, the turnips too hard stuck for the beasts to pull. I mean to write about spring plans – Lachlan and I looking at the lists of seeds and fertilisers, a good deal depressed at the steady rise in price of practically everything we need. Those worries and unpleasantnesses are very definite; they get into one's dreams. But my main depression, the thing that brings me nearest to just sitting down and screaming, is the farm accounts. I try and try to put down everything. Or at least I seem to myself to try, but possibly my subconscious with its profound dislike for arithmetic (matched by its distaste for anything connected with money, which was so unladylike when I was a girl) keeps on losing the account book at the critical moment. Besides, one does quite a bit of swopping and what we in the Highlands call obligements; and nobody who clings to the old ways will be in a hurry to send in the bill. I get a few lambs from Dunkie every year and have the greatest difficulty in getting him to admit that I owe him anything at all. On the other hand, anyone in the country who has a small business and not much capital is feeling the credit squeeze now. Odd, to think of the misery which Tory policy is causing to just those small exponents of private enterprise whom it would have us believe it loves and cherishes.

Even with a Labour Chancellor, I suppose I should have to do my farm accounts and valuations, and fill up that depressing buff form which is enough to arouse guilty feelings in an archangel. Dick asks me if I am sure I have put everything in. No, I say, I'm not sure, how can I be sure, this isn't the sort of thing I ought to be expected to be sure about. Then suddenly I remember I never put in the painting of the sheds. It was done by an outside contractor. I paid him out at the sheds and before I'd got back to the account book, something no doubt intervened; so that never got itself in.

There is always a fantastic amount for repair and upkeep, partly because when I took over eighteen years ago the place had been neglected for years. At least it looks like a farm now; and every year whatever profit I may have made goes for some essential farm implement. These count as capital expenditure and go on the back of the buff form. You get depreciation on them, and altogether they seem to be morally superior. This year I got a new mower to replace the old second-hand one which was always going wrong. The old henhouse was falling to bits round the hens and beyond repair, so I had to get a new one; and finally I got a roller of my own because, although I have been borrowing one all these eighteen years, it is handy to have one of one's own. But everything seems to be so dear to buy, and one doesn't seem to get the cost back on what one sells. I know I am bad at the business of buying and selling. I don't watch the markets and consider price trends; and I suppose only the farmers who do that are the successful ones. My main farm profits are cattle. My few sheep show a profit too; and there are odd sales of potatoes, wool, milk, eggs, articles for the *New Statesman* and so on. And then, of course, there are the subsidies.

If I had a few fields of good land – deep, rich earth like Northamptonshire – I wouldn't need the subsidies. But I would have to be a better farmer; for on rich, heavy land one has to choose the exact moment and weather for cultivation. Our casual Highland ways would leave the ground in a mess. But with good farming, decent land produces a crop that pays for itself. Up here we are almost or quite 'marginal', which is the justification for subsidies – unless one is going to argue that much of the marginal land would be better under forest. The unfortunate thing is that subsidies go equally to the farmer on land which doesn't need them; so some economically silly and wrong results turn up. For instance, lowland farms should be buying young store cattle from the upland and seaboard breeding areas, and finishing them off for market. But now, with the calf-rearing subsidy, they have taken to breeding calves themselves.

I get the calf-rearing subsidy, the hill cattle subsidy and the TT subsidy. We in Kintyre are rather proud of being one of the first 'designated areas', where there is no bovine tuberculosis. By now there are quite a number of such areas, and the standards of cleanliness are high. It makes me wonder if the policy of pasteurising and homogenising, or whatever wonderful thing it is they do to town milk, is justified. Personally I can't drink London milk and don't like even cooking with it. But all my subsidies together – there are others on lime and fertilisers, ploughing up and some kinds of improvement – don't come to one man's wages. And wages are, of course, the main thing on the debit side of the account. They would look even larger if I charged for myself. Then, again, one has to set off what goes into the house, which is a good deal better in quality than what one would be likely to buy for the same money. I suppose if I didn't have such a hungry – or is it greedy? – family and such a lot of friends, I might be selling more. But then, would I find such an easy market? All this gets into the realm of economics. Some people believe in economics; other people believe in fairies. I can't say economics is my first choice.

After the valuation (and my poor bull's leg is still swollen so I have had to depreciate him quite a lot) and the cash paid out and cash received and the allowances, it remains to consider debts owing and debts owed. On the one side there are a few dozen eggs; on the other solider things like the tractor fuel and Dunkie's lambs. But should I really count Dunkie's lambs as something owed, seeing he wouldn't dream, dear Dunkie, of sending me a bill for them? Better to shut one's eyes and think of a number – possibly doubling it. If only Dick won't ask me if I'm sure it's the right one!

The New Statesman and Nation, v. 51, 11 February 1956, pp. 144, 146

The cash-book for Carradale House Farm and Garden, 1941-59, is among Mitchison's papers in the National Library of Scotland, Acc. 9054.

The Cow and the Calf

(1956)

The cow had calved early in the day, a big whitish bull calf. In other years she had calved out in the field, with no trouble, but it was a cold, nasty day, and we thought she would do better in her stall until she had cleaned. So far she had very little milk. But now it was time for the afternoon milking; she had cleaned all right and her udder looked full. The veins were swelling. But she had hunched herself up right against the head of the stall, which was the end one of my little byre. When a cow gets to her feet she pitches forward slightly and this she could not do; her neck was twisted half round already.

We talked to her encouragingly: 'Come on, Vicky,' we said, 'Come on – hup, girl!' But Vicky shivered and rolled her eyes and bellowed a little and lay with her back firmly against the concrete partition of the stall. Vicky is a cow of character, as befits a V-day calf with a nice V sign on her brown and white Ayrshire face. At last Lachlan said: 'I'll need to get a rope on her.' He went off while I tried again to persuade Vicky to make an effort and listened to the pitiful bleating of the calf from the calf-pen next door.

He and Eddie came back with a rope, and a sack which they put over the middle to soften it. Then they got it round her chest. Immediately she got one leg over it and it had to be hauled out from under and the thing started again. I suppose a large Ayrshire cow weighs half a ton; we heaved and panted and things remained as they were; her hay bed was full of dung and blood and she went on trembling. I tried to get one of her hind legs back so that she could get a better grip on the floor; her udder was hot and hard to touch.

Lachlan moved the rope to a better position; we hauled again. Suddenly she seemed to realise what it was all about, let her hind legs slide back, and stood up mountainously, still very agitated. We tried to get her to take a drink, but no. I began to hand-milk her, while Lachlan brought in the other two cows. They stood in the doorway tossing their horns, worried by the mess in the grip and the smell of blood. However, they quieted down to the familiar hum of the milking machine, while I went on milking Vicky, trying not to get my head right into her flanks, which were plastered with dung. She was as quiet as a rocking horse, and when I had got half a pail of the thick yellow milk full of colostrum for the calf, I put on the milking machine. I wanted to get the rest of the milk for the house, to make into what we call 'beestie cheese'.[1]

The calf was very wild and strong for its age and with little idea of drinking. I got it into a corner and started it sucking at my fingers, then gradually got in a little milk. When it was really drinking its tail started wagging. A calf always has to be taught to drink from a pail. I was feeding it all that weekend and by Sunday evening it had the idea and would get its muzzle down into the pail and suck, though sometimes one would have to give it a finger to encourage it. I held the pail between my knees, and it butted into me, feeding, with its round muzzle and little blunt head.

The evening wasn't too cold, so we let Vicky out with the rest of the cows. She had stopped trembling and only gave an occasional bellow. Lachlan cleaned out the byre. Now that summer is coming and the cows are out at night we shall tidy it up and give it a new coat of Snowcem inside. And the little bull calf? Well, in the ordinary way we send them off in a sack in the back of the bus to Campbeltown, where they are slaughtered. But I decided to feed this one to six or eight weeks and then have it slaughtered for veal for ourselves. I shall be doing the same for one of the pigs; we shall get nice young pork and ham. They can all go in along with a yeld cow which I am now fattening a bit, so that she will grade better. A nasty business: yes. And nasty, essentially, in our own minds.

Lachlan had been killing a sheep. We have a humane killer. 'But a sheep's not just the same,' he said, making sure that I would be sending the calf in to the slaughterhouse and not expecting him to kill it. I said that maybe the calf would like to have the extra six weeks of life. The nasty bit was in our own minds, feeding the young beast and then betraying it to death. I feel rather the same about the pigs, which are attractive creatures enough. I don't like to be about when the pig is loaded up for Campbeltown. But Lachlan has to be. And anyway, with a calf, there is the curious bond of hand feeding. Yet, if the bull calves were not slaughtered, there would not be the milk which even our vegetarians drink. Nor is it much better to kill them as steers, even if it wrings the heart less.

I don't know what the answer is. Our whole attitude towards animals is unethical. Yet the alternative, Indian, one does allow cattle to be half-starved – though perhaps they are no worse off at that than their masters – and to die lingeringly of disease and broken bones. And everything is made to depend on our own attitude. We are brutal enough with rats, fish and hens, which do not appeal to the human heart; and I have yet to hear of the RSPCA interfering with an angler dragging a salmon around by a hook in its throat, though there would be a fuss if it was done in a laboratory. But we worry about animals which appeal to the child in us. You will notice that, in a Disney nature film, small, furry animals always escape.

Meanwhile, the calf has stopped bleating, though it is impatient enough for its dinner. The Easter calf, a pretty little quey, is out in the field with the cows, bouncing around, standing on its head with pleasure. Its mother occasionally smells at it but does not recognise it. And Vicky is milking well and looking in the best of health; she barely turns her head at the calf's bleating. I made my beestie cheese; one flavours it with salt or sugar and leaves it in a slow oven to bake. It comes out as a stiff custard, and those who like it at all are apt to like it very much. But hardly anyone from a town has ever tasted it. When they are told what it is made of, they may even find the idea rather revolting. When it comes to anything to do with animals we all behave rather irrationally because we are all rather guilty.

The New Statesman and Nation, v. 51, 9 June 1956, pp. 648, 650

[1] A dish made from the beestings, the first milk from a cow after calving.

Rough Weather

(1956)

Last year was a light crop of hay and fine weather. For once we didn't even have to turn the rows. They dried sweetly and were ready to put up after two days' sun. This year we had a heavy crop, full of clover and thick, strawy grass, even on the sown-out field, which seemed as bare as a desert when we took the nurse crop of oats off it last September. This year it was not easy weather, even for cutting the hay, and we were well into July before the first field was finished.

Everything had to be turned. I came back from the PEN Congress and blistered the inside of my thumb quick enough with the rake handle. Now I'm hard-handed again, but if this rain goes on … Sheneval, the upper field, is half cut. The rains began when the cutting was on, so there is a patch left, getting brown and seedy, the red clover like bushes. The cut hay has young grass growing through it already, so that raking will be extra hard.

The first field is in small conical ricks – the pikes of the west country. We rope these as we put them up, twisting the end of the stack ropes round a wisp of hay pulled out as in the start of a hay rope, but the next day they are slack and have to be tightened again. Round Tarbert they are netted with old fishing net and in some places one puts an opened-out sack over the top for extra protection. After our worst gales one or two had their tops off, but they should stand without getting too much rainwater blown into them. They need to wait at least a fortnight before we bring them into the stack-yard. There are forty of them in the Mains field, three big stacks, we hope, which means about two tons to the acre. This is a light crop on the national average, but better than average for our poor soil. Before we get them off the field there will be a heavy aftermath of new grass growing round them.

I had a lovely oat crop standing green and high in the lower part of the Mains field. It is 'Forward', a comparatively new oat which did well in the Kintyre field trials. It stood the first rain but now it is beginning to go down in the corners. It would be worse but that this field catches any wind there is and dries out quickly. But, as the rain goes on with autumnal force, I get more and more gloomy about its prospects. Between here and Campbeltown all the barley and half the oats are flat as though they'd been rolled on.

It all means so much more work, first the hay, then the corn. All the laid oats will have to be scythed out and bound by hand, a wet and back-breaking job. These hand-bound sheaves are the worst to dry when they are stooked, needing more shifting. And the coarse, much wetted, hay loses a lot of its feeding value. Some of this could be avoided by having silage and I keep thinking about the possibility. It is easy enough if there is a fairly dry piece of sloping land close to the steading, where one can dig out a pit silo and line it with cement. But my only bit of hill in the corner of Sheneval is not only very wet, but faces straight on to the main road which in summer, when one would be making silage, is full of car traffic. I would have to have a built-up silo, which is much more expensive and less easy to make a success of.

The old horse, now twenty-three years old, worked quite hard in the rake. I did the last bit of raking in the Mains field and brought him in by myself. It was so long since I had unharnessed him that I had quite forgotten what came first, and in fact the harness is very old and full of unexpected bits of rope fastening this to that. But Jo, tossing his head and making faces at me, managed to convey what I ought to do. He is very rheumatic, poor dear, but looks well and occasionally frolics ponderously.

When he has raked the hay into rows we pick it up with a 'tumbling tom' on the back of the Land Rover. But the Land Rover has a habit of getting hay wound round its most intimate guts and then we all have to crawl under it with knives. I have now got a buck rake to go at the back on the Ferguson tractor, and one of my neighbours is going to lend me a swathe-turner, which will first turn the hay and then, at the change of a gear, sweep two rows into one, ready for the buck rake. It would be nice if we could combine more with our instruments; and we are all willing, but the weather forces us all to use them at the same time. I may have to get a swathe-turner for myself – I can't think that Jo has much more work in him. But I am chipping in on one labour-saver: a scarifier and gapper which cleans the turnip drills up to the level of the seedlings and then knocks out gaps so that thinning is much easier. In past years thinning has been a tinker's job, but our local tinker family is going to Corby to work on steel instead of turnips. Some of my turnips were thinned by the skipper of a herring boat – one of the beautiful Clyde ring-netters, but got with a government grant and loan, which means that the Herring Industry Board has its eye on every shilling the skipper-owner can make. No herring in Kilbrannan Sound: no herring at the Isle of Man: chancy herring in the Minch and money to pay out before you get there. But insurance and interest mounts up and a paternal government is ready with the big stick.

Tarbert fair was wet, too. There was nothing faintly attractive about the draggled stalls with their coconuts and shoddy tableware prizes. Lachlan and I gave them a look over while we were waiting for our beasts to come up at the sale. I had seven Galloway bullocks and three Ayrshire queys in. But they came late in the sale and the prices were disappointing, especially for the three bigger bullocks, a nice little lot, but they only went to £73 10s. With beef prices the way they are, someone is going to make a good thing out of them after a few months' finishing. The yeld Galloway cow which I had fattened on grass alone did much better at the Campbeltown grading market.

I can never see myself getting good at the buying and selling side of farming. And just the same, some of my fishermen friends who are keen and hard working and good at their job will never be any use at the business side of it. And the Herring Industry Board, with its good old *laissez-faire* admiration of economic man at his most business-like, will judge these men accordingly and – unless it can be brought home to them that there are other criteria – weigh down the balance against them with a heavy fist.

The New Statesman and Nation, v. 52, 25 August 1956, p. 212

The Buck Rake

(1956)

It went on raining. Everything was soaked and battered, though my oats still had strength enough not to go down all over. In the occasional intervals we managed to get all the hay up into little ricks, though some of it was not in such good order as we should have liked. Then a storm would blow the heads off the ricks or knock them crooked. Sometimes one could shove the head on again with a fork and tighten the ropes, sometimes they had to be rebuilt. A thick aftermath of grass and clover grew up round them. If only we could get the cows on to it!

Then on Sunday it cleared. There was a heavy dew and no sense in starting early. I was feeling a bit upset because, after milking, I had gone out to feed the pigs, and there was the girl pig lying dead and dreadfully human looking from behind. Blood poisoning, the vet said, after testing for anthrax and finding it negative – but why should a pig that was perfectly well in the evening die of blood poisoning in the night?

By now I had my new buck rake on the back of the Ferguson tractor. Ideally I should have had two implements, a hay rake, to replace the old horse rake, and a rick lifter, fairly narrow with long prongs. But on a small farm like this it is quite uneconomic to get all the instruments one would like; and I felt this would have to do the job of both. First of all, we were surprised to find what a clean job it made of raking the windrows of hay. Lachlan was doubtful if it would lift the bigger ricks. But it manages, with weights on the front wheels of the tractor to balance it. The only difficulty is that there is the barest clearance through our farm gates, which, even so, are much widened from what they were when we came here, twenty years ago almost. I wouldn't much like bringing a load in myself, but Lachlan and Colin seem to have unerringly straight eyes where gates are concerned.

We started bringing the ricks into the stackyard from Mains field where they had been up more than a month. Some of them were wet in the head, with hay seed growing green, and sometimes wet and blackened in the south-west side where the gales had come from. Once we found that they were coming in safely, we developed a new system. In the old days two or three people had to be in the field to fork and load into a trailer – we used to have two trailers going at once if there were enough helpers. Then the trailers were forked off again on to the stack when they had been driven into the stackyard. But now our pattern was different. Colin went alone to the field, edged the buck rake in under the rick, tied it on and raced back with it. The rest of us concentrated on forking on and building. This way we must have halved the time this particular farm operation took.

Any really efficient bit of machinery must alter methods of working, setting its own pattern; the problem is to adapt oneself quickly. This, for instance, meant that there had to be two stack-builders to make the most of the hay coming in. Those forking on could also keep an eye on the stack, see that it was going up straight, point out a light corner where more had to go on, tug out a piece here or there and rake down the sides. They must also put in the stack props, so that the built stacks would settle evenly.

I have not done much stack building, because in other years I was usually driving one of the trailers. However it became clear that this must be my part of the new pattern. I cannot manage the really skilled part, the drawing in of the head of the stack, which ends with the builder on a ladder combing down the head with a rake. While Lachlan was doing this on one stack, I was building the lower part of its neighbour. A couple of friends were helping; in order to fork up to the head of Lachlan's stack, one had to stand on the trailer, which was now acting as scaffolding. Eddie forked up, while Roddie and Taggy forked from the little ricks, either to him or me. I moved round my stack tramping the hay as I went, doubling the long trails of hay, shoving the wetter bits on to the outside where they would do no harm, shaking the drier bits into the centre, getting the tickly hay seed into my hair and sticking all over me, so that the clothes I took off at night still smelt of hay in the morning.

When Lachlan's stack was finished he climbed down and went on with mine. The two of us building went up quick, level with the branches of the big pines. The tractor raced across the fields below us, trailing the dirty skirts of the lifted ricks. We broke off for tea. The evening church-goers ambled by, not, I think, any longer shocked by Sunday work. Then the midges came out. But we had the field finished off before dusk.

There is plenty of time for talk during hay and harvest. We all work hard, but there are bound to be breaks in one part of the work pattern or another, both when we are gathering the hay in the field and when we are bringing it in. This year, I think, we tended to talk about the Queen's visit,[1] and not with enthusiasm. I wonder how much the newspapers that write up the royal doings are aware of an increasing resentment and irritation among their readers? 'Aye, going too far altogether,' says Wal, shaking his head as he passes a rope carefully over one of the ricks. And this last visit, among places and people that we in the west know well, has considerably reduced royal popularity. We realise that ex-servicemen, wounded in the first war perhaps, but humble and ordinary, have been passed by, while jumped-up, successful so-and-sos have been presented and photographed. The kind-hearted feel that she has been ill advised, the poor woman, but others are beginning to come to the conclusion that the whole thing is a pack of nonsense and not worth the money that is being spent on it.

However, the weather and our neighbours' doings are still the most important. In the middle of the rains the river suddenly flooded, worse than it has ever been. Duncan had some sheep swept away. His hay was draped over fences that are ordinarily far enough from the river bank. Rory had to wade for his trailer, which was nearly carried away. We are all, I think, sorry for one another's difficulties, glad when things go right. We know the hard work that goes into what has to be done. And we respect it.

The New Statesman and Nation, v. 52, 22 September 1956, p. 340

[1] The royal family sailed up the west coast of Scotland in *Britannia* in several summers at this time, and in August 1956 had visited many of the islands.

The Price of a Binder

(1956)

In the west, the grass still goes on growing late into the back-end of the year, blue-green and cold and soaked. There may not be much feeding value in it, yet the cows still give a very high butter-fat content in their milk. Like most farms in Kintyre we are all set for the winter work, tattooing the calves, getting the dung out onto the fields, doing all the clearing up and tidying that has had to wait over harvest. It's the time, too, when next year's problems begin to take shape.

I bought my binder, reconditioned, some ten seasons back; before that I used to hire from the government depot – an endless nuisance, for it never came just when one wanted it. But now, in spite of new spares hurriedly telephoned for and sent on by plane, it is always having minor breakdowns. There was one evening in harvest when I knocked off at seven o'clock, in time for a village hall management committee, but was uneasily aware that two committee members were still at work on that binder, all because we were stuck for an hour in the afternoon.

So I've got to get, not only a small swathe-turner and hay-rake to replace my old horse rake, but also a binder. Like a true West Highlander by adoption, I always look the other way when financial trouble approaches, hoping it will have disappeared when I look round again. But the price of a new binder with a power drive – I shall need that in the next ley field, which is likely to be damp and put too much strain onto a wheel drive – remains inexorably at over £300. A reconditioned one might be less, but I'm afraid nobody in his senses will take my old binder in part exchange.

How necessary is harvest in the farm economy? I can't make up my mind. In many parts of the Highlands they cut the corn green to make hay, or, better, silage, concentrating on plenty of winter feed for more young cattle, whose selling price will pay for hen's meal instead of the oats that mine get as their main food. Equally, cattle cake will be bought in, instead of the crushed oats we give the dairy cows. One wouldn't, of course, have one's own delicious locally ground oatmeal for porridge, but, after all, there are all kinds of breakfast food in packets.

If corn is cut green, it needs only a mower. And that I have. So where do I go? What do I set against the price of a binder? I have an uneasy feeling that it is better national economics to grow one's own hen and cattle food as far as possible, rather than encourage the millers to take all the good out of our white loaves and re-sell us the remains at a high price. And then, I like harvest.

That, in a way, is rather peculiar. Evening after evening one is frantically tired, arms and back aching, watching the evening sky with worry, shaking one's head over the weather report, saying that this BBC crowd never know a thing about *our* weather. One finds oneself quite unable to think about Suez[1] and the future of the Labour Party; Critic's Diary is far too intellectual at harvest time – oh, am I beginning to arrive at why I like harvest? Isn't it that, for a time, one is concentrated on one apparently worthwhile and also attainable end? Attainable by struggle, by primitive human exertion and in companionship. This year I had a particularly enthusiastic crowd of visitors – surely it wasn't all just being polite to their hostess! They pitchforked nobly, drove the Land Rover with *élan*, and learnt quickly to distinguish between a damp sheaf and a dry one. Most people, I think, enjoy learning and using a new skill.

Ordinary agricultural work can be solitary. A day's ploughing, satisfactory in a way, may mean nobody to exchange a word with for hours. You can't even talk to a tractor the way you could to a horse. But harvest is all in a crowd. Even Lachlan on the stack, comparatively isolated, is the king of a busy stackyard, with the trailer loads coming in, Colin or Eddie forking, and Wal keeping the stack, that is to say going round the stack as it is building, knocking the butts of the sheaves in with a spade or a flat piece of wood on a handle, occasionally pulling one out a little, warning the builder if he is a wee bit light here or there, and putting in the props so that the whole thing doesn't shift before it settles.

Things went well. There are twelve nice stacks in the yard. The corn was in good order; one stack started heating slightly, but, with a couple of sheaves pulled out and a prop put in to open it up to the breeze, it cooled down quickly. Now the golden-brown stacks are thatched with green, glistening rushes, carefully tied down with stack rope, except for the ones which will be threshed soon; these have just a piece of fishing net over them. We can always make good use of any old piece of net the fishermen have done with.

It is the same all over Kintyre, though some of the corn was very difficult to cut where it went down after the July storms. We all made the most of the few days of good weather, working on until late. We could still see to pick up the sheaves in the field and pitch them in and the Land Rover could wobble over the road with headlights on and the dark heavy load behind, yet it was too dark to go on building and the last load had to be left with a tarpaulin over it, to start off the next morning. We all knew enough about conditions elsewhere to be very grateful for these few bright days.

As soon as the corn was off the ley field, Lachlan opened the gate to the Bay and drove in the Galloways. There was a good deal of corn lying which the binder had missed; it was grand feeding and set the spring calves on to box one another. Then I bought in some three score of lambs at the Tarbert sale and put them onto the second stubble field, but didn't leave them there too long in case they would tear up the young under-sown grass, in the way that sheep do. As soon as we got the ricks of hay off Sheneval – and we started on them as soon as the corn was in – we got the lambs onto the long green aftermath, just the thing for fattening up a hill lamb for the November sales.

Dunkie was a bit behind with his harvest, and not, indeed, for the first time. We went up the glen and gave him a day. We'll spin out Wal's potatoes with our machine in a morning. Then we shall borrow Duncan's tattooing iron for our calves, and so it goes. Lachlan says we should be doing more yet for one another and it is cheerier so. Meanwhile Dunkie has given me one of his black lambs, because I'm one for black sheep!

But what about the binder? I shall have hay enough to sell, but then, everyone round here had a huge hay crop so there is no local market. There will be corn to sell next month after the mill has been round. But again, the buyers will be on the mainland and my sacks of corn have to go more than a hundred miles by lorry before they get to the man who will pay for them; and that is a journey that takes a fat slice of the price off. So I doubt if the price of a binder will come out of that.

If I am lucky with the lambs there should be a profit there. I bought in more than usual just because I had so much extra grass; but then, so did everyone else and the auction prices rose accordingly, so that, for instance, some of the cross lambs – blackface mother and Border Leicester father – fetched nearly as much as their ultimate grading price. So I'm still left swithering about the new binder.

The New Statesman and Nation, v. 52, 3 November 1956, pp. 544-5

[1] The Suez crisis in October 1956, when British and French troops entered the Canal Zone.

Threshing in Carradale

(1956)

The big threshing mill has been working its way down the Glen, beginning right up at Auchnareoch and ending with me. We have had good enough weather, praise be. The wireless says there will be rain soon, but what do we care now? For the girnals are full and the big straw stacks built to feed the young beasts all winter. Most of us have cattle out-wintered and, in the early winter at least, this oat straw has good feeding in it; what they don't eat they will trample down to dung, back into the land.

A man comes from every farm, and the one where the mill is working provides a lavish dinner, soup, meat, pudding, and strong cups of tea. Some are pitching on from the stacks, some cutting the ties of the sheaves up on top of the mill, some building the straw stack with the battels of straw that come out at the tail of the mill, some filling the corn sacks at the front of the mill and taking them away, others just standing about. I'm one of the standers about, but one helps to hook on the corn sacks, and I put my hands up to the wrist in the generous flow of grain that fills a sack almost as quickly as it can be tied, with a skilful pleating of the neck, and a new one hooked on. There is only a trickle of seconds, especially when we get on to the stacks of new corn. This is 'Forward', an oat that has done well at the trials and that did well with me, standing up to storms, and with a very heavy head.

When they came in for their dinner everyone was speaking about the Harvest Home dance, which we shall have in the village hall to-night. It is the great dance of the year, none of your ladylike town dances, but two sweating accordionists and a set of drums, and the hard dances following one another, reels and three-steps, barn dances and strip the willow, till, by two in the morning, one feels exhausted and yet, in a queer way, light as a dancing leaf.

Johnnie is saying he would like to have something to announce – an engagement, maybe. I look round; there are one or two likely boys, but they only titter. Talk goes on to the *cailleach*, the last sheaf which I have standing in a corner of the kitchen. For my own part I feel that it is most appreciated by the mice, or even the birds which come in through the kitchen window as bold as brass. What should I do with it, I ask. It is generally agreed that it ought to go to the oldest horse. I have no choice, as my one and only horse is very old; indeed, he is past work, and his main useful purpose seems to be to stand in the stall next to the battery hens, generating a fine warmth for them. But when? At the first ploughing? That might be, but the general idea seems to be New Year's Day or maybe Burns Night.

I wonder when Burns Night began to be part of the farm calendar. It would surprise Robbie well enough. Of course, it is somewhere near the old New Year,[1] so maybe it has taken over. I catch myself wondering if some day people, even in Scotland, will have forgotten altogether who or what Burns was, but will still talk about his night as a mark in the year.

But, to return to the horse problem, almost all the ploughing round here is done with a tractor nowadays, and you can't give a tractor the last sheaf.

I churned yesterday and felt a bittie anxious as to whether these good judges would pass my butter. But it seems to be well thought of. I was using one of the wooden prints which Johnnie's grandfather made in the old days, and which Johnnie passed on to me, for nowadays the Brackley milk all goes to the creamery on the big lorry. The print has a cow's head, more of a Highlander than an Ayrshire I would say, with *Direach chon Fhraoch*[2] round it. I am not quite sure about milk coming straight from the heather, but it makes a handsome butter pat. There is another, even prettier print beautifully carved with rose, shamrock and thistle, but rather harder to use. What pride and pleasure it must have been to carve these prints up at Brackley, no doubt in the long winter evenings, before the days of wireless when the dark hours were full of singing, and Gaelic at that. For it is only in the past fifty years that Carradale has become completely Lowland in speech, though still with an odd Gaelic tag here and there. It was Johnnie's sister Jemima who taught me all I know of butter making, and she sang like a bird during the churning.

It is wonderful how quickly the stacks go down. It seems no time since we were building them, and the last couple of stacks none too dry. One of the stacks started to heat a little, but we pulled out a sheaf here and there to let the breeze through, and it was all right. They are rather too much under tree branches, but it is none too easy to find the right place for a stackyard, open and yet with access and dry ground round them, so that the heavy mill will not bog.

Meanwhile, the hens and runner ducks are having a real picnic. They are as pleased as the rest of us. For this marks one stage, and an important, a satisfactory one, in the farm year. The golden grain of the harvest is truly in now, waiting to be turned back into other life.

The Glasgow Herald, 24 November 1956, p. 3

[1] Old New Year: 12th January, still celebrated in some parts of Scotland.

[2] Correctly, *direach bhon fraoch* (Gaelic, straight from the heather).

Summer Work

(1957)

Any farm needs more labour in the summer. It doesn't matter how mechanised it is – unhappily the silly old machines don't work by themselves.It might be easier on a single crop farm, or it may be possible to shift crops and methods so that things are easier. But on our local type of traditional mixed farm, machinery makes work quicker and lighter, but doesn't end it. If we grow turnips, kale or carrots, all very useful crops, they have to be singled. A scarifier makes this much easier, but the gapper, doing one row at a time very slowly, has not proved itself worth while.

In the old days there were always the tinkers for the thinning, but the two main tinker families have now left. One of them is working in Corby, at the steel works. The sons have all done their army service, and the combined family income must be around £30 or £40 a week. I wonder what Bridget does with it. She used to keep the neatest possible tent on wattle hoops, where I helped her to bath her bead-hung babies. But I suppose she has dropped into the pattern of another income group. I only hope she has enlarged her cookery ideas. But probably she just gets lots and lots of tins.

However, there is spare labour this year for the thinning. We are in a bad way at Carradale. This used to be one of the most prosperous fishing villages of the west coast. It is so no longer. We have had a series of bad seasons, with no local herring. It is not the first time in history this has happened, but, earlier on, we managed to scrape through. This time the skipper-owned boats, which do not have to pay insurance, have just managed; but most of these are old and battered – will they be replaced even when we get our new harbour? Or are we merely one of the doomed fringes in the modern pattern of occupation, which gathers the old family units of production into bigger and more efficient and more highly capitalised centres, taking both the risk and the profit away from the individual and putting them into the hands of big companies or the state?

We aren't mad on the state here, having had a very poor deal from the Herring Industry Board, which started by financing a number of grant and loan boats on the Clyde and then, when they had got far in arrears with their payment, foreclosed on them. The fishermen, like the tinkers, have to go to Corby, leaving their hills and their sea, probably for ever. It is not as far as Nova Scotia was last century in an earlier clearance. Presumably it is not a forced movement of population, but merely a bit of economics. Still, we who are in the middle of it feel rather bitterly about the Herring Industry Board. They, being the principal creditors, scooped most of what could be got out of the forced sales. Local creditors, small businesses who can ill afford the loss and who went on giving the boats credit so that they could at least go out and fish, are left with debts which will never be paid. The boat in which I had a third share[1] sold for a better price; we had kept her up. We paid the Board and our creditors and are left with nothing – only the pain it is when the other boats are out and not our own. A beauty gone from our lives; a nagging reminder of the last interview with the then Secretary of the Board. Probably it was quite good for me being treated as the under-dogs have been treated throughout history; all the same it was rather a shock. When it was over I sat down and cried on the granite steps of the Board's Edinburgh office. But it was not good for the fishermen; they do not have the *hubris* that needs that kind of punishment.

So my turnips have been thinned by fishermen and one or two forestry workers in the evenings. They got through three acres at a good pace and cheerfully. This has cost just over £19, which compares well with other years. But the poor little turnips are sagging for want of rain. That isn't the only job that takes several people. This year I had over fifty hoggs bought in as lambs in autumn at the sales. Fifty sheep is a handful, and I had a septic thumb, so I couldn't help. Not that I would have been a good shearer; it is nearly ten years since I last did any shearing. That was the year I had tried running a small ewe flock and had a handsome and arrogant Border Leicester ram called Philip, who used to follow me into the house demanding pieces of bread. I duly sheared Philip but, when I turned him loose white and clean, he stamped and shouted at me in fury at the indignity and wouldn't come near me again for days.

However, the shearing went very well; two of the neighbours from up the glen, Rory from Auchanfraoch and Johnnie, Dunkie's brother from Kilmichael, came over, each with his own bench, shears and hone. Lachlan had already started, and a few of the sheep were capering about, very white after their grey and sordid months. Eddie hauled them over, protesting, to the benches and the three shearers got going, each with his own technique – though one always starts by opening the fleece down the front. What struck me is how different the fleeces are since the days of the modern dip. When I sheared, the fleeces were crawling with ticks and keds; now there isn't one to be seen. We scarcely ever get a sheep fly struck nowadays, though ten years back it was a constant summer nightmare, gripping a wretched sheep between one's knees, cleaning out the maggots and running in the dressing.

Rory was the quickest, taking less than five minutes over each sheep, but he has been doing it most of his life. These hoggs were worse to do than his own, as they like to burrow into the sand dunes when they are hot, and the fleeces get full of sand and take the edge off the shears. Each sheep, released, bounces and leaps in the twisty sheep fashion over the bracken. 'They'll be feeling the midges now!' says Rory.

As they come up on to the benches, we look for the marks, the brand on the horn and the nick on the ear which shows where they came from. Johnnie smiles quietly, when we see one of the Kilmichael lambs looking as well now as the ones that ran up to a high price at the Lochgilphead auction. His brother always puts in a wee black one specially for me! Rory advises us to grade the crosses separately. 'You'll be surprised!' he says. I made the mistake of trying some of them for the Christmas market, but I was competing with specially fattened beasts and got bad prices. Rory says we should try a load for the Monday grading in July.

At the end everyone comes up to the house and the beer that has waited in the fridge goes rolling down. It is all a neighbourly way of doing. Lachlan was up the glen the day before; none of us will see the rest stuck if it's a matter of lending a hand. It seems lighter, some way, to do a thing for someone else. One can take one's time and yet, for all that, one is showing off. Work is no longer just the thing which is paid by the hour, but something on its own: a social value.

The New Statesman and Nation, v. 53, 29 June 1957, p. 834

¹ *Maid of Morvern*: see the Fishing section later in this volume.

Beating the Rain

(1957)

The grass was cut earlier this year than I have ever known it, but after the hot, dry spell in June it was fully ripe, and indeed on the sandy bank towards the Bay fence the red clover was withering up. We put it up into pikes in the field, but smaller than usual, so as to be easily lifted by the buck rake. It went altogether easily, for I got a small swathe-turner this year, which did everything we have done other years with palm-blistering rakes, and in half the time it would have taken four or five of us. It costs £70 and can only be used for one job, once a year; but I think it is worth it. I hope, all the same, it is the last piece of machinery I shall have to get for a good while.

We were in no hurry, putting up the pikes, in that spell of dry weather, so early that the astonishing variety of young golden greens from the trees along the road and in Black Hill Wood had not yet melted into the uniformity of summer. Then the rain came and the aftermath grew dark and thick, full of clover. We are anxious to get the cows on to it; their two fields are eaten down, except for thistles and bennyweed, and the milk yield has dropped. I tried a hormone weed-killer on Sheneval, but it must have been too early in the year, before the thistles were up enough to be affected; it is rather disappointing and we must get those thistles out before the next corn crop; last time we had the most unpleasant time stooking thistly sheaves. I must get the cows off Sheneval, too, so as to give the Forestry Commission, my neighbours, a chance to mend the march fence. Part of it is leaning now, and the roe-deer come bouncing over. We never used to have roe, but they hide in the thick plantations. The Forestry Commission don't like them because they eat the tops off the young trees. I like them – especially to eat. They are not the same farmers' headache as the foxes, which are the other main hiders in the plantations and which eat the lambs. It is all a case of who eats who.

So now we have been watching for a good day to put the hay in. The morning is only fair and we put into the shed beside the byre, but in the afternoon it really seems promising and we start taking the pikes out of the stackyard. Colin comes tearing along on the tractor, with the hay neatly up on the buck rake like an untidy old lady with full skirts. Eddie forks it to Lachlan on the stack and is finished by the time the next one comes in. When the stack is six or seven feet high I come over and rake down the sides, and pull out the hay round the bottom, so as to give it a nice overhang. At this stage it is beginning to shape; it must not be allowed to develop hollows or lumps; a badly built stack may come down, and a slight lean at an early stage means a bad lean later on.

I go up on to the top of the stack and tramp it down; the hay is in fine order, sweet and nice coloured. If there is a bit from the bottom of one of the pikes which is damp we put it on to the outside, where it will do no harm. The driest hay goes in the middle. When it gets up a bit farther we take over the trailer and the pike is edged on to that. We work round and round the stack.

From the top we can see into the nest of one of the runner ducks, with eight blue-green eggs. She becomes terribly agitated and leaves it, then comes slowly back, quackishly chattering to herself and weaving her neck from side to side. But now we can also see up the glen, where a curtain of grey has crept across the farthest hillside. Slowly it comes towards us. 'Ach,' they say, 'we'll get on another two or three.' Eddie is keeping us right, holding a rake straight against the side of the stack, so that we can build it out when there is a hollow. 'Am I right?' says Lachlan. 'A wee bit light. Aye, a forkful will do it.'

There are still two of last year's haystacks left, which we shall use first this year for the cattle in the Bay; we are well above the eaves of them. But our own stack will sink a good bit in spite of my tramping. The rain has obscured all the farther hillsides; they look like drawings half rubbed out. Now it is between us and Dippen brae. But there is so little breeze that it will take its time to get our length.

Now Lachlan is beginning to draw the stack in for the head. But will he manage in time? I shout down to Geoffrey to bring over the stack-sheet in case we have to cover her before she's finished. 'Aye,' says Colin, 'there's wee spits coming.'

The rain is close now, over the garden; one can see the texture of it, the drifting, shining drops. I climb down from the narrowing head leaving Lachlan, working quickly but without the hurry that might spoil the shape; the rain is on us now, coming softly through the trees. It is milking-time. I am wondering whether Mistletoe is going to kick the milking machine off, or, alternatively, kick Geoffrey or me. She never seems to kick Lachlan, probably because he doesn't think she is going to. Cows are only too good at thought reading.

When I come back there is the stack finished, combed down, well shaped, with a nice, even head. 'Aye, the rain took off for a wee while and we got her finished.' But when are we going to get another fine day?

The Manchester Guardian, 26 August 1957

Lambs for the Fair

(1957)

But how it rained! Rattle and drum on the tin roof of the auction shed, and the thick sharp smell of sheep and sheep farmers. I had thought that perhaps the weather might have kept off some of the buyers and that blackface lamb prices would have been fairly reasonable – I was wanting some myself. But not at all. The dealers were all there, sitting on the bench that goes inside the ring. It was only the summer visitors who weren't there, the ones who always crowd into the auction shed for the big sale at Tarbert Fair. And naturally, the sellers, wearing black oilskins or black waders and cloth caps, had all come with their lambs.

The lambs weren't looking their best. They had been in the muddy pens for hours. They looked small and bedraggled. I had a hope that their appearance would be reflected in the price. Usually I buy my lambs at one of the later sales, but this year I had taken an early hay crop which had left me with a heavy aftermath, deep green with clover and thick stemmed grasses. There was too much for the cows, and if I left it to grow till the next sale, a month on, it would be too coarse; the lambs wouldn't eat it evenly but would just pick out the young grass and leave the rest. Even if I could get one lot now, it would help.

But the prices were high from the start. Most went to the dealers who were sitting round and indicating their bids apparently by thought transference, for one never saw so much as a finger being raised. The blackface lambs were coming in mixed lots and the bidding went quickly. There were ewe lambs with their pretty little light horns, well set back; there were wedder lambs, thicker and tougher looking; and usually a few riggs with the coarse, heavy horns that show them up. I wanted wedder lambs to fatten and sell later on to the grading market. But so did everyone. In fact, some of the ewe lambs were probably being bought for killing, not for breeding, and the farmers who wanted to buy a few to put out on the hills came away without them.

Most of the Glen were selling; this was the first pick of their lambs. They came into the ring with them and stood impassively, only perhaps a slight moistening of the lips as the price went up a shilling or two, which, of course, on a flock of thirty or forty means something considerable. The lambs leaped and bounced like wave tops, pouring in through one door and out by the other, stirred round with long ash sticks or handsome cromags if they coalesced. At a specially good lot the dealers would rise as one man from the bench and start feeling the lambs' backs, prodding at hindquarters and shoulders, poor little joints of mutton that they are.

Mr Weir, the auctioneer, welcomes us all as friends: it is a family affair. But some are more welcome than others: 'Ah, here's the news you're waiting for, the well-known Dippen lambs – ah, there's grand lambs!' Or again: 'Ah, there's strong lambs – look at that!' 'Straight off the hill – grand keeping lambs!' And then gobble, gobble, gobble as the prices go up, the last moment with the hammer waving. Rory, who is in with his lambs, turns to the desk with his hand up to say something – 'Watch your fingers!' says Mr Weir, and bang goes the hammer. The rest of us smile sympathetically with Rory and the nice price he has got.

Several times a single lamb is put in, usually a hand-reared one, which goes bleating to the nearest human to be stroked and fed. But its end, too, will be mutton, though its price is usually higher than the ordinary blackface lamb off the hill. Sometimes the lamb is the property of the farmer's wife, and, as it mounts up, I think, yes, that'll be her dress for the Young Farmers' Dance.

I only want second-grade lambs: they will grow in time once I get them on to the grass and I am not skilled enough on the selling end to try for Christmas fattening. I bid up two or three lots, finally get a few. They come from a neighbour and I only hope they won't try and get home – but I think not. They'll settle down among my clover.

At the very end of the sale there is a heifer calf, only a day or two old, a pretty little Ayrshire. Someone bids £1 and there is a pause. I lift my hand to Mr Weir and it goes up five shillings. I go on bidding up to £5 and then think that's enough. I hadn't thought of buying one but could manage on the milk I have. Five pounds, however, is all she is worth to me, and the main thing about an auction is to know when to stop. Still, it's a few pounds more to the seller, who is doubtless pleased!

Meanwhile my neighbours from the Glen are in fine fettle and a merry noise comes from the refreshment shed. They are highly pleased with themselves, but I have only half the lambs I want and will have to come back next month to the second sale and go through the whole business again, hoping that then there may be rather more of a buyers' market.

The Glasgow Herald, 31 August 1957, p. 3

Cattle Sales at Oban

(1957)

There is a subtle difference between the looks of the ring at a pedigree Highland sale and a pedigree Galloway sale. The breeders of the Highlanders, with their long silky coats and waving Celtic horns, tend to wear the kilt and carry decorative cromags. We Galloway owners are more likely to have plain sticks and sensible tweeds, or even the black oilskins which are practically uniform for the outlying farmers coming in to Oban with their mixed crosses off MacBrayne's boats, the herds of young beasts which cavort round the last of the summer tourists' cars.

For this is October and the tourists are drifting away like the bright autumn leaves from birch or rowan. The judging for both Galloways and Highland cattle is on a Monday morning, so most of us have broken the Sabbath bringing in our beasts. Both these are hill breeds, wild enough unless they have constant handling. The sedate prize-winners with their carefully combed coats and forelocks, the parting dead straight down the back, have obviously been handled a good deal, and have that extra gloss that comes with a few weeks' feeding with cattle cake. But in the other pens there is occasional turmoil, and Lachlan and I have considerable difficulty in getting the burrs combed out of my Peppermint's woolly ears and curly forelock. This is the first Oban sale of Galloways, and the organisers have taken a lot of trouble over it. Some of these heifers and cows have had a long journey, especially the Duchess of Westminster's handsome beasts from the far north-west. And there are buyers from all over, including the main Galloway country, down round Castle Douglas.

But while we are still combing our reluctant charges the Highland sale is going on. The catalogues for both sales have the full pedigrees of each animal: the Highland pedigrees ring with Gaelic names. The pedigreed darlings step in delicately, sniffing the air which must for them be polluted with humanity, for the ring is packed with buyers and lookers-on. If there are two together they may decide to quarrel, occasionally to charge the barrier, but more likely they wander round smelling at the human hands, hoping perhaps for the associated smell of bread or meal. They are lovely cattle, but not wholly practical, since they are slower maturing than others. The long hair, golden tawny, or deep russet, hanging over their eyes, gives them an air almost of fragility, and there is something of the feel of a flower show or a wine-tasting about the whole ritual. 'From the real old Ardtornish strain,' says Mr Jackson, the auctioneer, nostalgically.

One of my cousins is a breeder of Highlanders, the other of Galloways, both with namely herds, each, perhaps, looking down ever so slightly on the other's choice. My own little cow, Sonas – which means Luck – is related to the Achnacloich Highland beauties, for she is the result of one of those misalliances, inevitable in remote conditions, between a Jersey cow and a Highland bull, himself a prize-winner. She isn't a good milker on quantity, but her rich yellow cream colours my butter in a way that pale Ayrshire milk would never do in autumn. Some of these Neoineans and Baravallas[1] parading in the ring and exciting eager bids are upper-class cousins of hers.

Prices for Highlanders never run up to the fancy figures of the heavy beef breeds, shorthorn or Aberdeen Angus, nor yet of the main milk breeds. Perhaps the Tourist Board should do something about it, for what is a Highland landscape without the appropriate cattle on the skyline or down by the loch side? Galloway prices are higher and the ring as crowded. We take our cattle out of the pens and drive them through a complication of gates and hurdles, none of which they like, until they are in at the back of the ring. Here we do some frantic last-minute combing before going through to face the crowd. From where I am, under the auctioneer's stand, I can't make out where the bids are coming from. Nobody ever seems to want to start the bidding, which usually begins at a sadly low figure; one feels as embarrassed as a parent at a school prize-giving.

At this sale I am the only breeder to have sent in any duns, and I am lucky to have found two dun fanciers, one of them all the way from Oxfordshire, who bid up my dun heifer. The two cows don't do so well; I have half a mind to take them back, and turn to the auctioneer to say so, but this brings out another couple of bids to a reasonably acceptable price. I think myself that whoever got those cows got a bargain, as they have both been running with an Ichrachan bull all summer and are almost certain to be in calf. They are by no means my oldest, and should have a useful five or six years – perhaps longer – of calf-bearing ahead of them.

I stay on, in the hope that one Galloway cow, in from the islands, would go fairly cheap. However, I seem not to have been the only one who thought well of her and her price goes right up. But meanwhile the Oxfordshire bidder has been in touch; he will come over and have a look at my herd the next morning.

So we go back through the evening, and early the next day we get all my beasts together. How much better they look in Carradale Bay among their own rough grass and bracken than they did in the Oban ring! Lachlan and I keep saying to one another: 'She's no worse than that one that went for eighty guineas!' Duly my Oxfordshire friend turns up and we get down to bargaining, never an occupation I feel myself completely at home with. He wants a full lorryload; I hadn't meant to sell so many; on the other hand, we shan't have so much straw this winter, and maybe it would work out best if we fed the rest a bit more heavily. I try to think hastily in terms of turnips, kale, and hay. In the end he takes all the duns and a couple of others who have a dun strain in them and would throw dun calves to an appropriate bull.

And all the rest of the week other sales go on in Oban. I go back there for county council, and the days are still full of lowings and roarings and the smell of cattle. They are shouted at and hustled and frightened, but there is careful inspection and far less cruelty, intentional or unintentional, than there used to be. Most of the Highlanders stay in the north and west, though there are some fanciers elsewhere, but the crosses, the beef stirks or Island queys, go south and east to the richer, kinder grazings. And the money goes the other way, or is used in turn for fertilisers and feeding stuffs, or for that matter to pay MacBrayne, part of which is British Railways in a kilt. And at Oban station there is shunting and shouting as the cattle wagons get ready for the end of the sale.

The Manchester Guardian, 11 November 1957, p. 5

[1] Neòinean and Baravalla are prefixes used in the names of pedigree Highland cattle. *Neòinean* is the Gaelic name for the corn marigold. Baravalla, possibly from *barrabhalla* (battlement, parapet), may originally have been a local placename.

Building a Haystack

(1958)

There is a certain difference of opinion between those who fish and want a nice spate and those who farm and want some fine weather for harvest or hay. We would get a fine afternoon, and things beginning to dry up. 'Tomorrow,' we would say, 'we'll be at the hay.' But tomorrow one woke up to the drumming of rain or, worse, the kind of soft weather that is good for neither farmers nor fishermen.

We had got the hay up in the fields, with some difficulty. It was a good crop; the second-year field, though with less red clover, had done as well as the first. But the ricks were beginning to get soaked on the top and on the western side, however well made they had been. Then at last came two fine days running, though the ground was still wet underfoot. We thought we would make the best of it and put in.

Colin went off with the tractor and buck rake. You back the buck rake in under the rick, lift it, and come in with the rick trailing disreputable skirts like an old shawlie from the Gorbals. The rick is dropped, the buck rake slides from under, Eddie and Geoffrey fork on and Lachlan builds. I left them at it while I churned, but when I had finished my butter prints I came out. The stack was now shaping well, but the sides had to be combed down, as part of the process of keeping it in shape.

You might think that it was simple, making a haystack, but it is a piece of art. At first you can see what shape you are making it and can keep it round and even, but, as you go up, it gets harder to see, and those on the ground must help. 'She's a wee bit light here,' we'd say, reaching up a fork in a straight line so that the stack builder can shove out the hay and stop the stack from sloping inward. If it sticks out, one can comb it down with a rake. This shaping is essential if it is going to stand a Scottish winter of storms and violence. The narrow North-West Highland stacks have props inside them; they have to be narrow because the hay is not so dry, and this means there is need for extra support. But ours go straight up without props.

As the height increases, we fork on from the trailer, propped up and steadied: the versatile buck rake manages to get the ricks onto this, though sometimes Eddie and I have to give them the last shove. Lachlan begins to draw in from the eaves of the stack, gradually working in a smaller space. 'She's swinging a bittie,' he says, and we fetch heavy props to go into her sides and steady her. The stack has become a personality now.

This is skilled and pretty to watch; the builder has drawn in until there is only room for himself. Then one hands up a rake. He pushes the rake gently downward, getting the slope right and the dry stuff lying so that the rain will slide off it. It is like icing a cake. Then we lean the long aluminium ladder, one of those ingenious finger pinching devices, against the stack. A boot feels round for it, the last forkful must go into place on the top.

Eddie reaches it up carefully, Lachlan as carefully puts it on, then another. 'Aye, she'll do at that.' Eddie and I both make balls of stack-rope and throw them up; she has to be roped yet. Eddie's arrives accurately, but I, throwing in the proverbial feminine fashion, miss twice and get well laughed at. Finally I pass it up on a fork. 'That's cheating!' says Eddie. We are all feeling grand to have got the first stack into the stackyard; there is very little over from last year.

We decide to have a 'cup' and come out again. We can't be sure of tomorrow. All over the countryside there'll be overtime worked on an evening like this, and well worth it. Even in this short break the first stack has settled a little, and I get up on to the next one and trample it. That way we shall get another couple of ricks into it. We usually reckon to put eleven or twelve into a stack, but if it is trampled we may get fourteen or more, making a three-ton stack as against a two and a half ton.

Colin has left to the last the ricks at the near end of the field which were rather under the trees and are still very damp looking. But most of them have bad patches. Lachlan can usually work a damp bit into the side, but sometimes he or I throw out a really nasty, black, rotting lump of what was once good hay. The young cattle in the field next the stackyard seem to enjoy hay in almost any state of decay and bounce around cheerfully, eating and tossing it. It is not as good hay as last year's, but still, not bad at all.

We put the best hay, from the middle of the ricks, which is dry and sweet, into the middle of the stack, tossing it out a little before it is trampled, so that any dampish bits are separated.

It is Tarbert Fair, but our beasts had gone to an earlier market, so we had nothing in this time. However, we watch the lorries coming back, saying 'Aye, there's Jock, sober!' And then suddenly we notice that the young cattle are not in the field next the stackyard, but are all wandering down the road. Geoffrey dashes off and we watch him trying to edge the flighty little queys back through the gate.

Now we begin to look at the sky. The heavy rain clouds that have been haunting us for the past week seem to be away. There is light cirrus over the hills. We have got in the best of the ricks; the rest would be the better of another blink of sun and taste of breeze before they come in. We don't pay much attention to weather reports on the radio here; the weather always seems to be one ahead, and the clouds that break on the Kintyre hills drop their contents over us. But we all pride ourselves on being able to forecast, not that we are always very successful. Finally we decide to leave the stack, which is now up to the eaves, overnight. By morning it will have settled and we shall get on another couple of ricks before it has to be drawn in to the head.

Lachlan and I heap up the middle, so that if the weather does defy us and rain, the rain will slide off the tarpaulin. With any luck we shall get in the rest of the field tomorrow.

Every year now fewer and fewer stacks are built. In most of England, and the east coast, hay is baled in the field, and the bales are made into a square stack, like so many building blocks. But stack-building is a kind of creation and is also team work. There is satisfaction for eye and nostril and hand. How should that be valued? I don't know. I am only certain that the value is there.

The Glasgow Herald, 16 August 1958, p. 3

259

The Weather and the Crops

(1958)

Out of the wicked summer of south England, the flooded crops and rain-beaten grass, the train ran into bright sunshine beyond York. Edinburgh was baking. Flying over from Renfrew to Campbeltown I could see the stripped hay-fields, pale and pleased as new-shorn faces, even the tractors and men working. I was eager to get at my own hay, and sure enough there they were in the field at seven in the evening. 'Two minutes to change!' I shouted over the fence, threw my town clothes all over the room, and then I was back at the hay and the feel of a hay fork in my hands and my muscles stretching again.

The whole field had been cut and turned once, lovely, sweet hay with red clover thick through it. In a few places it had gone down, and had cut badly, but, once we could get the ricks off, the beasts would make short work of that. And there was the new tractor, the Massey-Ferguson which had only just arrived the week before, the day I went south. I had turned in my old one, while it was still good. The only thing I had against it was that it had a starter against which one needed to jam one's ankle while one tugged at the gear lever with both hands; somehow my ankles aren't built right for that. This had a hood, a car-type self-starter and various other improvements.

Lachlan, Eddie and Colin were there, and Wal had come over from Airds to help. When I thanked him, he growled that it was a pleasure, delicately adjusting the last forkful that crowns the conical rick and which makes all the difference to whether it will shed the rain during the two or three weeks it is standing out and maturing. Some people put split sacks over the tops of their ricks, anchored at the corners, but I feel that is a confession of partial failure. A rick should stand on its own. One cross ropes it, pulling out a wisp of hay near the bottom, twisting it as one does so, as at the start of a hay rope, tightens the end of the stack rope round it and then shoves the twisted end right into the stack and slightly upwards so that it holds.

It is curious how from year to year a manual skill remains in one, though I often think nowadays – for how many years? Given that we do not contaminate the atmosphere with radioactive products so that any green growing thing after rain is a menace. Twice already before this, in as long a ley as I can manage with the fields I have for rotation, I have taken first-year hay off this field, the Middle Park, between the two old drives. Another long rotation, possibly two, before rheumatism and age weaken my back completely, making it no longer a pleasure to lift a good forkful of sweet hay and twist the tines over for delivery with so little effort or thought and such assurance of the skilled action that one is free all the time to smell the hay, the cut ends of the grass underfoot and one's companions at work with the summer sweat running. I miss only the old smell of horse dung, for Jo is too old to go in the rake now, and besides we have the new side-turner.

'How long shall we go on?' I say, and Lachlan says, smiling: 'That's up to you'. There was a good weather forecast but I feel we might work on and manage the half of the field that had the heavier crop. The worst of it is that the midges are working overtime too, and there is nothing one can put on that will beat a hard-working Highland midge. It is nearly nine by the time we have finished seventeen ricks. It will take only a short day for us to get the rest of the field up.

I go in and wash my hair, then think I must get down to the Bay and talk to the Scout camps. We have one camp after another here in summer, anything from Boys' Brigade to the Young Communists. The little field in front of the house, always called the Cricket Field from days long past, is terribly light soil in spite of my efforts to better it, working with controlled grazing so as to enrich the grass. When it was ploughed this spring, I was even afraid it would blow. But now the oats, though a little patchy, are not at all bad. If it had been a dry season I might have had a repetition of one year when the stalks were so short that the binder couldn't catch them. But the rain has suited that field. The leaves are dark green and handsome, the heads have shot and look like threshing well.

Down in the Bay the Galloway bull calves, well fed by their mothers since March, are playing little public school games. One of the cows is pounding with her great head at Janitor, the young bull from Ichrachan. Suddenly he plunges into attention, but she walks out from under him – the first time, anyhow. Over the wall, the second-year grass in the meadow looks full ripe. It is not so thick as the first-year crop, for the red clover dies out, though the white clover at the base increases. The turnips and potatoes look good, I can't really think why, for I said to myself, when I put the potatoes in, that their only chance in the bottom of the meadow (which used to be a very damp field, and still isn't really dry in spite of draining) was a dry season. Nor were the earlies in until well on in March. But they are cropping well, and a nice-tasting potato.

The milk cows have nearly eaten their field bare, but we were told to keep them out of the other field for three weeks after the spraying. I had hoped to get the thistles out of that field before it was next under crop. I have painful memories of thistles in the sheaves! But I am not sure how much good the spraying did. The thistles and bennyweed look bent and uncomfortable, but are firmly going to flower. The dockens have twisted and shrivelled, but I don't put it past a big dock root to come alive again next year. What have been most affected by the spray are the ordinary daisies, the plantains and silverweed and, alas, the clover. I have been spraying my ley corn regularly now and usually one other field, but I don't see much change in the general weed situation. There is nothing yet like the near weedlessness of the regularly sprayed Danish farmland.

Naturally, the rain caught up with us early the next morning. We say now, if only we'd thought to put the turned hay into coils! But I would have made the same decision as Lachlan, to turn and leave. It is not hard rain, just the wee, odd shower that wets everything just when one thinks that in half an hour it will be dry. Yet it's bound to be fine soon, isn't it, and at least one's mind is on that and not on Mr Dulles and Mr Krushchev.[1]

New Statesman, v. 56, 16 August 1958, pp. 190-1

[1] John Foster Dulles (1888-1959), US Secretary of State 1953-9; Nikita Krushchev (1894-1971), First Secretary of the Communist Party of the Soviet Union 1953-64; adversaries in the Cold War.

The Calves

(1958)

It was a day of storms and rainbows. By now the bracken is broken down into brown heaps and, though there seems to be plenty of grass, it is sodden and tasteless and doesn't do the cattle much good. The Galloway calves were all driven into the cattle shelter, for it was time for the marking; and, besides, two important people were coming: Mr McSporran, the dealer, who wanted one or perhaps more of the bull calves, and my old friend Mr Lewis, the vet, who saw me through all my early difficulties and did all the tuberculosis tests I had to have before my farm became part of a tubercle-free area.

The cows were ranging round the shelter, bellowing, high and harsh, for their calves. Galloways are good mothers and even the early calves were still sucking. All calves must be ear-marked with their owner's number or brand. My registered farm number for the Galloway herd book is MNC, and my year number M. For the other cows the farm number is 4649 and the year X. The Ayrshires are easy to mark, with their pale ears, but the Galloways' ears are only a shade less dark than the rest of them. One rubs the inside of the ear with Zebo, avoiding the big vein; then one clamps on the branding pincers, while the calf tosses its head and tries to get away. It takes only a moment.

The calves look rather alike to me, but not to Lachlan. After the marking he leans over the slype where we have them penned, and fondles them. They seem to me to be in very good shape, thick and beefy, with splendid coats, black with bright shades in it, and often a golden dun colour in their ear tufts. These are the offspring of an Ichrachan bull called Kruger, and I have been a bit puzzled as to appropriate names for the heifers. The daughter of Kruger and First Lady comes out as Ladysmith,[1] but what about Cassandra? I am tempted to call her heifer calf Cry the Beloved Country,[2] but it is a bit long. Pedigree cows and bulls have names as fantastic as racehorses, but I notice with some pleasure that the heifer calf of one of my beasts which I sold in Castle Douglas a few years back, is called Naomi. There's fame for you!

A Galloway cow and her calf

The sun has been almost hot, but a sudden clap of thunder is followed by a chill wind and then hail, which lies in the calves' curly coats and drives us into the Land Rover. Mr Lewis and Mr McSporran arrive. It appears that Mr McSporran would like the three larger bull calves, but there is one we are just not sure about. When he came over a month ago to look at one, there was a curious lump in its navel that might have been a rupture. I didn't think it was, but we wanted Mr Lewis to make sure. He feels around and decides that it is merely loose skin, and might have come from the other calves sucking it, though this is rare with calves which are on their mothers. Two of these bull calves are fully pedigreed, the third is from a 'B list' mother, whose heifer calves would count for the herd book, but not her bull calves. However, Mr McSporran's customers won't bother about that; these little bulls will be used for crossing with Ayrshires or some other pedigree cow. Should anyone want a pedigree, I can get it for £2, by writing in later.

I ask and get £45 each for them. How I arrive at the price is this: the inspector will not come to pass them as stock bulls until they are at least ten months old, so anyone buying now takes the risk of their not passing. He will also, if he is wise, feed them up a bit with cake during the winter. If they pass as bulls he will be able to sell them for a good bit more, anything from £60 up, I should say, in February or March. If they do not pass he can claim the subsidy - £7 10s a head – and will then sell them as bullocks in May or June or perhaps fatten them himself and grade them. My own bullocks, sold last June at just over a year old, fetched £50 each. This would not be quite so profitable, but probably Mr McSporran knows his markets better than I do. He is a cheerful, friendly man, very unlike the wicked dealer of the stories. I hope, and think, the calves will pass as breeding bulls.

You might think I should keep them myself, taking the risk of their being turned down; but if I did, I should have all the complication of finding a buyer afterwards, sending them over and so on. Mr McSporran knows everyone and will have no trouble at all with this. But the fourth bull calf, who is smaller and less of the type? Well, Mr Lewis makes a bullock of him. At this age, the calves don't seem to worry much; the clamp which does it draws no blood, appears not to hurt. He trots off to his mother and has a good suck. The heifer calves, too, are back with their mother, but the three who have been sold are kept in the shed, to be picked up tomorrow on a lorry. The cows wander round uneasily, bellowing. It doesn't do to think of their feelings.

I have two heifers in calf. They will calve within a week of one another and one of them is very young. This was due to campers leaving a gate open, so that the Galloway bull got in. I feel I must keep the young one and look after her well, hoping she will have a small calf. I sell the other one to Mr McSporran for £50, though on the complete bargain there will be the 'luck-penny' back for him, the odd pound or two that usually gets asked for and given in local sales – though not, of course, at classy pedigree sales. I should get more if I kept her until spring; but there would be her keep, and this way I shall get more room in the byre. It is all a very friendly business.

I shall leave the Galloway calves with their mothers for a few weeks longer, then separate them and bring them into a field near the house where there is a shed, so that they can shelter at night and be fed. I used not to give them bought cake – the old cows do well on my own hay, straw and turnips – but it seems worth while to spend that much extra and get them well on by spring and the time of the new grass. They will get much tamer too and easier to handle. I think I know already which of the heifers will be Lachlan's favourite. Next autumn she will be walking sedately round the sale ring wearing a halter like a dairy cow and won't try to kick when she is brushed or combed. And her mother will have forgotten her.

New Statesman, v. 56, 25 October 1958, pp. 554, 556

---

[1] Paul Kruger (1825-1904) led the Boer resistance in the Second Boer War (1899-1902). The siege of Ladysmith (1899-1900) took place during that war.

[2] Alan Paton's *Cry the Beloved Country* (1948), a novel about apartheid in South Africa.

The Threshing Team

(1959)

Along Lomond side and across Rest-and-Be-Thankful the three-foot icicles were breaking off, tinkling and shattering on the road like badly handled Christmas decorations. It was the thaw beginning, right enough, but not getting very far yet. I have never known such a long cold spell, here in the west; by now the nobleanum hybrid rhododendrons are usually in flower – rather inappropriate banks of pink and scarlet. But not this year, and it is only in the last couple of weeks that the snowdrops have come bursting up.

Still it is wonderful weather for the threshing. The mill has rocked its way up Carradale Glen and today was at the farthest out of the farms, Auchanfraoch. That means the heather field; and Auchanfraoch is just on the edge of the rough hills, heather and whin at the back door. But Rory has a few goodish fields along the side of Carradale Water, where there is some alluvial land, better, really, than any of my own, and he has a nice stackyard.

We thresh twice in the year, first in early November, just as soon as we are finished with the autumn work; this gives us good straw for feeding our out-lying cattle, straw which has something of the value of hay. The straw from the second threshing is dryer and less palatable, but of course fine for bedding. We cannot thresh all our stacks at once, because the corn is not hard and dry enough. So we have a second threshing about now.

It is a pale blue day with mist lying soft in Carradale Glen; but Rory's farm seems to shimmer through the golden stour of the threshing, the bright, floating chaff. There are one or two men and boys from each of the seven farms in the Glen; and there are the mill men, who are old friends and stay, most of the time, on the top of their shaking, rocking, unstreamlined mill, cutting the bindings and feeding in the sheaves that are tossed up to them. Lachlan is doing that from a trailer when I come up pretending that I'm looking for a job but quite well aware that, as always, there are more people than are really needed, which makes the work go lightly and nicely, with time for talk and laughing.

We ourselves work it so that the mill comes right into the stackyard, but that isn't always possible. Here at Auchanfraoch the stacks are round at the back, and must be loaded onto trailers to take them to the mill, which is on one of the few pieces of hard and level ground and close to the stone-built barn where the straw is being piled in. Everyone wears blue overalls over a jersey or an old jacket, except for one of the MacKinnons, who works in his shirt sleeves and looks like a poster about agriculture. It's hot work, even in this weather, tossing the bales of straw up from the ground into the high opening of the barn, but no bother to a MacKinnon of Auchnasavil.

Dunkie and Johnnie from Kilmichael are there of course. I would be well content if, at Dunkie's age, I could smilingly pick up a full sack of corn and trot with it on my shoulders. But doubtless Dunkie will still be doing it just as easily ten years from now. 'Grand weather for the mill!' he says. The young Semple of Dippen is there, the same who, at six, managed to start his father's tractor and drive it quite a way before he was caught. I ask him if he isn't thinking of going to Agricultural College, but he seems to think it would be a waste of time. 'The hours are too short,' he says. And every moment away from actual farming is, for him, a waste of time.

Inside the barn the straw is being piled and trampled, to get it all in. Eddie is there, and Jimmie Strang from Auchnabreck, which is at the farthest limit for postie or the vans. By the end of the day the big barn is full, but it will all be used before the early bite comes on the hills. The corn trickles evenly into the sacks, plenty of big corn and not too much of the seconds. As each bag is filled the shutter is flicked to and another opened over an empty bag. Someone lifts the full bag and carries it across the yard to empty onto a golden pyramid. This interests Geordie, the pet lamb, who is now a large and respectable sheep. He keeps dodging in for a bite and nobody really minds. 'Aye, he's wise!' we say. On a day like this we can spare a mouthful or two for any comers. There are cups of tea going, too, and Mrs Beaton is getting stuff from the van for a grand high tea. You'll need two good meals a day, at the threshing!

When the weather is good there's nothing we like more than the threshing. It is skilled and varied and has something to show for it. Above all it is done with other people in an atmosphere of friendliness. I suppose it has certain of the qualities which made some people enjoy the wars. What is very disconcerting is that so little work has this quality. Harvest, of course, has it too, and so has fishing when there is a fairly small crew, all skilled and all with a direct, personal interest in the job. Peat-cutting, house building and such jobs used to have it.

But every modern political, economic and cultural trend is against it. The instrument of production which produces it, like the reaper-binder or the ring-net boat, is out of date. The same work can be done much more efficiently and using much less labour, both in the sense of muscular exertion and man-hours. All right, so what? Tell me what better thing Lachlan and Eddie, Rory and Johnnie and the rest would be doing? Going to lectures? Sitting easily on their backsides looking at the telly? Are they going to do anything which will use their capabilities and sensitivities more fully than in a day at the threshing? If they were more efficiently geared into fully productive modern industry, at which they would make more money, would that be what they would want? I doubt it.

Probably these small farms are out of date from the standpoint of modern efficiency, though less out of date than crofts. They sop up a great deal of the tax-payers' money in grants and subsidies, which means that the meat and eggs they produce (the oats are almost entirely for feed nowadays) may be dearer in a certain sense than imported meat and eggs. What is the alternative? Forestry? Or is timber going to be out of date too before it is mature? Or just being part of a national park, a place for tired city tourists and factory workers to gaze at and rest in? If that is so, do we all become tourist fodder, put on kilts and start learning the pipes? Or do we just go off to the cities, to efficient, unpleasant and comparatively well-paid factory work, visiting the country only for holidays?

It seems to me doubtful if the Labour Party has thought about all this, at any rate since the time of William Morris, who would have liked the threshing team – as soon as he realised that they were well fed, well clothed and not overworked. If I am the one to speak about it, some kind of bogus quality is assumed. What is it? I don't think it is bogus that I should assume that I am part of the threshing team. I have done a man's work on it in my time, and some years I have been at the kitchen stove making the dinner. But nobody wants me to be exactly the same. They would rather I was a bit different, but doing this funny job of writing about them. I get teased about it – I'm to be sure to put in this or that! But it is something they want me to do. It is part of the worth-while quality of this bit of teamwork. A typewriter is as genuine an instrument of production as a hay fork or a threshing mill. A different skill is needed, but not as different as you might think.

So, if the bogus quality which might have come in with me is ruled out, it remains that the Labour Party and others must take note of the threshing team and all that it implies.

New Statesman, v. 57, 21 February 1959, p. 250

Science and the small farmer

(1959)

Twenty years ago, even, we small farmers in Scotland lived mainly on farming tradition and old rules. No doubt it was different in the big east coast farms, the Lothians and the Mearns, or down in England. They could afford to try out these new ideas. For us, working on a small margin, mostly family farms or perhaps with one or two paid men in addition to the working owner, it was different. We moved cautiously along the old grooves.

No doubt we had come some way from eighteenth-century Scottish usage, when no farmer would have dreamt of keeping any but his worst corn for seed. We dipped our sheep instead of daubing them with tar. Not many of us believed in witchcraft. We had various simple implements, but we still did much of our work with scythes, rakes, snedders and forks; we use these still and keep our manual skills, but they are mostly for odd corners and special times. There were a few tractors then, though we still worked mostly with horses.

Today, almost all of us have tractors. When one of my neighbours got his and we all went over to have a look at it and congratulate him, he said 'Aye, well, she stays where she is.' That had not been so with his horse who was often, as he put it, 'away in the mist'. Some of us have a bad habit still of leaving our implements out in all weathers as though they were blackface sheep or Galloway stirks.

The old Fordson tractor was fairly simple to understand, and look after. A modern Ferguson, say, with all its gadgets, is more difficult; one has to have the sense of gadgetry which a technological civilisation gives to its children, if one is going to handle it properly. But that is expected of a modern farm worker, and his wage is, in consequence, higher.

We used to milk by hand; now almost everyone milks by machinery. There is a farmer I know whose wife had her first in the byre; she just couldn't be bothered to go in while she was in the middle of milking. Now they have a row of taps and rubber tubes. I don't think that machine milking is as clean or as good for the cows as first-rate hand milking. But first-rate hand milkers are as rare as lambs in October. Perhaps, too, we press our cows too hard

Mitchison milking an Ayrshire cow

for milk production, shorten their lives, and produce milk which is just up to required standard but seldom above it.

Probably the main impact science has on us is over animal disease. Nowadays a cow with mastitis can be cured very quickly; the deficiency diseases don't kill in the same way. There are inoculations against contagious abortion in cows and various sheep diseases. It is only the really terrible things like foot-and-mouth for which there is still no cure, only the wholesale slaughter that takes away what a man has loved and worked for over years of his life. Probably we don't know exactly what these massive doses of antibiotics or sulphonamide injections are supposed to do; but we do know they cure. I remember my Galloway bull with his badly cut leg, and how he wouldn't stand for his injections unless I went and stood by his head; then he leant on me, about a ton of him.

When I used to do shearing, ten years back, the fleeces were revoltingly full of ticks and keds; last year, when I was looking on, the fleeces all came away clean. Also, instead of expecting some of the sheep to be struck quite badly, and then having the filthy job of picking out the maggots with a knife point and dressing the wound, we are surprised if one is struck, and it never seems to get bad. All this owing to the new dips.

It is the same with poultry, which used to have so many horrid diseases and mysterious deaths. The little pellet in their water or whatever it is, and then, no bother. Perhaps we still look on it much as we used to look on the twist of straw against witches or the rowan branch over the byre door, that is to say with belief but without critical understanding. But, as more farmers' sons go to the agricultural colleges and as more semi-scientific articles get into the farming papers, so our understanding does increase.

The research behind all this comes from various quarters. There is the Animal Health Trust, the Veterinary Colleges, and a number of the big drug houses. Glaxo has done a great deal on drugs and preventives; so have Cooper's, British Oil and Cake, especially for poultry, Boots and half a dozen more. It is direct applied science.

So, of course, is the work on hormone weed killers and on fertilisers. But here I think we must be a bit careful. I am not one of the humus boys, but I think one can go too far with artificials. There may be a kick-back. In fact, it looks as though the increase of magnesium deficiency disease in cows may be due to some fertilisers doing funny things to pastures. I always try to have plenty of farmyard manure and also seaweed, rich in potash and perhaps in some of the needed trace minerals, on my fields. Then, I feel, they can take artificials. I think, too, that we may overdo hormone weed killers and find ourselves destroying something valuable. But I always use a spray on my young oats in the first year, when it is not undersown with grasses and clovers.

Naturally I get soil analysis done, especially as it is a free service by the West of Scotland Agricultural College. And their adviser is a welcome visitor to any of us. His analysis gives us an idea of what our fields need, though not perhaps an entirely certain one. He is also much rung up by people from pubs, wanting to have bets settled!

We are beginning to have a faint idea of what genetics is about. A lot of work has been done on poultry, which have reasonably short generations, but rather less on cattle and sheep, in this country at any rate, and when it comes to the sale ring, you see the prices going up for most unscientific reasons. 'A nice pair of ears, that!' Or 'good clean legs!' Not that this doesn't mean more than one might think, for certain groups of physical characteristics go together. But there is little accurate planning. Artificial insemination is making a difference, though. I have just been asked to lend a heifer from one of the AI bulls for progeny testing, and am delighted at the suggestion. That's the way to get somewhere! It also may be the way to keep down the really crazy, artificial prices that some of the big breeders get. One of our difficulties in this country is, oddly enough, the Breed Societies and the rules for bull licensing, which stops promising new crosses.

When it comes to choosing seeds, I always try to see what has done best in the experimental plots which the West of Scotland College has been trying out in Kintyre. I order my seed oats accordingly. Other farmers do much the same, and some of them look in the seed catalogue to see the parentage of their seed. When we use our own seed we always get it dressed with Ceresan, which stops smut and leaf-stripe. But I, at least, don't know what it is – mentally I treat it like a charm! Some, again, make up their own seeds mixture for grass, though I tend to use a standard mixture, only occasionally asking for something like a little more clover.

In our part of Scotland we can only grow potatoes which are immune from wart disease. Again, we are a tuberculosis free area for cattle, in fact we were among the first TT areas in Scotland. This meant a real struggle at first, testing all the cattle, at first twice a year, and throwing out those which did not pass. But we had splendid help with this, both from our vets and from the Animal Health Officer. I was fortunate; none of my cattle reacted, except to avian, which is almost impossible to stop on grazing where there are any amount of large birds such as seagulls. Now we have tests only once every two years, and no longer have to go through an elaborate system of permits when buying or selling.

We are all looking for some way of controlling bracken. I was fascinated to read in *The New Scientist* about the Welsh sheep which suddenly took to eating it; I only hope that a lot of research is going on at this point and that it will soon be available. One might at the same time consider rhododendron. The wild *Rho. ponticum* is a plague here, and my neighbour is always having trouble. Oddly enough (and touch wood) my own cattle, who cannot be protected from rhododendron as there is so much in the rough grazing and it is in fact a useful windbreak, do not seem to get upset by it, although I am sure they eat a little in winter. Is this something which an animal can accustom itself to?

It may be that we farmers are to some extent an easier prey for advertisers because we feel that a certain amount of science is necessary, and we are impressed with long scientific or, sometimes, pseudo-scientific words. We feel we must be modern at all costs, and even if we don't really understand what we are doing. This, of course, is a thoroughly unscientific attitude, but is as far as most of us can get. Yet, in so much as we cease to be frightened of the unknown, it is all to the good. The snag, perhaps, is that we have got into the attitude of feeling that there must be a cure for everything and being aggrieved when there isn't, feeling that science has let us down. Perhaps the children who have listened to lectures at the Young Farmers' Clubs and, later, gone on to agricultural colleges, will do a bit better and achieve a more scientific attitude when their turn comes to take over our small farms.

The New Scientist, 12 March 1959, pp. 586-7

The Sales

(1960)

This is the time of year when all farmers are thinking about the Sales. According to how things have gone, we will or won't be able to go on with our farming plans. But it's more than that. We have to measure our efforts against something, and unhappily money is the only standard that seems to count. So the sales are either encouraging or disheartening. I'm feeling a bit disheartened myself and I'm not the only one.

It was the Tarbert Sale a couple of weeks back. I sent in two Galloway bullocks and a cross heifer. Most of my bullocks had gone to the June sale, but these weren't up to it. Yet somehow a summer of good grazing hadn't done that much for them. I haven't the buildings or the skill for finishing them off: fattening cattle is a specialist's job. Still, if these are properly handled, they should fatten for Christmas and make a tidy profit for someone and meanwhile I've had the subsidy.

By the time I got to Tarbert with my Danish friends, one of them a farmer, the sale had been on for a while, but it was dragging. A good sale goes quickly, with sharp bidding; here the auctioneers had to coax the bids out, even with the lovely Ayrshire heifers: 'Aye, there's a milky-looking lass! There's a sweet heifer, a real swell!' Or again, to jolly them on: 'Extra teat, aye; but we'll no charge you anything extra!' The Tarbert ring is cosy and smoky, and occasionally a bidder comes back from the bar tent and bids in an apparent dream, but, alas, still cannily. Inside the ring the habitués sit round on a bench, risking an occasional kick for the sake of a better view.

Most are in the profession, buyers or sellers, muddy-booted. My Danish friend thought they were better-looking than the average rather pudding-faced Danish farmer, and certainly there was a fine Highland cragginess about some of them. On Danish standards the Ayrshire prices were high but the beef prices low. Myself, I thought they were all low, and so did most of my fellow sellers. Why? There's plenty of hay this year and splendid turnips if my own are any guide. Perhaps there have been too many calves kept for the demand; does that mean a mistaken calf-subsidy policy? It's funny, the way low beef prices don't seem to get down to the housewife!

I had half a mind to take my stirks back, but that would have meant hiring the lorry again. One or two people who had their own farm lorries did take their beasts back. But even if I had, did I really have the winter keep and housing for them? My old sheds are beginning to go. They have stuck together so far with new coats of paint, but the woodwork has got to the stage where a determined young stirk might bring the whole thing down on his head.

Lachlan and I had hopes of getting up to £40, at least, with the Galloway stirks, but as soon as we began to see the run of the prices, hopes faded. I decided to make my limit £25 – and I just got past it. Perhaps if I'd had the courage to say no when I was in the ring, I might have gone a few pounds better, but by the time I was there I was dead scared. I couldn't even see where the bids were coming from and goodness knows how the auctioneer did, since the bidding was done almost imperceptibly by the raising of an eyebrow or a single finger.

The hard quick patter of the auctioneer – how can they keep it up? – was sometimes almost drowned in the lowing or bellowing of frightened beasts. I think for some people half the point of an auction is in the sense of vicarious power over living, suffering flesh, the whack of the stick, the shouting and struggling. Was a slave market like this? Did the suffering flesh yell to its gods and mothers in Parthian, Thracian, Gallic, British – or more lately in Ewe and Fanti and Congolese? And did the bystanders equally flock to look on and laugh and enjoy themselves?

The Oban Sale had a different atmosphere altogether. There was much less protest from the cows and heifers; these pedigree beauties are, comparatively speaking, the ladies of the harem. Both my cousins were, as usual, prize-winners, one with a Highlander, a corn-coloured cutie with a long silken fringe over her eyes and under the sweeping horns – which are obviously for decoration, not for malice. The other had a superb curly Galloway.

But here again prices were disappointing. I think Ted had hoped for £200 or £300 for his champion Galloway, but the bidding was sticky. To get it going again at £150 I put in a couple of bids, and it went up nicely for a while, then stuck again. All his

Ichrachan heifers were beauties and fetched reasonable prices, but nothing outstanding. It was a buyers' Market. Lachlan and I had gone round looking at beasts before the sale began. We both felt we wanted new blood in the herd. The Arduaine beasts were fine, but I was sure they would be above my price, though I did bid one of them up. In the outcome some of them were withdrawn as they didn't make enough; in fact quite a number of owners withdrew. I wasn't impressed by the pedigrees of other beasts. Also I wanted particularly to get a heifer or cow from rough land which would stand up to our gales off the sea. Then I found a herd from Ross-shire being sold off. They were young cows, all in calf to a Lochur bull from the Westminster herd. I fancied two of them, big strong beasts with good coats. They were coming up late in the sale.

There is something very special about the Oban ring. It is partly that one always gets a smell of peat there, in spite of all the electric stoves and fires; and there is always a good deal of conversation among the farmers in Gaelic, a great language for not being understood by others. But there is also a modishness about the pedigree men and women; kilts, cromags and hand-woven tweeds are not out of order. And the place is packed. Many of the sightseers are knowledgeable, indeed a good many are up for other sales. A few are tourists. One has to squeeze one's way in; and, once in, the excitement grows. I had a feeling that my Danes were going to end up by bidding themselves!

Most of the heifers waited fairly patiently in the pens, advancing through one gate to another till they came to the last one just behind the ring. One stands there waiting for the gate to open and listening to the bidding and the reassuring friendliness of the auctioneer, who kindly said about my beasts: 'straight off the hill, as they should be', and seemed to put a tone of admiration into his voice – perhaps all owners feel this. At least I could see more or less where the bids were coming from. These of mine were bulling heifers ready for next year off an Ichrachan bull. I thought my first one went cheap, especially as I'd liked the look of her myself. The second went better, to £45, having started at £30. The third, whose agile hoof I had just avoided by jumping, went to £64. I have a feeling that she pleased people by trotting round the ring in an interested way and blowing in their faces. She had good big bones too.

Then came the turn of the Ross-shire farm. The first two or three went reasonably enough, though I think the seller was not too pleased. Lachlan and I found ourselves at opposite sides of the ring; I signalled urgently to him and he managed to wriggle round to confer with me. The two I fancied were better beasts and I thought – correctly – that they would go up towards the eighties. I wasn't going to bid that high after the prices I'd got myself. One had bad hoofs and I turned her down, she couldn't last. Then came one which I hadn't particularly noticed in the pen, but we both liked her; she looked tough and big-boned, fairly low-slung on sturdy legs. In the fifties I joined in the bidding and got her at £65. If only she gets me a heifer calf with the Lochur bull!

Or shall I have one more try at bringing up a bull calf? Of course one is nowhere in the pedigree world without bulls, but have we got the know-how? Or the buildings? I shall have to see about the buildings at once!

New Statesman, v. 60, 5 November 1960, pp. 688, 690

Namely Lambs at Tarbert Sale

(1961)

Our own wedders went off in a big float at seven o'clock on a dripping wet morning in company with a good few other local wedder and ewe lambs. I hadn't been sure whether to try them at Tarbert, or grade them, but some were riggs, which never make any kind of price as the meat is supposed not to be so good.

Anyhow, I decided to have a try. I wanted to buy in my next year's lambs and put them on to the thick grass and clover, the aftermath of the hay, which needs eating. The field in front of the house won't do for cows; it is too far for the dairy cows, and the fence isn't strong enough to keep a heifer in so long as I have my apparently irresistibly attractive young bull grazing in the Bay at the other side of it.

So that was settled, and the rain came slashing down. One doesn't know what number one has got in the ballot and the Tarbert Auction Market isn't on the telephone, so one feels one ought to be there on time. Of course I needn't have bothered. Eleven went past and it was near twelve before the Gigha lambs were put off the boat at the West Loch and brought up to the pens.

Fellow-farmers, their black oilskins running with rain, greet one: 'Usual weather,' 'A dirty, dirty day.' But it's cheerful enough, for friends are meeting all the time: – 'How's the man?' 'Come away and have a cup of tea.'

Then the bell rang and Mr Weir, the auctioneer, got up into the rostrum and started his non-stop sale talk. The lambs began pouring in from the pens like grey water, with one suddenly leaping from all four feet like a waterfall. The ordinary gait of a running sheep isn't pretty: they look too much like small mechanical mattresses. But the leap shows the kind of crag inhabitants they were before we started changing them for human purposes.

But they didn't look their best in the ring, wet and draggled as they were. Mr Weir praised them up: 'Nice keeping lambs,' and urged us not to be so slow to bid. 'You're seeing the sheep badly,' he'd say, 'you'll not know them dried out.'

Mitchison and a lamb

Many of them came from farms which sent in their lambs regularly to this market, and were well known. These would be singled out: 'Namely lambs from Culfuar'. My neighbour from Dippen got a good price for his first cut: even I could see that they were extra good. Yet I can't help thinking he'd expected to do better. It wasn't a very brisk sale; the rain seemed to press down on all of us.

Most of the bidders were inside the ring, though a few roamed round, and once or twice someone thought he'd bought a lot when it was really his neighbour who'd got it. The auctioneer exclaimed once rather sharply: 'I wish you'd stay in the same place!' But I wasn't just sure myself whether he was talking to a bidder or a sheep.

I had intended to get my usual blackface lambs but it seemed to me that the cross lambs were going cheap. I said so to Lachlan, who was standing beside me. He whispered back: 'It was going through my own mind.' There was a lot of these in the ring which looked to me nice and even, not too big and not too small. They were from Lossit, farther down Kintyre, a well known place. I didn't think I could go wrong. I bid them up to £4 16s, intending to drop out if they went any higher. However, I got them at that.

Then we got on to the wedders. While Lachlan brought them down from the pen I waited in the second pen from the one behind the ring, while lambs surged past me. Suddenly I felt one licking my hand; it must have been someone's pet lamb; I hoped no child was sorrowing for it.

My wedders had looked so well in the field, but now, like all the others, they had no appearance. When we got them into the field we moved them round; I hoped some one would feel the fat ones, and dug into their shoulders myself. But there was no great trade. They went at £5 6s 6d and I've a feeling that whoever bought them – and I had no idea which of the barely moving faces had bid – got rather a bargain.

After that the blackface lambs began to go through. 'Come on, come on,' said Mr Weir, encouraging us, 'you know the Gartnagrenach lambs.' Cups of tea were brought to the rostrum. In the middle of slow bidding, he called out to us, 'I'll take a half – I could do wi' one myself!'

I ended by buying in quite a nice little lot, the second cut from a farm down near the Mull. They would be my next year's wedders.

But I am hoping to fatten and grade a few of the crosses before Christmas. In any case, if I keep them, their wool is a bit more valuable. We shall have to keep it separately at the shearing. But that's far, far ahead. In June of next year. In sunshine.

Meanwhile the lorry-load of wet sheep have come back up the Tarbert road, and have been decanted into a field. They seem to be settling down, as if the auction ring had never happened.

The Glasgow Herald, 26 August 1961, p. 3

The New Shed

(1961)

The MacKinnons up the glen have a handsome new shed, a Dutch barn with one side open, made of shining corrugated iron. No doubt it would be a lot nicer, in a way, if it were Cotswold stone or Warwickshire timber framing and plaster. But at least it looked what it was, something which I myself increasingly needed.

At first I had thought merely in terms of replacement for my oldest shed. But, between Lachlan persuading me and myself thinking it over, and above all after some consideration of grants under the Farm Improvement Scheme, I decided to go ahead and get a Dutch barn which would do for the hay. This would mean more shed space for the calves. But it would also mean that the ricks could come in straight from the field; there would be no making of stacks with the slowing down as one gets to the top. There would not be the extra labour of cutting rushes and thatching with them, nor the difficulty of an old stack getting blown out of shape, losing its thatch and wasting.

But there was a lot to do before I got my shed. I had to decide how big it was to be and how it was to face. First of all I had thought of a square, facing towards my present range of sheds, which might have made a kind of sheltered yard for the beasts. But Lachlan reminded me that this would mean that the open side would face west, into our prevailing storm and rain wind. Better for it to face north, where it would get the shelter of the hill: we don't have very much rain from the north anyway. It would have to be on the flat, and not too much over the old stone condy, that drains off the hill water into our elaborate system of underground land drains.

The Glasgow contractor, A. & J. Main, sent down their representative, a nice, solid man who explained things slowly so that simple farming types like me, who get badly at sea over specifications, understood exactly – or not exactly, perhaps, but reasonably well – what had to be done. For we had decided to lay the foundations ourselves, so that Main's men would have to do only the erecting. We have plenty of sand and gravel on the beach, and Davie Oman at the pier had offered to lend us his concrete mixer.

We had decided to have three bays of fifteen feet each; it looked a lot paced out on the grass, but less would have been silly. Then I filled in the form asking for my proposed improvement to be approved; we couldn't go ahead till I got that. I called it an All-purpose Shed, for I had visions of tucking the pigs or perhaps a couple of calves into the end of one bay. Or, for that matter, quite a lot of things which now lie about could be kept there tidily. In time I was approved and we could start on the concrete.

The apparently level ground proved to be oddly unlevel, but earth from one end went on to the other. There were two layers of concrete, the second one raising the floor of the shed a little above ground level. Colin and Eddie worked on this with the borrowed concrete mixer, and at last it was ready for the erectors, who worked hard and quickly, joking down from the high steel cross pieces while they bolted the roof sections together. At the end it seemed very large and shining.

Then I had to fill in the form asking for the grant to be paid. This form was not, as a matter of fact, at all difficult, for the whole thing had been agreed. But it looked as if it was. I made the calculations on the basis of standard costs for our own work, plus the cost of the shed. On this, in time, I hope to get a grant of one third. The building itself cost £440; our own work and materials were valued at £130 15s. I don't know exactly what my labour costs were. The cement, bought through the Kintyre farmers' co-operative, cost £34 4s; but it's a bit hard to estimate the cost of labour, when it is often in half days, and always stopped early for Colin to feed the hens. Matthew, our local joiner, who does things for all the village (many of whom are related to him), had helped to measure out; then there was Davie's cement mixer, my own mental wear-and-tear on forms and so on. I think I did quite well.

Still, it was a pleasure to start putting in; the tractor, with a pike on the fork-lift behind it, looking a bit like a lady with a bustle, buzzed up and down from the field. We shall need, I think, to put down a few loads of gravel to firm up the ground outside, where the tractor tyres have already squelched deep into the mud.

Of course it might stop raining for a few days and then the mud might harden up. But the rain is on again. Another fine day and we could clear up the field and let the young beasts on to the foggage, the lush autumn grass with thick red clover in it from the seed mixture. Another fine day ... in fact we shall need two, for the pikes are soaking again. In the middle distance the Boy Scouts go dripping across their camping ground; their poor camp fire is out; and the caravanners huddle like chickens with a fine view of the rains.

New Statesman, v. 62, 6 October 1961, pp. 472-3

Happiness on the Farm

(1961)

We had a week of good weather for the threshing mill and the last day, when it was down with me, was the best of the lot, frost-crisp in the morning and an unclouded sun all day, but so low that the light and shadows always had something of evening colour in them. However, I spent quite a bit of the morning in the kitchen, as a big dinner for the threshing team is essential, and it had to be the traditional kind, with lots of carrots in the soup and turnips for a vegetable. I kept thinking how much nicer my stock would have been without the roots in it, but Emily knew what they like.

I had come back from the byre the evening before and seen the familiar humped shape of the tarpaulin-covered mill, not as always in the stackyard, but over by the new shed. And it is clear that the shed is beginning to pull us all its way. It certainly turned out much easier to pile up the straw into the remaining bay of the shed, where one won't bother about it getting wet. In this part of the world we think a lot of our straw and feed it to the cattle outside through the early part of winter.

When the mill first started coming to the Glen, you would get the lend of a horse and cart from one or two of your fellow users, but now everyone brings a tractor; and these raced to and from the stacks, taking the sheaves over to the mill. But next year, I begin to see, we shall have to have the stacks over by the shed and shall bring the stackyard itself into the field, which I am intending anyhow to plough up and reseed directly to grass. It is close to the house and the sheds are there. I'm thinking of running out a cable and having a couple of lights – or rather it was Lachlan who thought of it, saying it was a wee bit difficult working with a torch in one hand and a pitchfork in the other. But here again, it begins with our having collected some telegraph poles when the Post Office decided to put their cables underground. Once you start thinking what to do with a telegraph pole, you may end up anywhere!

The mill has worked its way down the glen, a day at each farm, and one or two men coming to help from each of the other farms. In the middle of it we had our Farmers' Dance in the Village Hall, starting off with whist and tea. The difficulty from my own point of view is that nobody dances with me till they have worked up a certain amount of confidence – and done all their duty dances with their own female relatives. And by the time the confidence is on them, some of them have lost the use of their legs. Though I always think it is quite amazing how some of my friends can dance when they can't stand. I suppose it is just that dancing is a nobler thing.

It had been a difficult harvest this year in our part; week after week of bad weather. Nobody's stacks were in very good order, and the corn is damp and will have to be turned rather often. The corn from the tops of the stacks, which is the worst, has been kept separately for the hens. But there was an odd sheaf sprouting here and there, even far down the stacks. There were fewer rats than usual. 'I've heard it said they see the mill arrive and go away,' said the mill man.

'Most of them seem to have got under my drawing-room floor,' I said. After a time, one stops minding the rats and only wonders about their life below one's feet. The rattle of their feet and the squeaks, which are clearly some kind of communication, are much nicer than a snake's slither.

Of course, what one asks oneself is whether it is sensible to grow oats at all. Would we not do better, instead of feeding oats to hens and cows, to have all the land under grass and buy in feeding stuffs? Some people even silage their oats green. We grow a cleaning crop one year between the two oat crops, but this year our potatoes were under water half the time and have a lot of brown spot through them. The turnips have done fairly well, and are less expensive to grow since we got a precision sower that eliminates a lot of the singling. But how would the whole thing compare with the cost of feeding stuffs?

If I were a real agri-businessman I would no doubt know the answer; and it would probably mean less labour costs, which ultimately means a fall in the rural population. A lot of people are aiming at just that. One can't be sure, but I think it would also be a fall in general happiness. Farm work has had the really back-breaking quality taken out of it, though cows have not so far been persuaded to take Sundays off. And it was the age-old cruel work that made the real case against farming as a way of life – at any rate for the farm labourer. My guess is that nowadays it may be less pleasant to work on an agri-business factory-farm than on a family farm. Once I asked Lachlan whether he noticed a difference in kind in the hours of work and the hours after work. He said no, and I think many people on small farms would say the same. But is that ever true of a factory?

New Statesman, v. 62, 22 December 1961, p. 956

The Fortunate Isles

(1963)

'The date of my death will come,' he said, 'before I forget this greenness.' He looked round, the hay-fork lightly in his hand. He had never used one before, but he had the instinct for it. We didn't have to tell him to keep the tines turned down, as we must for a Londoner. We were standing up in Sheneval among the heavy swathes, the green Forestry Commission wood behind us, larch and spruce, and ahead, between us and the blue sea, green oats, green grazing, green hedges soaked with rain.

Watching him, I hoped he had put on a bit of weight; I had tried to feed him with milk and butter and meat, knowing he was going back to a tough six months before the crops round Mochudi ripen if – and one dares only say if – the rain comes for the ploughing. Francis Phirie had never been out of South Africa before, had never been on a sea voyage before the Campbeltown boat brought him here to see the way of life of his tribal adviser. Perhaps in some ways he could learn more from my farm than at the splendid English agricultural institutes to which the Central Office of Information took him and his Batswana friends. Here the implements we use are a halfway step between the agriculture of those without capital, such as African tribesmen, and those who accumulate elaborate agricultural machinery in order to avoid taxation of profit. Buck rake, seed drill, row-crop grubber: they all made sense to somebody like him.

He didn't, of course, realise how abnormally difficult a year we were having. Spring had come so late that there was little growth on the grass until June, the only month when we had a run of fine weather. Had we cut near the end of June, we might have got the hay up safely, but it would have been a very light crop, and I have so many cattle now that I have to think hard about winter keep. The first cut with Mains field was in early July, but then it rained every day, or every other day, for three weeks, soaking the cut grass and matting the uncut hay crop, which filled up with tough red clover, difficult to dry and not such good food value as soft grass. It could be cut only one way, and even so it went well only when half a dozen people stood along the cut, turning over and pulling back the cut swathe, which otherwise just stayed as if it were still attached to the growing crop. It was as bad in the field of second-year hay, though Lachlan made an effort to get right round it. But the blades of the mower were continually choking up.

Still we began to get it up gradually into ricks, gratifyingly close to one another. It looked like being twice the bulk of last year. It was curious to find myself using a pitchfork and rick-building again with Eddie and Colin. I'd thought all that was over after I got tossed by the cow in the Oban sale-ring; last summer I just couldn't have done it, nor gone down on my knees to pull out the loose stuff from the base of the stacks. But the hot sun of Mochudi dealt with that; odd, at my age, suddenly feeling younger. And not to sunburn because one's skin has taken in enough melanin – probably a sign of hideous decadence in a white, according to the writers of anti-black anonymous letters!

The team work of rick-building goes with few words. Lachlan backs in a buck rake load of loose hay. Everyone knows what to do, how to steady someone else's forkful at the point of the rick, how to comb down the sides into a good shape to keep the rain from going into it, how to rope it at the end. 'Hae ye enough?' 'Aye.' 'Pull now.' 'She'll do.' And away we go to the next set of stacks, set up the tripod, begin to build.

The men are all extra friendly to Francis, with the politeness of Highlanders to a stranger, but above all feeling that he comes from folk who have had a hard do. One evening I took him up the glen to Kilmichael, the MacKeith farm, with my granddaughter who wanted the tune of one of the old Campbeltown songs, 'Flory Loynachan'. Dunkie sang it to her, in a voice less strong at eighty-plus than it must have been at forty, but with lovely feeling. In a couple of repetitions Francis picked it up and could hum it. I asked him, would he not sing something for us? 'Oh no,' he said. 'I cannot sing. I can only teach it.' For teaching is his life, although as Educational Secretary to the Bakgatla he gets less chance of doing it than he used.

I found out a lot I didn't know about the Mochudi schools and their organisation, including the fact that, on a directive from the Bechuanaland Education Office, children will now not be accepted for school over eleven years old. So twelve and thirteen-year-olds, whose parents happen to have kept them herding at the cattle posts, will be cut off from school, creating future adult education problems. The educational intention is fine, bringing the children in at a reasonable age and making life easier for the teachers. But meantime, in the tribal areas, school must still be paid for by the parents. Only a few shillings, but if you don't have a cash income that is rather a teaser. Or if you have had to spend every penny on a little meal or grain to tide you over.

Yet this isn't sufficient to build urgently needed new classrooms or take primary education off the two shift system. Couldn't the British taxpayer give a little more towards education in the Protectorate instead of acquiescing delightedly in a cut in the Colonial Development and Welfare funds paid by Britain?

I saw Francis off in the train at Glasgow with a box of film strip for his new projector, a small bottle of real sea-water, a pinch of sand and some mussel shells. He was horribly nervous about the Salisbury customs; for a moment I saw them through his eyes, those tough-looking, red-kneed Southern Rhodesians, who would think of him as – what? Not, I'm afraid, as a man and a brother, though perhaps that's too much to expect of any Customs Officer towards any traveller! 'Nonsense,' I said: 'You've got your letter from the Colonial Office, there's nothing to worry about.' And I saw the other people in the railway carriage obviously preparing to be nice to him.

What will Francis Phirie remember? I hope the general friendliness of the people he met, who perhaps didn't even know where Bechuanaland was, but who now see it as a real place with very real problems for which they are partly responsible. The farm supper at Kilmichael, with new strawberry jam on pancakes and girdle scones; the summer sea and Ailsa Craig tangling its top in clouds; above all the heavy swathes of grass, the fat cows in the wet pasture, the green, ah the green, of the rich and fortunate northern islands of Britain.

New Statesman, v. 66, 22 November 1963, pp. 738, 740

The Deadly Bracken

(1965)

The Highlands are covered with bracken, which nobody has found a cheap and effective way of eradicating, and we are encouraged to keep cattle. The numbers have been going up steadily, as has the price of beef, and one or two other things. In the last financial year, for instance, I notice that the hill cattle subsidy is edging up, a few thousand beyond the £1m mark. But from time to time these cattle eat that bracken; then there is trouble. Bracken contains an alkaloid which produces fever and extensive bleeding in all the body cavities. Cattle which have lived all their lives in bracken country with only a nibble here and there seem to get immunity. Yet sometimes it breaks down and there is an epidemic of bracken poisoning. There seem to be one or two every year in Kintyre. It was my turn now.

I have kept cattle since 1938, apart from a year when my beasts had a horrible attack of brucella (contagious abortion) so that I had to get rid of them. Nowadays we inoculate the heifers against brucella; this is a Ministry service and should clear up the disease, just as bovine tuberculosis was got rid of in its time. I have made various attempts at bracken destruction, cutting patches three years running, but it is a discouraging thing to try. Walking across the Bay, waist deep in bracken, I remember going up and down with the tractor and the old mower, trying to avoid stumps and hillocks that would jam the blades, getting down to free them and then starting again. The ground didn't stay clean for more than a couple of years after the cutting except in one or two places where whins have taken over instead.

But there is a big acreage. I feed in winter and spring until the grass comes. The kale is kept for the milk cows, but Lachlan takes the tractor and trailer down to the Bay, first with turnips and the oat straw after the first threshing. This must be used as soon as possible if it is to have any feeding value, and it certainly has some, partly because the sheaves in the sown-out fields have a good deal of grass and clover in the base, and partly that oat straw, cut fairly green, has not lost all its sap, as ripe wheat or rye straw has. In the south it shocks me to see the straw bales left after combining simply being burnt, not even used for bedding. This year English farmers have even burnt wet hay, so as not to use expensive labour in winning it. Here one begins to doubt whether there is any connection between economics and morals.

We give the out-wintered Galloways hay after Christmas and some compound feeding-stuffs mixed with our own crushed oats. But this year it was late on into April before there was any grazing on the Bay, and many of the cows had calved in February or March. Partly because I was uncertain of the temper of my new shorthorn bull, a sturdy white chap who should throw a crop of blue-gray calves, they were put onto the Point before the Glasgow fair fortnight and after, when the Bay is full of campers, bathers and so on. But the green on the Point is more rush and fern than grass. They must have been hungry and taken to bracken. Suddenly, within as many days, four of them were dead – four cows in calf – which in the sale ring would have fetched around £50 each.

Neither Lachlan nor I suspected bracken poisoning; both bracken and rhododendron flourish here and can't be got rid of, but we have never had any trouble. But we were a little scared of anthrax; there had been a case among our neighbours in spring, with all the quarantine, police action, burning the body and so on. The first diagnosis said red-water fever; it is quite something, doing a PM on a half-ton cow corpse. But then it became clear that it was bracken poisoning.

We took them back onto the Bay and tried to tempt them with hay, but they were not interested. There was plenty of grass, if only they would keep off the bracken, which by now they had developed a taste for! But there is an antidote, recently come on by chance. Mr Sutherland, the vet, brought it up, keeping it warm under his car heater, as otherwise it grows viscous and the syringe can't take it.

By now all the cattle were in the shed; one by one they were driven out through the slype, a strong wooden affair, too narrow for a grown beast to turn in. Each one had her tail held back and her temperature taken while she tossed and fidgeted and looked round wild-eyed. Mochele, a fellow Mokgatla from Bechuanaland, liking to be with cattle again, came and helped. Sometimes a cow can be quieted or distracted if one breathes into her face, others respond to a bit of handling. One or two were very wild, but Mr Sutherland didn't lose one thermometer! Some were a bit thin, others were in fine condition, with the wavy gloss of the Galloway coat, black shading to golden brown, but none of this was a clue as to whether or not they had been poisoned. The white bull was most amicable, but his coat had nothing silky about it; it was more like a polar bear hearthrug.

Five of the cows had temperatures over normal and each got a syringe full of the antidote into her behind. One was bleeding a little at the nose, a sign of danger. She was a young beast; they don't get to their full bulk until the second or third calf. One, which had looked to me ill the day before, was diagnosed as having worms, and an appropriate dose will go into her. Once they were through, those with older calves scattered, but the ones with young calves still in the shed came close and bellowed at us. The bull was calm and uninterested.

Some of the bull calves hadn't yet been castrated, so Mr Sutherland did this at the same time. Mochele obviously felt that it was unkind to do it so young, but here we think that the younger the less pain. If they are left until over four months they must have an anaesthetic. They kick as if they had six legs each and bleat piteously during the actual crushing of the cord by the vet's pincers, but then they bounce off and have a good suck at their mothers, or, for that matter, someone else's. These cows take over each other's calves, a good thing, especially if, as happened this time, the mother dies while the calf is still suckling. At least these calves are not shut into dark cells to be turned into veal; they have some rights as living, individual creatures.

Now we wait. Lachlan will go round them every day. He knows quite well which are the ones which had the poison and the antidote. I can't tell which is which, but he knows, just as a shepherd, even more surprisingly, knows individual sheep. Perhaps I was slightly overstocked for the carrying capacity of the ground. I doubt if bracken cutting pays; the grass which is uncovered is soft and unpalatable. Even the strip which we harrowed and limed after three years cutting is not much good. But there is a better hay crop this year; it is all up on tripods in the fields, ready to come into the Dutch barn. We should manage that before the oats are ready, though they are beginning to change colour a little.

The oat crop has stood up to the abominable weather. I still sow 'Forward', not the newest of oats, but it doesn't seem to go down. We shall need all the oat straw and most of the hay this winter, and trust that the Galloways will keep off bracken and lose the taste for it, let's hope for good.

New Statesman, v. 70, 27 August 1965, p. 282

The Day I Took a Fellow Tribesman to Tarbert Fair

(1966)

In a changing world Tarbert Fair changes little. The oldest farmers, the ones who still swear in the Gaelic, seem to be no older. The boots, clumping on to the wooden staging round the sale ring, are as solid and unfashionable as ever they were. The amicable hands one grasps are as firmly beefy.

I took my fellow tribesman from Bechuanaland to the sale. Better, surely, that one's overseas visitors should be shown not the prize beasts, that one can hardly believe oneself are really cattle, but the ordinary farm stock off the fields and hills. These are beasts they can compare with their own.

It is the same with farm implements. How pointless to take people from the poorer African countries and dazzle them with expensive and sometimes incomprehensible machinery! Yet this often happens on official tours. Those who come to my farm see things which are simple and not expensive, which they can easily imagine themselves using: a buck rake, a seeder, a hay tedder, and so on. Above all, they see us all working, and working cheerily; they see me with a hay fork – and how easily the movement comes back to one year after year, so that one spares oneself the extra effort which those who are not used to such things put into it.

I can explain to my African friends how when I first started farming we still sowed by hand from a sowing sheet – I was rather good at this, casting the light, shimmering hay seed evenly right and left. In those days we sowed in the plough furrows, harrowing afterwards. Now we sow with a seeder but the seed bed has to be prepared, hence these discs. That way, it all makes historical sense.

There is not much selling by auction in Bechuanaland. The dealers come round buying people's cattle, often at a poor price, since so many people only sell when they suddenly want money for some urgent matter like school fees or to buy the things they must have: meal, tobacco, sugar and tea, paraffin, matches.

Other cattle, if they are in decent condition, are sent to the abattoir and get a standard grading and the price that goes with it. A man who gets £20 for a beast thinks himself lucky. But we plan a buying and selling co-operative, and my Bechuanaland friend has already been to visit the Kintyre Farmers' Co-operative, thrilled to hear how small it started and how quickly and successfully it has grown. This might happen in Mochudi, our tribal capital, to which he is going back.

He watches the sales intently. He has a good eye for a beast and soon recognises the crosses; he knows the Hereford face, for there are a few Hereford bulls leaving their mark on the herds of Bechuanaland. Prices are good in the early part of the sale, dairy cows mostly. Of course they are not like prices in the really big markets; we don't go in for anything fancy. But they are far beyond what anyone gets out in Africa.

I suppose I have my eye in for African faces; I find myself struck, looking round me, by the extraordinary cragginess of the farmers' features, the jutting noses, the great bushy brows, the solid chins. And these pale blue or blue-grey eyes: isn't that an odd colour for eyes to be?[1] Yet they are kindly faces on the whole; what is lacking perhaps is imagination. Kindness is for a rather small circle.

The sale goes on, with the constant whack of the sticks, the din of the voices echoing from the tin roof, an occasional furious or frustrated lowing from one of the beasts, or the high voice of a pointing child. There are quite a few children, some with funny hats or toffee apples from the fairground down at the harbour. We move on to the young stock, the stots and heifers. My friend can hardly believe they are only eighteen months or two years old. 'Ours are still calves then,' he says, 'but if we could only sell them younger!'

My own are fairly far on in the sale and I begin to worry and watch the prices. There is one lot which has been fattened and fetch extra good prices; these are Aberdeen Angus crosses with their short legs and thick hindquarters, something altogether different from the bony Bechuanaland cows, Afrikanders mostly, which have to walk miles and miles for grazing and water. But the Angus crosses have had plenty of cake and will need more yet. By Christmas they may be into three figures.

My own are the last of my pure Galloway stirks. I am now working with a white shorthorn bull. Pedigree breeding is all very well, but it just doesn't pay. And there is a good deal of paper work with it, though I always rather enjoyed thinking up the names. But next year I shall have crosses, which are likely to be a good deal heavier and solider than my shaggy Galloways.

Lachlan is watching over them and having plenty of conversation; that's half the fun of a sale. I keep on meeting old friends, too, and having conversations and wishing to goodness that I could always put the right name to the face.

And now my own lot are being loosed out of the pen and coming round. I look in at the ring once more, trying to see how the prices are going, as always failing to see where the bidding is coming from. Then I go round to the far side to meet Lachlan. These are mild little beasts compared to the grown Galloway cows which will toss one with no bother if they've a mind to it.

There is a pretty little Ayrshire heifer, nicely shaped. I can't altogether get used to the hornlessness of the modern Ayrshire, but that's all the fashion now, and there's certainly something to be said for not getting a horn in one's eye.

Lachlan arranges them and the Ayrshire goes in first. She makes £45 and I do hope she will find a good home; I expect so; people are kind to their dairy beasts. I had sold the best of the young Galloways at the earlier sale, where on the whole one gets better prices. By July most people are stocked up, but still, there is any amount of grass and bidding is fairly brisk. They come in three separate lots, but there is not much to it in prices; the average works out slightly over £30.

I come out of the ring and rejoin my fellow tribesman, who has been watching with the greatest interest. Was it right that I shook my head at one point? Yes, indeed, I said. I wasn't going to let them go below £30 and if I hadn't said no the bidding could have stuck. Of course I might have been left with them, but one just has to judge it for oneself.

Lachlan said he'd go back with the lorry. He had just a few more friends to see. By now the singing from the bar was getting sadly out of tune. But there was a general air of wellbeing about both buyers and sellers. We went down to the harbour, the fishing boats in after a good night at the herring, and the fair booths set up all along the edge of the sea, with expectant squawkings and thumpings rising from the roundabouts.

But some way, like everything else, the fair has got very dear.

You'd need to pay out a whole shilling for almost anything, where it used to be pennies in the old days. My tribesman was a bit puzzled. Would he like to go on the merry-go-round? No, indeed he wouldn't! Or on the bumping cars? No, no! At the shooting booths he got the black every time, but not the irrelevant little white dot in the middle which would have entitled us to a coconut.

'If it had been a lion,' he said rather indignantly, 'it would have been dead now!'

The Glasgow Herald, 20 August 1966, p. 3

[1] An echo of Mitchison's observations in her African memoir *Return to the Fairy Hill* (1966).

Skills and Changes

(1977)

Today's agricultural worker is likely to spend most of his working hours on his own, driving a tractor or a combine, perhaps having to wear a mask, and with some fairly powerful, complex and potentially dangerous machinery attached. He must watch over this, so as to catch any developing trouble. If the recent anti-noise regulations are taken seriously, the driver is even more isolated; he will scarcely be able to hear if anything is going wrong with the mechanism which he is towing, still less when someone shouts from the far side of the field that a load of fertiliser has arrived – or the Man from the Ministry.

A few years back he might well have been in the seat of a smaller tractor, without a safety cab; but if, for instance, he was pulling an old-fashioned long-bladed mower or a binder, there was his mate perched on its seat to shout at him if there was s snag. If his binder was circling an oat-field he would be constantly passing the crowd of stookers, probably with cheerful, shouting children lugging sheaves their own size.

Another step back and you come to the pair of horses which were themselves a kind of companionship. The pairs of oxen in the Orkneys, wearing horse-collars for pulling but with the haims pointed downward to clear the dewlap, were perhaps less intelligent and friendly than horses, but still living beings in your own world. Further back takes you to the row of scythers working across a harvest field, as I remember them from my Perthshire childhood, the women binders going behind and the old and very young gleaners, including me, last. Yes, it was hard and heavy work. Yes, the pay was miserable and the hours long. We know. But a whole range of skills has been lost, and those that replace them are less varied and often just as heavy. I can work with most hand implements or build a stack, but I can't even lift some of the machine components and it's a struggle to carry a tight hay bale.

We used to carry tea out to the hay field or harvest, scones and new jam; there was talk and laughter, everyone a bit loosened up, the men and women pleased with one another's company. Now there's no time for that, everything goes at the machine's pace. Talk and laughing may come later among the men at the bar, now that everyone can afford a round, but it's not so friendly. It is seldom enough that a modern farm needs a crowd. While we all grew oats extra hands were needed, not only at harvest but when the threshing mill came round – a good neighbourly occasion, that, with a big meal provided by each farm it went to. But the threshing mill became uneconomic; it was old and spares not to be had. Now the combine rushes round our barley and in no time there is a beautiful heap of grain. Yet we do cooperate in the sense that we do contract work for one another among the local farms, sometimes share the dipping and are always ready to lend a piece of equipment to a neighbour.

Today, shearing is done by one professional shearer with his own electric shears, the farm supplying the outlet; he needs two others to catch and place the sheep. He comes to us all in turn, but we must be careful not to have him too early; you can't shear until the thick fleece has lifted away from the skin, leaving a layer of hairs to cut through. But in the old days there might be a small crowd of hand shearers working together. I remember shearing my much petted Border Leicester tup, and how, when I untied his feet, he stamped and roared furiously at me. The policeman is supposed to look in on the statutory dipping, but can't be everywhere at once and may well be afraid of being made to help. But, with the new dips, the fleeces, which used to be mucky with ticks and keds, now come off clean, ready to roll. I'm sure, too, that it is nicer for the ewes to have two minutes of professional shearing than one of us taking five times as long and probably nicking her into the bargain.

This is all part of the transition from comparatively small-scale farming run by, or in close association with, a knowledgeable owner or tenant, to factory farming. It seems clear that factory farming is short-term, immediate profit based, and has little use for conservation, including the stability and fertility of the land. What is the point of worrying about that if profits depend on an economic situation that has nothing to do with farming? Most small-scale farming, which is particularly appropriate in areas with narrowish fertile valleys between useable but difficult hill land, is very careful of the future.

Percy Edwards, gardener and friend, in the walled garden

Anthony Edwards (Percy's son) in the tractor, pulling up a section of fence

The small mixed farm is flexible. Probably several crops are grown on relatively small acreages (how inappropriate and irritating is this change to hectares in the forms we have to fill up!) so that we avoid devastating one-crop failures. Above all, people switch about and must have, at least, some of the old hand skills. On the factory farm the man on the tractor has one job; he is not taking in the whole thing, any more than the man on the assembly line is interested in the completed car. His primary interest is bound to be his pay and his mechanical skill. His machine attachments change, but the main job, up and down, is the same. He is not really sharing in the farm's purpose. There can be none of the old companionship, leaning over a gate, chatting away, master and man, deciding what a field needs and what it will give back if properly treated. Participation has become a boring word, but it is genuine in one kind of farming, not in another.

Nor is it simply between people. You can be skilled with machines but you don't really get a sympathetic response from them. You do get this from animals, especially milking cows. In the days before we had mains electricity and machine milking with those horribly heavy churns, my land girl Jean and I used to go out carrying a bucket of water and an old towel, our milking pails and stools, and call the cows who clearly enjoyed the process of hand milking and turned their heads to give us an occasional lick. Jean used to sing to them sometimes and they liked that. It took time, of course, but why not if one is in no hurry to do something else?

Let me remember one other thing from old, pre-tractor days: Lachlan ploughing with the pair, Jo and Echran, and twisting the furrow to save a peewit's nest. Is that laughable? And two other points. One is that every time you buy a piece of machinery in order to economise on working costs, you help to put someone out of work. The other is that there are a good many men and women, not drop-outs but competent people, who want to live and work, not in industrial cities but in the country, and not necessarily on an urban standard of living, because they do not have to make up for some of the less pleasant aspects of city life. They do not, however, want to do semi-industrial work on factory farms; they may not be interested in, or good at, mechanical skills. Probably they hope to work, partly at least, with stock on a mixed farm.

I would add that, in the Highlands, which I know reasonably well by now, there are just not enough small farm units for those, including farmers' sons, often with modern agricultural training, who want to make a start on their own and work their way up. The Department of Agriculture and Fisheries has been told this often enough! Perhaps also land-owners who might have let small farms on reasonably long leases – ten or twenty years – are unwilling to take a tenant who, today, has complete security of tenure, whatever he does, so that the landlord has no say at all.

Every year there are fewer voters outside the towns. The big farmers get their publicity and make their demands through the NFU. In Scotland the crofters' voice is listened to. But money is the only measure. Good land use is not only about economics, but about aspects of living which cannot be exactly quantified. Nevertheless, they exist.

New Statesman, v. 94, 19 August 1977, p. 235

No more porridge

(1982)

One of my old friends, sadly retired from his small hill farm to live in a council house, shook his head: 'There'll be nay mair parritch'. And sure enough, from where we stood there was nothing but barley fields, golden barley and the combine harvesters humming over them, moving from one crop to the next. Here, one farmer in a group will own a combine which he hires out, and this seems to work well enough with the earliest fields getting the first cut. Many of these fields on the Kintyre peninsula are steep, between hill and sea, and I catch myself worrying about some of the top-heavy-looking machinery, but the men on the tractors are always confident. Soon every field will be bare. Ploughing will start early, often for a crop of winter barley.

Over the last five years the visual pattern and below it, the actual pattern of work, has changed, following the cereal prices: barley, barley! Even more important, an oat crop cannot be harvested by combine; if it is left until the seed is ripe, it will shed. Above all, it means not one or perhaps two working, but a team. Harvest used to be a time of tension, often a race against the weather, with room for plenty of labour, skilled and unskilled. The oat sheaves were stooked, six together, in long beautiful lines, straight across the level fields or following the hill contours in eye-gladdening curves, pale gold on green, with the under-sown grass or clover quickly springing up. They had to wait a while to dry out before stacking. In a damp autumn the stooks would need to be shaken out and turned into the wind, a tedious job with the smell of mould beginning to creep through the good smell of ripe grain.

Once we started carrying, the work was mostly skilled. Five years ago was the last time I helped to build a stack, catching the sheaves as they were forked across, laying the driest snugly, heads to the middle, keeping any I suspected of damp well to the side as the stack rose above the level of its three props; and from up there one could see the clearing of the fields. Skilled friends from the village would come and help, two stacks at a time going up. At the end Lachlan would thatch them with green rushes pegged down to stand the weather until the big thresher came round.

All that has gone, except perhaps on a few small family farms where oats are still grown. At least in this part of the world, where it is almost all mixed farming, there is no burning of the stubble as there is in monoculture wheat lands. The barley is on short straw which does not go down, or if it does the combine picks it up easily. The oat straw was good for early winter feeding to stock; barley is poor food but is good enough for bedding.

It is not that barley-growing is new. At one time the Laggan of Kintyre, the flat, fertile land between the two seas, grew barley for the many Campbeltown distilleries. Now most of that acreage has been knocked out of cultivation by the NATO base. Instead of the stacks or the long potato or turnip clamps, those ridges you see are full of nuclear torpedo heads and such for the sinister games which are played nowadays. Also, of course, the two dozen or so local distilleries have been rationalised into two.

We see few turnip fields now and the potato ridges are mostly for home consumption. Both mean labour at two points, early cultivation and harvesting. It also means less and less work for the travelling people, the 'tinkers' who used to have a real place in the rural communities. The district council now tries to rehouse and settle them permanently. There are difficulties here. Existing tenants complain about tinker neighbours, not up to their own standards. This is often unfair when the tinkers are struggling for a place in society and when some at least of the children deeply want education and the better chances that go with it. But too many of the older ones are disheartened, not able to get their traditional work, with no turnip-singling nor potato-lifting and even their basket-making sabotaged by imports from Taiwan and Korea.

There are other problems in agricultural transition. Weed-killers and pesticides mean fewer butterflies; this year I did not even see the usual clusters of red admirals and tortoise-shells on my buddleias. Perhaps this is unimportant and we should feel guilty at regretting poppies and corn-cockle, or, for that matter, the social get-together when the big mechanical threshing machine used to come round, moving from farm to farm, a day or so at each, and the women-folk vying with each other to produce the best dinner for the helpers. Now one man can do the work of a dozen – that is, so long as his machinery doesn't break down.

My old friend who worried about his porridge meal ran his own farm but in a less profit-oriented way. He didn't like to be hurried. Once, asking the whereabouts of a heifer which might be for sale, I was told: 'Och, she's away in the mist'. There was, clearly, no hurry. Farming was less of a business and more of a way of life, something you were brought up to and expected to go on with. It still is in a way, but now there is much more watching over the profit margins. Equally you may be more susceptible to the advertisers. The sales are as important but perhaps less social affairs than they used to be when one's friends rolled in and out of the drinking tent, with no unseemly hurry to be getting home. I wonder, though, if some of the older people don't miss the companionship of the working horses. There was also the companionship of the milking shed; with hand-milking we got to have a real relationship with our cows, whether or not they were good milkers.

What other changes are we going to see? I think people here realise that wind-breaks are important. Farmers here are less likely than those in monoculture country to cut down hedges and trees. We still have a lot of good stone dykes left. But all kinds of oil-based fuel are going up in price. There may be changes in the air. But what will they be?

TThe Countryman, v. 87, Autumn 1982, pp. 66-70

PART IV

THE FISHING

Herring Country

(1961)

Go south along the loch from Inveraray towards Kintyre. Every hundred yards or so you may see a heron, standing and watching hump-backed in the middle of his own fishing ground. Wait till he takes off! With a single wing flap he unfurls into a shape of trailing beauty.

All along the south Argyll roads you see rare and lovely birds; handsome hawks, big buzzards, square-winged kestrels, hen-harriers, and even a golden eagle, high and far off. Not that their eyries are always hard to find; I have been close to one of them, perched so precariously on a cliff edge that I felt that, as a good county councillor, I ought to put up a danger notice or even a closure order. ... The white-feathered eaglet stared at me, the parents circled but realised I wasn't trying to harm them.

There are deer too, fallows and roes and an occasional red deer which has wandered down. The shallow end of West Loch Tarbert is full of wild swans which sometimes fly over, necks stretched, wings creaking. Greylags or pink-footed geese settle on a field and graze it. There are handsome eider duck, oyster catchers, mergansers, and many another, and on every sandy beach the charming and ridiculous little ringed plover, moving like clockwork toys.

Tarbert is the entrance to Kintyre. The old castle stands high above the harbour, the new boat-building yard, and the many small boats at anchor. Yes, and in the daytime the herring boats, asleep until early evening, when smoke begins to rise, and a smell of tea, and then, one by one, they slip out to the fishing grounds.

The main road to Campbeltown goes along the west coast, with marvellous views of the islands, small villages, and the ferry across to Gigha and a wonderful garden opened to visitors. Almost everywhere there is a narrow strip of cultivation and then the hills of central Kintyre, dotted with sheep. The road turns inland near the aerodrome, the famous golf course of Machrihanish, the coal mine where the tail end of the Ayrshire coal seams turns up again, and Campbeltown itself, the not-so-large metropolis of Kintyre, also asserting itself as a fishing town with nets draped along the harbour front and a good-going net factory which probably provides you with your garden pea nets. Most of the distilleries are shut, but it is still possible to get the pure Campbeltown malt whisky, dusky tasting and unmistakable.

But if you take the east road from Tarbert to Campbeltown, you see still more signs of fishing. The narrow, twisting road, diving in and out of light woodland, gives you a superb view of the great cloud-capped ridge of Arran, across the Kilbrannan Sound, which is one of the best herring fishing grounds in a good season. At night the boats, with their working lights, looks like clusters of villages far out in the dark, or the risen full moon makes a silver path between them.

Halfway to Campbeltown the road twists inland to the gentle and fertile glen with the Carradale river looping brightly down it. The new Forestry Commission plantations are varied and handsome, with a well-designed mixture of the different spruces and larches, the old Scotch pine, and decorative trees as well. The glen widens at the bottom to a long sandy bay, facing south, and a village which is much loved by summer visitors. But the new harbour at Carradale is the focal centre, highly utilitarian, steel piles and concrete, and the boats sheltering against it. On a good night they will take you out, and there will be the thrill of the great ring-net coming in, and the silver mass of herring – best of food when they are fresh – with the gulls swooping at them. That's something you'll not get except with the Carradale fishermen, and it's something you will never forget.

The Glasgow Herald, 30 September 1961, p. 2

Bringing Home the New Boat

(1949)

We came over from the west to fetch the *Maid of Morvern*, the fifty-three foot ring-net boat, newest of the Carradale herring fishing fleet. She had been built at Weatherhead's Eyemouth yard. Last time I had seen her she was three-quarters planked, the beautiful sea-going lines of the plain larch, curving from high bow to stern, the solid oak ribs and keel stark among blue sky and sea and flowering elder bushes. We had watched the steaming planks being laid in, bent as though they were plywood instead of heavy timbers that needed six men to carry them, each individual piece of wood curved down into part of something else, into the planned shape of a boat.

But now she was finished, the basic lines somewhat obscured by new paint and varnish. Yet in the end she had become not simply a boat, but a special kind of fishing boat.

Engine and winch were in, wheelhouse, fo'c'sle and hold, the echo-sounder being fitted. Some things were obviously on the point of going in, the brailer pole, one end shod, the other waiting for its fitting, was in the shed; then there were coils of rope and chain and the anchor. But a few major things, not the concern of the Eyemouth yard, were promised and overdue, mostly metal parts which had to be galvanised; most important of all, the rudder.

However, we had J.J. Robertson, MP, Joint Under Secretary of State for Scotland, due to christen her at high water, among his cheering voters and a lovely smell of claret! Then we had the traditional tea with all the men from the yard, led by Willie Weatherhead and Neen Black. We all said our piece, and even the teetotallers, just for this once, managed a wee glass of something! And then it was back to work, finishing her off.

We had hoped to sail next day, but the rudder, when it came from the galvanisers, didn't quite fit and the alterations took too long for us to make the tide. There were various things which couldn't be done until the rudder was fixed. The men in the yard started them as dusk was beginning to fall; Willie wading in below the boat to get at the rudder, Neen, on his knees, above, surrounded by tools and chips; and the rest hurrying and intent, but yet not driven – each an intelligent and skilled craftsman working in close harmony with his fellows, an encouraging and inspiring sight.

We all did what we could to help, but we were nervous, worried. This was Thursday. Denis was due to start the fishing on Monday. We must be back by Saturday. At last it seemed certain that we would. It was midnight past and we would need to make a start at four in the morning to get the tide.

There were too many of us for the fo'c'sle, so some of us slept down in the hold. Once it had been packed with herring the hold would be no place to sleep, but now it was comfortable enough, lying on blankets and the new sails which, in a modern diesel-engined boat, might never be used.

When we came on deck it was dark still, a high late moon, and the ugly yellow sodium lights dotted along the far side of Eyemouth harbour. The Weatherheads' car drove up; our loud voices broke the quiet night, and then the rattle of chains and the engine starting up at last. We towed her down carefully to the main basin. Suddenly the sodium lights clicked off and we saw it was dawn. We turned east out of Eyemouth harbour into a light jabble of sea, the place where the sun was to rise showing pink against the enormous grey of sky and water, and the moon gradually losing power. She began, for the first time, to rise to the waves.

Now we set the course to round the high cliffs of St Abb's Head. Colour spread and spread through all the sky and at last the gold finger of the sun pierced the waves and rapidly became a disc and lifted itself. The Weatherheads were coming with us for the first hundred miles to see that all was well. They watched her as closely as we did.

We were all keen to try our hand at the steering or else to start the echo-sounder. Denis was beginning to calm down, to feel that we were on our way home, that the boat was his own at last, that she was a lovely sea boat, faster than any fishing boat he had been on yet, that after all these years the thing had come true. He knew well enough that he could never have had her on his own, and he was saying in words what many fishermen feel and know – their real gratitude for the Herring Industry Board's loan and grant scheme. My share in the boat was of course completely paid up

Denis Macintosh, part-owner and skipper of the fishing boat
Maid of Morvern

and he was already making plans for making the very most of the herring fishing and repaying the loan as soon as possible.

Meanwhile, Fred was in with the engine. Rob at the compass was explaining to me about the true east and how to take bearings from the rising sun; like many of the Carradale men, he had just taken the new fisherman's examination. Then Lilla called us down to the fo'c'sle for a grand breakfast of kippers.

When we came up again the sun had gone in behind a sky of clouds. We could see Traprain Law and Berwick Law, and ahead of us the Bass Rock, small and odd-looking. I was sleepy by now, half slept, and woke when we were almost under the Bass, which was now suddenly huge; we were steering straight at it, for it rises out of deep water. There were solans all round us, so many that they looked small. One had to remind oneself that they have a wing span of six feet. We hooted at them, but the thousands on the rock ledges paid no attention. It must have been forty-five years since I was last on the Bass; what a heart-in-the-mouth business it must have been for my mother to stop me running over the edge!

Now we were heading into the Firth and the air was thickening all round us so that Edinburgh was half hidden with only an indication here and there of spires and the Castle Rock. Then we began to see the spidery threads of the Forth Bridge. It was here that the Carradale herring fleet had been fishing in '29, in the bad days of falling markets and dumping. The skippers of the boats were hardly able to get the price of a meal ashore, and it was worse for the share fishermen.

Denis was speaking of one bad week working from dusk to dawn and scarcely enough in the divide to keep them going at all, and then he had a letter from Lilla with half a crown and they had gone ashore and got cigarettes for the whole crew.

As we came up to the Forth Bridge a little train went trotting by overhead. It was difficult to realise that it was something real, not just a toy one could flip off. The houses at the root of the bridge where the painters live who spend their lives painting and repainting the framework, looked tiny too. The water here was no longer beautiful but thick with mud, and scummy with oil. A destroyer passed us, smart and pretty with modish touches of scarlet on grey. We waved to her and the Navy relaxed and waved back. Here we were in the thick of peculiar badges of Admiralty, old ships, targets, and whatnot.

We made for Grangemouth and the mouth of the Forth and Clyde canal. I have seen a good many ugly towns, but Grangemouth, crouching in its surroundings of mud like someone in the second circle of the Inferno, was just about the ugliest yet. Even the enormous lock gates were mud-coloured. Yet, as so often happens, the people were charming. We got provisions at the friendly and helpful Co-op, and the minor officials down at the dock couldn't have been nicer to us. Here we began the climb through the industrial part of Scotland, starting with the slums of Grangemouth and Falkirk.

The canal is old, almost derelict in parts, and is little used except by the fishing boats coming and going, and indeed it is almost too narrow for them.

It was hard to keep her straight, especially later in the day when there were sudden gusts of wind which caught her high bow; she was only lightly ballasted. We were lucky with our locks. Another boat must have been going in the opposite direction, and at first all the locks were open on our level. We went in very slowly, fussing about our new paint. Where the locks were close together it was easiest for the shore party to walk. We had to work the locks ourselves and secure the boat by ropes fore and aft. Some of the gates seemed so old that one was half afraid to push them. The *Maid* had stuck for a little in the Grangemouth mud, and we brushed down her sides vigorously. It would never have done to come home with a muddy face.

We were all doing our lock drill well when we came to a basin that had only a few feet of water at the bottom, and here we had to wait while the water was let in from the next reach. For several miles we had to go very gingerly, wondering whether we would stick, always ready to push her off from the bank.

At last we got into pleasanter country and longer stretches between locks. At Wineford there were two little girl pipers who played for us while the boat gradually rose, and after we had opened the gates played us away. I think one of them was the daughter of the lockkeeper and I only hope she and her father know what pleasure and encouragement they gave to a few West Highlanders.

Now we could see the line of the Campsie Fells, to the north. The sky had cleared and it was a warm evening. We hurried as much as we could, for the bridge-keepers of the electrically operated bridges go home at dusk. We could work the small swing-back bridges ourselves. Fred and Campbell would jump up on to the bridge before the bows quite touched, swing back the two halves, and then jump again after we had gone through. But at last we came to a great road bridge whose operator had gone to bed nine miles away. It was dark now and we tied up to the side, a last cup of tea and then to bed. I shoved back one of the planks of the hatch so as to feel soft air smelling of water weeds and harvest patting at my face whenever I half-woke in the night.

About six in the morning the bridge swung back and we were heading for Maryhill. Now we began dropping in a steep curve round the back of Glasgow. Here we passed backyards and ends of streets, sheds and cranes and tag-ends of industry. Colin and I went with the heavy can to get water and did badly by putting the filler in crooked and pouring all the water into the bilges. There was still a small leak in the quarter, probably where a plank had been strained in the launching. We watched for some time to see if it would right itself, as it did in time. A new boat is apt to have teething troubles and our gear chain slipped several times.

We still had to pick up our switchboard at Anniesland. If I were to write a detective novel, this underside of Glasgow would be the scene of it. Here the canal came down in steps, basin and lock one on top of the other, and here and there old boats or rusty boilers and engines. No fallen tree ever looks quite so forlorn and ugly as these man-made things do when they are no longer needed. In one lock I did think I had found a corpse in a sack, but Rob decided it was a dog. Even if it had been a corpse I don't think any of us would have wanted to interfere. It was the kind of place where it was better to pass by and say nothing.

Further on we came to housing estates and little gardens and once a shed full of pigeons. At the locks we were invaded by little boys and unwittingly took two of them a long way from home. Rob and Denis gave them pennies for their fare back, but I couldn't help wondering whether they didn't do it regularly when they got a chance. Down here bridges were all of the heavy electrically operated type and when we went through them we held up trams and lorries in a rather satisfactory way.

At last we got down to Bowling and the sea-lock. Rob and Colin and I got out here to get two or three bottles for the boat's hansel when we got to the pier. But, alas, everything was shut. I rang up home and explained our position so that the family could bring down bottles to meet us!

By now everyone had tidied up. The *Maid of Morvern* is a modern boat in which men will have to spend most of their working lives, and it seems a pity that such boats should perpetuate the old slum conditions. We have a washbasin and WC. So far there is no hot water except for the kettle which is usually on the stove, but I feel that it would be quite easy to have a hot-water attachment round the stove pipe.

The wind had freshened now, and as we came out into open water there was a fair jabble. We decided to go through the Kyles [of Bute] where there would be more shelter, and from there across into Kilbrannan Sound. We took turns at the wheel. The fishermen all steer on well-known landmarks, but I found it easier to steer a compass course than to keep my eye on some small lump on a far-off hillside.

When we came into rough water it became still clearer that the *Maid of Morvern* was a grand sea boat. She seemed to have just the right way of going through the water. It was cold on deck and most of us crowded into the wheelhouse and set the echo-sounder to working again.

We were off Lochranza and going well when Fred shouted up that the tail shaft was heating. We slowed down and the men all got into a state of agitation. They pulled some of the packing out and she began to cool down, but we didn't dare to go at full speed. It turned out afterwards that the whole thing was due to the packing and almost always happened with a new engine. But at the time we were all fearfully worried. Added to this, we couldn't possibly lie at Carradale; it was much too rough and the old pier is no protection at all. Carradale is one of the places that is asking for a new harbour, and we who live there can only hope that America does not insist on economies that include not giving us our new harbour.

We were coming in slowly now, in falling dusk, when Rob shouted that the pier was black with people. And so it was. All our friends had come down to watch us make our way in. As we tied up they were all cheering. There were fishermen, foresters, farm workers, and summer visitors.

We were still feeling rather agitated about the tail shaft, and somehow it was difficult to accustom ourselves to being back after the two days of our little special world. But soon enough I was busy pouring out the stuff for the hansel and half Carradale seemed to be on board, in and out of the fo'c'sle, and in and out of the engine-room. Everyone was admiring; perhaps a few were envying. It was Saturday night. And on the Monday she was fishing.

Scotland 33, November 1949, pp. 27-32

See also 'The Old Canal', later in this section.

Spindrift at the Citizens'

(1951)

For long years I had wanted to write for the ordinary man and woman in Scotland. But few of them read my books, since it is always easier to get a tuppenny 'book' from the wee shoppie round the corner than to go to the County Council Library book-box, let alone buying a book which might cost as much as a pair of good stockings, or a couple of drams even! Then at last I got my chance. The Citizens' Theatre in Glasgow gave it to me.

The beginning of it all was writing a play in collaboration with a fisherman: a play about his job, the fishing. We did it when he could get away from his work to share my own, and nobody but myself thinking it would ever really come to anything. Let all you ivory tower writers with your nice, undisturbed, regular working hours every morning, go and put your heads in a bucket! We worked at odd hours, mostly evenings when we were both tired. Time and again my co-author would get a message saying he must away over and help mend a net or take the boat round from one anchorage to another. And I'd be left cursing and swearing.

I had the Citizens' Theatre in mind from the beginning. Denny Macintosh had little idea, either of any special theatre, or of dramatic form and method. But he is a born story-teller and the good story is always dramatic. He knew before I did what was bound to happen in the play and, for that matter, what had been going on between the acts. He made the characters solid, living people for himself and me.

We sent the play to James Bridie.[1] I shall never forget how he helped us and encouraged us. We re-wrote it two or three times. At last he said it was right. It had meant, for me, the happiest visits to his house. There could never be anyone nicer to sit at the feet of. We called our play *Spindrift against the Women*, but we were advised to shorten it to *Spindrift*, the name of the boat in the play.

The stage set called for a pier and boat, and a cottage, the kind of wooden hut which the fishermen build for themselves – if they have a good house it is always for summer letting! John Russell, the brilliant young designer at the Citizens', came down to Carradale and went out with my fellow author, who was by now a skipper, with all the difficulties and joys of a boat of his own – exactly what we had been describing in the play. Yes, said Denny, he had been yarning away great with the boys. But he had also been drawing and measuring, and the result was a magnificently real set, just as ours was a completely real – and, I suppose, low-brow – play.

We were lucky to have seafaring folk as our producers, for John Casson[2] – now for a time lost to Scotland, but a gain to Australia – was an old Navy man and John Russell is a fine seaman, too. But before we were done with them, there wasn't one of the Citizens' players who couldn't mend or set up a net like a professional!

Spindrift went into production with a swing. Here, it seemed, was the genuine modern Scots play that the Citizens' Theatre had wanted from the beginning. Many of the players were Highland themselves, some Gaelic-speaking. The accents were genuine and lovely, Roddy McMillan's especially. I had all along had Duncan Macrae in mind for the chief character, half hero, half villain – like so many Highlanders.[3] After seeing *The Lass wi' the Muckle Mou*,[4] I had some idea of the others. But I didn't know how good we should find Marillyn Gray, the young actress who played the heroine.

There were all sorts of questions, most of which we tackled in the Business Manager's friendly, smoky little den. Would we, for instance, like a few words about the play on the programme? We decided not, but instead to have four lines from 'Caller Herrin'.[5] I went and verified them, for there is always someone waiting to catch one out on a minor point. How about clothes? Actors in rep. produce their own. Helena Gloag, for instance, found an entrancingly vulgar hat for the Glesgie wife going back to the village. Duncan Macrae's blue jersey, after being darned every night for three weeks, was a sight!

I went to the first rehearsal, prepared to steel myself to see the play hacked about, prepared to comfort my fellow author and to assure him it would be better later on. But already it had begun to take shape. The real set was to be all steps and different levels, people jumping down or reaching up, but this was all laid out on the flat with rods against an *As You Like It* back-drop.

Meanwhile we had brought up the props. My farm van drove into Tarbert for the boat piled with nets, baskets, scoops and sea-boots. MacBrayne's heaved the unusual luggage aboard amid considerable amusement. My porter at Glasgow Central couldn't have been more sympathetic as we stuffed the trailing net ends into a taxi; indeed, it was listening to him that I suddenly felt that perhaps he and his friends might come and see a play which was about ordinary folk like himself.

Spindrift opens with nets being hauled down and looked over for holes; my fellow author showed how it was done. A pity he couldn't be called in to give expert advice on the love-making, but that seemed to us to be good enough! One or two small points came up. We had not, considering the size of the stage, given enough dialogue for some of the exits. But the players were so well into their parts that it was no bother for anyone to put in an extra sentence – we scarcely knew whether it was ours or theirs. But in one scene Duncan Macrae was eating his dinner – bread crumbs soaked in Marmite, though it looked like 'mince with an onion through it', favourite food of the Clyde herring fleet. We wanted another bit of dialogue here and it obviously had to be about the new boat he was talking of. What was it to be? I had no idea myself, but seized hold of my co-author and a line half a page back. 'What was wrong with the man's brailer pole, Denny?' I asked. Immediately I got my answer – and the bit of dialogue, written straight down.

The first few rehearsals were so good that we realised we could perfectly well leave our play in the hands of a company who fitted into the thing like a hand to a glove. Some of them had been really afraid that we wouldn't like their interpretation or that we should be cross at occasional alterations or small cuts. I felt that some authors probably don't realise that a play is essentially an affair of collaboration. When I wrote my first play, at fifteen, I got furious if a word was altered. I'm afraid many authors never grow up beyond that stage! When writing a play, one must, of course, visualise it in a stage setting, but one must also realise that this will certainly change when the producer gets at it. Unless one is very unlucky, the change will be for the better, since the author almost always knows less about the reactions of an audience than the producer. And no doubt a Glasgow audience is different from a London one; certainly the Saturday one was different from the Friday one – it tended to laugh more and often very inappropriately, which meant that the actors must time their lines very carefully, never giving the titterers a chance with serious lines. Occasionally an author's original picture comes perfectly on to the stage, as it did here, for instance, in the case of scenes between Duncan Macrae and Eric Woodburn, the skipper. But this is as rare as it is delightful.

The Sunday before we opened was of course a frantically busy day at the theatre, as it always has to be in repertory, when one set is broken up and another one built; and the Sabbath was broken, right, left and centre. The stage hands were all busy hauling and shifting and climbing up impossible looking ladders. John Russell dressed in a gown of sacking like a lay brother was painting the wheel-house of the boat; two twelve-foot spars had been borrowed from our own boat, as well as a winkie – the guiding light that goes overboard with the net. Denny and I sat well back, so as not to inhibit John Casson when he wanted to swear. 'I was always thinking we fishermen worked harder than most,' said Denny, 'but now I can see these stage folk work harder than ourselves.'

There was no Sunday rehearsal, of course, but some of the cast came over and rehearsed among themselves. Then came the dress rehearsal. There was one rather startling sunset effect which, however, was put right before the evening. Inevitably a few things were not perfect. A couple more sou'westers were needed; I hunted Glasgow for them, finally running them down among naval surplus stores. Denny and I were warned that we must be ready for the curtain call, he with his Mod clothes – he is one of the bass line in the Carradale Gaelic choir – and I with my tartan scarf. Both of us, I'm afraid, enjoyed counting the posters, with our names in such very big print!

There was no need for us to be nervous on the first night. Everything went wonderfully; the press couldn't have been nicer – perhaps they liked being called 'You wild newspaper men' by Denis. Yet all the same I was scared and confused at the end. I have done plenty of public speaking, but never faced the curtain of up-pouring dazzle from the footlights that cuts off the audience, including that little-woman-in-the-back-row that a public speaker always picks out to speak to. We spoke haltingly and got back the warm, affectionate applause that must be the main encouragement for the actor, who, unlike the speaker or lecturer, can never see his audience.

Then came next morning and the press notices and the possibility of a third week's run. The Directors of the Citizens' came to the play and sometimes I had a quite overwhelming feeling that James

Bridie was just round the corner. Clyde fishermen came, skippers and share fishermen from all ports, large, solid men, unused to the theatre and astonished to see a boat and wheel-house so real and a crew just like a real crew. They also insisted on seeing likenesses to real men who had never been in our minds at all! They came back-stage through the strange tangles of scenery and props, and met the players, whom they mixed up inextricably with their stage parts. And the summer visitors to Carradale, who knew Denis as one of the fishermen who go out in the evening after the herring and stumble up from the boats dead tired in the morning, and knew me, very likely, as someone who gave them wrong change when they were buying garden fruit – for I am hopelessly bad at adding up two lbs. of rasps. and one of black currants – they came, too, and so did the ordinary Glasgow folk, for this was a play they could understand, about their own kind of problems and in their own fashion of speech. And what is more, one of the best places in the house is the front of the Grand Circle!

One of these days, perhaps, we shall have a play put on at some grand London theatre. There may be more money in it, but it will never – it *can* never – be half the fun that the Glasgow Citizens' Theatre was. We shall never feel ourselves part of it in the same way. We shall never get the same welcome. We could hardly bear it that last night when our stage boat was broken up and had to become no more than a splendid memory, back in our minds again, as it had once been, while we were writing the play.

Scotland's SMT Magazine, v. 47, December 1951, pp. 42-4

[1] James Bridie (1888-1951), dramatist, moving spirit in the founding of the Citizens Theatre and of what is now the Royal Scottish Academy of Music and Drama.

[2] John Casson (1909-91), director.

[3] Roddy McMillan (1923-79), actor and dramatist; Duncan Macrae (1905-67), actor; both in the Citizens Theatre company during its early years.

[4] Alexander Reid's *The Lass wi' the Muckle Mou'* had been premiered at the Citizens earlier in the 1950-1 season.

[5] 'Caller Herring', Scots song; words by Carolina Oliphant, Lady Nairne (1766-1845).

Winter Fishing

(1952)

The ground was white with frost as I walked down Campbeltown pier, on to the ring-net boat *Maid of Morvern*, of which I am part owner. At home, the big threshing mill would still be at it, but half the stacks were through when I left, and by now the pale, rustling oats would be settling down into heaps in the granary and the neighbours who had been helping would be on their way home. I had brought eggs and milk, and an extra jersey and duffle coat for myself. When I went down into the fo'c'sle, Willie was frying bacon and eggs and brewing tea and lamenting for the teeth – most of what he had – which had been pulled that morning.

The diesel-engined ring-net boats were streaming out of Campbeltown harbour towards the fishing grounds, less beautiful, perhaps, than in the old sail days, but I wouldn't know. I had thought our boat very beautiful from the day I saw her first, half built, on the slips at Eyemouth, and watched them laying the steaming curved planks into her sides.

Denny, the skipper, and Willie and I, ate our tea while a last-minute repair was made on the engine. When we left, it was getting dark and the Campbeltown sea front, so remarkably ugly by day, clothed itself in romance, a string of jewel lights against the dark shapes of mountains. As we went out, Denny, not for the first time, lectured me on navigation: 'green to green and red to red'. But I knew well enough that as soon as we got right into the fishing, he and everyone else would be racing across one another's bows like a fleet of dodgems.

The seiners were passing us in the entrance to Campbeltown loch on their way home – the boats that take their seine nets out to the white-fish grounds round the Craig [Ailsa Craig] and work there all day. I had been out often enough for a night with the ringers at the summer fishing, but never in winter. I had chosen a moonlit night because there were certain fishing operations which I could not quite grasp and I wanted to see them clearly – it seems almost impossible for anyone doing a job and thoroughly familiar with it, to make it clear in words to someone else. But a full moon in a cloudless sky is bad for the fishing; the herring see the nets, and perhaps the boats, and swim away from them.

Willie was mending the winkie, the light which marks the end of the shot net and must be picked up by the neighbour boat – ringers always work in pairs – when they make a ring. It ought to light automatically when it turns over into an upright position. Once he got it right he sealed the join with candle grease. Then he began to dress for the night's work, putting on layer after layer of trousers and knitted stockings.

Fred and the two Shaw boys – once little terrors, but now growing up into good-mannered, responsible, keen young fishermen – began on their tea. I steered for a while on the rising moon, enormous over Arran. A late returning seiner gave us news of a spot of herring and we cruised in the direction where it might be but never found it. We used the echo-sounder which makes an unmistakable dark blur over the bottom line which is being marked up with every rotation of the marker, and also the comparatively old-fashioned feeling wire, a long length of piano wire on which one can feel the fish knock and patter. There are other ways, too, of spotting herring, but not appropriate to a bright winter night; we use all of them. There was a fresh breeze from the North, and spray broke over the boat, but she made nothing of the waves, just danced across them, her hold empty and buoyant.

It was apparent that there was a big fleet of boats out, all fishing Kilbrannan Sound and down along the South of Arran. It has been a poor season so far, many of the boats are in debt, and everyone is out to make every penny he can. From a distance each group of boats looked like a small town, spread out in lights along the water. There must have been twenty or thirty pairs, from all the Clyde fishing ports. When we turned on the walkie-talkie we heard them calling to one another, interrupted sometimes by the English voices on the Fleetwood trawlers away out in the Minch.

Our neighbour suddenly turned north along the Kintyre coast, on rumour of a shot up by Saddell, and we trailed after her, since it does not do to get too far from one's neighbour. Every now and then we winked our lights at her to keep in touch. We found, right enough, that there had been two shots, both early on before the moon rose, but there had also been disasters. There were two or three 'bad nets' – nets which had been shot on a rocky bottom and torn. This is always a risk, and, the worse a season has been, the more risk a skipper and crew are prepared to run. But they risk anything from a tear which may take hours to mend to the complete loss of a ring-net costing about £350 at present prices.

Our own transmission belt, which fed the batteries, was broken, and Fred asked about over the walkie-talkie for the loan of one, or a piece for mending. At last he got it and went down into the engine room and mended the belt. Fishing boats will keep quiet, or even lie, about the whereabouts of herring, but nobody would dream of refusing a spare. We and our neighbour sculled about a good while more. In the moonlight the pale blue snow peaks of Arran were menacingly beautiful, remote from the frenzied couplings of the boats, each in a bridal wreath of eager, squalling seagulls. We had another brew of tea. The rocking of the boat had stirred up the bilges which smelt remarkably of ancient oil and ancient fish. But nobody was getting much now. So we decided to lie up for a few hours and cast anchor in five fathoms of water only a mile or so from my own house, but so magnificently remote – no possibility of being telephoned to, and, instead of the rambling, cold, lonely old house and myself isolated in it, I was tucked in a bunk in the warm fo'c'sle, the boys asleep or half asleep, Denny and Willie gossiping a few minutes in soft Highland voices, and then only the light from the stove. But Denny never slept; he was away up from time to time, watching the weather; he kept the stove going, and at last woke us, saying the breeze had taken off, and he thought we might try a shot at the far side.

The echo-sounder shows Kilbrannan Sound as a fantastic jagged valley, with sudden reefs and peaks. We saw a small spot of herring in one of those jags, but scarcely worth risking our net for. Then came thicker markings on a better bottom and we rounded up and shot. But we were in the middle of a fleet of boats, all tearing about, and the moon was bright. I believe Denny hardly dared to think the herring would have stayed in the ring; but fishermen have to be hopeful. The neighbour boat came alongside, all but one jumping on to our deck, the remaining man staying aboard the neighbour which kept a tow rope on us and enough strain to keep the net from slacking.

Nobody gave any orders, all moved quietly to their places, most wearing oilskins and high rubber boots, but any sort of old caps.

The winches take in the ropes, but when the nets begin to come in, everyone has to haul at the flow. It was cold now. Every now and then one of the men hauling silently would stop to flap his hands on his chest, then go on again. I waited behind, longing for the immediate breaking of the silence which would have come if there had been any show of herring – fish mashed by the gills in the net. But the net came in and in and there was nothing at all, not even a 'lift', a meal of herring at the bottom of the bag of the net. All that could be said was that the net was not torn. Quietly the neighbour crew went back to their boat.

Again we cruised around, the echo-sounder going, sometimes Denny in the wheelhouse and sometimes Fred; Willie was nursing his toothache in a muffler. For it seemed to be growing colder towards morning – or was it that we lacked the warmth which would have come with a good shot of herring? It must have been far colder in the snow and sleet of the Minch where the boat had been fishing in December. We picked up the news from the walkie-talkie and from what was shouted across the water from boat to boat. Out of some fifty boats, each with a crew of five or six, working that night, each pair must have shot at least once, perhaps two or three times. But only five or six of these shots had caught herring. These would be on their way to the Ayr market. Those crews would have a sweet sleep and a good divide the next day. The rest had nothing, but had used up oil and man-power. And overheads are heavy, as I, a part owner, know.

Yet a good fisherman is always hopeful; he knows there have been bad seasons before, but sooner or later, if he sticks to his boat and his skill, the fishing will take up. It is just this wee awkwardness of not, at the moment, having any money – money, this silly thing that the banks and the shops worry about but that is obviously so valueless compared with human courage and skill! Yet it was good to know the herring were there. When the moon goes back, the darker nights will come, and there will be good fishings.

And now the dawn was breaking, a pale rose light over the Ayrshire coast, and the land looking darker and solider. We made across for Campbeltown loch, and, on the entrance, met the seiners going out again to their day's fishing.

The New Statesman and Nation, v. 43, 15 March 1952, pp. 296, 298

A Lean Harvest

(1955)

The village is depressed. For three years the fishing has been bad. The herring have been scarce in the Clyde estuary and we are primarily a fishing village. In the old days most of the men got their living this way: maybe a hundred and fifty men and boys in half-decked sailing boats with a crew of four or five. From time to time there would be disasters; a home would be left without husband or sons – the boat herself uninsured. But that was God's will.

Then the skipper owners began to install auxiliary engines. By the 1914 war all the boats were engined, between forty and fifty feet long, fully decked, with a crew of five and a fairly high catching power. Winches for the net took away some of the heaviest labour from the crew, and meant that they could manage more shots in a night. Now most of the boats have powerful engines, are over fifty feet, have radio equipment and echo sounders, and are insured at a premium of about £300 a year; that is, some five per cent of their value. They carry a crew of six; but there are only five pairs of them now in the village.

That means sixty men employed. What happens to the rest? Some are with the Forestry Commission, which bought most of the old estate and has gradually acquired more land as it became available. There are a few other jobs going, between agriculture, small local businesses and the tourist industry, though that is seasonal and, in fact, employs mostly women and girls. But two families have recently moved down to the steel works at Corby. Another is going to Australia. They don't want to go, but the depopulation of the Highlands continues almost as of old. They'd like to be fishing. The boys at school paint fishing boats and are for ever at their fathers and uncles to take them out with the boats. It's only when they're old enough to see the cash side of it that they turn to something else – which usually means going away.

The few modern boats catch as much herring as all the older types, but an increasing proportion of the catch goes for fish meal. People don't seem to like herrings for their breakfast, so the herrings have, rather wastefully, to be turned into hens' food. Eggs are still eaten! People don't like kippers either – not until they meet Campbeltown kippers when they stay with me! Part of the fault here is that kippers don't keep indefinitely, any more than fresh fish. But most fishmongers put kippers into a fridge, take them out during the day and, if they aren't sold, put them back, and so on. A well-smoked kipper lasts longer, but it is only too easy for dye, harmless in itself, to be used to disguise poor smoking. Yet in the long run all lose by bad kippering.

At freshing and kippering prices a man can just get by at the fishing, even in a poor season. At fish-meal prices he can't, even though those prices are still subsidised. The boat's receipts are divided up, week by week, one share for each fisherman, four for the boat. As part-owner of a boat I get my divide, one and a third of a working share, in grimy, purplish Clyde [Clydesdale] Bank notes, shillings and pennies. It may be nothing; it may be £10 or more. But what's the good? Back it has to go into insurance, engine repair, replacement of nets, hire of radio equipment, paper for echo sounders. The share fishermen have averaged around £200 a year for many years. Possible for a single man, but it means running steadily into debt for anyone with a family. But some of them stick on, hoping for the herring to come back, as in the past.

Up till recently expert opinion was that herring could not be over-fished. Nothing that humans could do would more than touch the edges of a great shoal, nor would it compare with the damage from natural enemies and parasites. Now they are less sure. It looks as if the herring on the southern edge of the North Sea were being over-fished by the German and Dutch boats. In the old days, too, boats worked quietly, the engines barely turning over while the crew hunted with feeling wire or knocking mallet. Now they locate with the echo-sounder and rush full speed over the shoals. It may be that the herring are more sensitive than we think. 'Wise fish,' say the fishermen; 'aye, aye, wise altogether,' and talk endlessly about their ways.

When share fishermen do badly, skipper owners do worse, especially if their boats were partly bought on a recent grant and loan from the Herring Board. My own share of our boat was paid (since, naturally, the grant is only for fishermen), but my skipper and fellow owner has to try to meet loan charge and repayments. It has turned his black hair grey. Sometimes he shows me a 'thrown'[1] letter from the Herring Board, and I try to explain that they aren't being nasty on purpose, to him as a person. They, in turn, are harassed by the Treasury. Nor did all skippers really try to repay in the good years, since a Government Agency is always 'They' and comes last. But the honest (or, being in the Highlands, should one say those who make big, spasmodic attempts at honesty, which is not the most glamorous of the virtues, as compared, say, to courage or generosity?) suffer for the faults of the dishonest; and the Herring Board's attempts to get its money may break the very boats it helped to launch.[2]

Some boats, including my own, turn to white fishing as an alternative, though men who have been all their lives at one kind of fishing are very reluctant to turn to another. It would help us a great deal to have a small harbour; it is an extra charge on the boats to be in a harbour fifteen or twenty-five miles away, with bus-hire to get them there and no possibility of the crew getting home if there is a night of bad weather. If we had a harbour, some people might run small lobster boats, do local line fishing, and take out summer visitors. The fishermen started asking for a harbour at the end of last century. When I became County Councillor I was immediately involved. But it was turned down for one reason and another. A modified small scheme, which may not be completely adequate in all weathers, has now been passed by the Treasury; for the same amount, or less, a really good harbour could have been built ten years ago.

Still, we hope the harbour will start this year. That will mean immediate work for some of our people and help to pay off rent arrears. But after that, what?

The New Statesman and Nation, v. 49, 26 March 1955, p. 428

---

[1] This is probably the Scots word 'thrawn': stubborn, cross-grained.

[2] As happened with Mitchison's boat; see 'Summer Work' in the farming section of this volume.

The Crafty Darlings

(1956)

We are keeping our fingers crossed. We daren't hope it will last. Maybe they'll go away on us, the silver darlings, the way any kind of a darling may do. But – for this week at least, as for last week, the herring are back.

There have been five bad seasons running in the Clyde area, men drifting away, some to the Hydro Board works, but keeping on their homes, others permanently to the steelworks at Corby. Yet, even in Corby, their hearts are still at the fishing. 'The bairns miss going down to the harbour,' said one Campbeltown wife, and her man: 'Aye, everything's fine here, a good house and all, but if the fishing were to start, I'd not wait a day.'

But at least the crews can leave; there is nothing to stop them but their own wish. The skippers have had to stay, trying to keep the boats afloat, struggling with debts, insurance payments, and the Herring Board who started so many of them off with loans and grants during the last two years of the good fishing when it looked as though everything might be paid off in no time. They have been black years for the skipper-owners.

And now – it looks like a bit of light shining through the clouds. It looks like debts being paid, no more difficulty with the crews. We can't be sure – canny, now, canny! But a man comes back on the Saturday and is wearying for the Monday and a whole week of fishing to go – a strange feeling to have again after all this time.

There has been no good forecast for the Clyde for long enough, and this year the Isle of Man fishings were poor and nothing great in the Minch. But the herring have their own laws, which we have not got round to mastering. What is it that makes them move suddenly from one place to the next and disappear again, as suddenly? Where are they meanwhile? Are they deep under the Atlantic? We just don't know. Is there a change of temperature? Is it primarily something which affects their feed – the tiny creatures, some like very small shrimps, some that change the colour of the water, which populate the waters, rising and falling with night and day, followed by the herring? Or is it that there are fewer boats to catch them? Can we think that the darlings have enough craft in them to know that?

Whatever it is, there is a different feel to the fishing communities all along the Clyde. After all these years the herring are up again into Loch Fyne, as far, even, as Inveraray. They are up the lochs at the back of the Kyles [of Bute], in spots all along the shores and around Arran. On Saturday morning it was like a light on at Tarbert. There was money about, that blintering silver stuff that has been rare enough. Not that there can be any easy spending, not yet; we have far too much to make up. The local tradesmen have been long-suffering, most of them. Wives have done without all the kind of things that wives so much want. Rents have fallen behind. But everyone understood. Here, along the Clyde, there isn't a soul who is not, in some way, tied up with the fishing.

Maybe now the fishermen will be able to come again to dances and concerts; the choirs might start up; a whole new life may begin to stir. The news spreads through the village during the morning. 'Aye, there wasn't one of the boats but had a share.' 'Sandy had a hundred baskets, Jimmie had as much, your own crowd had a great shot.' They are small herring, most of them, and the prices not too good. The bulk of them go for oil and meal or for pet food – a shame, that, because the ones they bring back, though one can easily eat two or three of them, are sweet and fat, the best of food. I can't help wondering if the price of herring has gone down in the fishmongers' shops. Here we don't buy herring; either we have them given us or they've been forgotten – and a man can't be expected to bother with a few herring on shore when he's been working on them all night!

The Clyde is, and has always been, a nursery for young herring. But some of them stay. The question is, will some of these ones stay or come back? What brood do they come from? Is it just possible that they represent the slight, the tentative beginning of better times? After all these cruel years we were beginning to lose faith in the fishing. Perhaps, this time, it had gone for ever, as it seems to have gone in certain lochs and estuaries, notably the Forth. Yet a fisherman hates to think like that. It was making men unhappy and dour and mistrustful, like loss of any other faith.

There seem to be small herring in other small inlets up the west coast, places where in the old days the crofter fishermen would shove down their little sail boats and shoot a net when the herring were sighted, while their wives got out the barrels and salt. That doesn't happen any longer. The little boats rot, there is no barrel of salt herring behind the door. It has all become large-scale and professional.

A generation ago there were small fishing ports all up Loch Fyne, small places like Minard, where a sailing boat could be hauled up on shore, but where there is no harbour for the bigger, diesel-engined boats. There were plenty of boats at Inveraray too, but the herring have not been seen up that length for a long time. Yet now there they are again. 'Aye, they're loching right enough,' said one of the Tarbert fishermen, having seen the signs all up the shores.

The boats all have echo-sounders now, showing up even a deep shoal. But all of the fishermen watch for the old signs, the whales, the gannets striking, even the queer, light surface playing of a shoal of herring. How lovely to have them again, to be able to talk herring and think herring again! The nights of fishing are hard work, even in calm weather; a pair of boats may shoot the net four or five times in a night, each shot taking a couple of hours of hard work, with the smallest gap for brewing tea in between. Yet to have the hold deep in herring – so deep they'll slip over the top of your sea-boots! Men who have done without new oilskins for five seasons are getting them new, a real fashion parade. It is this rise in human happiness which is coming on us now, which is so clear and wonderful. If only it goes on!

The Manchester Guardian, 12 September 1956, p. 5

Twelve-mile Limit

(1958)

Any Highland west coast fisherman is bound to sympathise to some extent with the Icelanders who are trying to keep out foreign trawlers from an area twelve miles from their coast.[1] The Inner Minch at its narrowest between Vaternish Point on Skye and Henish Point on Harris is some fifteen miles across. Some of us have long thought there was a case for closing the Minch and giving the smaller, skipper-owned boats a better chance. It could be closed to English and Scottish trawlers, though I am not sure if this could be done simply by an amendment to the Sea Fisheries Act of 1883 or whether it would have to come up at an international convention. I cannot think it would be a major matter; there are not so many foreign trawlers there, though if British trawlers have to look for new grounds they might come in force. But if the Minch became a closed area we would not be pleased to see foreign warships coming in to protect their trawlers.

With the three-mile limit, as at present, there is a good deal of poaching. This may be partly because of increased economic pressure on fishermen and partly because modern boats can get away much more quickly than they could in the time of the old Sea Fisheries Act. If the limit were twice three miles it would be more realistic, as far as catching poachers goes. It may be that this was in the minds of the Icelanders, for certainly there has been poaching in and just outside Faxo Bay, which is one of the main grounds. From one headland of Faxo Bay, called after a ninth-century discoverer of Iceland, to the opposite one, is about the same distance as from Duncansby Head to Rattray Head across the Moray Firth. Now, the peculiar thing is that the Moray Firth is closed to trawlers, but only British trawlers. Foreign trawlers can, and do, fish there. The flourishing little ports along the northern coast of the Moray Firth, which used to have fleets of small boats, have all dwindled away.

The Clyde estuary, not quite as wide across as some of the closed Icelandic fjords, is, similarly, closed to British trawlers and open to foreigners. This is a funny bit of old-fashioned liberalism. If the

Icelanders start the ball rolling, we may all end up by closing such waters. The Danes are already worried about the Faroes agreement, which should normally last till 1967, and feel that, if Iceland gets away with it, they will have to ask for more room round the Faroes. Our own East Coast trawlers will have to fish somewhere if the fish and chip industry is to go on, and this worries us in the West Coast.

Everybody who knows anything about fish (this does not include the average shopper, who knows as much about fish as I do about Continental abstract art) is anxious about over-fishing. Not so long ago we all thought there could be no over-fishing of herring, so we went ahead with reduction factories where herring not used for human food could be turned into oil and meal. 'Overdays' herring, not completely fresh, can still make oil and meal, though 'sludge' needs fresh fish. This policy got a great lift during the immediate post-war shortage of fats, not only here but in all the continental fishing countries. Herring meal is used for animal food, oil for human and animal; some even goes into fertilisers. Whether we are justified in killing our fellow vertebrates in this wholesale way is not an economist's problem, though oddly enough it did in a certain way shock the fishermen themselves, though they are now used to it.

But now most of the experts think that herring are quite certainly being over-fished. I myself find the evidence impressive for the disastrous effect of fishing three-year-old herring on the Bløden grounds by Danish trawlers that land their catch in Esbjerg for conversion into meal. This is the argument in Hodgson's important book, *The Herring and its Fishery*.[2] Other scientific experts put rather more blame on the German and Belgian fisheries at the mouth of the Channel. Our old drift nets were biologically correct, in so far as they only caught mature herring which had already made their contribution to the fish population. But it is getting harder and harder even to find a place to shoot a fleet of drift nets from one boat, because of fast-moving trawlers dragging their nets all over the grounds.

Of course, if the fisheries experts of all fishing countries got together, simply to think out a fish conservation policy, they would have no difficulty, any more than the atomic scientists would have if they were asked to deal with radiation dangers. But, in practice, none of them is free. All have behind them pressure from their own fishing lobbies. In some countries these are particularly important; they must be in Iceland since there is virtually no other industry except growing carnations in geyser-heated greenhouses. It is quite clear that Icelandic policy is not primarily one of fish conservation, but rather of straight trade protection, for they have quite a large trawler fleet of their own, eat a lot of their own fish and sell the rest to Russia, eastern and central Europe and even, dried, to Africa.

On the other hand, the Icelandic fleet is certainly not as large as the combined fleets of all the fishing countries, so there is an element of conservation in it. I wonder what the currents were behind the congress at Middelfart: whether Iceland's representatives were told that they mustn't shift an inch but must behave like Gunnar of Lithend and other non-shifting heroes of Icelandic history. Did any British representative consider the counter-measure of closing the Scottish waters, or would the idea of the Minch being closed to all trawlers have been too unpopular with our own trawling lobby?

But whatever happens there are not only governments to convince, but fishermen. They, more than anyone, know about the dangers of over-fishing, yet they are always reluctant to do the very things that would help, like fishing with legal, large-mesh nets, instead of illegal, small-mesh ones. Some other boat got away with it, and so … Fishing is tricky and dangerous enough without this constant competitive urge behind the fishermen who are so often only just making a living. And this goes for fishermen of all countries, who are decent, grand folk to deal with except over this one thing.

Sometimes I wonder whether this is one of the industries which, for the sake not of economics, but of morality, should be in the hands of state boards which would not be desperate for dividends if this meant international complications, and which would take the immediate financial burden off the fishermen (who are not necessarily clever with money) and allow them to be honest.

New Statesman, v. 56, 23 August 1958, p. 218

[1] Refers to the fisheries dispute between Britain and Iceland (1958-61).
[2] W.C. Hodgson, *The Herring and its Fishery* (1957).

Carradale Harbour Opened
Climax of Years of Work

(1959)

The village of Carradale on the Clyde coast was gay yesterday with the flutter of flags; the fishing boats were all dressed with pennants. St Andrew's Cross flew grandly from the great crane which still stands at the harbour head because, though the fishing harbour is now officially open and has been used by the boats for a month past, there is some clearing up and shifting of rock to be done.

But this was the grand opening, the climax of years of work and hope, anger and despair, and then hope again.

The fishermen have been asking for a harbour for three generations. It could have been built at twice this size and a quarter of the cost in the years between the wars, but nobody bothered. Then, since the war, scheme after scheme has been put forward and cut down on economic grounds, so that some people thought it should be a red tape rather than a red, white, and blue ribbon which Mr Thomas Johnston cut yesterday at the opening ceremony.

Here it is finished at last. The fishermen's pennies steadily added up into thousands of pounds. The Government grant had taken solid shape, steel and concrete. This is an entirely new type of harbour and the result is ugly, but solid enough for centuries of wear and tear, and when the fishermen's nets are thrown over the black steel parapet, it won't seem ugly to them.

The official party was piped down to the harbour by the Campbeltown Pipe Band. The convener of Argyll County Council introduced Mr Johnston, and distributed much well-merited praise all round. The school children sang 'Eternal father strong to save,'[1] then Tom Johnston (for that is how all of us in Scotland think of him) spoke to us.

He began by telling us about the industrial and commercial finance corporation originally sponsored by a Scottish Secretary of State to provide long-term loans and how, when the scheme came into being, it turned out to be directed from London, with the Scottish banks putting up 11 per cent of the total capital of £34m, but with Scottish borrowers getting only 4½ per cent of the loan.

He spoke, too, of the affairs of Dundee, where the local people had hesitated in raising money for themselves, and had ended by not getting their road bridge. Here in Carradale, on the other hand, the fishermen had begun immediately to raise money, and had kept up the effort, even in the very difficult years. Now through the manifestation of local initiative they had their harbour.

His speech was followed by an appropriate prayer by the Rev. A. Murdoch Bennett, the Carradale minister. Then Mr C. Sim, Chief Fishery Officer of Scotland, who knows everything there is to be known about the fishing, spoke with knowledgeable friendliness and encouragement. He is held in respect and affection by all fishermen. He mentioned the possibility of Carradale becoming a landing port.

Then one of the leading fishermen, Mr John MacMillan, spoke on behalf of the fishermen, who had put so much effort into getting this harbour built.

There were presentations – a silver salver from the contractors to Mr Johnston, and a bouquet for Mrs Johnston from Mr MacMillan's little daughter.

Then came the splendid sight of the Carradale fleet coming round in brilliant sunlight in curves of colour into the harbour. There are ten boats now. In another two years, if the fishing holds, there may well be more.

To crown the occasion a spectator fell in, but fortunately surfaced with his bottle quite undamaged.

The whole party then followed the pipers up the hill to a party at the Carradale Hotel and later most of them went on to the village hall – another example of Carradale communal effort – for dinner and dancing, good food, and a splendid supply of the other thing.

The Glasgow Herald, 18 September 1959, p. 10

---

[1] A nineteenth-century hymn often associated with the sea and seamen; its refrain is 'For those in peril on the sea'.

The Old Canal

(1961)

We were taking the *Maid of Morvern* up from Eyemouth to Carradale on the west coast. She was our new ring-net fishing boat, 52 feet overall. We took her through the Forth and Clyde canal; later she went through it once or twice to the herring fishings on the east coat when there was nothing doing on the Clyde.

And now they say they are closing the canal! That's hard lines on the in-shore, west coast fishermen; but then, we're only the small folk and maybe we don't matter, not to that tune of money they'd need to put the canal in order.

It is 171 years old, and for the first 130 years or so it never flagged. In the twenties it had a revenue of some £120,000 a year and an expenditure of £40,000.

But it doesn't look as if those days would ever come back, or anything remotely like them. Even the year [1949] we took our boat up through the canal, things were getting into a bad way.

We sailed from Eyemouth on the early tide, north and round into the Firth, with the bridge enormous above us and the long smoky line of Edinburgh to the south. By now the tide had ebbed, leaving fantastic mud banks heaving out on each side of the channel into Grangemouth. We ran on to them and dirtied our nice new paint, and after that at every lock we'd have a go with mops to get her clean again. We paid our canal dues at Grangemouth and went ahead.

At first it's all town, the backs of houses and warehouses, filthy water scummed with rubbish, and smells you'd hardly credit. The locks take you up from Grangemouth to Falkirk where the narrow road bridge is pushed back and one works one's way between the lowering bonnets of lorries and the jibes of lorry men. It was all as ugly as could be, but gradually we got up into open country: green fields and trees slowly opening out at the boat's pace.

There was nobody at most of the locks; we had to make our own way through. Sometimes the iron bars that work the sluices were lying about where we could find them, but sometimes they were away, probably picked up by another boat for convenience sake and never returned. Now and again the sluices jammed, and the gates could be very stiff; they'll be worse now.

Still, we managed. We would edge our way into the lock, Rob and Denny shouting back and forth to one another, the rest of us fending her off the dark, slimy lock sides; the gates shut to behind us.

The water would be dark, the air dank, then we'd manage to open the sluices and the water would come bouncing in and up we'd swim into the sunlight again. But I never felt like dipping a hand into that water.

Occasionally we'd see a house, isolated among the fields; a small boy would come down and stare. But in one place word had gone ahead that the *Maid of Morvern* was a new fishing boat going west to the Clyde; and a young man came down and piped us through the lock and on our way. It was heartening, that.

There was one difficult stretch, almost at the top, where the canal is supposed to be fed from springs. By the time the lock was full, the basin ahead was almost empty, mud banks sloping down to maybe three feet of water. However, the lock beyond had some water in it which we let out, and just got ourselves enough to wriggle ahead on, while the gradual natural filling up took place.

I suppose this kind of thing is bound to happen on a canal which can't be properly looked after. Sometimes, too, bushes had trailed into the canal or the banks had slipped a bit. I think we met just one small boat in the whole day.

We camped at night by a road bridge, a bit before Kirkintilloch, and went on in the morning among the early bird song. We had a new diesel engine which was still running in, but nobody could have gone fast; even a light wash swept up on to the grass, and a 50-[foot] boat takes some managing on the bends, though the canal has taken bigger ones in its time, coal boats and timber boats and iron boats, heavy barges carrying all the goods which now career along the main roads. By now we were sailing into full locks and dropping down to a lower level.

Slowly the Campsies rose, ahead and to our right; there was industry to each side of us, factory buildings and chimneys, but most of it a field or two away, until we began to get down towards Glasgow, and buildings started closing right in on us.

The great curve of the canal round the back of Glasgow is extraordinarily dramatic; it goes steeply here, lock and basin, lock and basin, past the towering grey backs of tenements, like some alarming film set of murder and hate.

I kept feeling that, if a lock gate went – and they looked any age – we'd fall bow-on down someone's chimney; I was jumpy every time we knocked into the dark ancient woodwork. 'Look at that now!' shouted Rob and poked with a pole at some large sinister object that was swirling round half under water. 'That'll be a corpse,' said Denny, 'What'll we do?'

'Let's leave it alone!' I said, 'it'll not be a human corpse.' I was pretty sure it was a big dog or something of the kind, and even if it had been something worse, none of us wanted to get involved. You never know, with the police, and these wild Glasgow folk, what mightn't they be doing!

The great steps ahead of us flattened out; we had come to council flats and even an occasional attempt at a garden. Ahead was the main Glasgow-Dumbarton road, A7, the route to the west.

We slowed down and there was much shouting and hooting; barriers went up; the great bridge turned round slowly, and there was the *Maid* and her crew holding up two huge and growing processions of traffic, the back of it hooting like mad, for they didn't know what was holding up the front. Indeed it's the only time I've known that bridge to open.

It was tramcars in those days. Very high they looked from the canal, and we nipped past as quick as we could.

Here there were a few friends and relations; Rob or Denny would jump off the boat and shake hands. By now we'd got rid of all the Grangemouth mud and had become a respectable boat again. But it was mid-afternoon which is, alas, closing time, and it was important to get a bottle against the evening when we would get to Carradale and all the rest of the fleet would be coming aboard and must be properly welcomed. And here there wasn't a pub open. It would have been different nearer home, where one knows the back way to anywhere, but we were in strange country, and at last I had to go ahead and ring up Carradale to have the necessary ready for us.

We were tired of the canal by now; we'd had enough opening and shutting of gates and sluices. The last bit is through town again. And here at last we were coming down into Bowling; we could see masts and funnels ahead of us and smell the live waters of the Clyde after the dead water of the canal.

The sea lock at Bowling is big and well looked after. We were dropped down to sea level and then we were away on the Clyde, setting out for the west, the long length of the canal only now a memory to strip off over our shoulders.

The Scotsman, 12 August 1961.

See also 'Bringing Home the New Boat', earlier in this section.

PART V

THE GARDEN

Mitchison in front of the glasshouses in the garden of Carradale House

The Gale

(1953)

When I walked back from the Village Hall it was a calm, starry night, less cool than it has been. But there was a clouding over towards the north that didn't look too good and the glass dropping like a stone. I woke in the night and heard it beginning and buried my nose in the blankets again. Time enough in the morning to look round for what was bound to have happened.

Usually here we get north-westers, or sometimes the wet south-west gales. But this time there was more than a touch of east. It got the trees where they were unprepared. The beautiful tree rhododendrons that had lifted at the roots and almost gone in the north-west gale eleven months ago – they would have gone for good if we had not all rushed out of the house and held on to them, quivering and straining all up their trunks, till the worst of the storm was over – had not been affected. But one of the three great golden cypresses was gone, lying huge and beautiful along the grass, and beside it a cedar of Lebanon, the best of them, of course. Farther into the same wood there was havoc, pines and spruces lying anyhow. I did not dare to go too close, for everything was slipping and breaking like roofs after an air raid.

At the other end of the garden a big maritime pine had fallen over the top of some rhododendrons, Loderia and Campylocarpums mostly. I had been cosseting one of the campylocarpums and had at last induced it to make some good growth. Now all that was in shreds and splinters. We cut branch after branch, then got off the top of the maritime, but its huge trunk is far too big for us to handle. While we were cutting the wind kept on rising in gusts, usually with rain or hail which seemed to come straight out of the north-east, hardly falling at all, but streaming past the house so that the windows to the south were quite dry. It was a little worrying, because there was an Austrian just behind the maritime, which kept rocking in an ominous way, but it had not lifted at all so far and it may stand.

Meanwhile the buses had not got through because of fallen trees along the road and the telephone wires were all down. But we are well used to that up here. It would be nice – but expensive – to have all the wires underground.

One of the tall, hardy myrtles which grow against and above the walls was down, but not snapped off. I thought it could be propped up again if I took off the branches. There is plenty of young growth below. After I had lightened it we shoved it up again, with props to keep it in place.

All over the place there were other trees down, and in the part of the village near the harbour, where they are less protected from the north, roofs were off and windows blown in. In Blackhill Wood a few trees had been blown in the last gale and since cleared away; at the same time I had cut out a few larches which had the larch disease. That had opened a way for the blast and a quarter of the wood seemed to be down, including some grand Scots fir and mature larch which had escaped the disease and which, I had hoped, would stand for a few years more. This is valuable timber and should be taken to the sawmill as soon as possible, but trees will be down everywhere and it may be months before we can get it to Campbeltown. It is too big for us to handle ourselves. Meanwhile we will take the broken branches and smaller trees; luckily we can get at them through the field and the ground is hard enough for the tractor and trailer.

In another place a pine was struck by lightning; we took it down a month or so ago. Now the one just behind it has gone, doubtless because of this attack on a side which had been sheltered. One has to be desperately careful about cutting in Scotland, just because of this. The Hydro Board always has to cut broad belts where its lines go through trees and this always means that in the next gale another set of trees goes. Some of mine in the Bay have done just that.

It looks as if the beeches and oaks have stood fairly well, but none of us liked to do much exploring along the drives with the wild gusts coming. At best the whole thing will mean days of work, and we are behind already with the bad weather there has been. But still, we have not lost nearly so many slates off the roof as we did the last time. And only one pane of glass has gone.

Perhaps it is just as well that we should have a taste of these natural calamities from time to time. They give one the sense of urgency and working together – yes, and sometimes tragedy – that we get in wartime, but without hate. There is no enemy. You cannot hate the storm. Even if you are out in a fishing boat – all our fishing fleet were safely in shelter that night – you can be afraid and angry, but there is no entity there to hate. And it is something to talk about: 'A terrible wild day, that!' 'Aye, hellish altogether!' And we will speak of our narrow escapes from flying branches, just as we used to in cities after blitzes, and our sluggish country lives will seem a bit more lively; indeed, there may be a piece about our own part over the wireless, so it will be worth listening to the thing, for once.

The cattle and sheep don't seem to mind, though the wind blows a ridiculous permanent parting into the fleeces of the sheep. The Galloways shelter in the hollows, minding this less than they do heavy rain or frost. The robins, of which there are so many round here, are obviously muddled. They knew their own small territories, attacked any new arrival who came in, and on the whole welcomed the humans who were likely to dig their ground and turn up delicious worms for them. But now the boundaries of their territories are all over the place. There were two of them hopping about the branches of the maritime pine, their small worlds having come unstuck. How much more sensible is our kitchen robin, with its definite room territory, the bowls on whose edges it perches and sometimes goes to sleep, and the people it tolerates; the window is open, but the storm goes howling on outside. And the robin stays in.

The Manchester Guardian, 1 January 1953, p. 5

Highland Water Garden

(1955)

East of the dining-room window there is a long, high stone wall that finally loses itself in a tangle of rhododendrons and a very fine view of the peaks of Arran. Towards the end it has lost heart and toppled into various piles of ruin, over which the runner ducks invade from time to time; but near the house it still has pretensions to being a very fine wall and remembers the days when it had a rose bed at its foot and gardeners to tend it. It still supports old apples, once fan-trained, and pink ramblers; there are masses of daffodils in spring, but grass has eaten up the rose border, which anyway depended on cartloads of manure every year; now I need all that manure for the farm. However, it seemed to be a rather dull wall. Behind it there used to be the kind of outdoor water closet which happens behind so many Scottish garden walls. The water came from one of the many springs which never fail in a county with a rainfall of eighty inches, and rose high enough for us to run it in a lead pipe through the top of the wall. That was the beginning.

My son Murdoch then came over from his laboratory and took charge. He designed the shuttering for a small pond jutting out some six feet from the wall which forms its longest side. Concrete walls, two feet above the level of the water and six to nine inches thick, leave the stone at a fairly sharp angle, then come forward at a wider angle before they close in at the front. In the narrow angle behind the back and side walls wire holds in place heaped peat for irises. In the wide angles, where the concrete walls are broader, there are two little pockets of damp soil connected by pipes with the pond, which is about nine inches deep and has a concrete bottom. As this was not properly keyed to the stone wall, it is leaky. (Well, well, it was our first pond.)

The final coat was fine concrete, made with sand instead of gravel, and we thought we would make designs on it. We were working in winter – our mild, comparatively frostless winter near the western sea-coast – and the days were short. Suddenly we realised that the concrete was setting and the designs would have to be done that evening. We worked freehand by the light of an electric torch held by each in turn, mostly on studies of marine life (Murdoch is a biologist). There are some fine sea-horses, amoebas and starfish, joined by swirling seaweed, and a just-recognisable ship: child-art, we say to ourselves proudly, while visitors are politely baffled. My best fish is now shrouded in ramping *Iris kaempferi*.

Half-way up the wall we fixed a shell I had bought in the Persian Gulf for twopence, and the water drips from it on to a pile of large stones. On the bottom of the pond is a six-inch layer of turf, in which we planted three water-lilies – too many, as it turned out, for one of them, *Nymphaea froebeli*, would have filled the whole pond; in a reasonably sunny year it continues to produce masses of deep pink, gold-centred blooms until late autumn. In the corners we planted *Iris laevigata*, *I. sibirica* which starts flowering in May, and *I. kaempferi* which goes on into August. So far the little bog pockets have not been a great success, because they seem to go sour; but the local butterworts which I brought from the moors are very lovely. At one side the pond overflows by a little depression into a small bog with primulas and the monkey-flower or spotted mimulus, which looks as if someone had gone round with a brush dabbing a spot of orange paint on each yellow flower.

Once this first pond was achieved I found myself wanting a larger one, and a bigger and better bog. At the far side of the lawn the ground drops into a wilderness of rugosa roses, which are one of our main garden weeds; they have a wonderful smell and look rather fine when the carmine-purple flowers are all out in June, and again in autumn when they are covered with large red hips. Beyond the roses is a thicket of rhododendron and olearia, a sea-whipped hedge of escallonia and a five-acre field separating the garden from the dunes. I began to hack away at the roses till I made a gap in the bank about six feet wide, and a bigger gap below. In the hollow I made a square pond two foot six deep; it need not have been more than two feet, and I might have saved concrete by making a shallower rounded basin, but I was not sure how to do this and Murdoch was not there to advise me. This pond is a rather forthright affair with a square lip level with the ground, but I plan to have rock plants coming over the lip.

Then I dug a shallow trench across the lawn and laid two lengths of iron pipe into it. The plumber made me a kind of box with holes which screws into one end of the pipe and rests in the bog, well camouflaged with primula leaves; when he saw the pipes laid he said I ought to join the union. We put the turfs back within a few hours of lifting them and now there is no trace of the line of the pipe on the surface of the lawn.

I got all the friends I could to help to move a dozen or so large (two-man) stones with which we made a series of water steps in the bank. It took us days to fit them in so that the water trickled and dropped as we wanted; one needs slightly concave stones, preferably those which are water-worn already. At each side of the small waterfall we made flat stone pockets which I filled with peat and leaf-mould. At the bottom I dug out the sandy ground and replaced it with a foot or so of peat, of which we have any amount; and through this I made a meandering channel of concrete and flat rocks, leading to the lip of the pond.

We stretched wire netting across the back of the pond from hooks bedded in the concrete walls, and piled turf behind it. Here I have planted blue and white *Iris laevigata* and other bog plants, many of which, like the sagittarias, have strikingly handsome foliage. In the pond are two water-lilies and a water-hawthorn (*Aponogeton distachyos*) which has flowered continuously, almost from the time I put it in.

Before planting, the pond had to be filled with water and emptied by siphoning, to wash out the poisonous alkali from the concrete. I planted in gum boots, almost losing them, and gradually let the water trickle in, lifting the leaves of the lilies as they grew. It then became clear that I had made an ideal breeding ground for Highland midges. I could not use chemicals because of the plants, so I bought four hungry golden orfe; there still seems to be rather too much pond life, but the orfe go sculling around in a determined way. Over the plants Murdoch and I did not agree. I like collecting things here and there; he wanted to try those he had seen in and around other ponds, notably that in the Edinburgh botanical gardens. Some of my odd bits have certainly not been too successful. When one digs up an orchid or a bog asphodel, one usually digs up bits of rush and grass with it and they take control, though this way I got a pretty little bog scirpus and a trailing St John's wort (*Hypericum humifusum*) which is quite enchanting. My feeling is that the only weeds are wild flowers which suppress their cultivated neighbours; when they behave politely they are no weeds.

The Highlands are full of common and lovely flowers, lovelier often than the rarities which one would hate to remove from the places they have chosen. I know of a quarry by the road to Oban where the beautiful grass of Parnassus grows in sheets, and tried several times to get it to grow for me, but so far it has barely survived. On the other hand the summer-flowering yellow saxifrage, *Saxifraga aizoides*, which grows in great profusion along the shores of Loch Lochy, just above the main road to Inverness, has transplanted well and grows in corners of the little waterfall and in crannies of the stone wall. Bogbean came from the Moor of Rannoch, some ordinary little orchids – but how smartly they stand up and how their leaves shine! – from the nearest bit of moorland. For my 'garden' flowers I have Kurume azaleas and heaths. Every azalea fan has his favourite, and mine is Sakata, a lovely glowing brick-red. The heaths carry on through autumn and winter; one of the best is the dwarf *Erica cinerea atrorubens*, which has none of the muddy bluish colour so common in heaths. I got a mixed lot of primula seedlings, some of which turned out very well indeed; these I have left to seed.

There is a young silver birch at one corner of the pond, and I intend gradually to clear patches of rose to make room for shrubs and small trees. Meanwhile rose suckers rush cheerfully back; I am not sure whether even concrete is proof against them. In the grass edge I have planted spiraeas, which do well here and naturalise if given a chance.

An important part of my water gardening is still to come. I am going to run a pipe from the outlet of the pond through the old shrubbery and the hedge to a trough in the field, which at present has only the water that falls so abundantly from the sky. Nowadays there is no need to use iron piping with all the bother of corners and joints; I shall use some kind of plastic only lightly buried.

I suppose what one really does with this kind of ploy is to go back to childhood and endlessly happy days mucking around in the burn. Even the sound of the water is delicious. I was told that lilies must have completely undisturbed water, but the splash off my pile of stones does not seem to worry them. So far only one child has fallen in and he got out very quickly indeed without, apparently, worrying the fish. The difficulty is that nothing worries those fish. I would like them to come to the surface and circle slowly round if I played the harp to them. Only, for that, I would have to learn to play the harp.

The Countryman, v. 51, Spring 1955, pp. 85–8

Mitchison in her 60s with Prof Victor Gugenheim by the back door, with the big oil-tank painted by Sir Charles (Charlie) Brett.

The Golden Year

(1960)

This was the first year in twenty when the harvest was all in by the end of August. I have known years when part of it was still out early in October, or when we gave up the last few rotting stooks, slimy and sprouting, half eaten by mice and birds. The 1959 oats were a light crop but we didn't lose one sheaf.

In Sheneval the stalks had been twisted and broken, not by rain but by the fierce August gale; we could cut only one way. But my redd-land, that is the field which had a green crop last year and now is in oats undersown with grass, had been completely sheltered and the corn was in good order. The days blazed on; Lachlan took the binder off and cut for some of the neighbours. But, as always, we hurried over harvest as soon as it was ready. We needn't have done that in 1959, but we have got into the habit of not trusting our weather, whatever the forecasts say. Besides, agricultural workers are not the best paid, and the men wouldn't like not to get their bit of overtime.

Last summer I had little hard work myself, so easily it went and so many helpers. Before a drop of rain had fallen all the stacks were thatched, pale gold under blue-green rushes. The first to be threshed were just tied over with old pieces of net that the fishermen give us, but those that have to stand until the second threshing in the spring have a spider's web of stack-rope over the thatch, the spokes weighted with bricks.

Under the steady sun the potato shaws died off quickly, and we spun them out while the weather held, good Kerr's Pink and the best Golden Wonders I have ever had. I never expected them to do so well in the sandy cricket-field, but the ground was certainly helped by intensive grazing between electric fences during the grass ley, and they had a good dose of seaweed as well.

It was wonderful hoeing weather in the garden. We felt we'd got on top of the weeds at last. But the rhododendrons decided that next spring must have arrived early and far too many came into bloom. You don't expect to see a hillside of ponticum dotted with purple in October. One of the tender ones, a *bullatum-*

Johnsoneanum hybrid from Crarae,[1] which I planted six inches high two years ago and which has shot into a handsome bush, produced in mid-autumn a wax-like lily flower, gold blotched and scented. It lives in the old conservatory in a half wine-barrel, but it might do out of doors if I could get it out of the draught. Percy can sense draughts as if he grew tender leaves himself; and sometimes moving shrubs just a few feet takes them out of the killing current. But what can we do with all that glass? There are five greenhouses in various stages of decay, as well as the conservatory.

None of the greenhouses cost more than £100 to build, but repairing even one of them properly would take more than that now. Mice nest in the ruins of archaic heating systems, or did until Stumpy[2] came. But one side of one of them can be heated, enough for the early seeds, from an electric heater, with polythene sheeting tacked over a framework for the insulation. We are going, though, to improve on that, with a coil of soil-heating wire: all thanks to Tom Johnston's Hydro-Electric Board, which dammed the Lussa and brought us reasonably cheap power.

There used to be peaches and nectarines in most of the houses, but peach trees have a life of only about thirty years, after which the branches begin to die back. Most of the old ones are gone; so is the old laird's out-of-door water-closet. He usedn't to function without his 'pineapple' peaches and his special seat. But now, unroofed, the closet is a compost heap, and I have induced the water to trickle through the wall to a fountain on the other side. My son Murdoch and I built the fountain and basin, but the stones we used in the concrete were too big for a good key-on, so it leaks slowly. Also, we hadn't reckoned with such a quick set, so the child art with which we decorated the concrete had to be done by the light of a small torch in the middle of a jolly evening. It still, somehow, has that look.

Concrete is my least favourite material. Apart altogether from the fact that the pigs' bucket, once used for mixing it, is now twice as heavy as it should be, concrete wants you to think you can shove it around. But once give way to it, and you have twenty feet of something that is more immovable than any Establishment – Nissen-hut foundations still scarring the grass long after the huts have blown or rusted away, rocket platforms hideous in the flowery machair of Eoligarry [Barra] long after rockets are obsolete, the eastern corn counties of England cut to bits with enormous runways. Local opinion there holds that they are all built half as long again as they need be owing to the incompetence of American pilots in landing. My own feeling is that a change of armies of occupation might be a good idea; if we had the Russians for a bit, I'm sure we should all become pro-American.

But, unlike concrete, the greenhouses don't last. And they produce their own problems: how to hide the key so that it will be visible to the (good) grown-ups but not to the (bad, but sharper-eyed) grandchildren, still less the lads of Carradale. They raid such apples as I have every year. Last year they left none, and I had to buy monstrously bad cookers from the Co-op at a shilling a pound, the kind one sees rotting under the trees in southern England; but that's another problem. I suppose we all have to have our bash at authority, and, of course, the Big House is the traditional super-authority in any village. Still, they might have left me a few. Most years the Stirling Castle bears so well that I can easily spare some for the raiders; but last year there wasn't an apple, though, again for the first year in twenty, there was a fair crop of pears on the old espaliers, which I keep only for the sake of the blossom.

One can expect pears only in a hot and dry summer. But last year I might have had maize outside instead of growing it in one of the houses, a practice which always strikes my African visitors as deliciously crazy. 'You forgot to put it on the Suttons' list,' says Emily, 'so Percy and I just slipped into Woolworth's when we were in Glasgow for the rhododendron show, and got a packet of seed. But I wasn't going to tell you till I saw they'd do.' But would they have done it for anyone else? And, for that matter, did the summer have anything to do with it?

New Statesman, v. 59, 2 January 1960, pp. 9-10

---

[1] A notable garden in Argyll, generally open to visitors.

[2] The garden cat; see 'Winds and Seedlings' in this section.

Winds and Seedlings

(1960)

If I were keen to be in a really honest job, unlike writing, which could do no harm to anyone in the community, I would think seriously about seed-growing and nursery-gardening. It is a big industry now and assists in giving pleasure of a recognisably international kind to millions of people; our hearts beat as one with the delphinium experts of America and the prize paeony growers in the dachas of Moscow. Of course it gives pain sometimes: as *Shoppers' Guide* found out, the less reputable firms sell seed which isn't what it should be; but even with the best of seed the resulting flowers are not like the picture on the packet. Snobbism is catered for, though more discreetly than with some products. But at least the consumer is not just an open mouth or empty mind; he or she must co-operate with skill, hard work and green fingers.

As it is, I am a consumer, and of course, a swapper. Percy and Emily, however, know about both sides of it, since they used to work for one of the highly specialised nurseries which does not, like so many of them, depend for a number of the more ordinary shrubs on the Dutch growers. In Holland it is common to see cottage gardens with well grown and tended young shrubs, ready for marketing by the big firms. Dutch azalea growing is highly skilled, as the Ghent hybrids, as well as the Christmas specials, testify. And yet I ask myself if we couldn't do as well in parts of the Highland west coast.

Already Hebridean Bulb Growers, starting with quarter acres on crofts, but spreading wherever they find the combination of soil, climate and people ready to do the work, has shown what can be done. Unfortunately the few days of really intensive work coincide with haymaking. But not every crofter makes hay nowadays. So far, the more obvious sure selling bulbs have been grown, but perhaps we shall soon find something to specialise in.

And what about azaleas and the rare shrubs? Even in my garden, azaleas and many rhododendrons seed themselves; but so far I have trusted to wind pollination, so that almost all the azaleas have luteum parentage. I have been told that I ought to throw out all the golden honey azaleas and concentrate on the 'good' ones. But I can't, at my age, manage this professional ruthlessness. The Loderi seedlings, though sometimes pleasant enough, have never so far been like the seed parent. But Loderi flower at the same time as ponticum, which is one of our main problem plants. It is only the barbatum, blood scarlet in March, when little else is flowering – perhaps nothing it can cross with – that always comes true, as well as a triflorum which is late but probably does not cross with the larger-flowered species.

These seedlings have taken their chance, struggling with grass, heather, ponticum, a wretched little pink spirea which suckers away everywhere, and prickly masses of pernettya. Only a few ever get transplanted. Yet from the catalogues, which have been bed-time reading all the winter, I realise that people actually pay for pernettya-type rugosa roses and even rhododendron ponticum.

What couldn't we do with a seedlings industry in the peaty Highlands! Of course seedlings are not so easily harvested as bulbs. Half the cost of a shrub is its packing. But a co-operative society, handling orders centrally, should be able to send round a van with packers. The Forestry Commission could do it, and well. But they have a firmly blinkered policy about not competing with 'the trade' – not even for social reasons, such as bringing extra employment into the Highlands. Perhaps some public spirited estate, such as the Duke of Westminster's, would try shrub growing and see if it might be suitable for sheltered, peaty crofts near the sea. We desperately need alternatives.

It seems to me that deciduous azaleas have everything: an autumn blaze in the leaves, a reasonably attractive winter look, flowers with shape and colour – unlike, for example, most of the viburnums – and usually a scent – unlike the camellias, which have the best evergreen foliage of anything. With our big azalea bushes we can cut and come again; they last well indoors or revive after a journey. Also, once they have got their roots in, they stand up well to wind.

That is essential for us in the west of Scotland. My garden was fairly typical of the rather unimaginative layout of the 'big-house' garden a hundred years ago. There is a terrace in front of the house, grass lawns, not all of which can be kept up now, a walled kitchen garden with a rhododendron plot and a 'wild' garden dating from the turn of the century. The layout of the whole of the garden is done with an eye to the wind.

There is an enormous escallonia hedge as a windbreak between me and the cricket-field, just now unlovely with the remains of Swedes and kale stalks which the Galloways will polish off when they are let in. Beyond the field is the bay and the sea, which usually looks amiable enough, but off which comes the salt-bearing south wind, guaranteed to burn up the leaves of the toughest shrub or tree.

An English garden may have long, beautiful vistas, but a Scottish garden must be snug. Our walls do not really protect the flat two acres of kitchen garden, planned in the usual way, as four squares of fruit and vegetables, with paths and flower beds on their edges. When we took over, twenty-two years ago, there were various windbreak hedges. All round, immediately inside the wall, there was a series of boxes, mostly bedded out with French marigolds, petunias, asters and scabious, but interestingly hedged with tricuspidaria, various hebes and escallonias, kalmias and olearias. Down the middle, hedged in by dark escallonias, was a double border, bare earth most of the year, then a forest of green-painted stakes and then for a month magnificent with bath-sponge dahlias.

All the hedges needed constant clipping, the annuals constant bedding out. I did not yet know the West Highland climate and rashly rooted up most of the hedges, replacing geraniums, when the war came, with far too many cabbages. The head gardener, whom we took over with the house, was Calvinist-minded; he liked staking and clipping and mowing; he liked to leave vegetables till they were large and tough. I was so scared of him that I seldom went into the walled garden during working hours, but made myself a crescent-shaped bed at the far side of the house which nobody else worked on. This was exactly what my aunt, Elizabeth Haldane, similarly terrorised, had done at Cloan in Perthshire a generation before.

But that gardener went. He was unquenchably a head gardener, and we couldn't go on providing his cannon-fodder. Two single-handed gardeners came and went, each leaving the garden more of a wreck and turning the gardener's cottage into more and more of a slum. I coped with it alone for a matter of months, aided occasionally by visiting MPs, but it was a wet summer and the weeds were winning the battle.

Then, out of Cornwall, which also has an Atlantic climate, and from years in the garden which produced *Shrubs for the Milder Counties*,[1] Percy and Emily came, with Stumpy, that exceedingly wise cat who recognises the difference between small birds, which are looked at severely but let alone, and mice, which are no longer tolerated in the garden. Now everything is different. Unlike other gardeners who insist on having things in rows, Percy sympathises with all trailers, overlappers, untidy but romantic flowers. Only vegetables grow in rows now. The cottage is a picture; even the least promising, exposed bit of wall has Emily's cyclamens flourishing under it. I find myself welcome in the garden, and, goodness, what a lot I am learning!

When the war ended and one could again think of something other than cabbages, I began to regret my lost windbreaks. I planted the hedges again at each side of the double border, but with a grass path between them and it, so they don't immediately start sucking the good soil of the bed. This is a mixed hedge, with lonicera, beech, holly, berberis, darwinii, olearia and flowering currant, kept trimmed at one side and wild at the other. I put a couple of cypress seedlings into it, the *cupressus macrocarpa* which grows so much better with us than in its native Monterey. These are now very handsome but much too big; I keep on saying to myself that I ought to do something about them. Never mind, Percy will certainly know the answer!

In the cross-over, where the long beds are cut by the main path, there used to be lumps of stone, pathetic remains of a rockery, much overgrown with this and that. Now there are four young camellias, which will in time tower into deep green glossiness of leaves and profuse, formal flowers. Primroses and jonquils, followed by tulips, will nestle round their toes. I shall be eighty or so, but (assuming no H-bombs have dropped) I shall be surprised if I don't enjoy it, write about it, and tell off my great-grandchildren for treading on the flowers.

New Statesman, v. 59, 9 April 1960, pp. 516-18

[1] W. Arnold-Forster, *Shrubs for the Milder Counties* (Country Life, 1948).

Mitchison with *Sunflower*, a sculpture by Gertrude Hermes.

A Garden in Argyll

(1980)

Nothing is left of the North Oxford house where I spent my childhood, not the almond and apple trees I used to climb, nor the rockery which I used to climb too, though strictly forbidden. But the garden of our next, bigger house, Cherwell, is not entirely lost; I can trace some of the trees which used to stand at the far end, in the garden of Wolfson College. A pear tree is now in one of the quads – one up for the architect who stopped the builders from cutting it down as I am sure they wanted to. And the young walnut – what a beautiful tree it has made! Its parents, the three old walnuts, gave us enough nuts during the hard autumns of World War I to make the war-time economy bread palatable. My mother, a good Scot, was more interested in vegetables than flowers. Luckily the kitchen garden also included a large strawberry bed; I minded less having to weed that part. Oxford is very good rose soil, but our roses were dull; it was just before the big break in hybrid teas. We never had any but the most ordinary iris and paeonies although, again, Oxford is just right for them.

My grandmother's walled garden at Cloan in Perthshire where we went every summer was different. It is high on the north-west slopes of the Ochils, above Auchterarder, and needs all the shelter it can get. In front of the house was a double holly hedge with tropaeolum growing through it and in those days little beds deeply enclosed with wire because of the peacocks and presumably rabbits. And there was a small round pond with a fountain in the middle controlled by a tap in the grass, source of infinite pleasure in the various games which my cousins and I used to play, and annoying for mothers and nannies who had dressed us up for grown-up tea.

But the walled garden, up past the great beech and lime trees, had almost everything in the way of fruit if one could dodge the gardeners, flowers for the bees, and a long herbaceous border backed by espalier apples which separated it from the vegetables, a usual Scottish feature. Also the grape house, locked, but accessible from the roof if there was a bunch within reach of the skylight – and time to get away.

Later my aunt, Elizabeth Haldane, enlarged the garden, made yew hedges and planted many of the better rhododendrons. In the well-shaved lawns between the hedges there were always a few special flowers and our dogs' gravestones, carefully lettered.

Gardeners, of course, were easily come by in those days. When we moved to Carradale on the west coat in 1937, there was a head gardener, two competent under-gardeners and several aged retainers who swept paths. I found the first two summers deeply exciting; my London back-garden was not too bad, but in the thirties all London gardens were a bit grimy. However the conservatory next to the house was in a bad state and we cut it down in size; I did not realise then that we were losing beautiful indoor rhododendrons, but I doubt if we could have saved them. There were five other houses, in reasonably good condition, most with peaches or nectarines, all planted in the twenties before the owners who were selling had moved south. They cost £100 each to build and have been sufficiently good to survive with much patching, new ridges and plastic replacing glass.

Stone walls are not really enough shelter for a two-acre garden in the stormy Highlands. The garden was halved by a thick dark hedge of clipped *Cupressus macrocarpa* and along two of the walls there were boxes for flowers hedged in with various loniceras and hebes or the better escallonias. The whole front of the house is protected by a vast spreading hedge-belt of escallonia which stands up to salt spray from the sea, and a stretch of wild garden heavily infested with pink spirea and *Rosa rugosa*. Little beds had at one time been shaped like the letters of the owner's wife's name, but the clipped heath borders had gradually been squared. Inside the two main dark hedges there was a double row of green painted sticks. These waited for the dahlias which stretched from one end to the other. The bare beds were a bit off-putting in spring. However I let things go till 1939, thrilled with the rhododendrons, most of all the two great clumps, one of *R. barbatum*, the other of *R. shilsonii*; later in the year came the Loderi hybrids scenting the air and along the outer walls the tree rhododendrons; in another part of the garden yet more, including some very fine arboreums of all kinds, especially the old blood-red which, luckily, layers very successfully. This part got terribly overgrown, has a year's work to be done on it still, but only a few years back in the course of clearing brambles I came on a magnificent, hidden 'Dr Stocker', which is now spreading like mad.

Luckily, we managed to re-do all the cottages before the war; it had shocked me deeply to find that the pretty-looking cottage at the end of the garden had no inside water, a nasty old range and a leaking roof, all for a highly skilled man – but the total garden wage for everyone was, I think, well under £300 a year. Well, Hugh was a somewhat puritanical man; he decided that everything must be vegetables except for the big fruit cage which was fed yearly with seaweed as well as dung, for the soil is light except where leaf mould has thickened over it. Out went dahlias, roses – never very good – and the annuals started in the houses. Easier to plough the ground if the small hedges went! So they did and all the delphiniums. We grew far more cabbages and kale than anyone could eat. But the bush fruit was wonderful. That cage lasted until four winters ago when a heavy snowfall brought it all down. Now I have three smaller ones and do not net the gooseberries; the blackbirds get a lot but so do I.

We cut down to three gardeners, to two, finally to none and a struggle which I lost. We had more machines, and the family helped when they were there. Then came a happy twenty-five years with Percy Edwards who had been with Will Arnold-Forster at Eagle's Nest in Cornwall, with whom I worked in complete friendship, from whom I learned constantly and who never said anything harsher than 'We shouldn't have done that, should we?' After his death another gap, and now Phil Asherman, part-time but full of enthusiasm. By now I have managed to get paths through the wild garden where I have encouraged the azaleas, many now so tall that I can hardly reach them, planted hoherias and eucryphias which tower into bloom in September, and started some new groups of shilsonii and barbatum rhododendrons.

Mr Davidian came over from the Edinburgh Botanic Garden, named some I did not know and ran his hands lovingly over the red-gold bark of his favourites. Every year I try to get one or two new ones and now I have a bank of continuing interest from March to June; the brooms are constantly seeding really lovely colours, all on their own; I simply cut out the dull ones. I can count on hammamelis, flowering malus and in winter two big arching trees of *Prunus subhirtella autumnalis*. One quarter of the walled garden is Phil's, another quarter is grass but crammed with narcissus which spread and spread.

I only grow the easiest annuals, a few dahlias and chrysanthemums, but the peaches and nectarines – I replanted in the fifties – are a great success. So are the vines which I hack about and do not worry with, though they get a tar wash. I expect by now they have rooted well under the greenhouse walls. The ten-year-old fig has almost filled its house; we sell a lot of tomatoes.

There are problems, but such rewards. One year in five the frosts leave the camellias to flower. And how is my newly planted *Magnolia wilsonii* doing? And what about the planting where the two big cupressus trees heeled over in the November gales, crushing everything? Sooner or later it will all take shape again.

The Countryman, v. 85, Summer 1980, pp. 126–31

PART VI

KINTYRE (2)

The Tinkers and their Language

(1952)

We all have to have something to give us confidence and a decent pride. In fact, history is very largely that. We have a pride in even the less pleasant deeds of our forebears – so long as they *are* deeds! If people have not got this pride, this myth, this secret world, this underpinning of the fabric of reason, they will find life much less worth living. But different people get their pride in different ways. It is sometimes difficult for settled folk to realise that a tinker's life may be worth living. The joys of the open road in Scottish weather are not great. An encampment has little comfort as we know it. So, for the tinkers, pride and myth must be all the more potent.

There is a certain pride in just being the people of the road, and that is quite genuine. And there is pride in being wanted by the farmers, in knowing – as many of the tinkers know very well – that they work better than anyone else and are correspondingly in demand. But in the old days they were wanted for more than that. They were the carriers of news, both local and national. But now that buses are frequent, and wireless sets even more so, this use is almost gone. Nobody wants horn or wooden spoons now, or any of the other small household goods which they used to make but which are now easy and cheap to buy. It is easier to replace a saucepan than to get it mended. In one place and another they are beginning to assimilate with their neighbours, and to wear down the prejudice against them of those who consider themselves one rung up the social ladder. But to have a secret language is a great source of confidence and moral build-up, as those who remember their own childhood will know well. I hope that no tinker families will let this drop or be superseded by the hideous language of the movies; and I believe a study of this language will pose a few interesting historical questions.

It is, of course, partly used by the tinkers for talking to one another in hearing of other people, to conceal their purpose, but partly for no utilitarian reason. It has no grammar and consists mostly of substantives, a few adjectives and verbs to be used with auxiliaries. I am far from any comprehensive knowledge; but my small vocabulary (spelled more or less phonetically) will show five kinds of derivation, from English cant, from Romany, from Gaelic, from Scots and from a kind of children's make-up. The words I know are all Argyllshire, and probably would be the same as the Perthshire words. The Galloway tinkers or – as it should properly be spelled – tinklers, have various other words. Many of them are recorded in MacCormick's 'The Tinkler Gypsies'.[1]

Now, first there are the words of the old cant or slang (I have heard some of my tinker friends refer to it as gibberish), such as *mort* for woman – *kinchin mort* for a girl child is also used – and *prod*, a horse, from the eighteenth century cant word *prad*, still used by circus people. Some of these words were probably current in old English speech, at any rate the speech of the vulgar, as opposed to the courtly southern English speech which, on the whole, is what has come down to us. The derivations in the Oxford English Dictionary and in Eric Partridge's *Dictionary of the Underworld* are very conjectural, though sometimes one sees the Latin – the dog Latin – right at the back. Such words are:

Girl: *dell* (an old slang word, sixteenth century on).
Dog: *buffet* (from bufe, cant, sixteenth century on – yet there is also the colloquial Scots word for a dog, Bowfie, and bowf or bouf, to bark).
Knife: *cutlin* (from cuttle, sixteenth to eighteenth century, colloquial).
Fire: *glimmer* (cant, sixteenth century onward).
Watch: *clocka* (nineteenth century cant clock, for a watch, or it might just be made up).
Shop: *chova* (from chovey, costers' slang, nineteenth century).
Bread: *pennam* (cant, usually pannam from seventeenth century on – here the Latin derivation is plain).
Milk: *yarrum* (cant, sixteenth century on).
Cheese: *cassam* (cant, sixteenth century on – here again from Latin caseus. But sometimes *saum* – from what?).
Meat or bacon: *cornie* (from nineteenth century cant, carnish, either from Latin carnis or Italian carne).
Something to sell: *chaet* (from cant, seventeenth century on, used for thing or object).

House: *cain* (from cant, sixteenth century on, but probably in
      turn from the Eastern khan).
Go: *bing* (cant, sixteenth century on. Used as *bing here* for come
      here, but *bing avree* for go away).
Coat: *tug* (from cant tog – perhaps from toga? – eighteenth
      century on).

We know a good many of these words, because during the
eighteenth and nineteenth centuries there were a good many
popular books which used them as literary decoration, much as
American words are used now. But they must have had a wide
mouth-to-mouth circulation among the people of the road, so
that even a late word like *chovey* starts from London and ends up
some fifty years later in Argyll. Of course, there are other possible
derivations. Though Eric Partridge does not suggest it, it seems on
the cards that *chovey* might be related to the middle English word
chapfari (from which chaffer) or that *bing* might come from the
old Norse verb *bua* which is used for being somewhere. Naturally
there are a good many pure Romany words, or words derived from
Romany. Among these are:

Stockings: *hollovas* (Romany hoolavas).
Money: *lour* (Romany lovo).
Speak: *mang* (this is also cant, but comes from Romany *mong*, to
      beg).
Man: *gadgie* (Romany gaujo: a stranger).
Hen: *gannie* (Romany kauni).

Now this is all fairly straightforward; but one asks oneself what
and where is the connection. Are these folk with their predominantly
golden-orange hair (though there are some black ones) and usually
rather flat noses racially akin to the Romany people in the south?
Clearly they have not now got the matriarchal structure of the
gypsy encampment, though the older women are certainly of more
importance than they are, for instance, in the ordinary Highland
clachan. They themselves tend to disclaim Romany kinship, though
they are interested in books about the Romany – I found Borrow[2] is
a popular author to lend out. On the other hand they tend to speak

of ancient lineage, though it is the kings of Scotland or Ireland, rather than of Egypt, that they feel kinship with. Some of them say they are the remains of dispossessed Highland clans, possibly from the islands. This sounds to me not improbable. Most have cousins in Ireland, sometimes, too, in America. I rather think the main clan names may be adopted by people who are not really members of the clan or family, but have no very special names of their own.

One theory is that the present tinkers are descended from various wandering tribes, possibly pre-Celtic: people who had still the neolithic habit of wandering and had never picked up the corn-growing and fertility religions of the later people. It may well be that the early metal workers were such people, wandering from chief to chief in the civilisation of the broch builders, two thousand years back, surviving invasions and conquests, but not surviving the industrial revolution which brought their craft secrets to nothing. Perhaps the wandering bards were such people, and the *faas* and *cairds*. They may well have been established on the roads long before the gypsies themselves came, perhaps in the sixteenth century, certainly some generations later than they came to England. There has been plenty of inter-marriage. The Elliots of Minto have a black head on their coat of arms; and when I was a child I was told that this commemorated a marriage with 'the Queen of the Gypsies'.

When one discusses their speech with them, the tinkers sometimes say that it is derived from Gaelic. None of the younger Kintyre tinkers seems to have any Gaelic himself, and the only obvious Gaelic words in their language that I have recognised are:

Stone: *clach.*

Sheep: *megget* (from the Gaelic meigead: the bleating of a sheep or goat).

We now have a group of words which come from the look or use of an object and are rather like children's words. Here are some of them.

Duck: *quacker* (but quacking-chaet is the cant word for duck).

Cart: *whirlie* (from wheel? But to go for a hurl is Scots for a ride).

Tent: *wattle* (it is normally made on a basis of willow).

Bowl: *dripler.*

Pot: *blackie.*
Basket: *rushky* or *rishky* (from rushes?).
Foot: *trampler.*

There are one or two words which are closely related to English. A rabbit is a *cownie;* but this may either be coney, which was in use up to about two centuries ago both in England or Scotland, or the Gaelic *coinean.* A boy is a *ged.* This may simply be *get,* which is old colloquial, possibly from the Scots word caddy, which was in common use throughout Scotland and not merely specialised to the game of golf. A pot-hook is a *cleek,* which is quite good country English or lowland Scots. Soap is *sapler,* which might come through soaper, as dripler for bowl might come from dripper. Yet *saple* is Kintyre dialect for soap. A shawl is a *plasky,* something between the Scots (ex-Gaelic) *plaidie* and the Romany *plashta.* Blankets are *coories,* from the Scots word coorie, meaning to nestle. There are some very odd words. A potato is a *ned.* But the only cant *ned* is a guinea. But bagpipes are *stiumers,* and this may be a Shelta (Irish tinker) word.

These words have all coalesced from their various sources so as to make a secret speech; and now this speech is dying. More and more of the tinkers are settling down. They have, perhaps, understood that doing piece-work and undercutting the local agricultural labourer is not always popular. And many have been in the army or navy and seen other ways of life. They want to get decent houses like the rest of the world, and a modern tinker encampment is clean and tidy; there is a pram or a cot for the baby; the old whirlie may well have been replaced by a lorry. And the words will be dying out. When you are a citizen like the rest, with a steady wage and a vote and money in the Savings Bank, you no longer need a secret language. You are not against the rest of the world; you go with them to the cinema, and you pick up words of the slang which has now replaced the old cant. The words die, and the history dies with them.

History Today, v. 2, March 1952, pp. 181-4

[1] Andrew MacCormick, *The Tinkler-Gypsies of Galloway* (1906).
[2] George Borrow (1803-31, author of *Lavengro* (1851) and *The Romany Rye* (1857).

The Haldanes in Kintyre

(1979)

My great-grandfather, James Haldane, and his elder brother, Robert, came to Kintyre in the beautiful summer of 1800 to preach to the heathen Highlanders. They were in their early thirties and tough, as they had need to be. They had both been in the Navy, behaved with gallantry and good sense, then briefly settled down as landed proprietors, married and duly started begetting a suitable number of children. But several things happened to them; one was the French Revolution. The elder brother, writing later, tells how 'a sense of melioration and improvement in the affairs of mankind seemed to open itself to my mind, which, I trusted, would speedily take place in the world, such as the universal abolition of slavery, of war and of many other miseries ... I rejoiced in the experiment that was making in France ...' How many of us have felt exactly the same about later revolutions!

But the brothers gave up politics for religion; the two are very near and both brothers spoke of their mission work as campaigns. James was perhaps the quicker of the two brothers, with deep and generous affection. The two who had sympathised with the cause of the poor and dispossessed in the French Revolution, now saw it in a rather different way in India. They proposed a mission to India, with headquarters in Benares; all was to be paid for by the Haldanes and Robert sold his estate at Airthrey which he had loved and planted skilfully with trees round a winding artificial loch of his own making. All was set to go, but, fortunately, the Directors of the East India Company refused to allow them in.

But by this time the life of a country gentleman held nothing for either of the brothers, and about this time they fell in with little Mr Campbell, ironmonger, city missionary in Edinburgh, tract distributor. From then on the brothers were constantly in touch with, and influenced by, one or other fervent preacher, seldom in the Church of Scotland since no respectable institution could adequately cater for the spiritual demands of the Saved. It must all have been utterly satisfying for those who, not necessarily all the time, but at least for a great part of it, knew themselves to be in a state of Grace. But others may have found it quite simply too, too much.

During the next several years, the two Haldanes and their companions, usually Mr Campbell and also John Aikman, an educated and well-read young man who had spent part of his life in Jamaica, preached the Word according to their idea of it throughout northern and western Scotland. Sometimes they rode, sometimes travelled in a light gig, piled with tracts, and often enough walked; when I was a child I was much impressed with their large, knobbly walking sticks, kept in a glass case at home. And wherever they went they started Sunday schools or small churches – tabernacles – doubtless with the proceeds of the sale of Airthrey.

Clearly they had not originally intended to come to Kintyre, in fact they hardly knew it existed, but when they were preaching in Arran they observed a long neck of land. 'On enquiry,' Mr Campbell notes in his journal, 'we found it was Kintyre, towards the south end of which was Campbeltown ... hearing that there was not one Gospel preacher in the whole range of seventy miles, except in the chief town, we determined to pay it a visit.' No sooner said than done; they found a boat and crossed, finding 'a little inn' which must in all probability have been Dippen, marked in all old maps as an inn. The landlord was woken, made a light and cooked them ham and eggs; there was no great interest there the next morning, though a sermon was on offer, but Campbeltown was different. Here they stayed several days, preaching morning and evening 'on the green slope of a hill' with congregations of over a thousand. The villages round Campbeltown were visited during the day and then they sent a messenger up Kintyre intimating that they would preach four sermons a day at different places, a labour of faith indeed!

They had the lowest opinion of all the local Ministers who were 'deeply immersed in farming, fishing or trading in sheep or cattle'. But it was the land-owners who finally showed up, one of them sitting on his horse during James Haldane's sermon 'in a scarlet hunting-coat' – did they practise fox hunting in those days? There were threats of arrest, but James and Robert were not to be scared by a few Highlanders, though it meant that the audiences hardly dared to come close. Mr Campbell, courageous but rather small, was ordered back to Whitehouse – it sounds as if the population of Kintyre was considerably larger in those days – where James found a sealed warrant to take them to the Sheriff of Argyll. They set out in a leisurely way for Lochgilphead, preaching at the inn where they stayed the night. The Sheriff, an elderly man, was clearly embarrassed, wanted them to take the oath of loyalty to the Government but could not find the wording, finally released them.

This was a great victory for field preaching. Whether it would have been won had the preachers been other than class equals or superiors of those who wanted to arrest them, is something else. But everyone in the 'town of Whitehouse' turned out. Only the weather was unwelcoming; they arrived, soaking, at a very small inn, with only one fire where they could dry their clothes while ham and eggs were cooking in the kitchen. James was delighted, saying 'What a fine subject for a caricature – field-preachers refreshing themselves after a shower!'

All this was followed up by a young Campbeltonian, Mr MacCallum, who had studied at the seminary which the Haldanes had set up in Glasgow. Because the respectable Minister at Whitehouse had taken a different side from the landlord at a local election, the newcomer was given an acre of land for house and chapel. All went swimmingly. Mr Campbell, coming back to Kintyre again two years later, found a great change. The fiddler for wedding dances had seen the light, so had the members of a whisky-toddy group which had filled their evenings, up to the coming of the Word.

And now I ask myself how does this fit in with the young sympathisers with the French Revolution, the young Midshipman who insisted that the helmsman should teach him to steer (at that time no part of an officer's training), the Lieutenant who, being the only one on the *Foudroyant* who could speak French, took the unwilling surrender of the Commander of the *Pégase*,[1] or the other young Midshipman staying steadily aloft during a gale? Obviously they were still on the side of the underdog, though they saw him in terms of ignorance of those doctrines which had given them such courage and confidence. They had seen through the world of getting on, being a social success, which meant that, in the path they had chosen, they were immensely successful. Their particular theological convictions seem oddly unimportant now, but not the strength of character which carried them on, nor yet the easy comradeship with all who shared their ideals and hopes. I like to think of my great-grandfather wet through and laughing ready for the next bout in his campaign, whatever theological verbiage and unreality he chose to wrap it up in.

The Kintyre (Antiquarian and Natural History Society) Magazine 5, June 1979, pp. 25-7

[1] The Royal Navy ship *Foudroyant* captured the French *Pégase* in the Bay of Biscay in 1782.

Rural Reconstruction

(1942)

Carradale in Kintyre where I am living now, rather accidentally – for my own people are either from Perthshire or the Lothians – is like enough to other Highland or mixed Highland-Lowland communities, for its problems and possibilities to be common to most of rural Scotland, especially the west. I will describe it, and then say what we think is wrong, and how this could be remedied in any genuine reconstruction of Scotland. We talk about this kind of thing, some of us, and are disappointed that none of the grand schemes and plans have much in them for places like Carradale. We have, however, tried, and are trying now, to make some changes; people who try to change things are bound to make mistakes, but that can't be helped.

Several hundred men, women and children live here. Some are housed in modern bungalows, which are often let in summer, the owners moving into tolerably comfortable sheds at the back; some are in a new block of council houses, belatedly begun and still more belatedly finished, but quite pleasant to look at and live in; some are in a rural slum in the middle of the village, but-and-ben houses which have been responsible for plenty of death and disease, but which might be reconditioned; and some are in outlying farms and other houses, including the 'Big House' where I live. Almost all have gardens. Most Scottish villages suffer from a housing shortage and many have worse houses than ours.

Most of us in Carradale live by the fishing[1] and all have friends in the fishing and sometimes herring for tea. Some are forestry workers; the big estate here was mostly bought by the Forestry Commission; they are felling the grown timber and planting young trees high up onto the hills; some of the forestry workers are young girls who would be otherwise 'helping at home'. A few of us are farmers and farm workers; our main crops are oats, potatoes and turnips; there are good dairy cattle and fair hill sheep. I am market gardening. The country here is amongst the most beautiful in Europe; there is a sandy beach; so we have a considerable summer tourist trade. There are several small shops, a bakery, two post offices, a hotel and various boarding houses, two churches, a small golf course, a smithy, etc., besides a school which is at least three quarters of an hour's walk away for many of the children. In fact we are very typical; some similar villages might substitute quarrying for slate, stone or lime for fishing as a main industry. We have a fine Village Hall, of which more later on, and my husband owns the sporting rights here, including the fishing; more of that later on too.

Now, what is wrong with us as a community? Clearly, Carradale can't stand still; we must either grow and change or we perish, as so many Highland villages have perished. Immediately, there are not enough houses. Young couples have nowhere to set up house. And they want houses with reasonable facilities, proper ranges and water sanitation. Everyone would like electric light and the possibility of using electric appliances.

Next, our transport is very bad. There used to be a daily boat between our pier and Glasgow; this has been discontinued. Like many Highland villages we are a long way from a railway station. We are not in as bad a position as the Islands, but, in fact, the railway is little use to us, and the nearest aerodrome is eighteen miles away; the planes are useful for sudden illness or similar emergencies, but the fares are too expensive for most people. There are a fair amount of buses in the summer tourist months, but apart from these, it is very hard for us to travel or to market our goods or to get goods from Glasgow or elsewhere; this is particularly hard on farmers and shopkeepers. It restricts our markets, and unless there is Government control, we find ourselves obliged to sell cattle etc. to something like a ring of buyers who know we have no alternative. It is difficult to get coal or coke. That is to say, like most of the Highlands we are in the hands of MacBrayne. If MacBrayne were actually a man, he could be dealt with, and everyone would be delighted: unfortunately it is not as simple as that. MacBrayne is largely a railway company. In fact we are in the hands of a typical capitalist monopoly. The roads themselves are in a bad state; on the present rates nothing very much can be done to them. Our pier, like many others, is past service, nor can we, as a community, afford to rebuild it. Nor, even if it were new, would it afford adequate protection to the valuable modern ring-net boats. We want a safe harbour.

Next, we want various social services. Our schoolmaster and school mistresses are fine people, keen and good teachers; on an Intelligence Quotient measurement, with 100 as the normal score, we had two children in the 160 class, and a number of others over 130. But their education is hampered by large classes, sometimes two or three in one room, by lack of proper equipment and books; there is no playground and the lavatory accommodation, for instance, is intolerably old-fashioned. Only lately, after a petition by parents and an indignant village meeting, has the County seen fit to send the post-qualifying children in to Campbeltown, fifteen miles away, but the nearest secondary education, by bus. Before that, many of them, including the brightest, grew sick of school and applied to leave and go, usually to the fishing, before they were fourteen. Up till recently the disciplinary methods were old-fashioned and bad; under a new regime the strap is rapidly disappearing, but it still seems impossible to allow the children any kind of self-government or 'free work' in classes.

So far, there has been no attempt at adult education, evening classes, etc. Our bad transport facilities make it extremely hard for University Extension lecturers to come out from Glasgow; equally they have cut off the Gaelic Choir from its splendid conductor, who used to come once a week when we still had boats running to the pier. There are difficult children here, but no possibility of their attending a child guidance clinic. There are, of course, no other health clinics. Our doctor, even, has no surgery.

Our water supply is most inadequate; people pay water rates and all they get is a peaty trickle. For the first two years, the council houses' drains produced a horrible smell. This kind of thing is common in village life. It is not necessarily the fault of the sanitary inspectors; they have been helpful here, but there are limits to what they can do. Most Counties have their own bureaucrats, and voters do not pay enough attention to the County elections; to some extent we get what we deserve for being lazy. Part of the fault is that nobody wants to be the one to complain; it is always left to someone else. There is the difficulty of writing official letters or telephoning firmly. Country people are too used to things going wrong and nothing being done. Grousing is cheap and easy.

Finally, life is dull. There is little alternative employment for young men; those who are ambitious, especially if they are mechanically minded, go to the towns, where they are not necessarily happy. Whereas dullness drives young people away, it drives some of the older ones to drink. And it drives the girls and women into endless, pointless, gossip and quarrelling, family feuds, church feuds, feuds between the 'Rural' and the Gaelic Choir, one vast series of mole-hills talked into mountains![2] The discontent produced by dullness is very painful; we would be wrong to minimise it. It leads people to think ill of their own lives and to lose heart, to lose confidence and pride; it makes them listen to the sillier and easier items on the wireless, or go when possible to the cinema in the local town; it makes them admire – just because it is *different* – jazz and flashy clothes, and the international Hollywood culture of cities, a thing designed for no good end, but merely to make money for those who sell mass-produced anti-dullness mixture, guaranteed to take in the stupid for anything up to a lifetime.

Now, what can be done about all this? How is Carradale in another generation to be different to Carradale now?

We have to start by believing that rural life can be as good as or better than town life. In most ways the standards of the manual worker in the country are higher than those of the town proletariat; witness the difference between evacuees and their hosts. It seems likely that living among beautiful surroundings must have its effect, and it is plain that country people are very sensitive to natural beauty; the more one lives with them, the plainer it is. But some Highland communities are too small and find making a living too difficult, unless parasitically from some Big House. Possibly they might be sufficiently linked to one another and to market towns by bus services, telephones, etc., to make life in them tolerable to modern young people; but many are in areas which would best be turned into National Park land. At present the intelligent are bound to find life there intolerably small-scale, and will leave for anywhere with more scope. On the other hand, some Highland communities are artificially made and kept small, because the land-owners (unlike the original clan chiefs or tacksmen!) do not want houses or anybody not directly serving them, on their estates; where the laird will not feu land for village development, he is holding the pistol to his own head.

The scale, then, is important. But obviously communities of between 200 and 1,000 souls are worth planning for. How then can Carradale, typical of country living, be made as good as it might be?

First; we need the houses. Without them nothing can be done. But it is no use thinking they can be produced privately or let at an economic rent if they are. If we are to get enough houses in Scotland without intolerable waiting, we shall need a good deal of strictly temporary rural housing, using wood and pre-fabricated materials. Bye-laws and building trade rules will have to be correspondingly altered. Existing houses must be modernised, and this is especially true for outlying farms. The Forestry Commission has built houses for its employees in some places, and claims that its delays and neglects here are due to the war and will be remedied later. We hope so. But the Commission has no very good reputation as a landlord; it is primarily interested in trees, and not in people, nor in farming, although it owns much farm land. It was founded by people who believed in doing things from above, the laird's way; its insistence on an 'officer class' with a University theoretical education puts it out of touch with realities and discourages both foresters and small tenants.

Next we need better transport, both by road and sea, above all, a harbour. However herring are to be used, whether, as D. Macintosh suggests [*In chapter 11 of* The New Scotland. *See note 1]* by freezing and fresh sale or by processing in large Government controlled stations, one of which would obviously be sited in Campbeltown, or else locally, in smaller scale factories, there ought to be an all the year round possibility of landing them here. We could then increase our herring fleet and find immediate work for the young men coming back from the war who definitely want to fish. Detailed plans for such a harbour exist; if a Government loan were forthcoming, the harbour would doubtless be owned by the County Council, but if Carradale were constituted a special harbour district for rating purposes – and no rate-payer would grudge a little extra for necessary harbour repairs – there would be some local control.

This harbour is a necessity for fishermen, farmers, the Forestry Commission, and the tourist and ordinary passenger traffic; in view of present developments, a flying-boat jetty might be added, both for passengers and perhaps the quick transport of early vegetables, etc., to Glasgow. But, while the farmers consider the question of easier transport, they should also consider co-operative buying and selling. But if they are to practise this, and increase their present co-operation over farm machinery, they need one simple little thing and that is the telephone. We would do a great deal more neighbouring here, I think, but for so few of us being on the phone.

Transport is necessary for education too; as it is, some children cannot take advantage of the Campbeltown secondary school because they live too far beyond the present range of the bus. We would like a nursery school, but this is hopeless in a scattered community without some kind of conveyance. We would not ask for a permanent child guidance clinic, but we would hope for a visiting clinic to come, say, once a month; it should be possible for those who wish to space their families to get the necessary advice without going all the way to Glasgow, and there are other matters – especially those to do with women and children – which could be better dealt with by a travelling clinic than by a doctor. A travelling canning van for home-grown produce would encourage gardeners and housewives in the villages. All this means specially equipped cars, petrol and drivers; and more money spent on roads. It would also probably mean a garage here and employment for mechanically minded boys. Agricultural machinery and the diesel engines of the herring boats could also be sorted here instead of at Tarbert or in Glasgow. Radio repairs could be undertaken and batteries charged. There would be few slack times.

There are other problems, small, no doubt, but they must be dealt with. What is to be done with the village rubbish, especially tins? If they are not collected and taken away, villages in Scotland will become like villages in the United States, where the first thing that meets one is an enormous heap of old tins. We may come to use less tinned foods, but I think tinned fruit will go on being a winter necessity. Another problem is sewage disposal; this should be thought out in connection with the whole agricultural policy.

We must have new school buildings and the system of teaching several classes in one room must go. With smaller classes, discipline can be relaxed, and the children can practise self-government. Electric light and power are essential in a school, especially when much of the teaching is done – as it must be soon – by films.

But the thing that is wrong; the dullness and inferiority of country life – how are we going to deal with this? It is fundamental. We are still all individuals, at odds with one another, not a real community. We seem unable to co-operate successfully; we don't want to change. What, then? Here, I believe my own experience will be valuable. The first thing to remember is that it's no use at all talking about a thing; it has to be *done*. An hour of actual co-operation is worth a year of talk – or writing. Doing things is hard work, often discouraging; it is just fine to sit down and write. But that won't help. This book will only help if it makes people do things. We have had mostly plenty talk in Scotland already, and not only from the pulpit.

Dullness cannot be attacked straight, any more than drunkenness can. I was asking N.R., on his way back from leave, what he thought Carradale ought to be like after the war. He said he would like to see it developed as a seaside resort. But, I said, what are you going to do in it, Neil? Are you going to be a hotel manager or a croupier? Or do you see yourself taking visitors for half-crown rows across the bay? It wasn't good enough.

The first thing is fuller development of our own resources. Take farming. We don't even know what we could do. Probably we should specialise in early potatoes, perhaps we should do more with fruit and vegetables. There is plenty of high ground which might be reclaimed and made at least into good pasture. But none of us are prepared to take it on. That kind of thing must be done either by the Department of Agriculture, using its own machinery and its own workers – the ex-unemployed perhaps – or it must be done through loans to groups of farmers working in co-operation. None of us at present can afford the best types of machinery; I, for instance, am gradually cutting the bracken in the bay here, but I do it with a horse and a not very efficient cutter – it would be ridiculously extravagant for me to get a really good one for myself. Very few small farmers in Scotland have anything like enough capital; one way they save is abominably unfair – their children working for them only to get a little pocket-money; it is bad enough when they are young, and it often makes them hate the land; but the older they get the worse it is, practically and psychologically. Then the time comes when the old man dies and the eldest son can at last marry – but what about the rest of the boys, who have put their work into the farm too? What about the girls who have worked in the dairy? This particular source of unhappiness must go.

Kippering and net-making are possibilities. So might boat-building be.[3] Carradale Bay might be suitable for fish breeding, though this is still in the experimental stage. Our mainstays must be fishing and forestry. The Forestry Commission are planting 200 acres a year, which must be looked after, from the first draining to the last felling, employing a gradually increasing number of skilled workers. There are still some fine woods here, but we do not know what the Ministry of Supply will have left after the war. If enough timber is left, we would hope no longer to be used merely as a source of raw material; we would hope that soft wood could be used locally for box-making (especially herring boxes) and for toys which could be hand finished and painted, as in South Germany and Switzerland. Here some of our latent artists, who may find themselves lost and unhappy in ordinary village life, might find the beginnings of what they are seeking for. Hard wood, especially beech and ash, might be used for furniture, and bobbin making. None of this needs elaborate or expensive machinery. Carradale birches are small and twisted, but there are villages in the northern Highlands with forests of fine birch which could be used for the kind of furniture we used to admire and import from Finland. Almost all Scottish rural schools need re-equipping with pleasant modern furniture. Uses may even be found for sawdust and rhododendrons!

One obvious thing is the encouragement of Forestry nurseries; each forest should have its own. Fruit and flowering trees and other plants could well be grown; it seems ridiculous that the private nursery-men should be so thoroughly protected that the Commission is not allowed to sell a single tree privately or to make the profits that it needs in order to carry out some of its schemes! Each nursery should be allowed to sell within a certain area around it, at least. Home collection of wild seed should be done systematically, by skilled people.

Forest crofts, such as exist in other countries, should be

encouraged here; work could be arranged so that the men could do half a year in the forests, taking time off when they needed it most on the crofts; there are plenty of dispossessed country folk who would jump at the chance. If we had a group of forest-crofts here (and the Commissioners are not unfavourable), towards the head of the glen, I believe tenants could easily be found, here or in Campbeltown. If unemployed men from non-crofting stock were to come under the scheme, they might need training, partly to teach them agriculture – and they at least could start as a rural co-operative – and partly to see whether they really suited land work. If they did they might be very valuable newcomers. All this means that I want to see the Forestry Commission flourish, and grow like a Scots pine, but on rather different lines, working from below, from the forest districts and villages; it might mean more mistakes at first, yet I doubt if a good forester is likely to make fundamental ones, and as to a cultural background such as young men may (or may not) acquire at Universities, surely such things can also be acquired by adults. Even if they keep the Scots tongues in their heads.

There are other possible rural industries. Here we can use the oil and skin of basking sharks. One the western-facing seaboards, the incoming wrack can be made into the basis for every kind of thing from blancmange and face-cream to films, rayon, plastics and sizing. Milk Board activities might be extended; we could well have a larger choice of cheeses! Market gardening must be developed in the south-west of Scotland. In any scheme of rural industries, seasonal employment must be worked out. Weaving and dyeing could be encouraged, but not too much stress laid on it. At present there is little demand for the hard-wearing, hand-woven tweeds, which don't wear out in time to keep pace with the fashions. But it would be a pity if there were not one good hand-weaver within the reach of any group of villages. I believe there is plenty of mud of the right kind for oysters in some of our own sea lochs; the Scottish oysters which we already produce are of the highest quality and a larger supply might bring the price down.

But all this means electric power.[4]

We have plenty of Scottish water power, actual or potential, as well as power from coal; so far the water power has not been at all fully developed, and I, at least, hope it will not be except as part of a National (or super-National) plan, with due consideration both in use and amenities. At present it mostly goes to heavy industries, big towns, and even out of Scotland. The Highlands are left out.

In some places the local rivers can be used, but often it should come from a central supply, 'the Grid'. Some things should be run through the family group, many by the village group, some from the County or regional group, some nationally, a number internationally with no less a unit than the whole world; electric supply seems to be one of the few which should at present be run by the territorial block (here, of England, Scotland, and Wales, with representation of each country), but particular weight should be given to the undeveloped districts which need supplies most, though with a different kind of urgency to that of heavily industrialised districts.

So far (and inevitably in a society ruled by manufacturers) electricity has been considered mostly for its industrial applications, including the retail and amusement industries of the cities. As I, a woman, see it, a house with a water closet, a sink with running water and if possible a bath or shower, raises people one step in civilisation; electric light and power raises them another. Each step sets the family, and especially the mother, free from heavy, prolonged and sometimes disgusting work, and gives them leisure – to use or misuse. Rural electrification has gone slowly; its cash profits are difficult to calculate and may not result at once. Private supply companies tend to exploit other fields. But we have a few examples, notably the Dumfries scheme, put into operation by the County in 1933 with the help of a Government loan and probably due to the initiative and imagination of the County Engineer and a few like-minded colleagues. A public body can afford (but only just, considering the reluctance of most rate-payers to spend money even for their own good) to take a few risks for the public good. Here the risk was well justified financially; within a few years the Dumfries scheme was paying and is still doing well. But the County Council has to take it on trust that farms and cottages, as well as larger houses, would want electric lighting, cooking and sometimes heating, as well as mains radios, that farms would begin increasingly to use electrically driven machinery, that public buildings such as schools, halls and churches would come in, rural street lighting become commoner, while light industries would be attracted. All this happened in the County of Dumfries; it moved up one step in civilisation, perhaps in happiness.

We want that sort of scheme here, though at present it does not seem to be economically possible to have power lines run down the two sides of Kintyre, with sub-stations. Probably what is needed meantime is some system of rural co-operatives, which would own or hire diesel oil power generators, sufficiently large to meet the needs of a rural community, first for domestic use, then, as need might arise, for industries. Such co-operatives, working over an outlying area such as Kintyre, might have a travelling engineer, who could advise on break-downs and installations, although no doubt a local electrician could look after it normally. I do not think we need bother about amenities; in a village, surface wiring is efficient and inconspicuous. We would profit by the experience of the Dumfries scheme and others, over types of cooker or other domestic apparatus to be hired, over free installations, advertising methods, the use of slot meters, simplification of charges, and in the price per unit which could be charged, so that the Electricity Undertaking would amply cover its expenses, but no potential consumer be too poor to use electricity; at pre-war rates, something like ¾ d. a unit worked out all right in an area as scattered as this. But a diesel engine might not be as cheap as a supply from the 'Grid'. There would, of course, be a few very outlying houses and farms which could not economically be reached, anyhow at first. Later on, electricity might be supplied as an ordinary free public service, like roads and education, but not at once.

We would, I think, hope to see dairy and poultry farms in particular, whether private or co-operative, take advantage of power for milking, sterilising, heating poultry houses, etc. One of our transport problems – getting coal here from the Ayrshire fields – would be largely solved by cheap electric heating and cooking; we might well use nothing but our own peats or wood (including the throw-outs from the sawmill) for any other living-room fires we might want.

Above all, it would make our rural industries really practicable and stop them from spoiling the place. Agreed that natural beauty is only a mockery unless the people who live in it are economically secure, but even so, we see no reason for factory chimneys; our glens and burns need not be spoilt as the dales and becks of Yorkshire were by unplanned industrial development.

But I think I must now emphasise two things. First of all, I am not just saying (as with some justification I might) that we are a depressed and neglected area, and need to have Government money spent on us. We are not just standing with our mouths open. We do ask for a Government grant (not directly to ourselves, but through the appropriate bodies) for the housing and the harbour. The roads could probably be dealt with through a higher rate; the school might be. I am inclined to think that most rural industries might have to be started off with a loan from some central or regional body, though a kippering station, say, could be started for £50. But any such loan would be repaid; these industries would pay. Whatever system of monetary exchange may be in use after the post-war reconstruction period, our industries would be made to fit in. We can be reasonably prosperous and can, to my mind, combine prosperity with living the good life, being gay and creative, happy in our homes and confident in our culture.

I would also emphasise that none of these industries is likely to employ many people. Our shark oil factory employed a dozen or so on sea and shore; a kippering shed would employ, say, three men and twenty girls. A garage would take a dozen, and quite a number, both of men and women, could be employed in intensive market gardening. The forestry is slightly more complicated, as it would take longer to build up; you cannot hurry a tree, though, oddly enough, you can to some extent hurry a forest. If it included hard woods, it would take two generations to get going. It is difficult to look as far ahead as that.

But the preliminary plans for rural industries here would not mean any influx of town population, except perhaps for a few technicians, who might be needed at first; if they became part of the community, they would stay and contribute their own ideas and ways of life; if not, they would move on. But it would mean that the children who are at school now, instead of having to go off and seek their fortunes, could, if they wanted to, stay at home with no waste of talents, and that the young men who are now away in the Navy and patrol boats, could come back to interesting jobs and enough security to marry. We do not want to take men who are suited to fishing and agriculture away from them – especially if fishermen and farm workers are going to get the new deal we and they are asking for – but we are sure that we can easily double our population without losing character or ceasing to be a village community. I at least am not arrogant enough to try and plan in any detail beyond that.

Yet some of these industries need a long term solution. Agriculture itself clearly does; even on an ordinary farm one cannot plan ahead for less than seven years; a farming co-operative must plan further, a district or region further yet. We must work in touch with research stations, and some at least of these must be in the West of Scotland. A hasty visit from Professor Stapledon[5] is not, as he would be the first to admit, nearly enough. It takes years to breed new varieties of beasts or crops.

I have already indicated the kind of local autonomy that I want to see taking the place of the present Forestry Commission organisation. I want to see some Carradale children going on to take the forestry or agricultural courses, from their secondary schools, and others taking technical courses which would make them able to go into industries such as ours, not just as 'hands' – unorganised country labour – but as skilled workers with all the dignity and security that skill can give. For we want to run our own industries ourselves, not from outside either with State or private capital and ideas, but with our own ideas, which we shall have increasingly as we see chances of using them, and with loans at first, which will be repaid when our industries get onto their feet. Is that plain enough?

No doubt each industry will mean the coming in of experts, bringing advice and the latest results of research. I am sure that experts who really want to help and who are not too proud to learn themselves, or to do things slowly, are always popular. Such men and women, going from place to place, will help to keep things moving and lively; and, by telling one community what another one is doing, in terms of actual achievement, will help to bind Scotland together with the kins of serious yet friendly rivalry which the Gaelic choirs felt, competing at the Mods.

All these rural industries imply central marketing; I am taking it for granted that this is being dealt with somewhere else in this book.[6] Also, of course, there must be adequate transport by road or sea, with equalised freights. But some of the finished stuffs are not bulky. For instance, twenty tons of seaweed make only one ton of manucol, the gelatinous product which has so many and varied uses.

Each new industry will mean more security, something else that people can turn to and make their daily bread by. If you have no security you admire and envy and try to imitate those whom you suppose must have it. London civilisation is imagined from far-off as secure and superior; even a second-rate imitation of it seems desirable, better than anything of your own. At present a thing which is Scottish or local is by that condemned.

All this seems to me to point steadily towards more responsibility for everyone. At present most Highland villages are stilled into a kind of despair, an inability to do anything for themselves. They take what they can get, but, if it is not of the kind they want, they will have nothing to do with it. Leverhulme[7] tried to bring prosperity to the Islands, but his could never be the way of it; he failed. The same sort of thing, done from within, might succeed. We will make mistakes; we will quarrel. But that is Democracy; that is how we will learn. We have the ability; our schools IQs show as much. It is a city legend that country people are stupid. But all responsibility has been taken from us. We do not even have Parish Councils! Of course the Parish Councils were actually collections of old ladies and ministers, and little use to anyone; but they need not be like that. We can call such Councils what we like, names matter little. We must deal first with the means of production, but there are plenty of other things to deal with. And it will all be a fine cure for the dullness which we complain of now.

There are more direct ways of dealing with dullness. We might, for instance, have public houses like those one sees in any English village: not shameful places where a man rushes in, to get drunk as quickly as possible; but friendly and comfortable, fit for any family to go to, where a man or woman can have a glass of beer and a game of draughts or darts. Perhaps some of the Scots who have been quartered in England will come back with the idea of a new kind of pub, no longer associated with filth and drunkenness and the scunner that so many decent Scots women have at the very smell of whisky.

We have to decide how much we shall lay ourselves open to the tourist traffic. True, the summer visitors spend money here and some of them are welcome on other grounds; some have connections or relations in Carradale. But when a village is partly used as a holiday resort, its interests are split. Take the business of rural industries, for instance, necessary for the life and planned growth of a community such as ours. Clearly, all but the most public-spirited of the hotel or boarding house keepers will oppose them; in the interests of their visitors, they will want to keep the village old world, unspoiled, in effect – in subjection. For that matter my own reaction, from the Big House and the big view and the privacy of garden and woodland, might be against factories. But for one thing I am convinced that properly planned factories need not be ugly. For another, I love my neighbours more than my view, though theoretically and supposing that market were to continue, the market value of Carradale House might fall.

Yet we do not want to be selfish about our beauties; we know that Glasgow needs to get right away for its holidays. Only we do not altogether care for some of the summer visitors. They are arrogant, censorious, stuck-up; they say Carradale isn't what it was, the fishermen are so uppish; they are friendly enough here, but when they see us in Glasgow, they in their city clothes and ourselves in our fishing clothes, they walk across the street so as not to meet us! We would do better perhaps with another kind, even if they dropped rather less money into our hats – for one can go near to selling one's honour; suppose we had a Youth Hostel here, and young hikers, our own class, more?

And then again, there is the sport. And here I am treading on delicate ground, surely. Let me start by assuming that it is a bad thing that sport should be monopolised by any one class, or, in a given district, by any one person. Equally, if anyone at all can kill game by any method, then it is spoilt for everyone. It is a pity to kill off game altogether, except possibly deer, in agricultural districts; but if I see a pheasant eating my turnips or my tulip bulbs (which they love, the beautiful wretches) I shoot it. When my husband bought the tail end of Carradale Estate, he also bought shooting and fishing rights. Neither of us realised at the time that there were plenty others in the place as interested in sport as ourselves. Now, to my mind, there are three kinds of poacher. There is the man who is out to do it commercially, who will get five hundred pounds worth of salmon from the mouth of a river at the tail of a spate and spoil the river for everyone else that season; he is no sportsman and should be dealt with like any other thief. Then there is the man who likes killing and hurting things, who is naturally cruel; he should be dealt with by the doctor perhaps. But the most of the poachers are folk who like their bit of sport, and who often enough pride themselves that they have never sold a bird or a fish, but have given them away to their friends like gentlemen; they are some of the best men in any community and must be catered for. A good keeper knows the difference between them, but a bad laird does not.

These latter people are adventurous, good with their hands, though perhaps not much interested in machinery, but rather in animals and the way of nature; in fact good country-men. It may seem to them a wee bit tame if the kick is taken out of their sport by legalising it; but there are other fields for adventure, and will be increasingly in the new Scotland – and they will feel themselves to be citizens – for good poachers tend to be men with a strong sense of comradeship. They are good enemies too, but equally there will be enough persons and institutions left to fight, unless the millennium comes quicker than any of us can hope it will. Probably shooting and fishing should be done by clubs, connected perhaps with whatever is the community centre; these clubs should have a reasonably low membership charge, but one which would cover costs – for clubs would need to have their own keepers to keep down vermin and so on; and surely such clubs would be able to deal with whatever might go wrong, by more effective methods than any laird's! There are already fishing clubs in some parts of the Lowlands; fly-fishing appeals particularly to miners, who traditionally go in for skilled hobbies. There are other methods of catching salmon, some of which are equally skilled and even more exciting; but it would be a pity to spoil the rivers altogether for the fly-fishers. Such things could be arranged with a little good will; so far in the past there has been little enough good will over sporting rights. We tried at first running a shooting club in connection with the Village Hall on some of the land where my husband has the sporting rights; it did not work well, mostly because so many young men are away and others have less leisure; we will see what can be done after the war. At present it is hard to see local people paying high enough membership charges to cover upkeep, or taking enough trouble over it; yet something must be tried out. I think it may be on more than one estate I can think of; the bourgeoisie do not enjoy taking risks or sharing, but there are other traditions going back, in Scotland, to a time, not too long ago, before the industrial revolution, and to a society which was never feudal, as England was, and as the pro-English Whig historians have wrongly pictured it.

There are plenty of other leisure activities which should be possible, and should take the dullness out of life. It is always a help if there is a central place where people can meet and where some at least of the activities can be carried out. Village halls are often rather shabby; everything has had to be done on the cheap. That is a pity. The better the hall, the more people like being in it and the more money it brings in. Our own hall is constantly let for dances, concerts, sales of work and so on; it pays its way largely because it is a very attractive building to start with; we spent an extra £30 on a hardwood dance floor instead of the usual pine; that has been worth it over and over again. Here we have games in afternoons or evenings or both; carpet bowls, table tennis, billiards, etc., and sometimes badminton. We have a cinema once a fortnight with a 16 mm projector; the hall was designed with a projection room. Our reading room must probably wait until after the war, though we have a few shelves of books in a corner. We have a Games Committee, Social Committee, Cinema Committee, and so on; so far, a few people do most of the work – but the younger generation will grow up to an increasing sense of responsibility. The older people here have never taken responsibility, most of them; they are shy about it. That has to wear off, and will do so with practice *and only with practice.* It is very important that clubs and managing committees should not get into the hand of any clique; that has happened too much here. It would happen less in the Lowlands, where it would not be necessary to cope with one of our difficulties – the very real laziness of the West Highlander, due to various historical, and possibly climatic, causes. But even here, we hope to do better when our young men come back after the war, especially if we can show them a new Carradale to come back to, as alive as any city. Only the doing of things, and successfully, will begin to cure the laziness which is really, for the most part, deep discouragement.[8] One thing is certain: the Highlands cannot afford to be betrayed even once more. I doubt if the West will ever have the grim, twenty-five hour a day, tenacity of Aberdeen (which makes the migrant Scot into the kind of civil servant or employer whom the decent English hate). It would be awful if the whole of a country were good at engineering and none of it at poetry!

There are things to be learnt from the Highlands and a chance for Scots writers and musicians and painters that they would do well to take before it is too late. We still have the tradition of the ceilidh, the evening gathering in one house or another for stories and music and games, perhaps now for political discussion too. Once it must have been part of good village life everywhere: a thing opposed to the tight family binding of the isolated farm or for that matter the suburban villa, equally isolated, but by respectability and suspicion worse even than distance. Perhaps the Norse halls and the Celtic duns saw the first ceilidhs; here we do what comes to hand. Twice, now, I have written a play for Carradale; the first was tentative, a try-out for actors; but the second one has now been acted five times. Sometimes I wonder what my fellow highbrows would have made of it. For, as I wrote it, people began to be interested; they suggested things; they asked for parts for their friends; they altered the wording; songs were put in or taken out; in the end it was not my play, but Carradale's play. And yet what a satisfaction it was to me as a writer to see my thing come alive in this fashion. The great pleasure I have had in hearing the songs I have written sung by the folk I wrote them for, the greater pleasure to hear one of them, my own words to Faililoiriag,[9] being sung elsewhere, thirty miles along the coast! Surely there are enough Scots writers to supply their own country-side? We have a great tradition of song writing, both in the Gaelic and in Lowland Scots; but people have been discouraged. They feel that 'home-made' songs and tunes are inferior. Equally they want to dance to the latest dance tunes (which they do very badly, because they can't help hopping a bit) instead of the traditional ones. Perhaps this stage has to be gone through, yet in doing so much will be destroyed: you cannot break a tradition in the middle and hope that it will go on growing and blossoming, any more than you can a lily.

We are not archaising, we are not trying to hold back the future. But we believe that the ceilidh tradition means something which, if it went, wo (Editorial note) Mitchison refers the reader to chapter 11 in The New Scotland, 'The herring fishing in a reconstruction period', by the Carradale fisherman Denis Macintosh, with some advice from Mitchison; see Among You Taking Notes (1985), pp. 159, 183. uld just have to be re-invented. It was a way in which we co-operated: not in work this time, but in happiness and friendship. It was a way of breaking down the barriers, stopping houses from being prisons; it was a way for the women to meet as well as the men – the women whose work is so often within the walls, by its nature not co-operative. It went on for centuries unconsciously, not changing much; now it must happen consciously and with constant growth and change. Now people must consciously make their own songs, their own tunes, their own plays, their own pattern of life. They cannot quite do it themselves, because there is a constant pull away from it towards the cheap, publicised thing, easy to buy and saving the trouble – and joy – of making, the almost universal Hollywood culture of cities. But there are some of us who have knowledge of something different, the civilisation of capitals; and we can help. Our best writing, music, films and painting is usually inacceptable in the places where we have tried it out; it is not cheap enough, nor does it put immediate cash into the pockets of the amusement monopolists. If we turn back to our own people, we may have to think out some values afresh; we may have to be very patient, to accept for a time what we may consider childish criticisms. Yet, if we choose, we can make something of Scotland beyond what we dream. Only we must be whole-hearted; we must be willing to drop the highbrow's cry 'nothing but the best', to say instead 'the thing we make ourselves, and, given our heart's blood, it will be good.'

The New Scotland (London Scots Self-Government Committee, 1942), pp. 92-107.

[1] *(Editorial note)* 'The herring fishing in a reconstruction period', by the Carradale fisherman Denis Macintosh, with some advice from Mitchison; see *Among You Taking Notes* (1985), pp. 159, 183.

[2] (Editorial note) See Mitchison's novel Lobsters on the Agenda (1952)

[3] (Mitchison's note) Would home-grown timber ever be suitable for this? Forestry wood has a bad reputation; I believe this is partly because it is not graded and seasoned. I am now myself seasoning some good forestry boards and hope to prove they may be as good as imported wood if they get a chance.

[4] (Editorial note) Mitchison refers the reader to chapter 5, 'Electrical and economic planning in Scotland' by Hugh Quigley.

[5] (Editorial note) Olaf Stapledon (1886-1950), philosopher and science fiction writer, friend of Mitchison.

[6] (Editorial note) Mitchison refers the reader to chapter 7, 'Co-operation in Scotland' by Neil Beaton.

[7] (Editorial note) William Hesketh Lever, 1st Viscount Leverhulme (1851-1925), soap manufacturer and philanthropist, bought the islands of Lewis and Harris in pursuit of plans (ultimately unsuccessful) to improve the life and conditions of the crofters.

[8] (Mitchison's note) For instance, I was discussing this matter of re-organising the sporting rights with one of my poachers, and he was rather discouraging, saying that a club could never be arranged, they would never be able to trust one another, everything would be killed out. My answer was that people would develop a sense of responsibility towards one another and the community and any communal activities they were engaged in; when, and only when, they had been given a few years of it. They would then see that if, for instance, they wanted pheasants (which most of them do – grouse shooting can never be so popular, as it is essentially a whole day sport for the strong and leisured) they would have to protect them from vermin and keep to the right season for shooting them. If they didn't do that, they would lose their own birds. They may do so to start with: then they will have all the expense of rearing before they can have their sport again.

[9] (Editorial note) Mitchison's poem 'Carradale Poacher's Song'; see the collection *Five Men and a Swan* (1957).

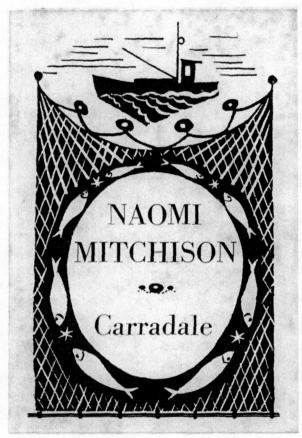

NAOMI
MITCHISON

Carradale

A fishing-themed bookplate

Title Index

A Binder of One's Own (1951)	178
A Garden in Argyll (1980)	363
A Lean Harvest (1955)	330
A Small Farmer Looks at her Farm (1942)	123
A Year's Work Done (1955)	220
Beating the Rain (1957)	248
Big Mill, The (1955)	223
Bringing Home the New Boat (1949)	313
Buck Rake, The (1956)	235
Building a Haystack (1958)	257
Calves, The (1958)	263
Caravans to Carradale (1979)	114
Carradale catch (1987)	118
Carradale Harbour Opened (1959)	339
Cattle Sales at Oban (1957)	254
Cautionary Story (1955)	216
Christmas at the Big House (1951)	53
Cow and the Calf , The(1956)	229
Crafty Darlings, The (1956)	333
Day I Took a Fellow Tribesman to Tarbert Fair, The (1966)	297
Deadly Bracken, The (1965)	293
Does this make sense? (1963)	101
Down on the Farm (1943)	134
End is the Beginning, The (1942)	131
Farmers' Dance, The (1955)	85
Fortunate Isles, The (1963)	290
Gale, The (1953)	347
Garden Fete (1950)	50
Garden Opening, The (1955)	71
Golden Year, The (1960)	355
Haldanes in Kintyre, The (1979)	374
Happiness on the Farm (1961)	287
Harvesting in Kintyre (1952)	188
Herring Country (1961)	311

Highland Funeral (1953)   57
Highland Water Garden (1955)   350
Hogmanay in a Fishing Village (1955)   80
I'll Never Forget (1952)   181
In Sight of the Sea (1964)   25
Kintyre News (1944-5)   12
Lambs for the Fair (1957)   251
Leaning on a Gate (1955)   204
Life Begins at Balloch (1957)   95
Living in Scotland Today (1955)   62
Lovely, long Kintyre (1960)   20
Maggots and Potatoes (1955)   207
Marginal Field (1947)   169
Marginal field: hay crop (1947)   166
Marginal Land (1) (1944)   140
Marginal Land (2) (1946)   163
Marginal land crop (1945)   150
Marginal land harvest (1944)   147
Marginal land: second year (1945)   155
Marginal land: sowing out (1946)   158
Mild Winter (1954)   197
Mistress Jean and I (1956)   89
My Farming and My Neighbours (1944)   143
My weeds (1946)   161
Namely Lambs at Tarbert Sale (1961)   280
New Shed, The (1961)   284
No more porridge (1982)   306
Old Canal, The (1961)   341
On the Council (1957)   98
On the Edge of the Highlands (1944)   3
Philip Ram (1945)   153
Pigeon Shoot (1955)   68
Planning a Kitchen Complex (1972)   107
Platform Party (1953)   59
Price of a Binder, The (1956)   238
Rough Weather (1956)   232
Rural Reconstruction (1942)   378
Sales, The (1960)   276

Science and the small farmer (1959)   271
Sheneval (1952)   185
Skills and Changes (1977)   301
Spindrift at the Citizens' (1951)   321
Summer Work (1957)   245
Think of a Number (1956)   226
Thoughts on Growing Grass (1955)   210
Threshing (1949)   172
Threshing in Carradale (1956)   242
Threshing Team, The (1959)   267
Tinkers and their Language, The (1952)   369
Trials and Rewards of Becoming Attested (1953)   193
Twelve-mile Limit (1958)   336
Village Play-Making (1941)   33
Visitor (1954)   202
Wartime at Carradale (1991)   27
Weather (1955)   76
Weather and the Crops, The (1958)   260
Wet July (1954)   200
What to Do with the Big House (1943)   42
Winds and Seedlings (1960)   358
Winter Fishing (1952)   326
Year of the Good Hay, The (1955)   213
Year of the Late Harvest, The (1950)   175

Sources

These articles have previously appeared in

Country Life;
The Countryman;
Good Housekeeping;
The [Manchester] Guardian;
The [Glasgow] Herald;
History Today;
The Kintyre [Antiquarian and Natural History Society]
          Magazine;
The New Scientist;
New Society;
The New Statesman [and Nation];
Piobaireachd;
Scotland;
Scotland's [SMT] Magazine;
The Scotsman;
Scottish Field.

'The Garden Opening' appeared in
The Scottish Companion, ed. Rhoda Spence (Edinburgh: Richard
          Paterson, 1955),
and
'Rural Reconstruction' in
The New Scotland (London Scots Self-Government Committee,
          1942).

Index

NOTE: Variant forms of Gaelic and Norse place names have been indexed as they occur in the text. Page numbers followed by n indicate a reference to text in a note. The abbreviation NM refers to Naomi Mitchison.

adult education, non-existent 380
African tribesman
    common ground with Scottish
        farmer 297–300
    taken to Tarbert Fair 297–300
    visit to his tribal adviser (NM)
        290–2
agriculture, *see* farming
Animal Health Trust 273
antibiotics 273
Ardrishaig 3, 5
Argyll County Council
    local reluctance to complain 380
    NM a councillor 62, 66, 179
    post-war housing scheme 13, 17
Argyll, Earl of 23
artificial insemination 274
Auchanfraoch 267
Auchnabreck 8, 268
Auchnasavil 68, 224–5, 268
auction sales, *see* cattle sales; lamb
    sales
azaleas 358–9

barley growing 190–1, 306–7
barley harvesting, contrasted with
    oats 306–7
Bechuanaland (later Botswana)
    education 291–2
    exodus to South African mines
        102–3
    need for local industries 102–3
bees 92
'beestie cheese' 230, 231
Bengullion, Piper's Cave 12, 19n
bennyweed 161, 162, 248, 262

Big House
    being neighbourly 42–9
    children welcome 65
    Christmas 53–6
    fire in the kitchen wing 107
    garden fete 50–2
    garden opening 71–5
    maintenance 66
    planning a kitchen complex
        108–13
    and sense of duty 47, 62, 143
big mill, *see* threshing
binder
    a binder of one's own 178–80,
        238–41
    Government binder 175
    repairs 186–7
birds 7, 24, 25, 79, 311
    in December 197
Black, Neen 313–14
Border Leicester tup 153–4, 181–4
borrowing farm machinery 145,
    159, 166, 206, 207–8
Botswana, *see* Bechuanaland
bottling 90
bovine tuberculosis, Kintyre an
    attested area 193, 195, 275, 293
Bowling 319, 343
Boy Scouts 213
bracken 161, 211–12
    search for way to control 175
bracken poisoning, in cattle 293,
    294–5
Brackley 150, 151, 174
Bridie, James 321, 324–5

brucella (contagious abortion) 194, 208, 273
  inoculation against 293
buck rake 233, 235–7, 248, 257
business, rural reconstruction 378–9
business transactions, payment in kind 46
butter-making 93–4, 222
  butter prints 243
byre, meeting required standards 194–6

Cadell, Bill 108, 112
cailleach, the last sheaf 242–3
Campbell clan 7–8, 21
Campbell, Mrs, cooking 66
Campbeltown 311–12
  distilleries 3, 23, 124, 312
  economy and infrastructure 101
  exodus of unemployed 101–2, 103
  fishing port 4, 8–9
  founding of 21
  Haldane brothers preaching 375
  Maid of Morvern leaving harbour 326
Campbeltown Cross 26
Cara House 8
Cara Island 7, 22
caravans to Carradale 114–17
Carradale
  in 1942 378–9
  castle 21
  fishing port 4, 20
  post-war rural reconstruction needs 378–97
  Village Hall 33, 71, 72, 394–5
  village life 63
  wartime at Carradale 27–30
Carradale Dramatic Club 33
Carradale Gaelic Choir 33, 37, 43, 324, 380

Carradale Glen 10, 68, 312
Carradale Harbour
  harbour scheme 17–18
  need for 332, 382–3
  the new harbour 20, 339–40
Carradale Point 3, 10
Carradale River, angling club 118–19
carrageen moss jelly 93
Casson, John 322, 324
cattle
  'a mixture' 69
  beef and dairy 65, 193
  breeding 209
  calf taught to drink 230
  cow and the calf 229–31
  Galloway calves 263
  health matters 208–9
  milking 196, 220–1
  slaughtering bull calves 203, 223, 230–1
  see also milking
cattle sales 234, 254–6, 276–7
ceilidh tradition 395–6
choirs
  girls' choir 43
  see also Carradale Gaelic choir
Christmas, at the Big House 53–6, 80
churning 222
Citizens' Theatre, Glasgow 321–5
class divisions in Scotland 126
clearances 5
clegs 76
Cloan, Perthshire, NM's grandmother's garden 363–4
Clyde estuary, closed to British trawlers 336
Clyde Fishermen's Association 15
Clyde River Purification Board 115
coal mining 3, 101, 311

contagious abortion 194, 208, 273
  innoculation against 293
cooking 89
  see also food
Corby steelworks
  tinkers going to 234, 245
  work for Kintyre fishermen 66,
    102, 246, 330, 333
corn
  ripening in the stooks 147
  short corn 175, 186
  'something very beautiful' 187
  stacks heating 216–19
  see also harvest; threshing
country-dancing class 42–3, 48
County Agricultural Executive
  127, 134
Crinan canal 5, 20
crop rotation 124
crowdie (cheese) 93
cutting, deciding when to start
  147–8, 200, 210, 216–19

dairy, meeting required standards
  194–6
dairy farming 7, 29
  becoming attested 193–6
  NM's reluctance 145
dancing
  classes in the Big House 42–3
  the Farmers' Dance 85–8, 287
  harvest home 164–5, 242
  Hogmanay 81–2
Davaar Island 8
daylight saving, double summer
  time 43, 135, 148, 167
deer 10
  digging into potato pits 220
  noble animals or vermin 202
  roe 248
depopulation, of the Highlands 330
derris powder 208

dipping 136
  cleaner fleeces at shearing 247,
    273, 302
diseases, impact of science on 273
distilleries 3, 23, 124
dockens 262
double summer time, daylight
  saving 43, 135, 148, 167
drainage 204
  marginal land 158–60, 171
  the meadow 140–1, 179
dramatics, village play-making
  33–41
drought 76
Drumlemble, coal pit 13, 16, 18
dullness of life 380–1
dulse (seaweed) 93
Dunaverty Castle 9, 21, 22
dung 274
  spreading 132, 206
Dutch barn 286

economic arguments, for efficiency
  104
education 16–17, 19
  in Bechuanaland 291–2
  rural reconstruction needs 380, 383
Edwards, Percy, gardener,
  Carradale House 361, 365
electric fencing 127
electricity supply 14, 53, 356, 379
  opening of Lussa Hydro
    Electric scheme 59–61
  rural reconstruction proposals
    379, 384, 386–9
employment
  fewer job opportunities 330
  rural reconstruction proposals
    378, 389–90
ethical dilemma, 'farming is
  savage' 203, 223, 230–1
Eyemouth 313, 314, 341

farm equipment
  progress of 271
  sharing with neighbours 207–8,
    215
  see also names of specific
    equipment
farm work, NM's childhood
  137–8
farm workers
  children 136
  labour shortage 134
  relations with 125–6
  skills and earning power 123
  summer work 245
  town people 136–7
  wartime shortage 143
farmers
  government lack of response to
    small 305
  relations with neighbouring
    126, 127, 223–5, 240
  science and the small 271,
    273–5
Farmers' Dance 85–8, 287
farming
  becoming more solitary 301–2,
    304–5
  evolving methods and
    equipment 123
  factory 302
  keeping the accounts 226–8
  long-term planning 129–30
  'looking up' 24
  NM's own farm 27–30, 64–5,
    123–30
  prospects for ex-servicemen 18
  rural reconstruction needs 383,
    384–5, 390
  small mixed farms 302, 304–5
  viewed as savage 203
  wartime at Carradale 27–30
  way of life or business 308

fencing 123–4, 168
  electric 127
fertilisers 273
51st Highland Division, 'Kintyre
  News' 12–19
fire, at the Big House 107, 170–1
first-footing 55–6, 80, 83
fish conservation, need for
  international policy 337–8
fish meal 330, 331
Fisheries group, Highland Panel 62
fishermen, summer work on farms
  246
fishing 3–4, 6
  see also herring fishing
fishing boats 4, 6, 63, 312, 330–5,
  340
  smaller crews 330
  see also herring boats
fishing community 9
fishing industry
  lack of herring 245–6
  need for canning factory 15, 18
  refrigeration 18
fleeces, cleaner due to dipping
  247, 273, 302
flowers 358–61
  an early spring 198
food
  for harvest workers 139, 173,
    201, 206
  local produce 65–6, 90
  for man and beast 174
  for the threshers 223–5, 242,
    268, 287, 302
foot-and-mouth 196, 273
forestry 10
Forestry Commission 10, 23
  being neighbourly 145
  employment and housing 64,
    330, 382
  rural reconstruction needs 385–6

Forth Bridge 316, 341
Forth and Clyde Canal 317–19,
    341
fruit 90
funeral, Highland 57–8

Gaelic
    in funeral service 57
    in village play 35, 37
Gaelic choir, *see* Carradale Gaelic
    Choir
gaffer and scarifier 233–4
Galloway sale 254–6
Galloways 145
    calves 261, 263, 265–6
    health matters 195, 208–9
garden fete 50–2
garden opening 71–5
gardening 350–4, 358–61
    arrival in Carradale 364–5
gardens, NM's childhood 363–4
genetics 274
Glasgow 318
Glasgow Fair 13
Glen Lussa 59
goats, wild 10
government, lack of response to
    small farmers 305
Grammar School, taken over by
    Admiralty 16
Grangemouth 317, 341
grass
    growing 210
    meadow sown in permanent
        grass 197
grass seed, sowing 158–60

Haldane, Archie 27
Haldane, Elizabeth 62
Haldane, James 10, 23, 374
Haldane, Robert 10, 23, 374
Haldane brothers, itinerant

preachers 374–6
harvest 28–9, 30
    best conditions for cutting 200
    between storms 163–5
    bunching sheaves 202
    cautionary story 216–19
    feeding the workers 139, 173,
        201, 206
    from marginal land 147–9
    with Glasgow boys and girls
        135
    in good weather 139
    a good year 166–8, 213–15, 355
    with new Ferguson mower 214
    pros and cons 238–40
    rough weather 232–4
    'winning' a crop 188, 190
    in wretched conditions 131–2
    year of the late 175–7
Harvest Home, dance 164–5, 242
haystack
    a piece of art 257–8, 259
    stack building 191, 201
hedges 168, 360–1
    quickset 124, 168
herring boats 4, 6, 26, 63, 326–9
    hard times 245, 331-2, 332n
        333
    see also fishing boats
herring fishing 4, 6, 312
    a changing industry 330–2
    dumping of fish 13, 15
    'Kintyre News' 12, 13, 14
    over-fishing 331, 337
    processing 14, 15, 18, 330, 382
    scarcity of herring 330, 331, 333
    silver darlings are back 333–5
    time of change 63–4
    see also ring-net fishing
herring industry, rural
    reconstruction needs 382, 385
Herring Industry Bill 13

Herring Industry Board, 245-6, 314, 331-2, 332n 333
Highland Division, 51st, 'Kintyre News' 12–19
Highland Panel 62
Highland pedigree cattle, Oban cattle sale 254–6
Highlands, depopulation of 330
historical writing, NM's 'job' 126
history 20–3
hitch-hiking home 95–7
Hogmanay 55, 80–4
Home Guard 12, 14–15
hormone weed killer 273, 274
horse-rake 214
horses 28
housing 13, 17
  rural reconstruction 378, 379, 382
Hurst, Mike 115
Hurst, Trish 115
Hydro Board, opening of Lussa Hydro Electric scheme 59–61

Iceland
  fishing industry 338
  twelve mile limit 336–8
industries, *see* rural industries

jam and jelly making 92
Johnston, Tom 14, 19n 339

keds, fleeces full of 273
Kilbrannan Sound 63, 234, 312, 328
Kilkerran castle 21
kilt, the wearing of the 60
Kintyre
  on the edge of the Highlands 3–11
  landscape 20, 24, 25–6
Kintyre District Council, NM a councillor 98–100

Kintyre Farmers' co-operative 24
'Kintyre News', for 51st Highland Division 12–19
kippers 331

labour, *see* farm labour
Lachlan (farm worker) 27–30, 143
  dancing 87
  dung spreading 132
  leaning on a gate 204–5
  shearing 182, 183
laggan of Kintyre
  barley for Campbeltown distilleries 3, 20, 307
  dairy production 20, 25
  flooding 15, 198
  NATO base 307
  with poles against enemy landing craft 8
lamb sales 251–3, 280–1, 282–5
lambs, fattening for sales 240
landlords, oppression 5
language
  tinkers and their 369–73
  west coast Scots 66–7
Largie Castle 7, 22
Leicester tup 153–4, 181–4
Leslie, General 21–2
Lewis, Mr, vet 263, 265–6
library, absence of a 44, 72
limestone 3, 7
  liming the soil 124–5, 170
living standards 380–1
Loch Caolisport 5
Lochgilphead 3, 4, 5
Lussa Hydro Electric scheme, official opening 59–61

MacAlister, Duncan, neighbour 159, 164, 173, 228
MacBrayne, 'typical capitalist monopoly' 379
MacDonald clan 7–8, 22

McFarlan Shearer, suppliers to
farmers 185
machines, encroachment of 103–6
Machrihanish 9, 311
Macintosh, William, of Borlum
123, 126
MacKinnons of Auchnasavil
224–5, 268, 284
MacMillan, John, Carradale
fisherman 340
McMillan, Roddy 322
Macrae, Duncan 322, 323
McSporran, Mr, cattle dealer
255–6, 263
maggots 208
on sheep 181, 182, 247
magnesium deficiency disease 274
Magnus, King of the Danes 20, 25
Maid of Morvern
bringing home the new boat
313–20, 341
winter fishing 326–9
malt whisky 191
manure, *see* dung
marginal land
crop 150–2
harvest 147–9
hay crop 166–8
keeping up the acreage 140–2
second year 155–7
sowing out 158–60
subsidies 227–8
marriage celebrations, NM's eldest
son 45–6
A Matter between MacDonalds,
village play-making 33–41
meadow, plans to crop the 140–2
mechanisation
increasing on farms 134, 138, 144
reducing employment 304–5
medical services, doctor with no
surgery 380

milk production 193
milk products 93
milking
during potato lifting 220–1
electric machines 221, 222
relationship with the cows 196,
250, 304
Minch, case for closing the 336, 338
Ministry of Supply, being
neighbourly 145–6
Mitchell, Chuck, Glasgow School
of Art 109
Mitchison, Gilbert Richard
(Dick) 27, 66, 118
Mitchison, Murdoch 350
Mitchison, Naomi, reflecting on
her life 62–7
Mochele, from Bechuanaland 294
Mochudi, Bechuanaland 290, 291
Moray Firth, closed to British
trawlers 336
Mull of Kintyre 9, 20
mushrooms 91

Narrachan 8
National Farmers' Union,
Carradale branch 163–4
neighbours
help/irritation 144–6
relations with 126, 127, 240
teamwork for threshing 223–5,
267–70, 302, 307–8
nets, illegal and legal 337, 338
New Year 45, 55, 80–4
Norsemen 21
North Sea, over-fishing of herring
331
nurses, district 50

oat crop 127–8
oatmeal, for porridge 91, 190

oats
   harvesting contrasted with
      barley 306
   milled at Southend 190
   seed oats 175, 185
   threshing, *see* threshing
Oban cattle sales 254–6, 277–8
   'something very special' 278
Oxfordshire, gardens of NM's
   childhood 363

Paterson, Archie 107
Philip Ram 153–4, 181–4
Phiri, Francis, from Mochudi,
   Bechuanaland 290–2
pigeon shoot 68–70
Piper's Cave 12, 19n
plague 22
ploughing
   Government ploughing outfit
      132
   with horses 129
   the meadow 141–2
   with tractor 144–5
poaching 336, 392–3
   avoiding the Sabbath 45
   on Carradale River 118–19
potato growing 15, 18, 91, 124,
   127–8
   giving a drill in exchange for
      help 65, 128, 205, 220
   wart disease 275
potato lifting 29, 128–9, 220
   best crop yet 155–7
   with Glasgow boys and girls 124
potato varieties 155
potatoes
   pressure to grow more 134, 152
   as stock feed 90
poultry diseases, impact of science
   273
prawn fishing 26

public conveniences 99
public houses, 'a new kind of pub'
   391

quality of life, rural reconstruction
   needs 380–1, 384

rabbits 124, 127
ragwort 161
raking 213, 214
   with a buck rake 235–7, 248, 257
   with the old horse 233
rats 30, 66, 173, 224, 288
reconstruction, proposals for post-
   war Carradale 378–97
Reginald (Rognvald) 21
research, and applied science 273–4
rhododendrons 5, 24, 275, 358–9
   search for way to control 175
Rhunahaorine, battle site 22
ricks
   bringing ricks into the stackyard
      235–6
   see also stacks
ring-net fishing 312, 328–9
   see also herring fishing
roads
   Argyll Road Board 96
   in a bad state 379
Robertson, J.J., MP 313
roe-deer, good to eat 248
Rognvald 21
roller, borrowing a 145
rotation of crops 124
rural industries, reconstruction
   proposals 386
rural reconstruction, proposals for
   post-war Carradale 378–97
rushes 161–2
Russell, John 321, 322, 324

Sabbath observance 44–5
Saddell Abbey 9, 21, 26
  Highland funeral 57–8
salmon fishing, with a net 66,
    73–4
scarifier and gaffer 233–4
science
  impact on animal disease 273
  and the small farmer 271,
    273–5
scone-making 93
sea tangle
  on the marginal field 151
  potash-rich field dressing 7, 20,
    205
  for young grass 65, 198, 200
  see also seaweed
seals 8, 24, 25
seaweed 125, 274
  see also sea tangle
seed barrow, loaned by Duncan
    159
sewer repairs 98–9
shearing 181–4, 246–7, 273
  changing methods 302
sheaves
  bunching 202
  stooking 203
shed, the new 284–6
sheep 29–30
  Border Leicester tup 153–4,
    181–4
  clipping 181–4
  NM trying sheep 146
sheep-dipping 135–6
shellfish fishing 26
Sheneval
  'my one good pasture field' 140,
    210
  a successful crop off 185–7
shooting 392–3
shrubs 358–61

silage making 188, 190
  always put off 201, 213, 233
Sim, C., Chief Fisheries Officer 340
skills
  lost with changes on farms
    301–2, 304–5
  maintaining manual skills 260–1
  of the threshing team 268–70
slaughtering 230–1
social services, rural reconstruction
    proposals 380, 383
social/ economic factors,
    influencing happiness of
    people 105–6
Society of Improvers in
    Agriculture 126
soil, top-dressing 125
soil analysis 170, 274
soil quality, reviewing progress
    204, 206
sowing seed 158, 205
Spindrift, at the Citizens 321–5
spinner, for potato lifting 155, 157
spreader, Duncan's mechanical 206
spring flowers, in January 198
stacks
  building 191, 201, 236–7, 249
  haystack a piece of art 257–8, 259
  heating 172, 218–19
stooking sheaves 203
straw, for the Galloways 151
subsidies 227–8
sulphonamide injections 273
Sunday observance 44–5
Sutherland, Mr, the vet 294–5
swathe-turner 248

Tarbert 3, 4, 6, 311
Tarbert Auction Market 282
Tarbert Fair, taking an African
    visitor to 297–300
Tarbert lamb sale 280, 282–3

telephone exchange, very
    sympathetic 179
telephone service, rural
    reconstruction needs 383
thistles 184, 187, 248, 262
threshing
    after summer drought 172–4
    in Carradale 242–4, 287
    team work with the big mill
        223–5, 267–70, 302, 307–8
    using Government thresher
        132, 144, 150, 163
    with water-wheel and old mill
        133
ticks, fleeces full of 273
Tighnabruaich 17
tinkers
    assimilation with community
        307, 369, 373
    basket weaving 64
    connection with Romany people
        371
    from thinning to steel work
        234, 245
    language 369–73
    less work for 307
    lineage 372
    overcoming prejudice 369
    potato lifting 155–7, 220
    pride in their lifestyle 369
    summer work 245
    in transition 307
top dressing 125
tourism, rural reconstruction
    needs 378, 392
tractor 29
    bracken cutting 161
    new Massey Ferguson 260
    ploughing with caterpillar 141
transport 26
    rural reconstruction proposals
        382–3

'very bad' 379
tree planting 64
tuberculosis, cattle free of 193,
    195, 275, 293
turnip drill
    borrowing a 145
    thinning 233–4

undulant fever 194

vaccination, of cattle 194
valuation, farm accounts 228
vegetables, home-grown 91
veterinary tests, for attestation
    status 195
village hall 33, 71, 72, 394–5

warble fly 208
wart disease 275
water garden 350–4
water mill, producing porridge
    oatmeal 91–2
water supply 76
    inadequate 380
water wheel, threshing 133
weather 76–9
    and the crops 260–2
Weatherhead, Willie 313
wedding party, NM's eldest son's
    45–6
weeds 161–2
Weir, Mr, auctioneer 252, 280,
    282
West of Scotland Agricultural
    College, soil analysis 274
whisky
    Campbeltown malt 312
    Campbeltown's distilleries 3,
        124
    Highland malt 191
Whitehouse 375, 376
wildlife 25–6, 68–9

women, attendance at funerals
57, 58
World War 2
entertaining the forces 44, 45
'Kintyre News' for 51st
Highland Division 12–19
wartime at Carradale 27–30
writing, NM on historical writing
126

Young Farmers' Club 18, 176, 275
Youth Hostels 13

LaVergne, TN USA
01 April 2010
177926LV00006B/94/P

9 781849 210119